Technology, Productivity, and Economic Growth

NATIONAL BUREAU of ECONOMIC RESEARCH

Studies in Income and Wealth
Volume 83

NBER

NATIONAL BUREAU *of* ECONOMIC RESEARCH

Technology, Productivity, and Economic Growth

Edited by

Susanto Basu, Lucy Eldridge, John Haltiwanger, and Erich Strassner

The University of Chicago Press

Chicago and London

The University of Chicago Press, Chicago 60637
The University of Chicago Press, Ltd., London

Published 2025
Printed in the United States of America

34 33 32 31 30 29 28 27 26 25   1 2 3 4 5

ISBN-13: 978-0-226-83908-0 (cloth)
ISBN-13: 978-0-226-83909-7 (e-book)
DOI: https://doi.org/10.7208/chicago/9780226839097.001.0001

Library of Congress Cataloging-in-Publication Data

Names: Basu, Susanto editor | Eldridge, Lucy editor | Haltiwanger, John editor | Strassner, Erich editor
Title: Technology, productivity, and economic growth / edited by Susanto Basu, Lucy Eldridge, John Haltiwanger, and Erich Strassner.
Other titles: Studies in income and wealth v. 83.
Description: Chicago : The University of Chicago Press, 2025. | Series: Studies in income and wealth ; volume 83 | Includes bibliographical references and index.
Identifiers: LCCN 2024056936 | ISBN 9780226839080 cloth | ISBN 9780226839097 ebook
Subjects: LCSH: Technological innovations | Research, Industrial | Industrial productivity
Classification: LCC HD45 .T39683 2025 | DDC 658.4/063—dc23/eng/20250207
LC record available at https://lccn.loc.gov/2024056936

♾ This paper meets the requirements of ANSI/NISO Z39.48-1992 (Permanence of Paper).

Relation of the Directors to the Work and Publications of the NBER

1. The object of the NBER is to ascertain and present to the economics profession, and to the public more generally, important economic facts and their interpretation in a scientific manner without policy recommendations. The Board of Directors is charged with the responsibility of ensuring that the work of the NBER is carried on in strict conformity with this object.

2. The President shall establish an internal review process to ensure that book manuscripts proposed for publication DO NOT contain policy recommendations. This shall apply both to the proceedings of conferences and to manuscripts by a single author or by one or more co-authors but shall not apply to authors of comments at NBER conferences who are not NBER affiliates.

3. No book manuscript reporting research shall be published by the NBER until the President has sent to each member of the Board a notice that a manuscript is recommended for publication and that in the President's opinion it is suitable for publication in accordance with the above principles of the NBER. Such notification will include a table of contents and an abstract or summary of the manuscript's content, a list of contributors if applicable, and a response form for use by Directors who desire a copy of the manuscript for review. Each manuscript shall contain a summary drawing attention to the nature and treatment of the problem studied and the main conclusions reached.

4. No volume shall be published until forty-five days have elapsed from the above notification of intention to publish it. During this period a copy shall be sent to any Director requesting it, and if any Director objects to publication on the grounds that the manuscript contains policy recommendations, the objection will be presented to the author(s) or editor(s). In case of dispute, all members of the Board shall be notified, and the President shall appoint an ad hoc committee of the Board to decide the matter; thirty days additional shall be granted for this purpose.

5. The President shall present annually to the Board a report describing the internal manuscript review process, any objections made by Directors before publication or by anyone after publication, any disputes about such matters, and how they were handled.

6. Publications of the NBER issued for informational purposes concerning the work of the Bureau, or issued to inform the public of the activities at the Bureau, including but not limited to the NBER Digest and Reporter, shall be consistent with the object stated in paragraph 1. They shall contain a specific disclaimer noting that they have not passed through the review procedures required in this resolution. The Executive Committee of the Board is charged with the review of all such publications from time to time.

7. NBER working papers and manuscripts distributed on the Bureau's web site are not deemed to be publications for the purpose of this resolution, but they shall be consistent with the object stated in paragraph 1. Working papers shall contain a specific disclaimer noting that they have not passed through the review procedures required in this resolution. The NBER's web site shall contain a similar disclaimer. The President shall establish an internal review process to ensure that the working papers and the web site do not contain policy recommendations, and shall report annually to the Board on this process and any concerns raised in connection with it.

8. Unless otherwise determined by the Board or exempted by the terms of paragraphs 6 and 7, a copy of this resolution shall be printed in each NBER publication as described in paragraph 2 above.

Contents

Prefatory Note

This volume contains revised versions of the papers presented at the Conference on Research in Income and Wealth titled "Technology, Productivity, and Economic Growth," held in Washington, DC, on March 17–18, 2022.

We are grateful for support for this project from the Bureau of Economic Analysis. Support for the general activities of the Conference on Research in Income and Wealth is provided by the following agencies: Bureau of Economic Analysis, Bureau of Labor Statistics, the Census Bureau, the Board of Governors of the Federal Reserve System, the Statistics of Income/Internal Revenue Service, and Statistics Canada.

We thank Susanto Basu, Lucy P. Eldridge, John C. Haltiwanger, and Erich H. Strassner, who served as conference organizers and as editors of the volume.

Executive Committee, February 2023

Introduction

Susanto Basu, Lucy Eldridge, John Haltiwanger, and Erich Strassner

Today's economy is experiencing an explosion of technological advances that are far beyond what was imaginable even five years ago. This fast pace of innovation is pervasive across industries and countries. This volume considers if there are new and better ways to conceptualize and model these advances and improve our measures of productivity and economic growth to capture this changing landscape. Before delving into the expert essays that comprise this book, it seems only right to define what "productivity" is. Productivity is an economic measure of efficiency that shows how effectively economic inputs are converted into goods and services. A standard measure is total factor productivity (TFP), which is output growth minus share-weighted input growth. That is, the growth in output that is not the result of using additional inputs of labor, capital, energy, materials, or services. This concept is also known as "the Solow residual" (or just "the residual"), from the famous paper in which Solow (1957) showed that under certain assumptions it measures technological change in an aggregate production function.

A year before Solow gave the residual its most popular interpretation, Abramovitz (1956) had defined it in a less hopeful manner, calling it "a measure of our ignorance." For if the residual is the share of output growth that is not explained by input growth, it must measure something that is important for economic growth but is (as yet) unexplained by economics.

Susanto Basu is a professor of economics at Boston College, and a research associate of the National Bureau of Economic Research.

Lucy Eldridge is Associate Commissioner for Productivity and Technology at the Bureau of Labor Statistics.

John Haltiwanger is a professor of economics at the University of Maryland, and a research associate of the National Bureau of Economic Research.

Erich Strassner is chief of the Real Sector Division in the Statistics Department of the International Monetary Fund.

This challenge set a large branch of the productivity literature on a quest to transfer more and more of the sources of economic growth from the unexplained residual to inputs that were deliberately chosen by optimizing entities, either households or firms. This research program was laid out in the landmark paper of Jorgenson and Griliches (1967) and attained its modern form in the book by Gollop, Fraumeni, and Jorgenson (1987).

This research program was extremely successful by its own lights. In a larger context, however, the task became a Sisyphean one. The growth accounting started by Solow (1957) and reaching its full flowering in Gollop, Fraumeni, and Jorgenson (1987) was typically set in the context of neoclassical growth, with its assumptions of perfect competition and constant returns to scale. Only in such a setting would the easily measured factor income shares correspond to the necessary output elasticities of each factor input. But in a neoclassical setting, with its assumption of diminishing marginal products to all accumulated factors of production ("capital," in a broad sense), per capita growth in the long run could come only from exogenous technical change.

Growth accounting measures only the direct impact of technical change, holding capital fixed. But in the long run, higher exogenous productivity growth should also induce capital accumulation. In the neoclassical growth model with endogenous saving developed by Ramsey (1928), Cass (1965), and Koopmans (1965), as long as preference parameters were stable, *all* of long-run per capita growth in output and consumption come from exogenous technical change. As growth accounting reached new heights, it transferred more of the proximate causes of growth from the "residual" to the "capital" column. But decreasing the importance of the residual by increasing capital's share in production could not illuminate the deeper sources of growth in the neoclassical framework. In the Ramsey-Cass-Koopmans model, the reduction in the immediate impact of the residual on output growth only increased its long-run impact via induced capital accumulation, leaving the "exogenous technical change" still the sole source of per capita growth in the long run.

The tension between "exogenous technical change" and the "measure of our ignorance" remains. That is, mismeasured or missing components of labor and capital are a continued focus of research in this area. Relatedly, it has been increasingly recognized that technical change is in fact endogenous with technological innovation arising from investments in some form of R&D broadly defined. One approach is to treat R&D capital as just another form of capital. However, such endogenous innovation may be subject to spillovers or externalities (e.g., Romer [1990] and Jones [1995]) so that such R&D or "innovation" capital is not the same as other forms of private capital accumulation. Hulten (2001, 2009) emphasized the importance of distinguishing between the "costless part of technical change" and the endogenous components that may be subject to externalities. Hulten

(2009) writes, "Growth accounting formulated in this way is no longer a story about technology versus capital formation, but a story about costless advances in technology versus different types of capital formation, including those that promote technical change. Costless MFP growth arises from serendipity, inspiration, or the diffusion of technical knowledge from the originator who bears the development cost to other users." This perspective suggests that TFP is more than the measure of our ignorance and is susceptible to institutions and economic policy.

Building on this perspective is the recognition that accounting for intangible capital in terms of both output and input measurement is important for quantifying TFP (see Corrado, Hulten, and Sichel 2005 and 2009). This perspective is an expansion beyond the recognition that R&D capital is an important part of the dynamics of growth, to include additional intangible capital investments, such as investment in business practices, databases, and software. Research in the measurement of intangible capital highlights how difficult it is to measure these assets, not only in terms of nominal expenditures but in terms of depreciation rates and price deflators that capture quality adjustment. Yet, even with these challenges, quantitative analysis suggests that growth in intangible capital dominates growth in tangible capital substantially over the post-2000 period (Corrado et al. 2022). Intangible capital investments in the increasingly globalized and networked economy also involve scale effects that provide advantages to large firms—such as for example, the investment in databases. Perhaps relatedly, the productivity slowdown in the United States since the mid-2000s has been accompanied by a rapid rise in market concentration. These changes in turn raise questions about the perfect competition assumptions in output and input markets underlying standard growth accounting used to compute measures of TFP.

In March 2022, the Conference on Research in Income and Wealth (CRIW) of the National Bureau of Economic Research (NBER) held a conference in Washington, DC, to provide a forum where economists, data providers, and data analysts could present research on the state of our understanding of changing technology, productivity, and economic growth. The conference invited participants to present papers from a theoretical and empirical perspective with a focus on the ongoing measurement issues and challenges on these topics. The conference drew participants from academia, government, and non-academic research institutions. This volume includes the papers presented at the conference.[1]

The various views of productivity discussed above are a good way of classifying the papers that appear in this volume. Several chapters further the Jorgenson-Griliches program of classifying portions of the productivity residual as input growth, either through better measurement or by expand-

1. The papers have undergone review and, in some cases, substantial revision since their presentation at the conference.

ing the range of inputs considered in productivity analysis. Other papers look for the deep sources of productivity growth that remain. Still others remind us of the "costly" portion of productivity growth, where the costs may be paid in labor disruptions or the resources consumed in producing complementary innovations.

We have grouped the papers into three broad but related categories. The first set are papers that examine issues for tracking recent changes in advanced technologies such as artificial intelligence and implications of these changes for productivity and for the workforce. The second set of papers focuses on puzzles and measurement issues associated with measuring productivity. The last grouping of papers focuses on measuring productivity through the lens of issues associated with measuring input growth in novel and broader ways.

I. Changing Technology

The adoption of advanced technologies by firms often takes time and exhibits considerable heterogeneity across firms. In addition, the pace and nature of such adoption will have significant impacts on economic outcomes for both firms and workers. Given recent advances in advanced technologies, the US Census Bureau teamed with researchers to develop modules in the recently developed Annual Business Survey (ABS). The paper "Automation and the Workforce: A Firm-Level View from the 2019 Annual Business Survey" by Daron Acemoglu, Gary Anderson, David Beede, Catherine Buffington, Eric Childress, Emin Dinlersoz, Lucia Foster, Nathan Goldschlag, John Haltiwanger, Zachary Kroff, Pascual Restrepo, and Nikolas Zolas explores the adoption of advanced technologies by US firms across all economic sectors by leveraging a new module introduced in the 2019 ABS. The module collects data from over 300,000 firms on the use of five advanced technologies: AI, robotics, dedicated equipment, specialized software, and cloud computing. The share of firms that have adopted one or more of these technologies is low (especially for AI). For example, as of the time of the survey in 2019, the AI adoption rate is only 3 percent. However, since larger firms have higher adoption rates, about 13 percent of workers are exposed to using AI in the workplace. Adoption rates for AI are significantly higher in sectors such as the Information sector with about 10 percent of firms having adopted the technology and more than 20 percent of workers exposed in this industry. Similar trends can be observed in the adoption of other advanced technologies. Firms report a variety of motivations for adoption, including automating tasks previously performed by labor. Consistent with this motivation, adopters have higher labor productivity and lower labor shares. Adopters report that these technologies raised skill requirements and led to greater demand for skilled labor but brought limited or ambiguous effects to their employment levels. Periodic tracking of the adoption patterns of advanced technologies and the implications for productivity and productivity by the US statistical agencies will remain vital given the continued developments of these technologies.

With the explosion of advances in artificial intelligence (AI), there is increased attention on understanding the nature and pace of adoption of general-purpose technologies (GPT). In the paper "Similarities and Differences in the Adoption of General Purpose Technologies," Ajay Agrawal, Joshua S. Gans, and Avi Goldfarb provide guidance about the role of GPTs in productivity growth. Much of the literature focuses on the commonalities of GPTs as well as the required co-invention costs for productivity growth. This paper highlights that these components of GPTs are distinct and idiosyncratic. The implication is that for us to understand the impact of AI on future productivity growth we need to identify and quantify the distinct benefits and costs of the technology. The authors emphasize that AI can help predict the next word in a sequence with a host of possible applications. It can also provide predictions about likely outcomes in settings such as health care, enabling guidance about tests and treatments for observed health indicators. The benefits of such predictions and the co-invention costs all depend on the specific application. The authors highlight that without identification and quantification of these distinct benefits and costs it will be difficult to understand the ongoing nature and pace of adoption of AI. This paper provides perspective and insights relevant for the more empirical papers in the volume on AI in particular, and more generally about the dynamics of the development and adoption of new technologies elsewhere in the volume.

The paper "Firm Investments in Artificial Intelligence Technologies and Changes in Workforce Composition," by Tania Babina, Anastassia Fedyk, Alex He, and James Hodson, assesses the impact of investments in artificial intelligence on the workforce. The authors take a unique approach and combine worker resume and job posting data sets to identify firm-level workforce composition and AI investments. The authors use AI themselves to develop this very impressive data set. They find that firms with higher initial shares of highly educated workers and STEM workers invest more in AI. Moreover, as firms invest in AI, they tend to increase their shares of workers with college degrees and more specialized IT skills. Using the same data set, the authors are able to look at the firms' organizational structures and discover that firms with more AI tend to have a flatter hierarchical structure, with significant increases in the share of workers at the junior level.

II. Puzzles and Challenges in Measuring Productivity

Two papers in this volume explore the puzzling dynamics of productivity in the construction sector. While aggregate productivity has exhibited slower growth since the early 2000s, it has still been robustly positive. Although cyclical fluctuations can yield periods of measured negative productivity growth at the aggregate and sectoral level, in the presence of technological progress, long-run productivity growth is anticipated to be positive. Hence it is a puzzle that there have been large and persistent declines in productivity for the US construction sector. Moreover, because construction is a large sector in the United States, it has acted as a drag on aggregate productivity. The paper "The Strange and Awful Path of Productivity in the US Construction Sector" by Austan Goolsbee and Chad Syverson explores the sources of this puzzling long-run decline. They find some evidence of measurement issues but their analysis suggests that this is not the whole story. Using measures of physical productivity in housing construction, they find that productivity is falling or, at best, stagnant over multiple decades. In addition, they present evidence of a decline in the efficiency with which construction firms translate materials inputs into output, and a corresponding shift toward more value-added-intensive production. They also find some evidence that reallocation activity across states has, if anything, been productivity detracting. At the end of the day, they don't fully identify the key factors that have led to this large and puzzling decline. Given the importance of residential and commercial construction in the economy, this paper highlights that devoting attention to this puzzle should have a high priority.

The anemic performance of productivity growth in the US construction sector is matched in many respects in the United Kingdom. For the United Kingdom, the evidence for construction is more consistent with flatlined labor productivity and mildly declining TFP. In the paper "Digital Concrete: Productivity in Infrastructure Construction," Diane Coyle and Rehema Msulwa explore the impact of digitization on the structure and productivity of the UK's civil construction sector. This study is motivated by the greater use of digitization and outsourcing in this sector. The authors approach the evidence from two perspectives: the possibility that there are simply delays in the resulting productivity gains showing through; and the possibility of mismeasurement. They present evidence that both of these factors are likely to contribute. For example, in the architectural and engineering component of construction, they argue that the evidence suggests digitization has led to a greater decline in prices than in the official statistics. They also present evidence in favor of "J-curve" effects which implies that investments in new technologies take time to show up in productivity statistics. Part of the J-curve effect is that intangible capital investments don't get properly accounted for in output as they are difficult to measure. Another component of the J-curve is that there is experimentation and learning in the use of new technologies.

The US and UK papers on construction taken together highlight that the puzzling anemic (even negative) productivity growth in this sector is not country specific. Both papers explore measurement issues that are present in the industry with somewhat different approaches. The US paper seeks to overcome the output price deflator mismeasurement issues by using physical quantity productivity measurement and yet find declining or stagnant productivity persists. The UK paper emphasizes the increased use of digitization in the industry yielding measurement issues along with the aforementioned potential J-curve effects that arise in the presence of the adoption of new technologies. Some caution is needed in comparing the results in the two papers as the US paper focuses on overall construction while the UK paper on the civil construction sector. In any event, both papers argue that the puzzling performance of productivity in the construction sector is not due to measurement issues alone.

As we seek to better understand sources of growth in productivity, it can be useful to disentangle production between primary and secondary products within the same industry, particularly if secondary products are substantively different from primary products. When an industry includes establishments engaged in secondary production, measured TFP growth at the industry level reflects the joint production of the primary and secondary products. In addition, reallocation of resources between these products within an industry can obscure analysis of the underlying reasons for changes in aggregate TFP. In "After Redefinition TFP Accounting," Jon D. Samuels develops estimates of TFP growth for single product-based industries. This redefinition in TFP accounting facilitates analyzing international competitiveness where trade is driven by product competitiveness. These data are particularly useful for the analysis of global value chains (GVCs) and measuring trade in value added (TiVA). Samuels finds that distinguishing between primary and secondary production is important for measuring TFP growth, but only for a small subset of industries, including computer and electronic products and data processing, internet publishing, and other information services sectors.

III. Improved Measurement of Key Inputs: Capital and Labor

As artificial intelligence takes off, the need for increasingly large stores of data is growing and thus defining and measuring data have become vital to understanding growth in the economy. "Data, Intangible Capital, and Productivity," by Carol Corrado, Jonathan Haskel, Massimiliano Iommi, Cecilia Jona-Lasinio, and Filippo Bontadini, analyzes how the increased use of data throughout the world affects productivity. The authors conceptualize data as an intangible capital asset, which is a storable, nonrival factor input. Using the Corrado, Hulten, and Sichel (2005, 2009) intangible capital framework and the recently developed EUKLEMS & INTANProd database, they develop measures of industry-level investments in data assets for nine European countries.[2] The authors find that about 50 percent of intangible capital is, in effect, data capital. Incorporating these measures of data/

2. See https://euklems-intanprod-llee.luiss.it/.

intangible capital in a TFP framework the authors assess the recent global slowdown in TFP. Corrado et al. argue that the increased data intensity of intangibles weakens knowledge diffusion and diminishes TFP growth. They find that the increase to labor productivity from data capital is offset by an appropriability effect, which may have shaved 0.3 and 0.4 percentage points off 2010–2019 TFP growth in Europe and the United States.

As economists continue to dig into the measurement of productivity, it is increasingly recognized that data are an asset that should be incorporated into capital accounts and in turn productivity. During the last revision of the System of National Accounts (SNA) the agreement is to treat databases as a subcategory of software in capital formation.[3] The challenge is how to measure data as an asset. The paper "Valuing the US Data Economy Using Machine Learning and Online Job Postings" by José Bayoán Santiago Calderón and Dylan G. Rassier explores novel methods to achieve this objective. The approach taken in this paper is to measure the value of own-account data stocks and flows for the US business sector by summing the production costs of data-related activities implicit in occupations. Production costs include labor costs, capital costs, and intermediate consumption. The authors apply a markup to an estimate of the wage bill for data-related activities, which is consistent with the Bureau of Economic Analysis (BEA) methodology for own-account software. The method in this paper augments the traditional sum-of-costs methodology for measuring other own-account intellectual property products (IPPs) in national economic accounts by proxying occupation-level time-use factors using a machine learning model and the text of online job advertisements. The experimental estimates indicate that annual current-dollar investment in own-account data assets for the US business sector grew from $84 billion in 2002 to $186 billion in 2021, with an average annual growth rate of 4.2 percent. Cumulative current-dollar investment for the period 2002–2021 was $2.6 trillion.

An ongoing challenge for tracking productivity growth is distinguishing between lower frequency secular trends and high frequency cyclical dynamics. Complicating the latter is that measured TFP tends to be procyclical due to failure to account for variation in capital utilization. Many methods have been suggested and used to adjust for capital utilization with only limited success. This issue became especially relevant in the pandemic since output and hours declined sharply but standard measures of capital were largely unaffected. In the paper "An Occupation and Asset-Driven Approach to Capital Utilization Adjustment in Productivity Statistics," Josh Martin and Kyle Jones explore an extension of traditional methods which focus on variation in labor hours to capture capital utilization. The authors use hours worked for especially relevant occupations for specific assets and introduce a conceptual framework to motivate and guide this alternative approach.

3. See https://unstats.un.org/unsd/nationalaccount/sna.asp.

Applying their method to the pandemic, they find a decline in capital utilization of around 9 percent in the UK market sector in the height of the coronavirus pandemic, recovering over half of this by the end of 2020. This approach mitigates, but does not eliminate, the fall in TFP through 2020. However, the authors find this alternative method produces less-promising results prior to 2020, particularly during the global financial crisis.

As discussed above in the context of changes in advanced technologies, such changes are accompanied by changes in the manner in which firms organize themselves and accomplish tasks. The paper "Opening the Black Box: Task and Skill Mix and Productivity Dispersion" by G. Jacob Blackwood, Cindy Cunningham, Matthew Dey, Lucia Foster, Cheryl Grim, John Haltiwanger, Rachel Nesbit, Sabrina Wulff Pabilonia, Jay Stewart, Cody Tuttle, and Zoltan Wolf explores the measurement challenges of tracking the changes in skills and tasks by firms as the economy evolves with changing technology. This paper highlights that tracking the changing task content of production at the firm level has been elusive since the firm-level data on productivity at the US Bureau of the Census does not readily include information on the skill mix or the mix of tasks. A joint project between the Bureau of Labor Statistics (BLS) and the Census Bureau is seeking to alleviate the data and knowledge gap. The objective of this collaborative project is to open the black box of tasks, skills, and productivity by combining establishment-level data on occupations from the BLS with a restricted-access establishment-level productivity data set created by the BLS-Census Bureau Collaborative Micro-productivity Project. This paper takes a first step toward this objective by exploring the conceptual, specification, and measurement issues to be confronted in this data integration. The paper also includes empirical analysis that shows within-industry productivity dispersion is strongly positively related to within-industry task/skill dispersion.

IV. Conclusions

It is an exciting time for the field of economics that is focused on measurement of technology, productivity, and economic growth. Rapid changes in technology such as artificial intelligence appear to be on the cusp of generating rapid changes in how businesses organize themselves, including their workforce and stimulating a period of accelerated growth. At the same time, there has been an explosion of big data from administrative and private data that enable tracking and studying these topics in novel ways that enable shedding light on both long-standing and new questions. New methods for using and integrating disparate data sources using techniques such as machine learning are developing in tandem with the development of new data sources. As emphasized by the papers in this volume, there are also many core open questions about technology, productivity, and economic growth that involve both conceptual and measurement issues. It is our hope that the community developing and studying the data on these topics can use the accumulated knowledge and wisdom embodied in the papers in this volume to make progress on these issues in the years to come.

The conference organizers and attendees thank those who made this conference a success and this volume possible: the Bureau of Economic Analysis, the Bureau of Labor Statistics, the NBER and CRIW for financial support; and the NBER, especially Helena Fitz-Patrick, for assistance in compiling this volume. For acknowledgments, sources of research support, and disclosure of the authors' material financial relationships, if any, please see https://www.nber.org/books-and-chapters/technology-productivity-and-economic-growth/introduction-technology-productivity-and-economic-growth.

References

Abramovitz, Moses. 1956. "Resource and Output Trends in the United States Since 1870." *American Economic Review* 46 (05): 5–23.

Cass, David. 1965. "Optimum Growth in an Aggregative Model of Capital Accumulation." *Review of Economic Studies* 32: 233–40.

Corrado, Carol, Charles Hulten, and Daniel Sichel. 2005. "Measuring Capital and Technology: An Expanded Framework." In *Measuring Capital in the New Economy*, Studies in Income and Wealth, Volume 65, edited by C. Corrado, J. Haltiwanger, and D. Sichel, 11–41. Chicago, IL: The University of Chicago Press.

Corrado, Carol, Jonathan Haskel, Cecilia Jona-Lasinio, and Massimiliano Iommi. 2022. "Intangible Capital and Modern Economies." *Journal of Economic Perspectives* 36 (3): 3–28.

Corrado, Carol A., Charles R. Hulten, and Daniel Sichel. 2009. "Intangible Capital and U.S. Economic Growth." *Review of Income and Wealth* 55 (3): 661–85. September.

Hulten, Charles R. 2001. "Total Factor Productivity: A Short Biography." In *New Developments in Productivity Analysis*, Studies in Income and Wealth, volume 63, edited by Charles R. Hulten, Edwin R. Dean, and Michael J. Harper, 1–47. Chicago, IL: University of Chicago Press.

Hulten, Charles. 2009. "Growth Accounting." NBER Working Paper No. 15341.

Jones, Charles. 1995. "R&D Models of Economic Growth." *Journal of Political Economy* 104 (4): 759–84. August.

Koopmans, Tjalling C. 1965. "On the Concept of Optimal Economic Growth." In *(Study Week on the) Econometric Approach to Development Planning*, chap. 4, 225–87. Amsterdam: North-Holland Publishing Co.

Jorgenson, Dale W., and Zvi Griliches. 1967. "The Explanation of Productivity Change." *Review of Economic Studies* 34: 249–83. July.

Gollop, F. M., B. M. Fraumeni, and Dale W Jorgenson. 1987. *Productivity and U.S. Economic Growth*. Harvard University Press.

Ramsey, Frank. 1928. "A Mathematical Theory of Saving." *Economic Journal* 38 (152): 543–59.

Romer, Paul. 1990. "Endogenous Technological Change." *Journal of Political Economy* 98 (5, part 2): S71–S102.

Solow, Robert M. 1957. “Technical Change and the Aggregate Production Function.” *Review of Economics and Statistics* 39 (3): 312–320.

Find out more about the Annual Business Survey at https://www.census.gov/programs-surveys/abs.html.

Find productivity data for the United States at https://www.bls.gov/productivity.

Find information about BEA methods for own account software at https://www.bea.gov/sites/default/files/2018-05/Estimation-of-Software-in-the-US-National-Accounts.pdf.

1

Automation and the Workforce
A Firm-Level View from the 2019 Annual Business Survey

Daron Acemoglu, Gary Anderson, David Beede, Catherine Buffington, Eric Childress, Emin Dinlersoz, Lucia Foster, Nathan Goldschlag, John Haltiwanger, Zachary Kroff, Pascual Restrepo, and Nikolas Zolas

1.1 Introduction

Advanced technologies, including robotics, artificial intelligence (AI), and software systems, are thought to be spreading rapidly in industrialized economies.[1] These technologies are argued to increase productivity, automate tasks performed by labor, and raise the demand for skills, contributing

Daron Acemoglu is the MIT Institute Professor at the Massachusetts Institute of Technology and a research associate of the National Bureau of Economic Research.

Gary Anderson is a senior economic advisor at the National Center for Science and Engineering Statistics of the National Science Foundation.

David Beede is the Knowledge Transfer Officer of the Federal Statistical Research Data Center program in the Center for Enterprise Dissemination (CED), US Census Bureau.

Catherine Buffington is the Chief of the Economic Indicators Division at the US Census Bureau.

Eric Childress is a statistician at the US Census Bureau and a PhD student at George Mason University's Schar School of Public Policy.

Emin Dinlersoz is a principal economist at the Center for Economic Studies at the US Census Bureau.

Lucia Foster is Chief Economist and Chief of the Center for Economic Studies at the US Census Bureau.

Nathan Goldschlag is a principal economist at the Center for Economic Studies at the US Census Bureau.

John Haltiwanger is a professor of economics at the University of Maryland, and a research associate of the National Bureau of Economic Research.

Zachary Kroff is an economist at the Center for Economics Studies at the US Census Bureau.

Pascual Restrepo is an associate professor of economics at Boston University, and a research associate of the National Bureau of Economic Research.

Nikolas Zolas is a senior economist at the Center for Economic Studies at the US Census Bureau.

1. See Brynjolfsson and McAfee (2014), Ford (2015), Susskind and Susskind (2015), and Schwab (2017).

to rising inequality and declining labor shares. There is little direct evidence, however, on how widespread these technologies are, and which firms are adopting them, especially in the United States.

This paper leverages a new module introduced in the 2019 Annual Business Survey (ABS) conducted by the US Census Bureau in partnership with the National Center for Science and Engineering Statistics (NCSES) to shed light on these questions. The module focuses on the adoption of five advanced technologies: artificial intelligence (AI), robotics, dedicated equipment, specialized software, and cloud computing. The 2019 ABS module sampled over 300,000 employer businesses and collected information on firms' adoption and use of these technologies for the 2016–2018 reference period. The module also asked questions on firms' motivation for adoption, allowing us to measure the extent to which these technologies are being used for automating tasks, and on firms' assessments of the impact of technology on their employment level and skill requirements. Using the ABS module, we describe the adoption of advanced technologies by US firms in all economic sectors, documenting for the first time the extent to which these technologies are being used for automation and how they affect firms' production processes and demand for skills.

We first document that adoption remains limited when measured by the share of firms using these technologies in their processes and methods. This is especially the case for AI and robotics: only 3.2 percent of firms used AI and 2 percent used robotics during 2016–2018. There is wider adoption of the remaining technologies, with 19.6 percent of firms using dedicated equipment, 40.2 percent using specialized software, and 34 percent using cloud computing. Still, half of US firms did not use any of these technologies during 2016–2018. Firms identify the lack of applicability and high costs of deploying and integrating these technologies as the main factors limiting wider adoption.

Despite the low shares of user firms, adopters account for a sizable share of employment and economic activity. This is because adoption concentrates in large firms. 12.6 percent of US workers were employed at firms using AI during 2016–2018 (even though these are only 3.2 percent of firms). The shares of employment at adopting firms are 15.7 percent for robotics, 36.4 percent for dedicated equipment, 64.4 percent for specialized software, and 61.8 percent for cloud computing. These high shares indicate that advanced technologies have been an important force affecting US labor and product markets, despite their limited adoption by small firms.

After presenting these aggregate facts, we document differences in adoption rates between and within industries. Adoption rates vary substantially across industries, which is in line with firms' reports that these technologies have highly specific applicability. Detailed industry differences account for 10–30 percent of the employment-weighted variation in adoption rates across firms. Within industries, adoption concentrates in larger and younger firms, presumably reflecting large fixed costs and organizational barriers involved in adopting these technologies.

The ABS module allows us to document for the first time the extent to which US firms use advanced technologies for automation. Firms report a number of motivations for their investments in advanced technologies, including most commonly improving process quality, upgrading existing processes, and automating tasks performed by labor. The use of AI and robotics is closely related to automation. In terms of employment shares, 55 percent of AI users and 65 percent of robotics users report adopting these technologies for automation. Dedicated equipment and specialized software have more diverse uses, with 30–35 percent of users (in employment shares) adopting these technologies for automation. Other uses of these technologies, such as expanding product offerings or meeting industry standards, are less common.

The fraction of the US workforce exposed to automation-related uses of advanced technologies is sizable, with 30.4 percent of US workers employed at firms using advanced technologies for automation. Worker exposure to automation is particularly high in (though not exclusive to) manufacturing, where 52 percent of workers are employed at firms using these technologies for automation.[2] Although AI and robotics stand out as the two technologies that are more closely related to automation, most of workers' exposure to automation comes from dedicated equipment and specialized software due to their wider adoption.

Consistent with the importance of automation as a major application of these technologies, adopters have higher labor productivity and lower labor shares than other firms in their industry, size class, and cohort.[3] Also, consistent with higher incentives for automation when wages are higher, we find that high-wage firms are more likely to adopt these technologies.[4]

We estimate that the use of advanced technologies is associated with a 11.4 percent higher labor productivity (and a 21.2 percent higher labor productivity for firms using all five technologies surveyed in the ABS). From a pure descriptive viewpoint, the adoption of advanced technologies accounts

2. When interpreting these measures, one should keep in mind that not all workers currently employed at firms using these technologies are subject to the effects of automation. Our numbers do not imply that 30 percent of US workers are or will be at risk of having their jobs automated. Nevertheless, these high shares suggest that past and future changes in the demand for skills at automating firms associated with automation will have sizable effects on labor markets (see Acemoglu and Restrepo 2022 for evidence on the aggregate effect of automation on inequality).

3. This is in line with recent papers that emphasize the role of automation as a key driver behind the labor share decline in some sectors, most notably in manufacturing (see Acemoglu, Lelarge, and Restrepo 2020; Acemoglu and Restrepo 2022; Dauth et al. 2021; Cheng et al. 2021; Kogan et al. 2021.)

4. See Acemoglu and Restrepo (2021) and Dechezleprêtre et al. (2021) for evidence on how high wages drive the adoption of automation technologies across countries and firms, respectively.

for 16–30 percent of the labor productivity differences between small and large firms in each industry—the so-called *superstar firm* phenomenon (see Autor et al. 2020.)[5]

Finally, we explore firms' self-assessments of the implications of advanced technologies for their demand for labor and skills. Most firms report that advanced technology adoption did not change their employment level, and among firms that report a change, the reported direction of change is split. These findings point to limited and ambiguous effects of advanced technologies on firm employment.[6] Instead, a significant share of firms (between 30 and 40 percent depending on the technology surveyed) assess that advanced technologies increased their skill demands, while almost no firms report a reduction in their demand for skills. These self-reports are consistent with theories in which advanced technologies increase the demand for skills.

Our paper contributes to a growing literature on measuring the adoption of advanced technologies across firms and industries and understanding their implications for firms and workers. Our first contribution is on data collection and the measurement of technology use and adoption. In this we build and expand on the work using the 2018 ABS, summarized in Zolas et al. (2020). Due to data limitations, prior research on the effects of modern automation technologies on firms and workers has relied on indirect proxies of technology, or on data sets with limited and coarse coverage. Earlier work focused on industry-level robot adoption measures, from the International Federation of Robotics.[7] A more recent series of papers uses data on robot imports and in some cases detailed surveys of manufacturing firms in order to explore firm-level outcomes for robot adopters in manufacturing.[8] Our paper extends these efforts by collecting comprehensive data for the entire economy, not just manufacturing, and including AI, dedicated equipment, specialized software, cloud computing, and robotics. In doing so, we confirm

5. This is consistent with the results of Acemoglu, Lelarge, and Restrepo (2020) from French manufacturing, which indicate that a sizable portion of the covariance between labor share changes and size is related to robotics investments. It also aligns with the conclusions in Hubmer and Restrepo (2021), who use a calibrated model of firm dynamics with differences in fixed costs of technology adoption to show that automation technologies adopted by large firms contributed to the rise of superstar firms.

6. We also caution that, as documented in Koch, Manuylov, and Smolka (2021) and Acemoglu, Lelarge, and Restrepo (2020), the expansion of firms adopting automation technologies might come at the expense of competing firms that do not automate. Hence the increases in employment and the lack of negative employment effects reported by adopters are consistent with potentially negative industry or market-level effects as found in a number of studies, such as Acemoglu and Restrepo (2020), Dauth et al. (2021), Acemoglu, Lelarge, and Restrepo (2020), or no positive aggregate effects, as in Graetz and Michaels (2018).

7. See, for example, Graetz and Michaels (2018) and Acemoglu and Restrepo (2020).

8. See for example Humlum (2020), Bonfiglioli et al. (2020), Rodrigo (2023), Dixon, Hong, and Wu (2021), de Souza and Li (2023) for papers using data on robot imports to measure firm-level adoption of robotics in various countries. Acemoglu, Lelarge, and Restrepo (2020) combine imports data and detailed accounting information to construct a somewhat more complete picture of robot adoption in French manufacturing. Aghion et al. (2020) also complement these data with accounting information on the use of motor equipment.

and extend four findings that several papers have documented for robotics and extend it to the other technologies in the ABS: (1) larger firms are more likely to adopt these advanced technologies; (2) adoption is associated with higher labor productivity; (3) adoption is associated with lower labor shares; and (4) advanced technology adoption is associated with an increasing demand for skills (for example, in the form of reductions in the share of production workers for robotics).

There is also a nascent literature using various proxies for firm-level adoption of AI and new technologies obtained from the text in job postings, conference calls, and patent data. For example, Alekseeva et al. (2021), Babina et al. (forthcoming), and Acemoglu et al. (2022) use data from online vacancies, specifically from postings including AI-related skills, to estimate establishment-level AI activity. Bloom et al. (2021) combine job-postings data with the text data from patents and conference calls to measure the diffusion of AI and other novel technologies across US firms. Mann and Püttmann (2019), Dechezleprêtre et al. (2021), and Martinez and Moen-Vorum (2022) use patent texts to identify and measure the diffusion of automation technologies. The ABS module contributes to these efforts as it is more representative and offers a more direct measurement of technology use at the firm level. The ABS also distinguishes between users and providers of technology—a distinction that approaches based on patent data and job postings miss.

The ABS technology module complements new surveys that have been recently used to measure technology adoption in other countries. For example, there are similar surveys measuring firms' investments in advanced technologies and automation for Germany (Genz et al. 2021), Italy (Calvino et al. 2022), South Korea (Cho et al. 2023), the Netherlands (Bessen et al. 2019), and manufacturing in Spain (Koch, Manuylov, and Smolka 2021).

Finally, we expand on work using previous Census surveys devoted to measuring technology use in specific sectors. These include earlier work using the Survey of Manufacturing Technology, conducted in 1988, 1991, and 1993, which collected data on robots, automated storage and retrieval systems, automated guided vehicle systems, and automated testing equipment for a subset of manufacturing industries (Doms, Dunne and Troske 1997; Dinlersoz and Wolf 2024); work on computer use in manufacturing using the Annual Survey of Manufacturers (Dunne et al. 2004); work on telecommunication technologies using the Information and Communication and Technology Survey (ICTS) (Eckert, Ganapati and Walsh 2022); work on e-business practices using the Computer Network Use Supplement (CNUS) (McElheran 2015); work on self-service gas stations using the Census of Retail Trade (Basker, Foster, and Klimek 2017); and work using the Management and Organizational Practices Survey (MOPS), which collects detailed information on firm organization and management practices (Brynjolfsson, Jin, and McElheran 2021).

The rest of the paper is organized as follows. Section 1.2 describes the ABS module. Section 1.3 outlines the conceptual framework that motivates our empirical work and interpretation. Sections 1.4, 1.5, 1.6, and 1.7 provide our analysis of the ABS data. Section 1.8 concludes, while the appendix includes additional details on the design of the ABS module and empirical results.[9]

1.2 The Technology Module in the 2019 ABS

The 2019 technology module is the second module on technology collected as part of the ABS. The first technology module featured in the 2018 ABS focused on questions regarding firms' digitization of information along with the adoption of some specific business technologies (see Zolas et al. 2020 for an analysis of the data collected by the 2018 ABS technology module). The 2019 technology module features questions related to the use of five advanced technologies that are relevant for automation. In addition, the module collects data on firms' motivations for adoption, asking firms to report whether they are using these advanced technologies for automation, and their assessment of the effect of these technologies on the size and composition of their workforce. Finally, the module asks firms about the bottlenecks limiting their adoption of advanced technologies.[10]

The five technologies surveyed in the 2019 ABS were defined as follows:

- Artificial Intelligence: Artificial intelligence is a branch of computer science and engineering devoted to making machines intelligent. Intelligence is that quality that enables an entity to perceive, analyze, determine response, and act appropriately in its environment.
- Robotics: Robotic equipment (or robots) are automatically controlled, reprogrammable, and multipurpose machines used in automated operations in industrial and service environments.
- Specialized Software (excluding Artificial Intelligence): Software dedicated to performing a particular business function.
- Dedicated Equipment (excluding Robotics): Equipment capable of automatically carrying out a pre-specified task.
- Cloud-Based Computing Systems and Applications: Computing resources available on-demand via the internet.

According to these definitions, AI algorithms powering a chatbot would count as **artificial intelligence**. Industrial robots used in manufacturing would be considered **robotics**. A software system for document discovery or handling appointments would be **specialized software**. And an automatic

9. http://www.nber.org/data-appendix/c14741/appendix.pdf.

10. Appendix A (http://www.nber.org/data-appendix/c14741/appendix.pdf) provides an overview of the development of the 2019 ABS module.

retrieval system for warehouses would be **dedicated equipment**. On the other hand, **cloud computing** is typically used together with the other technologies to satisfy their demand for computing power. For example, a firm using a software system for trading would host the algorithms and data on the cloud.

The 2019 ABS data were collected from June through December 2019. The module starts by asking firms about their use of these technologies during the reference period of 2016–2018.[11] For each technology, a firm may respond that it did not use the technology; tested the technology, but did not use it; used the technology with a specified degree of intensity (low use, moderate use, or high use); or do not know whether the technology was used during the three years 2016–2018. Conditional on responding with some degree of technology use (low, moderate, or high), firms are then asked about the motivations for adopting or using the technology. Respondents may choose from the following list of motivations: "automate tasks performed by labor," "upgrade outdated processes or methods," "improve quality or reliability of processes or methods," "expand the range of goods or services," "adopt standards and accreditation," and "some other reason." In addition, the module asks firms whether they are using the technologies as part of their production processes and methods, or whether they are providers of these technologies (or goods and services that embed these technologies).

The module then dives into the workforce effects of technology. First, respondents reporting some degree of technology use are asked about the effects of the technology on overall employment, overall skill level, and STEM skills of their workers. Firms may respond with "increased," "decreased," or "did not change" ("not applicable" is also an option for STEM skills in the case that the firm did not employ any workers with STEM skills). Next, firms are asked about how technology use affected four types of workers—production, non-production, supervisory, and non-supervisory. Firms can respond that technology use either increased, decreased, did not change the number of each of these types of workers (again, with the additional option "not applicable"). These questions, while qualitative in nature, provide a broad assessment of various effects of the technology on a firm's workforce size and composition.

Finally, all firms—regardless of reporting technology use or not—were asked to assess all factors adversely affecting adoption and utilization of each technology. The factors included represent a wide variety of considerations and concerns, including applicability ("technology not applicable to this business"), the cost and maturity of technology ("this technology was too expensive," "lacked access to capital," "this technology was not mature"),

11. The exact wording and organization of the questions is available in the official survey instrument for 2019 ABS on the ABS website: https://www.census.gov/programs-surveys/abs/technical-documentation/surveys-instructions.2019.html.

inputs needed to deploy the technology ("lacked access to required data," "required data not reliable," "lacked access to required human capital and talent"), regulatory environment ("laws and regulations"), and security considerations ("concerns regarding safety and security—physical and cyber"). A response option of unhindered adoption and utilization was also included ("no factors adversely affected the adoption of this technology").

The set of firms sampled in the technology module was determined by the general sampling scheme for the 2019 ABS, a primary goal of which is to provide tabulations of collected data by various ownership characteristics.[12] The ABS sampling universe was created using Census Bureau's Business Register administrative data from 2018, which provide the information on industry classification, receipts, payroll, and employment for the construction of the ABS universe. The ABS universe was stratified by state, frame, and industry, where *frame* refers to categories of ownership characteristics for businesses. The Census Bureau used several sources of information to estimate the probability that a business is minority or women-owned. These probabilities were then used to place each firm in the ABS universe to one of nine frames that span key race and ethnicity categories, plus gender and public ownership status. Large companies were selected with certainty based on volume of sales, payroll, or number of paid employees.[13] The remaining universe was subjected to stratified systematic random sampling.

Because of these sampling procedures and selective survey completion, the set of firms that responded to the technology module does not constitute a nationally representative sample of firms, when compared to the full set of employer businesses in the Longitudinal Business Database (LBD).[14] We therefore construct firm weights based on the 2018 LBD to make the sample representative of the universe of employer businesses. These weights are calculated using a methodology similar to the one used in Zolas et al. (2020).[15]

The response rate for the portion of the survey used in this paper was 68.7 percent, which is comparable to the 2018 ABS technology module response rate, and similar to the response rate for other modules of the 2019 ABS. Still, about 5 percent of respondents claimed not knowing whether they used

12. For details on the sampling methodology, see https://www.census.gov/programs-surveys/abs/technical-documentation/methodology.2019.html.

13. More specifically, certainty cases satisfy the following criteria: firms with more than 500 employees; firms responding to the 2016 Business R&D and Innovation Survey for Microbusinesses (BRDI-M) survey with R&D costs of $1 million or higher; and firms larger than stratum-specific payroll and receipt cut-off. The certainty cutoffs vary by stratum, depending on the number and the size distribution of firms in the stratum.

14. The LBD contains the universe of non-farm employer businesses (or firms) in the United States (see Chow et al. 2021 for details).

15. We first stratify firms in the 2018 LBD and 2019 ABS by the same size, age, and industry categories (12 size categories, 12 age groups and 19 two-digit NAICS sectors). Each firm in a stratum in the ABS is then assigned the same weight calculated by dividing the firm count in the corresponding 2018 LBD stratum by the firm count in the 2019 ABS stratum.

some of the technologies in the survey and 9 percent of respondents missed answering some of the items in the questionnaire. We remove firms that responded "Don't Know" or missed an item when tabulating the responses to a specific question in our analysis.

1.3 Conceptual Framework

This section sketches a partial-equilibrium version of the model in Acemoglu and Restrepo (2022), expanded to include firm competition within an industry, in order to frame our interpretation of the results from the ABS technology module. In our framework, firms complete tasks to produce output, and their key decision is the assignment of these tasks across workers with different skills and specialized capital equipment or algorithms (e.g., AI, robotics, specialized software, etc.). Automation is the use of specialized capital in order to perform tasks previously assigned to labor. The results presented in this section follow from those in Acemoglu and Restrepo (2022) and their proofs are omitted.

1.3.1 Production, Tasks, and Demand

We consider a partial equilibrium model of a single industry. To save on notation, we omit industry subscripts, with the understanding that all objects and technologies might vary by industry. Firms are indexed by f and engage in monopolistic competition, facing a demand curve for their products given by

$$y_f = y \cdot \left(\frac{p_f}{p}\right)^{-\sigma}, \text{ with } \sigma > 1 \tag{1}$$

and charge a constant markup of $\mu = \sigma / (\sigma - 1)$. Here, y is industry output and p the industry price index.

Output is produced by completing a mass M of tasks indexed by x and belonging to some set T. The production function for firm f is

$$y_f = z_f \cdot \left(\frac{1}{M}\int_{\mathcal{T}} (M \cdot y_f(x))^{\lambda-1/\lambda} \cdot dx\right)^{\lambda/(\lambda-1)},$$

where z_f denotes the (factor-neutral) productivity of the firm, $y_f(x)$ denotes the quantity of task x completed, and $\lambda > 0$ is the elasticity of substitution between tasks.

All firms in the industry complete the same set of tasks, T, but differ in their productivity z_f, the factor prices they face, and how they assign tasks to different factors. Specifically, task x can be performed using workers from different skill groups, indexed by g,

$$y_f(x) = \sum_g A_g \cdot \psi_g(x) \cdot l_{g,f}(x).$$

Here, $l_{g,f}(x)$ is the quantity of labor of type g employed by the firm at task x, A_g denotes the productivity level of these workers across all tasks, and $\psi_g(x)$ denotes their productivity at task x. Task-specific productivities $\psi_g(x)$ capture the comparative advantages of groups of workers across tasks (e.g., less educated workers might have a comparative advantage in manual tasks).

Firm f can pay a fixed cost $\kappa_f(x)$ to adopt and integrate the technology required to automate the production of task x. Depending on the task, this may involve the use of AI, robotics, dedicated equipment, or specialized software to complete the task. We denote the specialized capital used for this purpose by $k_f(x)$, which yields the automated production of task x for firms that pay the fixed cost as

$$y_f(x) = A_k \cdot \psi_k(x) \cdot k_f(x),$$

where A_k gives capital productivity across all tasks and $\psi_k(x)$ is the productivity of specialized capital at task x. The fact that automation takes place at the task level, using task-specific specialized equipment or algorithms, aligns with the way in which industrial robots, narrow AI algorithms, dedicated equipment, and specialized software are used in practice. This also underscores that automation technologies are not "general-purpose" but highly customized for certain applications and tasks.

We close the model by assuming that firms pay exogenous wages given by $w_{f,g} = \tau_f \cdot w_g$, where w_g is the common component of the wage for workers in skill group g, faced by all firms in the industry, while τ_f is a firm-specific component, reflecting differences in the labor supplied faced by firms or the way they share rents with workers. On the other hand, we take the user cost of capital, w_k, to be common across firms and tasks.

1.3.2 Costs of Automation and Differences in Technology Across Firms

In the benchmark case in which wages are identical across firms and there are no fixed costs of automation, all firms would make the same cost-minimizing automation decisions. Differences in the factor-neutral productivity term z_f do not impact automation decisions and simply translate into differences in firm scale. In this benchmark, despite having different scales, all firms in an industry would employ the same bundle of workers, machines, and software to produce, and would have the exact same labor productivity and labor share.

As described in the introduction, however, there are sizable differences in adoption rates across firms, both between and within industries. We view these differences as being due to three factors:

- The nature of tasks required in an industry and firm determines the applicability of automation technologies. For example, industrial robots are not useful in most non-manufacturing industries, and within manufacturing, they are most suitable for various manual tasks involved in heavy industry, such as welding, painting, sorting and assembly, while certain fine-motor tasks, such as stitching of shoes, are harder for robots. Yet, other manual tasks involved in spinning, weaving and stitching in textile industries can be automated using dedicated equipment. Likewise, a range of white-collar tasks in services can be automated using specialized software and increasingly AI.

- Firms that compete in the same industry may face different wages, contributing to differences in adoption decisions.
- The fixed costs of adopting and integrating automation technologies will preclude some firms from using them. These fixed costs depend on industry (e.g., because it determines the engineering complexity of the tasks to automate), firm age (e.g., because they might face less organizational barriers), and other firm-level characteristics (e.g., how digitally savvy or informed the management may be and whether the firm needs to customize its products). For this reason, younger firms might have lower fixed costs, while the same fixed cost will make automation technologies less profitable for smaller firms in industries with limited applications for advanced technologies. Integration costs can be sizable. For example, in manufacturing, integration costs associated with the use of industrial robots can add up to four times the cost of the actual equipment (see, for example, Leigh and Kraft 2018).

1.3.3 Automation, Factor Shares, and Labor Productivity

Let $T_{f,k}$ denote the set of tasks that firm f has automated, while T_g denotes the set of tasks for which production by worker of type g would minimize costs in the absence of automation. Following Acemoglu and Restrepo (2022), define the *task share* of workers of type g and capital at firm f as

$$\Gamma_{f,g} = \frac{1}{M}\int_{\tau_g - \tau_{f,k}} \psi_g(x)^{\lambda-1} \cdot dx, \; \Gamma_{f,k} = \frac{1}{M}\int_{\tau_{f,k}} \psi_k(x)^{\lambda-1} \cdot dx.$$

The unit cost of production for firm f is then

$$c_f = \frac{1}{z_f} \cdot \left(\sum_g \Gamma_{f,g} \cdot w_{f,g}^{1-\lambda} + \Gamma_{f,k} \cdot w_k^{1-\lambda}\right)^{1/(1-\lambda)}.$$

Although this unit cost resembles the standard constant elasticity of substitution price index (which would result when firms have CES production functions), the shares are now endogenous and depend on $T_{f,k}$—the set of tasks that the firm has automated. Input shares are also related to $T_{f,k}$. As a result, the share of labor in costs, which is proportional to the share of labor in value added, is

$$s_{l,f} = \frac{\sum_g \Gamma_{f,g} \cdot w_g^{1-\lambda}}{\sum_g \Gamma_{f,g} \cdot w_g^{1-\lambda} + \Gamma_{f,k} \cdot w_k^{1-\lambda}}.$$

Likewise, the share of labor of type g in the wage bill can be computed as

$$s_{g,f} = \frac{\Gamma_{f,g} \cdot w_g^{1-\lambda}}{\sum_{g'} \Gamma_{f,g'} \cdot w_{g'}^{1-\lambda}},$$

and labor productivity (defined as sales per worker) as:

$$\textit{labor productivity}_f = \mu \cdot \underline{w}_f \cdot \frac{\sum_g \Gamma_{f,g} \cdot w_g^{1-\lambda} + \Gamma_{f,k} \cdot w_k^{1-\lambda}}{\sum_g \Gamma_{f,g} \cdot w_g^{1-\lambda}},$$

where $\underline{w}_f$ denotes the average wage paid by the firm. These expressions show that the labor share, the share of each skill in costs, and labor productivity are shaped by task shares and which tasks are automated.

In summary, labor shares and labor productivity will differ across firms because of variation in task shares. In particular, firms' automation decisions, summarized by the set of tasks they have automated $\{T_{k,f}\}$, determine their factor shares and labor productivity. In turn, firms will automate different sets of tasks depending on the fixed costs $\kappa_f(x)$, firm-specific wages, and industry differences in the nature of tasks.

1.3.4 Implications

The framework delivers the following implications:

- The adoption rate of automation technologies could be low because of the high specificity of the tasks that can be effectively automated, high integration costs, or organizational barriers to new technology.
- There are large differences in adoption across industries driven by the applicability of advanced technologies to production tasks.
- Because of the fixed cost of adoption, large firms are more likely to adopt automation technologies. If the fixed costs of adoption, κ_f, are lower for younger firms, then we expect younger firms to also adopt these technologies at a higher rate, conditional on their size.
- All else equal, higher-wage firms—those with larger T_f—are more likely to adopt automation technologies as well.
- Adopters of automation technologies will have lower labor shares and higher labor productivity.
- Automation, by reducing production costs, always expands firm sales but has an ambiguous effect on firm employment. The overall employment effect depends on whether the productivity effect (the higher sales induced by the cost reduction generated by automation) dominates the displacement effect (the fact that the firm becomes less labor intensive). Independently of which effect dominates, firm employment effects of automation overstate the industry-level implications, since automating firms expand in part at the expense of their competitors.
- If automated tasks used to be performed by lower-skill groups (which is

what we would expect to the extent that routine tasks are more likely to be automated), then advanced technologies will also increase (average) skill requirements directly.

- The implications of each technology (AI, robotics, etc.) for labor productivity and the demand for skills depend on the types of tasks that it automates. Technologies automating tasks performed by workers with lower skill levels will lead to a greater increase in labor productivity and demand for skills.

Our framework also underscores a key distinction between automation and other forms of technological progress. For example, a technology that simply raises productivity in a factor-neutral way—z_f in our model—would also raise firm sales and employment by the same amount, but would have no impact on the labor share, skill requirements or labor productivity (measured as sales per worker).[16] Hence, automation technologies have very distinct effects than factor-neutral technologies on firms' demand for skills, factor shares, and labor productivity. As we will see, the correlations in the data are consistent with the implications we expect from advanced technologies being used for automation, and not simply to increase TFP in a factor neutral way.

1.4 The Adoption of Advanced Technologies

This section documents the aggregate patterns of adoption by technology, differences in adoption between and within industries, and the main bottlenecks limiting wider adoption.

1.4.1 Adoption Rates by Technology

Table 1.1 reports the share of firms using each of the technologies as part of their processes and methods. Column 1 shows that the share of firms using these advanced technologies is low for AI and robotics (with 3.2 percent of US firms using AI and 2 percent using robotics), and moderate for the remaining technologies (19.6 percent for dedicated equipment, 40.2 percent for specialized software, and 34 percent for cloud computing).[17]

16. It might at first be counterintuitive that higher z_f has no effect on labor productivity. To understand this result, first note that higher z_f increases TFP, but labor productivity, defined as (dollar value of) sales divided by labor, is invariant to it. To see this, take the simple example in which there is only one type of labor, no capital, and the firm's production function is simply $z_f \ell_f$, and the firm still faces the demand curve given by (1). In this case, an increase in z_f increases real output per worker, but reduces price by exactly as much, so labor productivity remains constant. As this example clarifies, this holds so long as firms face a demand curve with constant demand elasticity.

17. The adoption rates of robotics and AI are close to the rates obtained in the 2018 ABS technology module: 1.4 percent and 5.8 percent, respectively (see Zolas et al. 2020), even though there are some differences across the two modules in the way technologies are defined and the survey reference periods for measurement (2017 in the 2018 ABS versus 2016–18 in the 2019 ABS).

Table 1.1 **Technology adoption rates for processes and methods and as part of goods and services, ABS data for 2016–2018**

	Technology users		Technology providers	
	Share of firms using technology (1)	Share of workers employed at firms using technology (2)	Share of firms selling technology (3)	Share of workers employed at firms selling technology (4)
Artificial Intelligence	3.2%	12.6%	0.5%	2.2%
Robotics	2.0%	15.7%	0.3%	1.8%
Dedicated Equipment	19.6%	36.4%	2.5%	4.8%
Specialized Software	40.2%	64.4%	4.3%	7.8%
Cloud Computing	34.0%	61.8%	3.5%	7.1%
Any Technology	47.6%	69.9%	6.3%	11.1%

Note: Data from the 2019 ABS technology module and authors' calculations. Technology use rates are based on firms' answers to questions E3 of the ABS: "During the three years 2016 to 2018, to what extent did this business use the following technologies in production processes for goods or services?" The table provides the share of firms that report using the technology in any capacity (low, moderate, or high use). Technology provision rates are based on firms' answers to questions E20 of the ABS: "During the three years 2016 to 2018, did this business sell the following technologies or goods or services that included the following technologies?" We exclude firms who either responded "do not know" or did not respond to these questions from our calculations.

In total, 47.6 percent of US firms had adopted at least one of these technologies by 2018.[18]

Even though a moderate share of firms uses these technologies, these firms are among the largest in the United States and account for a sizable share of employment. As a result, the share of workers *exposed* to advanced technologies is significantly higher than the share of firms using these technologies. Even though only 2 percent of US firms use robotics, 15.7 percent of US workers are employed at firms using robots. As shown in column 2, the employment share of users is 12.6 percent for AI, 36.4 percent for dedicated equipment, 64.4 percent for specialized software, and 61.8 percent for cloud computing. These employment shares are informative of the aggregate importance of these technologies for labor and product markets.

A key advantage of the ABS module is that it distinguishes between *users* and *producers* of technology. Columns 1 and 2 reported the share of firms and workers at firms *using* these technologies as part of their production processes. But the ABS also asks firms whether they sold goods or provided services that embedded these technologies (e.g., whether the firm produces

18. The 2019 ABS also queries firms on the intensity of use (low, moderate, or high use). The most heavily adopted technologies turn out to be also the most intensively used. Specialized software has the highest intensity of use with 44 percent of users reporting high and 35 percent reporting moderate use, followed by cloud and specialized equipment, each with 32–33 percent high use and 36–39 percent moderate use. AI and robotics have the lowest intensity of use with only 15–18 percent of users reporting high use and 33–35 percent moderate use.

Table 1.2 **Conditional adoption rates of multiple technologies, ABS data for 2016–2018**

	Share of firms using technology Y (column) conditional on using X (row)				
	Y = Artificial Intelligence (1)	Y = Robotics (2)	Y = Dedicated Equipment (3)	Y = Specialized Software (4)	Y = Cloud Computing (5)
X = Artificial Intelligence	100%	19.3%	54.4%	90.0%	85.8%
X = Robotics	30.2%	100%	87.7%	89.6%	73.1%
X =Dedicated Equipment	8.7%	9.0%	100%	82.9%	59.8%
X =Specialized Software	7.1%	4.5%	40.7%	100%	68.2%
X =Cloud Computing	7.9%	4.3%	34.4%	79.9%	100%
Unconditional rates	3.2%	2.0%	19.6%	40.2%	34.0%

Note: Data from the 2019 ABS technology module and authors' calculations. The table reports the conditional probability of a firm using technology Y (reported across columns) given that it uses technology X (reported across rows). Technology use rates are based on firms' answer to questions E3 of the ABS: "During the three years 2016 to 2018, to what extent did this business use the following technologies in production processes for goods or services?" These conditional probabilities exclude firms who either responded "do not know" or did not respond from our calculations.

and sells robots or provides cloud-based solutions to customers). Column 3 shows that the supply side of these technologies is more concentrated than their use, with only 0.3 percent of firms selling robots, 0.5 percent providing goods and services embedding AI algorithms, and 3.5 percent of firms selling cloud-based solutions. Column 4 shows that suppliers account for a small share of US employment too, so that more workers are employed at firms using these technologies than at firms producing them. In the rest of this paper, we will focus on users of advanced technologies.

Firms adopt multiple technologies at the same time, which points to complementarities between technologies. Table 1.2 shows that 86 percent of the firms that use AI also use cloud, and 90 percent of the firms that use robotics also use specialized software. Columns 4 and 5 of table 1.2 show that this is particularly the case for cloud computing and specialized software, which are typically used to control and handle the computing needs of robotic systems and dedicated equipment.[19]

1.4.2 Differences in Adoption by Sector and Industry

Figure 1.1 summarizes the differences in adoption rates both in terms of the share of firms using the technology (Panel A) and the share of workers at using firms (Panel B) across sectors.

19. Likewise, some specialized software products such as Customer Relationship Management (CRM) or Enterprise Resource Planning (ERP) systems as well as some cloud services (e.g., AWS) have (or are planning to incorporate) some built-in AI capabilities. 59 percent of early AI adopters report using such tools to implement or test AI applications, according to a survey conducted by Deloitte (Loucks, Davenport, and Schatsky 2018).

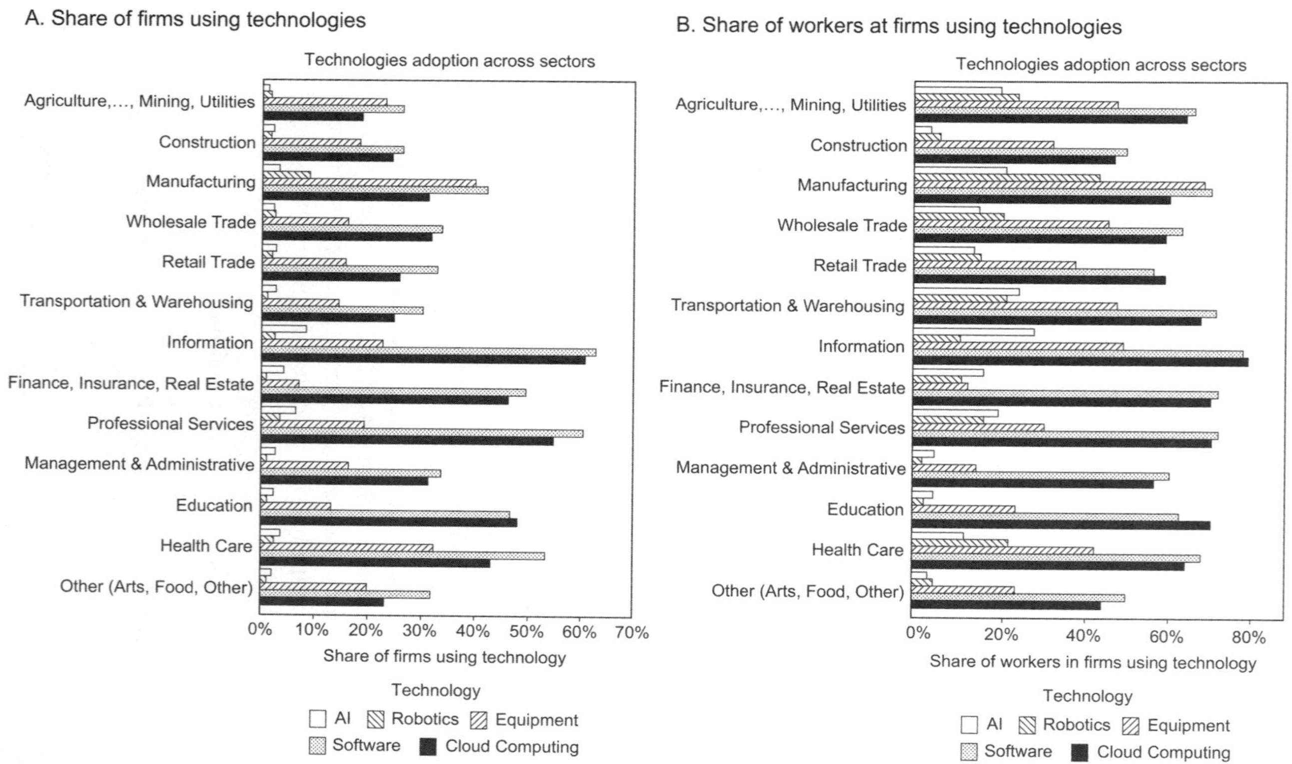

Fig. 1.1 Technology use across US economic sectors, ABS data for 2016–2018

Technology use rates are based on firms' answers to questions E3 of the ABS, "During the three years 2016 to 2018, to what extent did this business use the following technologies in production processes for goods or services?" excluding firms who responded "do not know" or did not respond.

The adoption of advanced technologies is particularly high in manufacturing, the information sector, professional services, healthcare, retail, and wholesale. The exception to this pattern is robotics, which remains highly concentrated in manufacturing, with 8.7 percent of manufacturing firms using robotics and 45.1 percent of all manufacturing workers being exposed to this technology, while firms in other sectors exhibit much lower adoption rates.

The ABS data reveal large variation across detailed industries in the same broad sectors. Figure 1.2 and table 1.3 illustrate this variation. The figure plots a histogram of the number of 4-digit industries by mean adoption rate for all industries, manufacturing, and non-manufacturing. The table complements this information with coefficients of variation for the adoption rate of each technology across 4-digit industries. It shows that there is sizable dispersion in adoption of AI and robotics across industries, and considerable (but less) dispersion in the adoption of dedicated equipment, specialized software, and cloud computing.[20] One explanation for the importance of detailed industry in determining adoption patterns is that the nature of products and tasks varies across detailed industries, and this determines the applicability of advanced technologies to specific tasks in those industries.

1.4.3 Adoption Rates by Firm Size and Age

Even though industries play an important role in determining adoption, there is sizable variation in adoption across firms within detailed industries. Figure 1.3 explores the role of size and age, which our framework identifies as important dimensions that mediate adoption decisions. For each technology, we report adoption rates in 36 size–age categories, defined in terms of employment and age percentiles within detailed 6-digit industries.[21] The figure also reports the average adoption rate for firms by size.

Adoption rises significantly with size across all technologies. For example, 5.5 percent of firms in the top percentile of industries' employment distribution use AI, 5.1 percent use robots, 31.4 percent use dedicated equipment, 67.4 percent use specialized software, and 63.5 percent use cloud computing. In contrast, the adoption rate among firms in the 50th to 75th percentile of industries' employment distribution is much lower: 3.1 percent for AI, 1.7 percent for robots, 18.6 percent for dedicated equipment, 39.6 percent for specialized software, and 33.4 percent for cloud computing. These facts support the idea that automating tasks, or adopting advanced technologies

20. For example, in manufacturing, 87.4 percent of the workers in hardware manufacturing (NAICS code 3325), 81.8 percent of the workers in forging (NAICS 3321), 67.2 percent of the workers in motor vehicle manufacturing (NAICS 3363), and 75.4 percent of workers in dairy product manufacturing (NAICS 3115) are employed at firms using robotics, which are much higher than the manufacturing sector mean of 45.1 percent.

21. We assign firms to their predominant 6-digit NAICS industry in terms of payroll across all its establishments. In this and all subsequent exercises, the employment percentiles are defined based on the employment distribution from the LBD in each industry.

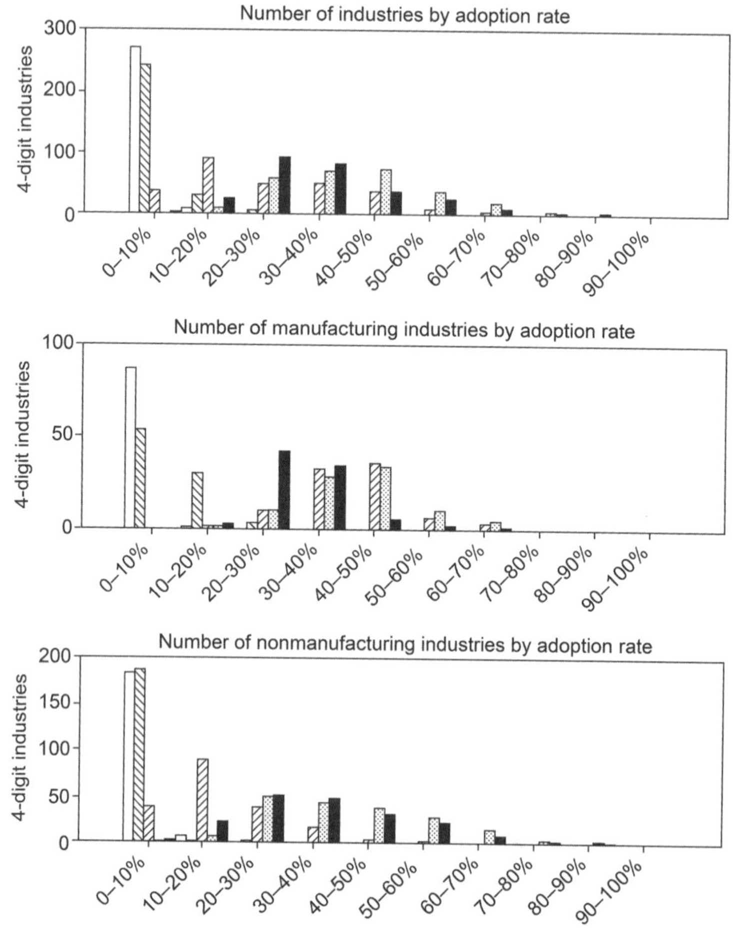

Fig. 1.2 Technology use across 4-digit NAICS industries, ABS data for 2016–2018
Adoption rates based on firms' answers to questions E3 of the ABS, "During the three years 2016 to 2018, to what extent did this business use the following technologies in production processes for goods or services?" excluding firms who responded "do not know" or did not respond. The figure plots histograms with the number of industries by adoption rate in bins 0–10 percent, 10–20 percent, . . . , and 90–100 percent.

more generally, involves large integration costs, which imply that large and growing firms will select into adopting these technologies.[22]

Although not as strong as the pattern for size, we see that among firms

22. In a companion paper, Acemoglu et al. (2023), we provide additional evidence in support of this interpretation. In particular, we document that adopters have had larger establishments than non-adopters from their same cohort at every age and that, for many cohorts, these differences preceded the arrival of advanced technologies. Moreover, these size differences between adopters and non-adopters have become smaller for more recent cohorts, presumably as these technologies become standardized and the costs of integration falls.

Table 1.3 **Coefficients of variation for technology adoption rates across 4-digit industries**

	Coefficient of variation	
	Adoption rates by industry	Employment-weighted adoption rates by industry
	Panel A. All sectors	
AI	0.83	1.26
Robotics	1.25	1.13
Equipment	0.57	0.55
Software	0.33	0.25
Cloud	0.39	0.29
	Panel B. Manufacturing	
AI	0.64	1.10
Robotics	0.54	0.56
Equipment	0.22	0.22
Software	0.25	0.21
Cloud	0.25	0.27
	Panel C. Non-manufacturing	
AI	0.91	1.30
Robotics	1.73	1.45
Equipment	0.57	0.58
Software	0.37	0.26
Cloud	0.42	0.30

Note: Data from the 2019 ABS technology module based on authors' calculations. Column 1 reports the coefficient of variation (standard deviation divided by mean) for adoption rates across 4-digit industries. Column 2 reports the CV for employment-weighted adoption rates.

of a given size, adoption tends to decrease with age. For most size classes, younger firms are more likely to adopt advanced technologies than older ones.[23] The declining adoption rates by age is in line with the idea that younger firms face fewer organizational barriers or do not have to pay a cost to reallocate workers as they automate tasks. The patterns in figure 1.3 also suggest that new entrants play an important role in the diffusion of advanced technologies, as is commonly assumed in models of technology diffusion (see, for example, Perla, Tonetti, and Waugh 2021; Hubmer and Restrepo 2021). Likewise, these patterns point to the slowdown in entry as potentially contributing to the low adoption rates observed at the aggregate level, especially for smaller firms (see Decker et al. 2020 for evidence on the decline of entry and dynamism).

23. One exception to this pattern is that technology adoption rates for firms in the 95+ age percentile group are higher than that of the 90–95 group. One difficulty in interpreting the results for the oldest firms is that the LBD only extends back to 1976, meaning that we cannot identify precise age values for firms born before 1977. Thus, the age distribution of firms in our ABS sample is truncated from above at 42 years, with all firms of age 42+ being assigned to the highest age percentile group.

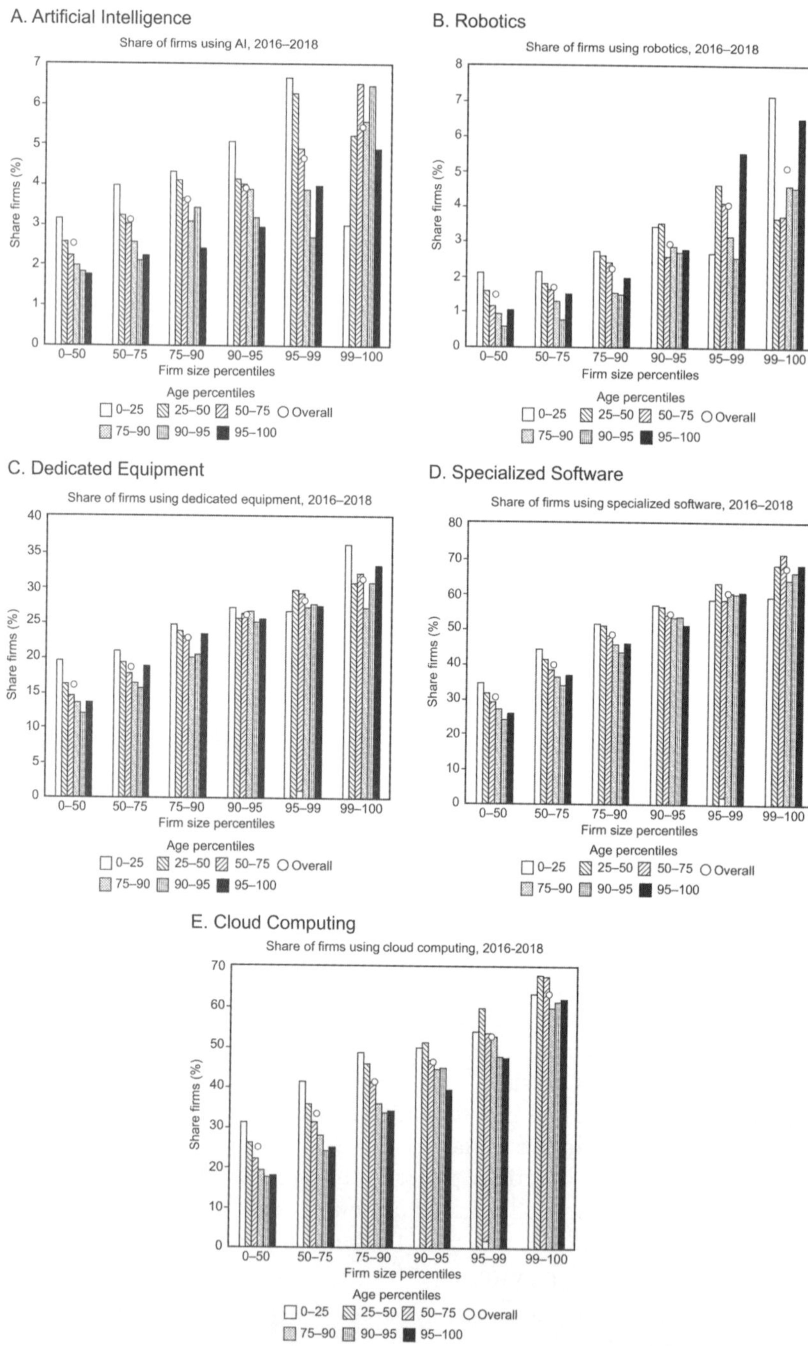

Fig. 1.3 Adoption rates by firm size and age classes within detailed 6-digit industries, ABS data for 2016–2018

1.4.4 Factors Adversely Affecting Technology Adoption

The ABS data reveal that a majority of firms, especially small firms, have not adopted advanced technologies. The 2019 ABS asked firms to identify all the factors limiting adoption from a list of 10 options (including costs, lack of data or skills, concerns about safety and regulations), or to indicate that no factors limited their adoption. Half of the firms that did not adopt technologies reported at least one factor that limited their adoption. As summarized in panel A of table 1.4, 45–50 percent of non-adopters (the majority of firms that reported some limiting factor) report that the advanced technologies in the ABS module are not applicable to their business. Besides lack of applicability, the main adverse factor discouraging adoption is its high cost, with 7–8 percent of nonusers (about an eighth of the firms that reported some limiting factor) identifying high costs as the main bottleneck for adoption.

For firms that adopted the technology, the adverse factors listed may be interpreted as discouraging further adoption or the intensity of use. As summarized in panel B, adopters faced fewer limitations as a whole, with 52–77 percent reporting no bottlenecks. On the other hand, some adopters identify lack of applicability (7–13 percent of firms) and high costs (6–17 percent) as the main factors limiting further adoption. The case of AI and robotics is particularly interesting, since these are the technologies with the lowest adoption rates and for which users reported the most bottlenecks (48 percent of AI users and 36 percent of robotics users reported some adverse factor that limited their adoption, compared to 25 percent of users for the remaining technologies). In contrast to the remaining technologies, users of AI and robotics see these technologies as lacking maturity, and identify the lack of human capital and financing as important bottlenecks for their adoption and more intense use.

These findings suggest that these advanced technologies have had limited applicability and require a high cost of adoption. This view aligns with our model, which sees advanced technologies as applicable to specific tasks—rather than general purpose technologies increasing the productivity of all firms at all industries irrespective of their task structure—and recognizes that there might be a high fixed cost of adoption. These two factors limit adoption but also imply that adoption concentrates in specific industries (those with the greatest applicability) and among large firms.

1.5 The Use of Advanced Technologies for Automation and Other Motivations

This section documents the extent to which US firms use advanced technologies for automation and the role of other uses and motivations for adoption.

Table 1.4 Factors limiting the adoption of advanced technologies, ABS data for 2016–2018

	Artificial Intelligence (1)	Robotics (2)	Dedicated Equipment (3)	Specialized Software (4)	Cloud Computing (5)
Panel A: firms not using the technology					
No adverse factors	41%	41%	44%	43%	42%
Technology not applicable to this business	49%	50%	47%	46%	44%
Technology too expensive	7%	7%	7%	8%	7%
Technology not mature	2%	1%	0%	0%	1%
Lacked access to required data	1%	0%	0%	0%	1%
Required data not reliable	0%	0%	0%	0%	0%
Lacked access to human capital or talent	1%	1%	1%	1%	1%
Laws and regulations	1%	0%	0%	0%	0%
Concerns regarding safety and security	1%	0%	0%	0%	3%
Lacked access to capital	1%	1%	1%	1%	1%
Panel B: firms using the technology					
No adverse factors	52%	64%	72%	77%	75%
Technology not applicable to this business	13%	8%	8%	7%	7%
Technology too expensive	17%	17%	12%	9%	6%
Technology not mature	10%	4%	1%	1%	2%
Lacked access to required data	4%	1%	1%	1%	1%
Required data not reliable	4%	2%	1%	1%	1%
Lacked access to human capital or talent	6%	4%	2%	2%	2%
Laws and regulations	4%	2%	2%	2%	2%
Concerns regarding safety and security	6%	3%	2%	3%	7%
Lacked access to capital	7%	7%	5%	3%	2%

Note: Data from the 2019 ABS technology module based on authors' calculations. The table reports the share of non-adopters (Panel A) and adopters (Panel B) that report each of the factors listed in the rows as adversely affecting their adoption of each technology, with separate technologies in different columns. The estimates reported above are based on responses to the following question in the 2019 ABS: "During the three years 2016 to 2018, indicate which factors adversely affected the adoption or utilization of the following technologies to produce goods or services. Select all that apply for each technology."

1.5.1 Motivations for Technology Adoption

A common view is that advanced technologies facilitate the automation of tasks previously performed by labor. Industrial robots and dedicated equipment are being used in manufacturing to automate tasks such as welding, painting, and assembly. AI is being used to create algorithms capable of achieving human proficiency at predictive tasks, such as controlling automated vehicles, trading, and medical diagnostics. And specialized

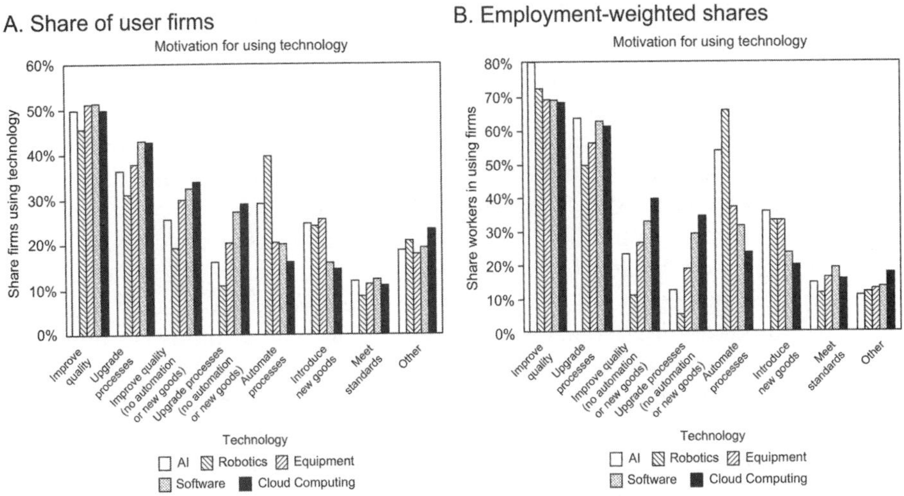

Fig. 1.4 Motivation for technology adoption, ABS data for 2016–2018
Tabulations based on questions E4 of the ABS, which asked firms, for each technology, "During the three years 2016 to 2018, why did this business adopt or use [technology]? Select all that apply."

software systems are capable of handling payrolls and sales. While these examples abound, we do not know the real extent to which firms are using these advanced technologies for automation. It could well be the case that firms use these technologies to control the quality of their processes, replace older vintages of machinery (instead of workers), or expand their offering of goods and services—alternative uses which do not involve the automation of tasks previously performed by labor. The distinction is consequential. As our theory demonstrates, the use of a technology for automation generates distinct effects on firm and worker outcomes.

To understand the importance of automation and other uses of advanced technology, the ABS module asked adopters to identify their motivations for adoption from six possibilities: (1) to automate tasks performed by labor; (2) to upgrade outdated processes or methods; (3) to improve the quality or reliability of processes; (4) to expand the range of goods and services provided; (5) to adopt standards and accreditation; (6) some other reasons. Adopters were able to select all the motivations that applied.

The share of adopting firms stating these motivations by technology is shown in figure 1.4. Panel A reports the share of user firms reporting each motivation, while panel B reports an employment-weighted share. Improving quality and the reliability of processes is the most common motivator. The employment-weighted shares in panel B show that 68–80 percent of all users cite this as a motivation for using advanced technologies. About 50–64 percent of firms report using these technologies to upgrade outdated processes or methods, and 20–36 percent report using these technologies to expand the range of goods and services offered. Adopting standards and accreditation is the least common motivation for all technologies.[24]

In both panels, but especially in panel B, we see that a significant share of adopters report using advanced technologies to automate tasks performed by labor. AI and robotics are the two technologies with the greatest automation component, with 54 percent of firms using AI and 66 percent of the firms using robotics (in an employment-weighted sense) doing so to automate tasks. On the other hand, 37 percent of the firms using dedicated equipment and 32 percent of the firms using specialized software do so to automate tasks. Cloud computing is the technology least connected to automation, with 24 percent of firms using it to automate tasks.

The comparison between panels A and B also shows that, conditional on their adoption, large firms are more likely to use these technologies for automation. For example, the 40 percent of robotics-using firms adopting the technology for automation (panel A) account for 66 percent of employment among robot-using firms (panel B).

How important is automation as a driver of technology adoption? One challenge in answering this question is that firms were able to select multiple motivations. Most of the firms that report adopting advanced technologies for automation or for introducing new products also indicate that these involved an increase in the quality and reliability of their processes and an upgrade of their methods. To remove this overlap, the figure shows the share of firms that report using the technology to improve the quality of their processes and upgrade their methods but not for automating tasks or introducing new goods and services (firm shares in panel A and employment-weighted shares in panel B). We view these shares as measuring other uses of technology different from automation or the introduction of new products. For example, these numbers would capture firms purchasing new dedicated machinery to replace older machines, or using AI algorithms to replace existing software systems—upgrades to their processes that improve quality and reliability but do not involve automation or a change in their product mix. For AI, robotics, and dedicated equipment, automation is more important than these alternative uses of technology. For specialized software, automation is as important as these other uses of technology. For cloud computing, automation is less important than these alternative uses of technology.

In sum, the ABS points to automation being a distinct and important driver of the adoption of advanced technologies. The ABS data also highlight that the extent to which advanced technologies are being used for automation varies by technology, with AI and robotics being more closely

24. The ranking of motivations for technology adoption reported by firms matches the results from the 1991 Survey of Manufacturing Technology. The top benefit from technology use stated by plants in that survey was quality improvement, followed by labor cost reduction and flexibility increase (see figure 3 in Dinlersoz and Wolf 2024).

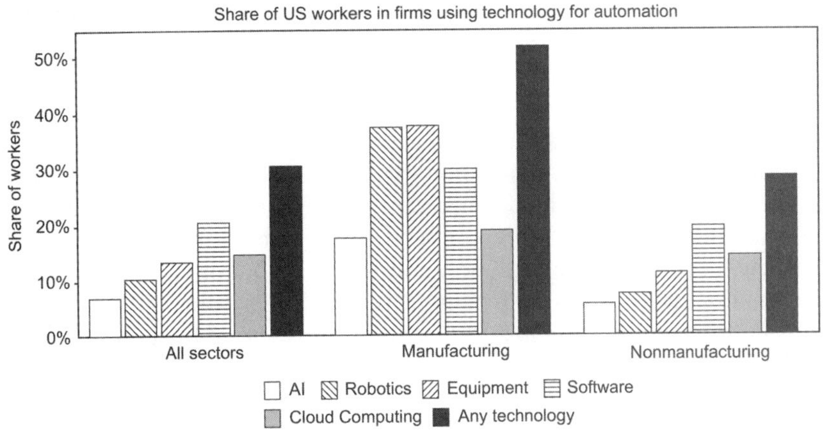

Fig. 1.5 US workers' exposure to automation via advanced technologies, ABS data for 2016–2018

This exposure measure is computed as the share of the US workforce currently employed at firms using each technology for automation.

linked to automation and software and cloud-computing systems having more diverse uses.[25]

1.5.2 The Exposure of US Workers to Automation

Using the ABS information on motivation, we can compute the *exposure of US workers to automation*, defined as the share of workers employed at firms using advanced technologies to automate tasks. This measure is informative of the extent of automation in US labor markets.

Figure 1.5 reports our estimates of worker exposure to automation. 6.8 percent of US workers are employed at firms using AI for automation, and this number rises to 10.4 percent for robotics, 13.5 percent for dedicated equipment, 20.5 percent for specialized software, and 14.7 percent for cloud computing. Even though AI and robotics are more likely to be used to automate tasks, automation via dedicated equipment, specialized software, and cloud-based systems have been more important contributors

25. There are two interpretations of these findings. On the one hand, this could reflect some fundamental and permanent differences across technologies. For example, it might be the case that dedicated equipment and specialized software simply have more diverse applications, while most applications of robotics and AI entail automation. This would also explain the wider adoption of software and dedicated equipment relative to AI and robotics. On the other hand, these differences might be temporary and reflect the maturity of these technologies. For example, it could be the case that technologies are initially deployed with an emphasis on automation, since these applications are more salient and easier to conceive. Over time, and as the technology matures and diffuses, new and more diverse applications of the technology emerge. While the cross-sectional ABS data do not allow us to tease apart these two explanations, we view this as an important question going forward.

in the aggregate due to their wider adoption. In total, 30.4 percent of US workers are employed at firms using advanced technologies for automation.

The ABS data also allow us to gauge the importance of automation in manufacturing and outside of this sector. This is important because most studies have focused on automation via robotics in the manufacturing sector, and relatively less is known about the extent to which automation takes place in services, retail, and other sectors. Exposure to automation is higher in manufacturing, with 52 percent of manufacturing workers employed at firms using at least one of these technologies for automation. However, automation is not exclusive to manufacturing: 28.3 percent of US workers outside of manufacturing are employed at firms using at least one of these technologies for automation.

Not all workers employed at firms using these technologies are (or have been) subject to the effects of automation. Still, these high exposure measures suggest that the use of advanced technologies for automation is a relevant force affecting the US labor market, despite their limited adoption across firms. This is because large firms are both more likely to adopt advanced technologies and to use these technologies for automation, and these firms account for a large share of labor demand.

1.6 Advanced Technologies, Wages, and Labor Productivity

This section documents systematic differences between firms that adopt and use advanced technologies and non-adopters in terms of their labor productivity, labor share and average wages.

1.6.1 Firm Correlates of Adoption

We first explore the correlation between technology use in 2016–2018 and baseline firm-level characteristics in 2015—a date that preceded the reference period of the ABS.[26] For each technology, we estimate the linear probability model:

$$Adopter_{f,i,s,a}^{tech} = \alpha_i^{tech} + \gamma_s^{tech} + \lambda_a^{tech} + \beta^{tech} \cdot X_f + \varepsilon_{f,i,s,a}^{tech}. \quad (2)$$

The dependent variable is a dummy for whether firm f in industry i size class s and age a used a given advanced technology during 2016–2018.[27] We explore

26. This timing choice does not imply any causality. First, adoption may have taken place prior to the reference period (the ABS only asked firms if they used the technology in 2016–2018, not if they adopted it during this period). Second, even firms that adopted during 2016–2018 might already be different in terms of unobservables by 2015. We interpret the estimates simply as describing the main cross-sectional differences between users and other firms.

27. We generate separate samples for each technology by dropping firms that answer either "don't know" or left blank questions regarding the intensity of their use of that technology (e.g. a firm that answers "don't know" to whether it uses robotics is not included in the sample for which we analyze robotics adoption). We also generate a separate sample for "any technology" by dropping firms that answer either "don't know" or left blank all technology use intensity questions.

if adoption correlates with firm characteristics from the LBD, including firm size, age, and average wages paid in 2015 (salaries and wages/employment). We also include two measures that capture the industry diversification of firms and the importance of manufacturing as part of their activities. The first one is a dummy variable that equals 1 for firms that have some (but not all) of their establishments engaged in manufacturing activities. This dummy identifies firms with some manufacturing activity. The second computes for these multi-sector firms the share of firm's employment classified in manufacturing based on its establishments' industry codes.

All of our specifications control for 6-digit industry dummies α_i^{tech}, size categories γ_s^{tech} defined by employment percentiles in each 6-digit industry, age categories λ_a^{tech} defined by age percentiles in each industry, and firms' employment shares in each US state to account for their location. All regressions use firm weights that are constructed to make the ABS sample representative of the universe of employer firms in the LBD.

Table 1.5 presents the estimates of equation (2), with a separate panel for each technology. In line with the theoretical framework and the fact that a significant share of firms use advanced technologies for automation, we find that adopters paid higher wages in 2015. This holds even when comparing firms in the same industry and of similar size and age.

The fact that adopters paid higher wages in 2015 has three plausible interpretations. A first interpretation is that, as emphasized in our theory, higher wages generate incentives for automation. A second interpretation of this finding which is also consistent with firms' assessments in section 1.7 is that automation leads to a reallocation of labor from automated tasks to other roles, such as managerial, design, and engineering jobs that typically pay higher wages, which explains the higher mean wages. This effect could be present for firms that adopted some of these advanced technologies before 2015. A third interpretation is that firms that adopt advanced technologies had a more skilled workforce to begin with, as in Doms, Dunne, and Troske (1997), which facilitated the adoption of advanced technologies.

The even columns in table 1.5 explore the role of industry diversification and the importance of manufacturing in firms' activities. Adopters tend to be diversified and have some manufacturing activities. Still, their share of manufacturing is lower than other multi-industry firms (with the exception of dedicated equipment for which the association is positive), though this relationship is not precisely estimated.[28]

In all specifications, adoption rises with size and decreases with age (with the exception of the oldest firms). Although not reported, all regressions control for detailed industry dummies and employment shares by state. 6-digit NAICS industry dummies account for 66–88 percent of the explained varia-

28. Continuing manufacturing firms have increased their employment of non-manufacturing workers over time, contributing to the process of structural transformation in the economy (see Fort, Pierce, and Schott 2018). Our findings suggest that this firm transformation has coincided with the adoption of advanced technologies.

Table 1.5 **Regressions accounting for the variation in the use of advanced technologies for 2016–2018, ABS data**

	Artificial intelligence		Robotics		Dedicated equipment		Specialized software		Cloud computing	
Dependent variable:	(1)	(2)	(3)	(4)	(5)	(6)	(7)	(8)	(9)	(10)
Employment percentile	0.008	0.008	0.007	0.007	0.056	0.056	0.109	0.109	0.096	0.096
50th−75th	(0.002)	(0.002)	(0.001)	(0.001)	(0.004)	(0.004)	(0.005)	(0.005)	(0.004)	(0.004)
Employment percentile	0.012	0.012	0.015	0.014	0.091	0.090	0.170	0.170	0.154	0.154
75th−90th	(0.002)	(0.002)	(0.001)	(0.001)	(0.005)	(0.005)	(0.006)	(0.006)	(0.005)	(0.005)
Employment percentile	0.016	0.016	0.025	0.024	0.108	0.107	0.222	0.222	0.208	0.208
90th−95th	(0.003)	(0.003)	(0.003)	(0.003)	(0.008)	(0.008)	(0.009)	(0.009)	(0.009)	(0.009)
Employment percentile	0.016	0.016	0.028	0.026	0.122	0.121	0.254	0.253	0.258	0.256
95th−99th	(0.004)	(0.004)	(0.003)	(0.003)	(0.009)	(0.009)	(0.010)	(0.010)	(0.010)	(0.010)
Employment percentile	0.033	0.031	0.044	0.038	0.173	0.167	0.311	0.309	0.329	0.327
99th+	(0.005)	(0.005)	(0.004)	(0.004)	(0.022)	(0.022)	(0.022)	(0.022)	(0.022)	(0.022)
Age percentile	−0.005	−0.005	−0.002	−0.002	−0.014	−0.014	−0.024	−0.024	−0.045	−0.045
10th−50th	(0.002)	(0.002)	(0.002)	(0.002)	(0.005)	(0.005)	(0.006)	(0.006)	(0.006)	(0.006)
Age percentile	−0.009	−0.009	−0.004	−0.004	−0.034	−0.034	−0.053	−0.053	−0.090	−0.090
50th−75th	(0.002)	(0.002)	(0.002)	(0.002)	(0.005)	(0.005)	(0.006)	(0.006)	(0.006)	(0.006)
Age percentile	−0.012	−0.012	−0.007	−0.007	−0.040	−0.040	−0.060	−0.060	−0.117	−0.117
76th−90th	(0.003)	(0.003)	(0.001)	(0.001)	(0.006)	(0.006)	(0.007)	(0.007)	(0.007)	(0.007)

	(1)	(2)	(3)	(4)	(5)	(6)	(7)	(8)	(9)	(10)
Age percentile 90th–95th	−0.017	−0.017	—	—	−0.051	−0.051	−0.083	−0.083	−0.136	−0.136
	(0.003)	(0.003)			(0.009)	(0.009)	(0.010)	(0.010)	(0.010)	(0.010)
Age percentile 95th–99th	−0.022	−0.022	−0.005	−0.006	−0.070	−0.070	−0.123	−0.123	−0.187	−0.187
	(0.005)	(0.005)	(0.002)	(0.002)	(0.012)	(0.012)	(0.015)	(0.015)	(0.014)	(0.014)
Age percentile 99th+	−0.011	−0.011	—	—	−0.045	−0.046	−0.077	−0.078	−0.125	−0.127
	(0.003)	(0.003)			(0.009)	(0.009)	(0.010)	(0.010)	(0.009)	(0.009)
log of average wage in 2015	0.003	0.003	0.002	0.002	0.014	0.014	0.047	0.047	0.050	0.050
	(0.001)	(0.001)	(0.001)	(0.001)	(0.002)	(0.002)	(0.003)	(0.003)	(0.002)	(0.002)
Multi-sector dummy		0.036		0.144		0.137		0.061		0.069
		(0.011)		(0.014)		(0.027)		(0.029)		(0.025)
Manufacturing employment share		−0.045		−0.020		0.155		−0.200		−0.334
		(0.029)		(0.048)		(0.105)		(0.127)		(0.104)
R-squared	0.016	0.016	0.051	0.053	0.118	0.118	0.139	0.139	0.142	0.142

Note: The table reports results from a regression of firm-level adoption on firm characteristics, 6-digit industry dummies, and employment shares by state. Columns 1–2 report results for the adoption of artificial intelligence. Columns 3–4 report results for the adoption of robotics. Columns 5–6 report results for the adoption of dedicated equipment. Columns 7–8 report results for the adoption of specialized software. Columns 9–10 report results for the adoption of cloud computing. To protect confidentiality, in columns 3–4 the coefficients for firms in the age percentiles 75th to 90th and 90th to 95th are pooled together, as well as firms in the age percentiles 95th to 99th and above the 99th percentile. These coefficients are reported under the row corresponding to firms in the 75th to 90th and 95th to 99th age percentiles, respectively. Robust standard errors are reported in parenthesis.

tion in adoption; while firm size classes explain 6.3–23 percent. On the other hand, once size and industry are accounted for, the geographic location of a firm (measured by its employment shares across states) plays a small role in determining their adoption decisions.

The appendix provides related exercises and checks.[29] Tables A.1 to A.2 repeat the regression analysis for manufacturing and non-manufacturing industries separately, uncovering similar patterns across sectors, and finding a significant role of wages in 2015 in explaining the use of these technologies in 2016–2018.[30]

1.6.2 Technology, Labor Productivity, and Superstar Firms

We now explore the link between technology use, labor productivity (measured as revenue per worker), and the labor share (measured as payroll over revenue). We document that the use of advanced technologies is associated with higher labor productivity and a lower labor share for adopting firms, both inside and outside of manufacturing.

As noted in section 1.3, adopters should achieve higher labor productivity for two reasons. First, when used for automation, advanced technologies allow firms to produce in a more capital-intensive way, by relying more on specialized equipment and software and less on labor. Second, these technologies may reduce employment of less-skilled workers and increase the hiring of skilled workers, and this effect on skill composition can also increase labor productivity. This is very different from a factor-neutral technology, which increases TFP but does not alter labor productivity.

We estimate regressions of the form

$$(3) \qquad \textit{Log labor productivity}_{f,i,s,a} = \alpha_i + \gamma_s + \lambda_a + \beta \cdot \textit{Technology User}_f + e_{f,i,s,a}\,.$$

This regression explains labor productivity in 2018 (measured from the LBD) as a function of 6-digit industry fixed effects α_i, 2015 size and age categories defined in terms of industries' percentiles γ_s and λ_a, and measures of technology use for 2016–2018 from the 2019 ABS.[31] We interpret this regression as descriptive and emphasize that this approach does not necessarily recover the causal effect of technology adoption on labor productivity.

Table 1.6 presents our estimates of equation (3). The specification in column 1 explains labor productivity with the size and age percentile categories. Starting at the median firm, there is an increasing relationship between firm

29. http://www.nber.org/data-appendix/c14741/appendix.pdf.

30. To protect confidentiality, the oldest age group now contains firms in the 96+ percentiles of the age distribution within an industry, rather than the 99+ category used in table 1.5 for the general samples that include all sectors.

31. For this exercise, we winsorize the labor productivity and labor share data at the 5th and 95th percentiles of the distribution of these variables by size bin.

Table 1.6 **Regressions explaining firm labor productivity in 2018 as a function of technology use in 2016–2018, ABS data for 2016–2018**

	Dependent Variable: Log of Labor Productivity in 2018				
	(1)	(2)	(3)	(4)	(5)
Employment percentile 0th−50th	0.047	0.059	0.061	0.062	0.395
	(0.007)	(0.007)	(0.007)	(0.007)	(0.008)
Employment percentile 75th−90th	0.030	0.024	0.022	0.022	−0.184
	(0.008)	(0.008)	(0.008)	(0.008)	(0.008)
Employment percentile 90th−95th	0.065	0.053	0.050	0.048	−0.348
	(0.012)	(0.012)	(0.012)	(0.012)	(0.013)
Employment percentile 95th−99th	0.137	0.120	0.115	0.111	−0.488
	(0.015)	(0.015)	(0.015)	(0.015)	(0.016)
Employment percentile 99th+	0.229	0.208	0.201	0.195	−0.781
	(0.032)	(0.031)	(0.031)	(0.031)	(0.033)
Age percentile 10th−50th	−0.016	−0.013	−0.012	−0.011	−0.052
	(0.010)	(0.010)	(0.010)	(0.010)	(0.010)
Age percentile 50th−75th	−0.047	−0.039	−0.037	−0.035	−0.095
	(0.011)	(0.011)	(0.011)	(0.011)	(0.010)
Age percentile 75th−90th	−0.057	−0.047	−0.045	−0.042	−0.123
	(0.012)	(0.012)	(0.012)	(0.012)	(0.012)
Age percentile 90th−95th	−0.119	−0.108	−0.105	−0.101	−0.178
	(0.018)	(0.018)	(0.018)	(0.018)	(0.017)
Age percentile 95th−99th	−0.100	−0.085	−0.080	−0.076	−0.168
	(0.031)	(0.031)	(0.031)	(0.031)	(0.028)
Age percentile 99th+	−0.084	−0.073	−0.070	−0.067	−0.180
	(0.014)	(0.014)	(0.014)	(0.014)	(0.013)
Technology user		0.108			0.058
		(0.006)			(0.006)
One technology			0.063		
			(0.009)		
Two technologies			0.120		
			(0.007)		
Three technologies			0.139		
			(0.009)		
Four technologies			0.173		
			(0.018)		
Five technologies			0.192		
			(0.033)		
Artificial intelligence				0.020	
				(0.016)	
Cloud computing				0.102	
				(0.007)	
Robotics				0.061	
				(0.017)	
Specialized software				0.046	
				(0.008)	
Dedicated equipment				−0.008	
				(0.008)	
log average wage 2015					0.279
					(0.004)
R-squared	0.323	0.326	0.327	0.327	0.395
Observations (rounded)	103,000	103,000	103,000	103,000	103,000

Note: The table reports results from a regression of firm labor productivity in 2018 on size and age groups, 6-digit industry dummies, employment shares by state, and measures of technology use from the 2019 ABS for 2016–2018. To protect confidentiality, the number of observations has been rounded. Robust standard errors are reported in parenthesis.

size and labor productivity, with the largest firms in each 6-digit industry achieving 22.9 log points (or 25.7 percent) higher labor productivity than the middle firms in their industry (firms in the 50th–75th employment percentiles). This is the *superstar firm* phenomenon: the rise of large firms with high labor productivity documented by Autor et al. (2020).[32] In addition, labor productivity declines with age (with the exception of the oldest firm group).

Column 2 explores the contribution of advanced technologies to the observed differences in labor productivity by including a dummy for firms that adopted any of the advanced technologies in the ABS. Technology adoption is associated with a 10.8 log points (or 11.4 percent) increase in labor productivity.[33]

Column 3 shows that the number of technologies that a firm uses is positively associated with its productivity. Firms using a single technology have a 6.3 log points higher labor productivity than firms with none. Firms using all five technologies have a 19.2 log points (or 21.1 percent) higher labor productivity than firms with none.

Column 4 includes separate dummies for each of the five technologies in the ABS. Cloud, robotics, and specialized software have positive and significant association with labor productivity, whereas AI and dedicated equipment are not correlated with labor productivity. One possibility is that the effects of AI on labor productivity and the labor share had not fully materialized by 2018, which aligns with the conclusions in Acemoglu et al. (2022). An alternative interpretation is that the individual technology coefficients are hard to interpret given that many of these technologies are adopted jointly.[34]

The estimates from column 4 imply that, from a descriptive viewpoint, the adoption of advanced technologies by large firms explains between 16 percent to 30 percent of the superstar phenomenon. Conditional on the technology measures from the ABS, the largest firms in each industry have a 19.5 log points higher labor productivity than mid-sized firms (as opposed to 22.9 log points when technology is not accounted for in column 1). Thus, technology explains 16 percent of the labor productivity difference between

32. Although not reported, these specifications also control for detailed 6-digit industry dummies, which shows that the superstar phenomenon is visible within detailed industries. Industry dummies are the most important factor accounting for differences in labor productivity in our analysis, accounting for more than 80 percent of the explained variation in all cases. This is not surprising, given the large differences in intermediate input use across industries. Within industries, differences in labor productivity are more comparable. For example, Foster, Haltiwanger, and Krizan (2001) present evidence that within detailed industries there is a strong positive correlation between value added per worker and gross output per worker across businesses.

33. These findings are consistent with earlier studies that documented a positive connection between labor productivity and automation technologies in the 1991 *Survey of Manufacturing Technology* (Dinlersoz and Wolf 2024).

34. In line with this interpretation, we find that the coefficient on AI rises to 0.041 (se=0.015) once we drop the highly correlated dummy for the use of cloud computing. This is not the case for the labor share regressions, however.

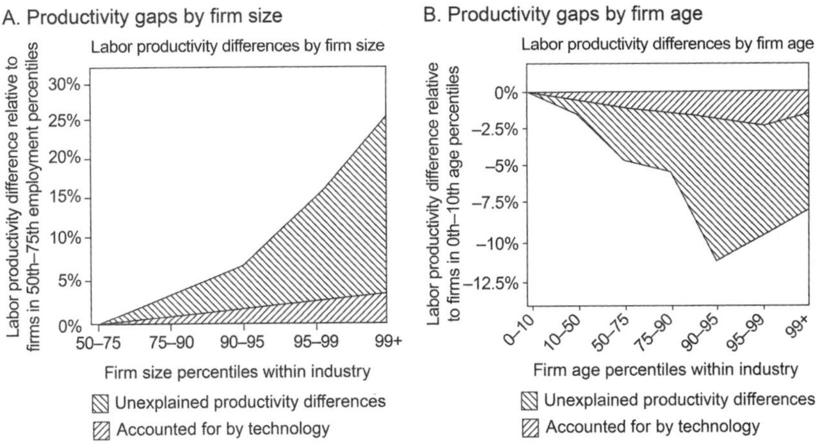

Fig. 1.6 Estimates of differences in labor productivity by size and age and the share of these differences explained by the adoption of advanced technologies, as measured in the 2019 ABS

firms above the 99th employment percentile and mid-sized firms. Likewise, technology explains 20 percent of the labor productivity difference between firms in the 96th to 99th employment percentile and mid-sized firms, and 30 percent of the difference between firms in the 90th to 95th employment percentile and mid-sized firms.[35]

For age, we find that differences in technology use between young and old firms account for 27 percent of the labor productivity difference between firms in the 96th to 99th age percentiles and the youngest firms in the bottom decile of the age distribution in each detailed industry.

Figure 1.6 illustrates our findings by plotting labor productivity differences as a function of firm-size and age, indicating the share of these differences explained by the measures of technology adoption from the ABS and the part left unexplained.

One concern with the results presented so far is whether they capture the fact that higher productivity firms pay higher wages, and, as we saw in table 1.5, higher-wage firms are more likely to adopt these advanced technologies. The last column of table 1.6 explores this issue by controlling for the logarithm of the average wage paid by the firm in 2015. The results in this column have to be interpreted with caution, since some of these technologies may have been adopted before 2015, and wages in 2015 are endogenous to past technology adoption, attenuating our estimates of the effects of technology

35. The same calculations show that technology use explains 30 percent of the labor productivity difference between firms above the 99th employment percentile and firms in the bottom half of the employment distribution, and 60 percent of the difference between firms in the 96th to 99th employment percentile and firms in the bottom half of the employment distribution.

on labor productivity. We find that there is still a sizable positive association between technology use and labor productivity, though it is attenuated relative to earlier specifications.

Tables A.3 and A.4 in the appendix show similar relations between the use of advanced technologies and labor productivity for manufacturing firms and non-manufacturing firms.[36]

Table 1.7 turns to estimates of (3) using the labor share from the 2018 LBD as outcome variable. Adopters have a 0.7 pp lower labor share by 2018. The more technologies a firm adopts, the lower its labor share, with firms that use all five technologies having a 3.1 pp lower labor share than firms that use none. When we look at the effects of different types of technologies separately, the use of robots has the largest negative association with the labor share, though we also estimate negative coefficients for all other technologies except AI.

Finally, we once again control for the log of the average wage in the firm in 2015, despite its potential endogeneity. In this case, the relationship between technology use and the labor share becomes more negative. Presumably, this reflects the fact that adopters paid higher wages to begin with, which masks the effects of automation on their labor shares.

Tables A.5 and A.6 in the appendix show similar relations between the use of advanced technologies and firms' labor shares in manufacturing and non-manufacturing.[37]

1.7 Technology and Changes in Demand for Workers and Skills

This section summarizes firms' self-assessments of the impact of advanced technologies on their workforce. The ABS asked adopting firms to assess the impact that advanced technologies have had on their employment level. Respondents were given 3 options: "Increase," "Decrease," and "Did Not Change." Figure 1.7 plots these answers separately for each technology. The figure provides the share of firms (both the simple share and an employment-weighted version) reporting an increase or a decrease in employment (with the share of firms reporting no change given by the complement of these two). For brevity, we focus on the employment weighted shares in our discussion.

Across all technologies, most firms claim that the use of advanced technologies did not change their employment levels in recent years, with 67–78 percent of firms selecting this response. A small share of firms reports positive or negative employment changes caused by the adoption of the technologies in the ABS. The employment-weighted share of firms reporting an increase in employment is 26 percent for users of AI. Robotics is the technology most

36. See http://www.nber.org/data-appendix/c14741/appendix.pdf.
37. See http://www.nber.org/data-appendix/c14741/appendix.pdf.

Table 1.7 **Regressions explaining firm labor share in 2018 as a function of technology use in 2016–2018, ABS data for 2016–2018**

	Dependent Variable: Labor share in 2018				
	(1)	(2)	(3)	(4)	(5)
Employment percentile 0th–50th	−0.060	−0.060	−0.061	−0.061	−0.001
	(0.002)	(0.002)	(0.002)	(0.002)	(0.002)
Employment percentile 75th–90th	0.022	0.022	0.022	0.022	−0.014
	(0.002)	(0.002)	(0.002)	(0.002)	(0.002)
Employment percentile 90th–95th	0.044	0.045	0.045	0.046	−0.026
	(0.003)	(0.003)	(0.003)	(0.003)	(0.003)
Employment percentile 95th–99th	0.047	0.049	0.049	0.049	−0.058
	(0.004)	(0.004)	(0.004)	(0.004)	(0.005)
Employment percentile 99th+	0.046	0.047	0.049	0.049	−0.126
	(0.008)	(0.008)	(0.008)	(0.008)	(0.009)
Age percentile 10th–50th	0.002	0.002	0.002	0.002	−0.005
	(0.002)	(0.002)	(0.002)	(0.002)	(0.002)
Age percentile 50th–75th	0.011	0.011	0.011	0.010	0.001
	(0.003)	(0.003)	(0.003)	(0.003)	(0.002)
Age percentile 75th–90th	0.021	0.020	0.020	0.020	0.007
	(0.003)	(0.003)	(0.003)	(0.003)	(0.003)
Age percentile 90th–95th	0.034	0.033	0.032	0.032	0.021
	(0.005)	(0.005)	(0.005)	(0.005)	(0.005)
Age percentile 95th–99th	0.038	0.037	0.037	0.036	0.023
	(0.008)	(0.008)	(0.008)	(0.008)	(0.007)
Age percentile 99th+	0.038	0.037	0.037	0.037	0.018
	(0.003)	(0.003)	(0.003)	(0.003)	(0.003)
Technology user		−0.007			−0.016
		(0.001)			(0.001)
One technology			−0.002		
			(0.002)		
Two technologies			−0.005		
			(0.002)		
Three technologies			−0.013		
			(0.002)		
Four technologies			−0.022		
			(0.004)		
Five technologies			−0.031		
			(0.008)		
Artificial intelligence				0.000	
				(0.004)	
Cloud computing				−0.006	
				(0.002)	
Robotics				−0.019	
				(0.004)	
Specialized software				−0.002	
				(0.002)	
Dedicated equipment				−0.005	
				(0.002)	
log average wage 2015					0.049
					(0.001)
R-squared	0.300	0.300	0.301	0.301	0.338
Observations (rounded)	103,000	103,000	103,000	103,000	103,000

Note: The table reports results from a regression of firm labor share in 2018 on size and age groups, 6-digit industry dummies, employment shares by state, and measures of technology use from the 2019 ABS for 2016–2018. To protect confidentiality, the number of observations has been rounded. Robust standard errors are reported in parenthesis.

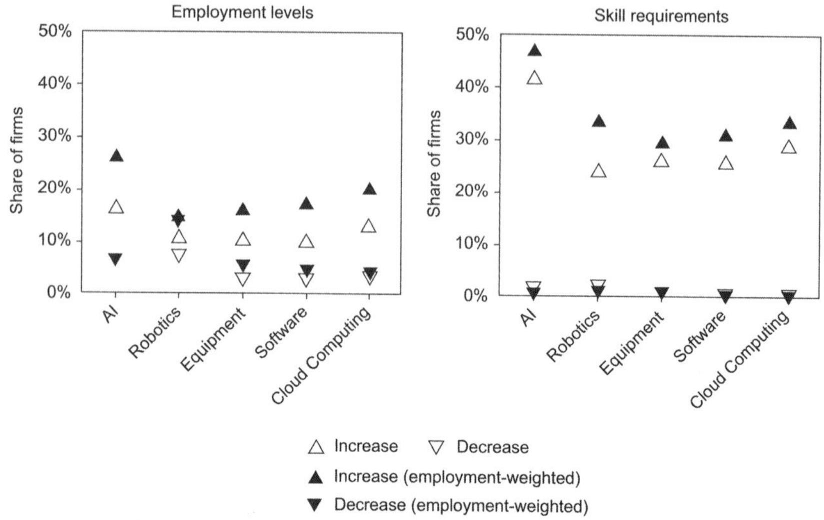

Fig. 1.7 Reported changes in employment levels and skill demand by firms adopting advanced technologies, firm- and employment-weighted shares from 2019 ABS

closely associated with employment decreases: the employment-weighted share of firms reporting a decrease in employment due to the use of robots is 14 percent (the same share reporting an increase in employment attributed to this technology).[38] One caveat is that these responses reflect self-assessments by firms, and some firms may be particularly reluctant to divulge information on workforce reductions through technology adoption; while other firms might default to reporting no employment changes.

We interpret firms' assessments as pointing to limited and ambiguous employment effects of advanced technologies at the firm level. This finding aligns with the theoretical framework, which highlights the fact that automation will have an ambiguous effect on firm employment. The framework also clarifies that it is reasonable to expect automation to increase employment in some firms while at the same time it reduces employment in others.

The possibility that advanced technologies have a limited effect on employment also underscores the importance of the displacement effects from automation. Consider, for example, a technological improvement that increases productivity in a factor-neutral way but does not involve the automation of tasks performed by labor. Our model shows that these factor-neutral

38. Figures A.1 and A.2 break down these answers by firm size and age. The 2019 ABS technology module also asked firms to assess the effect of technology on the number of production workers, non-production workers, supervisory workers, and non-supervisory workers. Here too, most firms report no changes in employment levels for these workers. One notable case is that of robotics, where the employment-weighted share of firms reporting a decrease in the employment of production workers exceeds the share reporting an increase.

technological developments should always increase sales and employment proportionally.[39]

The 2019 ABS technology module also provides information on firms' self-assessments of the impact of advanced technologies on their demand for skills. Firms were asked whether the skill level of their workers changed as a result of technology use, with the response options of "Increase," "Decrease," and "No Change." Panel B in figure 1.7 plots the share of reported changes in skill attributed to technology adoption (again, weighted by employment). A sizable share of firms, ranging from 30 percent to 50 percent of users in an employment-weighted sense, reports an increase in their demand for skills. Almost no firm reports a reduction in their demand for skills.

Firms' self-assessments indicate that the use of advanced technologies has resulted not so much in changes in firm-level employment but in changes in employment composition, with firms increasing their demand for skills. This finding is in line with the theory, which suggests that the use of advanced technologies involves a reassignment of labor from automated tasks to other complementary roles, including the maintenance, programming, and operation of specialized machinery. Firms' responses also align with recent work highlighting the fact that the adoption of advanced technologies and robots is associated with significant changes in the workforce composition of firms, measured in terms of their occupational structure or the skill level of their workers (see, for example, Dinlersoz and Wolf 2024, Humlum 2020, Bonfiglioli et al. 2020, Rodrigo 2023).[40] The relatively high incidence of skill upgrading reported by firms suggests that the use of advanced technologies might be an important force contributing to the observed changes in the occupational and wage structure of the US economy over the last 40 years, though quantifying the contribution of these technologies to these shifts is beyond the scope of our paper (see Acemoglu and Restrepo 2022 for more on this question.)

1.8 Conclusion

A lack of comprehensive data at the firm level has precluded a detailed assessment of the current state of advanced technology use by US firms and these technologies' impact on productivity and the workforce. Recent

39. In the simple model of section 1.3, this is always the case since firms face a constant elasticity of demand and have a constant markup, which makes their passthrough of marginal cost to price equal to 1. In practice, firms might expand their sales more than employment if their passthrough of marginal cost to price lies below 1. But for most reasonable values of the demand elasticity and passthrough, we would expect an expansion of both employment and sales in response to higher firm TFP.

40. These findings contrast with previous work by Doms, Dunne, and Troske (1997) using data from the US Survey of Manufacturing Technologies, which suggests that the adoption of new technologies does not increase firms' demand for skills (even though firms that had a more skilled workforce are more likely to adopt these technologies).

surveys conducted by the Census Bureau in partnership with the National Center for Science and Engineering Statistics (NCSES) as part of the 2018 and 2019 ABS fill this gap and offer new insights. Using the data collected by the technology module included in the 2019 ABS, we have provided new measures of the adoption of five key technologies—AI, robotics, dedicated equipment, specialized software, and cloud—and documented the relationship between their adoption and firm characteristics and workforce outcomes. While these technologies (especially AI and robotics) have low adoption rates among firms, a significant fraction of the US workforce are employed in firms using these technologies.

We documented a number of descriptive facts, which are mostly novel and complement previous work by Zolas et al. (2020):

1. We document that adoption remains limited when measured by the share of firms using these technologies in their processes and methods. This is especially the case for AI and robotics: only 3.2 percent of firms used AI and 2 percent used robotics during 2016–2018. While there is wider adoption of the remaining technologies, half of US firms did not use any of these technologies during 2016–2018.

2. Despite the low shares of user firms, adopters account for a sizable share of employment and economic activity. This is because adoption concentrates in large firms. 12.6 percent of the US workforce is employed in firms using AI technologies between 2016 and 2018, and this share rises to 15.7 percent for robotics, 64.4 percent for specialized software, 36.4 percent for dedicated equipment, and 61.8 percent for cloud computing. In manufacturing, worker exposure to advanced technologies is even higher: 22.6 percent for AI, 45.1 percent for robotics, 70.7 percent for dedicated equipment, 72.3 percent for specialized software, and 62.3 percent for cloud computing.

3. Large firms are more likely to adopt advanced technologies than other firms in their same detailed industries and cohorts. Conditional on size, younger firms are more likely to adopt advanced technologies than older firms in their same industries.

4. There is considerable variation in adoption rates across detailed industries even within manufacturing.

5. Firms identify automation as an important motivation for the adoption of AI and robotics, and to a lesser extent for dedicated equipment and specialized software. In total, 30.4 percent of US workers are employed at firms using advanced technologies for automation.

6. In line with the use of advanced technologies for automation, we document that adopters have high labor productivity and lower labor shares, and paid higher wages than the firms with similar age and size in their same detailed industries.

7. Firms' self-assessments point to an increase in the relative demand

for skill but limited or ambiguous effects on their employment level. These reports weigh against the view that automation technologies increase employment opportunities for low-skill workers.

Moving forward, there are several directions for future research. Many of these directions will also benefit from future planned ABS modules, which will add a longitudinal dimension. Here we list some of these directions:

- Future work can explore both whether the correlation between advanced technologies and labor productivity is causal at the firm level and how it aggregates to the industry and the economy. Composition effects and impacts of new technologies on markups will be particularly important in understanding these implications.
- Industry-level and aggregate employment implications of new technologies need further study as well. To do this, one can estimate the impact of advanced technologies not just on adopting firms' employment and skill demand, but on their rivals. If effects on rivals are negative and large, advanced technologies can have negative consequences, and whether they do or not and how this varies across different classes of technologies are central questions for future research.
- It would also be interesting to explore how advanced technologies impact the economy by expanding the range of goods and services and enabling quality upgrades. The ABS points to automation being an important driver of the adoption of advanced technologies, with automation being as important as expanding the range of goods and services offered by firms in driving adoption. However, the ABS data also highlight that the extent to which advanced technologies are being used for automation varies by technology and across firms, with a sizable share of firms reporting not using these technologies for automation. Understanding the determinants of these different motivations and uses is a fruitful area of research.
- Another important area is the study of whether labor shortages, such as those caused by the COVID-19 pandemic, trigger further automation and how permanent such shortage-induced adoption decisions will be.[41]

41. Examples of research predicting an increase in investment in automation technologies in response to the COVID-19 pandemic shock and forecasting related impacts include Autor and Reynolds (2020) and Chernoff and Warman (2023). Data enabling direct measurement of the association between the pandemic and technology adoption are still rare. Exceptions include Comin et al. (2022) (conducting a survey of firms in three developing countries and finding that pre-COVID digital technology adopters were better able to weather the pandemic and more likely to increase use of digital technologies than less advanced firms) and Alekseev et al. (2022) (conducting a survey of small businesses and finding that about one-half dealt with the pandemic by providing online services and about one-third expanded digital payments). The US Census Bureau added a question to Phase 7 (November 2021–January 2022) of its experimental Small Business Pulse Survey on whether firms changed any of eight business practices since the onset of the pandemic, including adoption and expansion of digital technologies US Census Bureau (2021).

Acknowledgments

Any opinions and conclusions expressed herein are those of the authors and do not reflect the views of the US Census Bureau. All results have been reviewed to ensure that no confidential information is disclosed. The Census Bureau's Disclosure Review Board and Disclosure Avoidance Officers have reviewed this data product for unauthorized disclosure of confidential information and have approved the disclosure avoidance practices applied to this release. DRB Approval Numbers: CBDRB-FY21–058, CBDRB-FY21–316, CBDRB-FY22–057, CBDRB-FY22-ESMD006–011, CBDRB-FY22–411, CBDRB-FY23–034. We thank Laurence Ales, Chiara Criscuolo, Eric Donald, Christina Patterson, and participants in the 2021 AEA session, 2021 Meetings of the Society for Economic Dynamics, and NBER CRIW conference for comments and suggestions. Acemoglu gratefully acknowledges financial support from the National Science Foundation, the Hewlett Foundation, Schmidt Sciences, and the Smith Richardson Foundation. Restrepo thanks the National Science Foundation for its support under award No. 2049427. For acknowledgments, sources of research support, and disclosure of the authors' material financial relationships, if any, please see https://www.nber.org/books-and-chapters/technology-productivity-and-economic-growth/automation-and-workforce-firm-level-view-2019-annual-business-survey.

References

Acemoglu, D., G. Anderson, D. Beede, C. Buffington, E. Dinlersoz, L. Foster, N. Goldschlag, J. Haltiwanger, Z. K. P. Restrepo, and N. Zolas. 2023. "Advanced Technology Adoption: Selection or Causal Effects?" *AEA Papers and Proceedings* 113: 210–14.

Acemoglu, D., D. Autor, J. Hazell, and P. Restrepo. 2022. "Artificial Intelligence and Jobs: Evidence from Online Vacancies." *Journal of Labor Economics* 40 (S1): S293–S340.

Acemoglu, D., C. Lelarge, and P. Restrepo. 2020. "Competing with Robots: Firm-Level Evidence from France." *AEA Papers and Proceedings* 110: 383–88.

Acemoglu, D., and P. Restrepo (2020): "Robots and Jobs: Evidence from US Labor Markets." *Journal of Political Economy* 128 (6): 2188–2244.

———. 2021. "Demographics and Automation." *Review of Economic Studies* 89 (1): 1–44.

———. 2022. "Tasks, Automation, and the Rise in US Wage Inequality." *Econometrica* 90 (5): 1973–2016.

Aghion, P., C. Antonin, S. Bunel, and X. Jaravel. 2020. "What are the Labor and Product Market Effects of Automation? New Evidence from France." Discussion paper, CEPR Discussion Paper No. DP14443.

Alekseev, G., S. Amer, M. Gopal, T. Kuchler, J. Schneider, J. Stroebel, and N. C.

Wernerfelt. 2022. "The Effects of COVID-19 on U.S. Small Businesses: Evidence from Owners, Managers, and Employees." *Management Science* 69 (1): 7–24.

Alekseeva, L., J. Azar, M. Giné, S. Samila, and B. Taska. 2021. "The Demand for AI Skills in the Labor Market." *Labour Economics* 71: 102002.

Autor, D., D. Dorn, L. F. Katz, C. Patterson, and J. Van Reenen. 2020. "The Fall of the Labor Share and the Rise of Superstar Firms." *Quarterly Journal of Economics* 135 (2): 645–709.

Autor, D., and E. Reynolds. 2020. "The Nature of Work after the COVID Crisis: Too Few Low-Wage Jobs." Discussion paper, The Hamilton Project.

Babina, T., A. Fedyk, A. He, and J. Hodson. Forthcoming. "Artificial Intelligence, Firm Growth, and Product Innovation." *Journal of Financial Economics*.

Basker, E., L. Foster, and S. Klimek. 2017. "Customer-Employee Substitution: Evidence from Gasoline Stations." *Journal of Economics & Management Strategy* 26 (4): 876–96.

Bessen, J., M. Goos, A. Salomons, and W. Van den Berge. 2019. "Automatic Reaction-What Happens to Workers at Firms that Automate?" Discussion paper, Mimeo, Boston University School of Law.

Bloom, N., T. A. Hassan, A. Kalyani, J. Lerner, and A. Tahoun. 2021. "The Diffusion of New Technologies." NBER Working Paper 28999. Cambridge, MA: National Bureau of Economic Research.

Bonfiglioli, A., R. Crinò, H. Fadinger, and G. Gancia. 2020. "Robot Imports and Firm-Level Outcomes." Discussion paper, CEPR Discussion Papers No. 14593.

Brynjolfsson, E., W. Jin, and K. McElheran. 2021. "The Power of Prediction: Predictive Analytics, Workplace Complements, and Business Performance." *Business Economics* 56 (4): 217–39.

Brynjolfsson, E., and A. McAfee. 2014. *The Second Machine Age: Work, Progress, and Prosperity in a Time of Brilliant Technologies*. New York: Norton & Company.

Calvino, F., S. DeSantis, I. Desnoyers-James, S. Formai, I. Goretti, S. Lombardi, F. Manaresi, and G. Perani. 2022. "Closing the Italian Digital Gap: The Role of Skills, Intangibles and Policies." OECD Science, Technology and Industry Policy Papers 126. OECD Publishing.

Cheng, H., L. A. Drozd, R. Giri, M. Taschereau-Dumouchel, and J. Xia. 2021. "The Future of Labor: Automation and the Labor Share in the Second Machine Age." Working Paper 20–11, FRB Philadelphia.

Chernoff, A. W., and C. Warman. 2023. "COVID-19 and Implications for Automation." *Applied Economics* 55 (17): 1939–1957.

Cho, J., T. DeStefano, H. Kim, I. Kim, and J. Paik. 2023. "What's Driving the Diffusion of next- Generation Digital Technologies?" *Technovation* 119(C).

Chow, M. C., T. C. Fort, C. Goetz, N. Goldschlag, J. Lawrence, E. R. Perlman, M. Stinson, and T. K. White. 2021. "Redesigning the Longitudinal Business Database." Discussion paper, National Bureau of Economic Research.

Comin, D. A., M. Cruz, X. Cirera, K. M. Lee, and J. Torres. 2022. "Technology and Resilience." NBER Working Paper 29644. Cambridge, MA: National Bureau of Economic Research.

Dauth, W., S. Findeisen, J. Suedekum, and N. Woessner. 2021. "The Adjustment of Labor Markets to Robots." *Journal of the European Economic Association* 19 (6): 3104–3153.

de Souza, G., and H. Li. 2023. "Robots, Tools, and Jobs: Evidence from Brazilian Labor Markets." Working Paper 10813. CESifo.

Dechezleprêtre, A., D. Hémous, M. Olsen, and C. Zanella. 2021. "Induced Automation: Evidence from Firm-Level Patent Data." Discussion Paper 384, University of Zurich, Department of Economics, Working Paper.

Decker, R. A., J. Haltiwanger, R. S. Jarmin, and J. Miranda. 2020. "Changing Business Dynamism and Productivity: Shocks versus Responsiveness." *American Economic Review* 110 (12): 3952–90.

Dinlersoz, E. M., and Z. Wolf. 2024. "Automation, Labor Share, and Productivity: Plant-Level Evidence from U.S. Manufacturing." *Economics of Innovation and New Technology* 33 (4): 604–26.

Dixon, J., B. Hong, and L. Wu. 2021. "The Robot Revolution: Managerial and Employment Consequences for Firms." *Management Science* 67 (9): 5586–605.

Doms, M., T. Dunne, and K. Troske. 1997. "Workers, Wages, and Technology." *Quarterly Journal of Economics* 112 (1): 253–90.

Dunne, T., L. Foster, J. Haltiwanger, and K. R. Troske. 2004 "Wage and Productivity Dispersion in United States Manufacturing: The Role of Computer Investment." *Journal of Labor Economics* 22 (2): 397–429.

Eckert, F., S. Ganapati, and C. Walsh. 2022. "Urban-Biased Growth: A Macroeconomic Analysis." NBER Working Paper 30515. Cambridge, MA: National Bureau of Economic Research.

Ford, M. 2015. *Rise of the Robots: Technology and the Threat of a Jobless Future*. New York: Basic Books.

Fort, T. C., J. R. Pierce, and P. K. Schott. 2018. "New Perspectives on the Decline of US Manufacturing Employment." *Journal of Economic Perspectives* 32 (2): 47–72.

Foster, L., J. C. Haltiwanger, and C. J. Krizan. 2001. "Aggregate Productivity Growth: Lessons from Microeconomic Evidence." In *New Developments in Productivity Analysis*, edited by Charles R. Hulten, Edwin R. Dean, and Michael J. Harper, 303–72. Chicago, IL: University of Chicago Press.

Genz, S., T. Gregory, M. Janser, F. Lehmer, and B. Matthes. 2021. "How Do Workers Adjust When Firms Adopt New Technologies?" Discussion paper, IZA DP No. 14626.

Graetz, G., and G. Michaels. 2018. "Robots at Work." *Review of Economics and Statistics* 100 (5): 753–68.

Hubmer, J., and P. Restrepo. 2021. "Not a Typical Firm: The Joint Dynamics of Firms, Labor Shares, and Capital-Labor Substitution." NBER Working Paper 28579. Cambridge, MA: National Bureau of Economic Research.

Humlum, A. 2020. "Robot Adoption and Labor Market Dynamics." Working paper, University of Chicago.

Koch, M., I. Manuylov, and M. Smolka. 2021. "Robots and Firms." *Economic Journal* 131 (638): 2553–2584.

Kogan, L., D. Papanikolaou, L. D. W. Schmidt, and B. Seegmiller. 2021. "Technology-Skill Complementarity and Labor Displacement: Evidence from Linking Two Centuries of Patents with Occupations." NBER Working Paper 29552. Cambridge, MA: National Bureau of Economic Research.

Leigh, N. G., and B. R. Kraft. 2018. "Emerging Robotic Regions in the United States: Insights for Regional Economic Evolution." *Regional Studies* 52 (6): 804–15.

Loucks, J., T. Davenport, and D. Schatsky. 2018. *State of AI in the Enterprise. 2nd edition*. Deloitte Insights.

Mann, K., and L. Püttmann. 2019. "Benign Effects of Automation: New Evidence from Patent Texts." *Review of Economics and Statistics*, 1–45.

Martinez, J., and J. Moen-Vorum. 2022. "A Long-run Anatomy of Task Exposures to Technology." Discussion paper, Mimeo, London Business School.

McElheran, K. 2015. "Do Market Leaders Lead in Business Process Innovation? The Case(s) of e-business Adoption." *Management Science* 61 (6): 1197–216.

Perla, J., C. Tonetti, and M. E. Waugh. 2021. "Equilibrium Technology Diffusion, Trade, and Growth." *American Economic Review* 111 (1): 73–128.

Rodrigo, R. 2023. "Robot Adoption, Organizational Capital, and the Productivity Paradox." *Academy of Management Proceedings* 2023 (1).
Schwab, K. 2017. *The Fourth Industrial Revolution*. Currency.
Susskind, R. E., and D. Susskind. 2015. *The Future of the Professions: How Technology Will Transform the Work of Human Experts*. Oxford University Press, USA.
US Census Bureau. 2021. "Questionnaire for Small Business Pulse Survey, Phase 7."
Zolas, N., Z. Kroff, E. Brynjolfsson, K. McElheran, D. N. Beede, C. Buffington, N. Goldschlag, L. Foster, and E. Dinlersoz. 2020. "Advanced Technologies Adoption and Use by U.S. Firms: Evidence from the Annual Business Survey." NBER Working Paper 28290. Cambridge, MA: National Bureau of Economic Research.

2

Similarities and Differences in the Adoption of General Purpose Technologies

Ajay Agrawal, Joshua S. Gans, and Avi Goldfarb

Economists recognize the central role of productivity in economic growth. At the same time, economic models provide little insight into when the next big idea and its associated productivity dividend will come along. Once an important technology is identified, however, the next steps are more within the domain of economic analysis. The economist's toolkit can provide an understanding when firms will adopt a new technology and for what purpose.

Bresnahan and Trajtenberg (1995) emphasize one category of important technologies, which they label "General Purpose Technologies," or GPTs. These technologies have the potential to generate sustained productivity growth through a positive feedback loop of innovation in producing and using industries. They note that "[m]ost GPTs play the role of 'enabling technologies', opening up new opportunities rather than offering complete, final solutions. For example, the productivity gains associated with the introduction of electric motors in manufacturing were not limited to a reduction in energy costs."

Since Bresnahan and Trajtenberg's article appeared, a growing literature has explored the diffusion and impact of general purpose technologies. Some of this literature takes a historical perspective, for example examin-

Ajay Agrawal is the Geoffrey Taber Chair in Entrepreneurship and Innovation and Professor of Strategic Management at the Rotman School of Management of the University of Toronto, and a research associate of the National Bureau of Economic Research.

Joshua S. Gans is Jeffrey Skoll Chair in Technical Innovation and Entrepreneurship and Professor of Strategic Management at the Rotman School of Management of the University of Toronto, and a research associate of the National Bureau of Economic Research.

Avi Goldfarb is Rotman Chair in Artificial Intelligence and Healthcare and Professor of Marketing at the Rotman School of Management of the University of Toronto, and a research associate of the National Bureau of Economic Research.

ing how the steam engine and electricity diffused (e.g., Lipsey, Carlaw, and Bekar 2005; Moser and Nicholas 2004). Much of the literature focuses on more recent technologies, particularly computers, the internet, and artificial intelligence (e.g., Bresnahan, Brynjolfsson, and Hitt 2002; Brynjolfsson and Hitt 2003; Forman, Goldfarb, and Greenstein 2005; Cockburn, Henderson, and Stern 2019).

Regardless of the technology studied, the focus of the literature has been on commonalities across each type of GPT. This focus is natural, given that the goal of the literature has been to identify generalizable insights across technologies. The main commonality has been the role of complementary innovation, or co-invention. For example, Bresnahan and Greenstein (1996) examined the diffusion of client/server computing systems in large companies. They emphasize the role of co-invention, the invention of new technologies and processes that enable the technology to generate growth. Looking at a different information technology, enterprise resource planning software, Aral, Brynjolfsson, and Wu (2012) emphasize complementary innovations related to organizational structures. Broadly, this literature emphasizes heterogeneity in co-invention costs. Organizations with lower co-invention costs, whether because of internal or external advantages, are more likely to adopt.

Each GPT, however, provides a distinct benefit. Steam provided a new power source. The internet facilitated communication. Recent advances in artificial intelligence reduce the cost of prediction (Agrawal, Gans, and Goldfarb 2018). The differences between GPTs are important for understanding adoption patterns. Co-invention costs do matter, but so do the benefits. The distinct benefits of GPTs determine why a particular GPT might be useful to a particular firm. Therefore, in order to understand how GPTs diffuse, and how they impact economic growth, it is necessary to consider the barriers to adoption common to all GPTs, as related to co-invention costs. It is also necessary to consider the benefits from adoption, which tend to be different with each GPT. These benefits often define the particular type of co-invention needed, as well as providing an understanding of which firms and industries will gain most from adoption.

Using the examples of the internet and artificial intelligence, we will discuss how both co-invention costs and distinct benefits determine the adoption of technology. The discussion of the internet will be grounded in the empirical literature on internet adoption, particularly a re-framing of Forman, Goldfarb, and Greenstein's (2005) *Journal of Urban Economics* paper. The discussion of AI will build on a theory literature and an extrapolation of Mullainathan and Obermeyer's (2021) study of AI in emergency departments. For both technologies, we demonstrate that discussions of the impact of a GPT on productivity and growth need to emphasize the benefits as well as the costs. The goal of this paper is therefore to link the literature on co-invention costs with an understanding of the distinct benefits of each GPT.

2.1 General Purpose Technologies

There has been a renewed interest in GPTs over the last few years. Figure 2.1 tracks citations to Bresnahan and Trajtenberg (1995) over time. Citations grew steadily until 2010, flattened through 2016, and then grew again. Many of these more recent citations discuss the potential of artificial intelligence to be a GPT.

Bresnahan and Trajtenberg (1995) note that "[w]hole eras of technical progress and growth appear to be driven by a few 'General Purpose Technologies.'" These GPTs generate follow-on innovations through what they label "innovational complementaries." This perspective mirrors a larger literature on the economics of technology that emphasizes the importance of a handful of innovations in driving economic growth. Such innovations have received different labels, with varying definitions, elsewhere. Mokyr (1990) emphasized the role of "macroinventions" in generating the potential for growth and innovation, and the role of follow-on "microinventions" in catalyzing the growth. This literature builds on studies that examine technological change in specific industries, such as David's (1990) examination of electrification and the reorganization of factories and Rosenberg's (1963) documentation of the breadth of innovations underlying the productivity increases in the 19th-century US machine tools industry. Here we emphasize the particular framework provided in Bresnahan and Trajtenberg (1995) and in Bresnahan's (2010) review paper.

GPTs are defined by their "potential for pervasive use in a wide range of sectors and by their technological dynamism" (Bresnahan and Trajtenberg 1995). The technological dynamism is not limited to the industry or sector that produces the GPT. GPTs have an outsized impact on long-term economic growth because they also generate innovation in using, or application, industries. The initial innovation in one sector generates productivity in the R&D in a downstream sector. This, in turn, generates further innovation in the upstream producing industry. This creates a positive feedback loop that

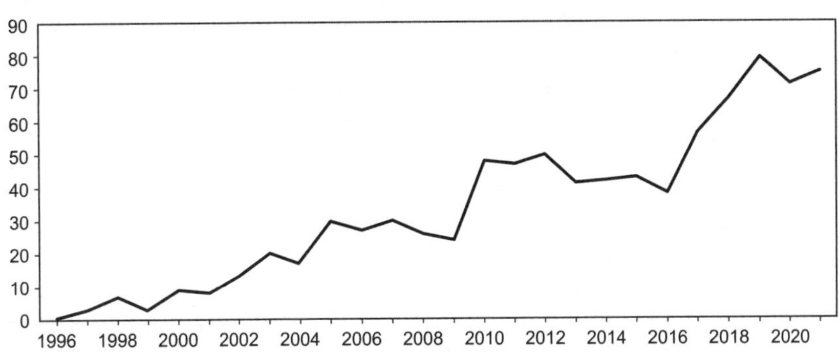

Fig. 2.1 Citations to Bresnahan & Trajtenberg (1995) in Web of Science

pushes against decreasing returns to innovation. This positive feedback loop between producing and using industries defines GPTs as distinct from other useful technologies.

Bresnahan and Trajtenberg attribute the increase in downstream R&D productivity to "innovational complementarities." These complementarities generate what Bresnahan and Greenstein (1996) label "co-invention." Gans (1995) and Aral, Brynjolfsson, and Wu (2012) note that these innovations can also occur in management and organization, and so they label them "organizational complementarities."

An empirical literature on information technology adoption has emphasized the costs associated with co-invention. Bresnahan, Brynjolfsson, and Hitt (2002) demonstrate that it takes several years for the productivity benefits of information technology to appear. They argue that this delay is caused by the challenges in developing new processes. Forman, Goldfarb, and Greenstein (2008) show that early adoption of advanced internet technologies was more likely in large firms or in large cities. They argue that this was driven by differences in co-invention costs. It is easier to undertake co-invention in firms with more resources, and in cities with more expertise. Dranove et al. (2014) further explore this hypothesis in the context of electronic medical records. They find that larger hospitals, and hospitals in cities with a large pool of health information technology workers, are more likely to gain from adopting electronic medical records, as measured by a reduction in hospital costs. As with Bresnahan, Brynjolfsson, and Hitt (2002), this cost reduction appeared after several years. Dranove et al. (2014) also show that many adopters fail. Even six years after adoption, hospitals that adopted but did not have access to a large local pool of health information technology workers experienced a substantial increase in costs with little benefit. Brynjolfsson, Rock, and Syverson (2021) take a more macroeconomic approach. They measure the relationship between IT investments and firm productivity in a cross-industry firm-level panel data set. They demonstrate a "productivity J-curve" in which measured productivity falls in the early years after IT investments but eventually rises. Their evidence suggests it is investments in intangible assets that lead to the short-term decrease in measured productivity. These investments generate complementary innovation.

Broadly, this empirical literature on IT adoption and its consequences has emphasized the common thread of co-invention costs leading to a lag in the productivity benefit to adoption and higher levels of adoption in firms that could adapt their processes efficiently.

The empirical literature on GPTs has emphasized commonalities in the costs of adopting different GPTs. In contrast, there has been little discussion of the benefits. That might be because the benefits are, at the surface, different across GPTs. Steam engines and electricity enabled new power sources. Interchangeable parts enabled production at scale. Railroads and the internal combustion engine enabled new forms of transportation. The internet enabled new forms of communication. In each case, these benefits are different.

Models simplifying these benefits provide insight into which firms will benefit the most. There is literature on new technologies, separate from the GPT literature, that emphasizes how technology reduces economic frictions. Shapiro and Varian (1999) emphasized the internet as a technology for cheap communication, reducing the costs of copying and of search. Goldfarb and Tucker (2019) noted how the internet also reduced the cost of transporting information and of tracking behavior. More broadly, Nordhaus (2007) linked computing advances to a drop in the cost of computation or arithmetic. For AI, Agrawal, Gans, and Goldfarb (2018) emphasized that it can be seen as a drop in the cost of prediction.[1]

Adding this perspective on a common model of the benefits of a GPT provides insight into which firms will adopt early and experience a productivity gain. It also provides insight into the types of co-invention needed. Put differently, co-invention is necessary, and is the source of the positive feedback loop that generates sustained productivity growth. Nevertheless, that productivity growth depends on adoption and co-invention in the industries that use the technology. As a technology makes a particular process cheaper, whether computation, search, or prediction, then that process will be used more broadly. How much more broadly depends on the elasticity of demand. Thomas J. Watson, then-CEO of IBM, allegedly declared global demand for five computers. That implies a very inelastic model of demand. As computers reduced the price of machine arithmetic, the number of applications grew rapidly.

In the remainder of this paper, we attempt to connect these two streams of literature. This attempt builds on work in economic history that emphasizes the particular benefits of a technology along with the challenges in co-invention. For example, David (1990) discusses how electrification provided a new way to power factories, but substantial co-invention was required for the new way of providing power to affect aggregate productivity. Similarly, Mokyr (1990, 82) emphasizes that during the Industrial Revolution, "a clustering of macroinventions occurred . . . thus creating a complementary flow of microinventions." For the macroinvention of the steam engine, Mokyr (1990) describes several microinventions. These microinventions were in the producing industry, making the engines more efficient. They also occurred downstream, applying the engines to provide power in new industries such as shipping (e.g., Fulton). Mokyr details innovation in a competing power

1. This framing can apply to a variety of technologies, even those that are not widely seen as GPTs. For example, for blockchain, Catalini and Gans (2020) saw it through the lens of a fall in verification costs.

source, water, for comparison. Understanding the diffusion and impact of the technology requires understanding the challenges to innovation, but also the benefits.

We use examples from relatively recent technologies in order to demonstrate how the impact of a GPT is best understood if the costs of co-invention and the benefits with respect to reducing a particular economic friction are taken into account. To do so, we first examine the diffusion of the commercial internet. Specifically, we re-interpret Forman, Goldfarb, and Greenstein's (2005) paper in internet adoption using this framework. We demonstrate how an emphasis on both co-invention costs and the benefits of the technology provides a useful lens for interpreting the results. Second, we describe emerging research on the usefulness of artificial intelligence. We combine the theoretical framework in Bresnahan (2020) and in Agrawal, Gans, and Goldfarb (2021) on AI systems with the empirical setting in Mullainathan and Obermeyer (2021). In doing so, we demonstrate a feedback loop between the benefits of prediction technology and the need for a particular type of co-invention.

2.2 Internet

Forman, Goldfarb, and Greenstein (2005) examine internet adoption patterns by 86,879 US business establishments, measured in the year 2000. The paper takes an economic geography perspective, examining whether the internet was adopted more by rural or urban business establishments. The main result of the paper is that establishments in larger cities were more likely to adopt relatively advanced internet technologies such as enterprise resource planning (ERP) and customer relationship management (CRM), but they were somewhat less likely to adopt the basic technologies such as email and web browsing.

The paper emphasizes that the result for advanced internet—which urban firms are more likely to adopt—supports the hypothesis that co-invention costs are important drivers of adoption. The other main result, that basic internet is more likely to be adopted in rural areas and smaller cities, received less focus in the paper and in the literature that followed. This is the result about the benefit of the technology, that the internet reduced communication costs and therefore has a distinct benefit for rural firms compared to urban firms. The authors wrote two additional papers with the same data set that only looked at the advanced internet, emphasizing co-invention cost differences in urban and rural areas (Forman, Goldfarb, and Greenstein 2008; Forman, Goldfarb, and Greenstein 2012).

Table 7 of the 2005 paper (replicated here as table 2.1) provides the most important results for understanding the difference between co-invention costs and the particular benefits of internet technology for facilitating communication. To do so, the paper further categorizes basic and advanced

Table 2.1 **Effect of population size and density on adoption of WEI firm and CEI adoption (standard errors in parentheses)**

	WEI			CEI		
	(1)	(2)	(3)	(4)	(5)	(6)
Participation						
	A. Coefficients from (weighted) probit regressions					
Small MSA	–0.000307	–0.00472	0.0318	0.019097	0.0209	0.0334
	(0.00222)	(0.0173)	(0.0294)	(0.0317)	(0.0200)	(0.0417)
Medium MSA	0.0138	0.00497	0.0303	–0.0356	–0.0294	–0.0244
	(0.0160)	(0.0138)	(0.0215)	(0.0200)⁺	(0.0153)⁺	(0.0260)
Larg, MSA	–0.00678	–0.00747	–0.0013	–0.0492	–0.0208	–0.0572
	(0.0127)	(0.0119)	(0.0151)	(0.0169)**	(0.0133)	(0.0238)*
Log likelihood	–30431.8	–52357.1	–17680.6	–15356.3	–34342.7	–8625.6
Observations	53231	86879	30260	53231	86879	30119
	B. Marginal effects from (weighted) probit regressions					
Small MSA	–0.000102	–0.00181	0.0107	0.00280	0.00489	0.0048
	(0.00736)	(0.00661)	(0.00978)	(0.00459)	(0.00462)	(0.00587)
Medium MSA	0.00457	0.00190	0.0102	–0.00536	–0.00700	–0.0036
	(0.00528)	(0.00527)	(0.00717)	(0.00308)⁺	(0.00369)⁺	(0.00393)
Larg, MSA	–0.00225	–0.00285	–0.000431	–0.00727	–0.00490	–0.0084
	(0.00423)	(0.00457)	(0.00513)	(0.00256)**	(0.00316)	(0.00361)**
Enhancement						
	C. Coefficients from (weighted) probit regressions					
Small MSA	0.0801	0.0724	0.114	0.0330	0.0379	0.0183
	(0.0236)**	(0.0222)**	(0.0330)**	(0.0194)⁺	(0.0159)*	(0.0268)
Medium MSA	0.0841	0.0931	0.0992	0.0462	0.0172	0.0370
	(0.0163)**	(0.0154)**	(0.0230)**	(0.0174)**	(0.0131)	(0.0192)⁺
Large MSA	0.130	0.147	0.125	0.0334	0.00703	0.0013
	(0.0135)**	(0.0125)**	(0.0164)**	(0.0109)**	(0.00920)	(0.0138)
Log likelihood	–24608.8	–27269.8	–12499.4	–29910.4	–46272.2	–16510.5
Observations	53227	86872	30260	53227	86872	30265
	D. Marginal effects from (weighted) probit regressions					
Small MSA	0.0217	0.0116	0.0274	0.0108	0.0117	0.00570
	(0.00662)**	(0.00372)**	(0.00841)**	(0.00642)⁺	(0.00498)*	(0.00848)
Medium MSA	0.0226	0.0148	0.0235	0.0151	0.00530	0.0116
	(0.00456)**	(0.00261)**	(0.00570)**	(0.00577)**	(0.00404)	(.00611)⁺
Large MSA	0.0340	0.0224	0.0285	0.0108	0.00215	0.0004
	(0.00367)**	(0.00208)**	(0.00393)**	(0.00356)**	(0.00282)	(0.00433)

Reprinted from Forman, Chris, Avi Goldfarb, and Shane Greenstein. 2005. "How Did Location Affect Adoption of the Commercial Internet? Global Village vs. Urban Leadership." Table 7. *Journal of Urban Economics* 58 (3): 389–420. https://doi.org/10.1016/j.jue.2005.05.004.

Note: All regressions include dummy variables for three-digit NAICS, whether it was a multi-establishment firm, employment and employment squared as controls. Robust standard errors, clustered by MSA, are in parentheses. Non-MSA is the base for these regressions.

(1) & (4) include only establishments that received the supplementary Harte Hanks survey.

(2) & (5) include entire sample.

(3) & (6) include only establishments from single–establishment firms who received the supplementary Harte Hanks survey.

⁺Significant at the 90 percent confidence level.

*Idem., 95 percent.

**Idem., 99 percent.

internet into those that involve communication outside the establishment and those that facilitate only within-establishment communication. This leads to four broad types of internet technologies:

1) Basic cross-establishment internet: These are applications of the internet that involve communication between establishments and do not require much expertise to use. Examples include email and web browsing.
2) Advanced cross-establishment internet: These are applications that involve communication between establishments and require considerable expertise to implement. Examples include using the internet for commercial transactions between firms, or between firms and customers.
3) Basic within-establishment internet: These are applications that primarily involve communication within an establishment and that do not require much expertise to use. Examples include internal web pages and networking services run through an intranet.
4) Advanced within-establishment internet: These are applications that primarily involve communication within an establishment and require considerable expertise to implement. Examples include ERP and CRM systems.

Basic cross-establishment internet is more likely to be adopted in less populated areas (panel A columns 4–6). Advanced within-establishment internet is more likely to be adopted in bigger cities (panel C columns 1–3). The other two categories are in the middle, with no consistent significant difference between urban and rural firms for advanced cross-establishment internet and basic within-establishment internet. Together, as noted in the paper, these results are consistent with evidence of co-invention: advanced technologies are more likely to be adopted in urban areas. These results also show that less populated areas are more likely to adopt cross-establishment internet, conditional on whether the technology is basic or advanced. Even for advanced technologies, small cities are as likely to adopt as large ones. Adoption is determined by more than co-invention costs. It is also determined by who benefits most from being able to communicate more efficiently across establishments.

Taken together, these results suggest that the internet is a GPT, but of a particular type. There is evidence that adoption is more likely in cities, but there is also evidence that the applications most related to communication technology were also likely to be adopted in rural areas.

This gives a hint of what kind of co-invention was necessary and which types of firms benefited most. While co-invention is easier in cities, a key benefit of the technology is cross-firm communication. Several papers by Chris Forman examine the co-invention needed for this cross-firm communication, although the papers do not frame it as such. Forman and Gron (2011) show that internet adoption was faster for insurers that were vertically integrated with their agents, and therefore non-vertically integrated adopters need to adapt their systems to avoid "opportunistic behavior," such as agents selling competitor products to consumers acquired through an insurer-funded electronic commerce system. The benefit of the communication technology is clear, but the incentives to adopt may not be aligned. Langer, Forman, Kekre, and Sun (2012) show that the successful addition of an internet distribution channel requires a change in product offerings that appeal to the more diverse set of customers that become feasible through digital communication. Forman and Van Zeebroeck (2012, 2019) examine within-firm knowledge flows after internet adoption. They show that internet connections increase collaboration and citations across inventors at different locations within a firm, but primarily for researchers with overlapping interests. They then suggest changes to the geography of the research group within the firm.

Each of these papers documents how the internet changed communication patterns. This, in turn, meant that firms needed to change their processes to take advantage of the change. While not labeled as such, this is co-invention. Put differently, the literature on internet adoption by businesses has emphasized co-invention costs (as in Forman, Goldfarb, and Greenstein's papers) and it has discussed how easier communication benefits certain types of businesses (as in Forman's other work). Our goal in this paper is to connect the two and point out that understanding co-invention and how a GPT might have an impact on productivity and growth requires an understanding of the benefits of the particular technology.

2.3 Artificial Intelligence

We proceed by assuming that AI is a GPT (whether part of a broader GPT or distinct), in the sense that AI technologies are defined by their "potential for pervasive use in a wide range of sectors and by their technological dynamism" (Bresnahan and Trajtenberg 1995). There has also been substantial innovation in both AI-producing and AI-using industries over the past 10 years, suggesting potential for a positive feedback loop. AI patenting has growth rapidly since 2010 (Bloom et al. 2021). AI is frequently mentioned in earnings calls and job postings in a variety of industries (Bloom et al. 2021; Goldfarb, Taska, and Teodoridis 2021).[2]

In our prior work (Agrawal, Gans, and Goldfarb 2018, 2019), we have emphasized that it is useful to see AI as prediction technology, and so advances in AI can be understood as reductions in the cost of prediction, where prediction is defined in the statistical sense. AI makes it easier to fill in missing information. Just as the internet is communication technology,

2. Artificial intelligence technologies are still diffusing, and it remains an open question as to whether they represent a new GPT (Agrawal, Gans, and Goldfarb 2019), an extension of the information technology GPT that has been diffusing since the 1950s, an aspect of data science as a GPT, or not a GPT at all (Goldfarb, Taska, and Teodoridis 2021).

steam provides an energy source, and the railway is transportation technology, AI enables prediction.

AI has been developed to address a number of prediction problems. It underlies Google's search engine, predicting which website a user wants in response to a query. It underlies Facebook's news feed, predicting which information a user is most likely to engage with. It underlies Amazon's recommendation engine, predicting which products people are likely to purchase. It is also an important component of business processes in a variety of other industries. It helps banks, credit card companies, and other financial institutions detect fraud. It helps insurance companies determine risks. It helps healthcare providers with diagnosis.

Bresnahan (2020) argues that only the information technology companies have received a substantial productivity benefit from AI so far. Google, Facebook, and Amazon had processes that could adapt to the opportunities in AI relatively quickly. They had data tools in place to enable good prediction, and they had the ability to adapt workflows to accommodate the predictions. Bresnahan emphasizes that this requires a system-level approach to using AI. A system-level approach involves changing workflows, adding new products, and providing new forms of value to customers. In other words, co-invention around the technology was easier. Therefore, IT companies adopted the technology early and with success.

In contrast, many other industries that have adopted AI have found relatively narrow applications within existing workflows. Financial services have used AI for fraud detection. As a result, fraud detection has improved, but the overall workflow has changed little. There has been relatively little innovation, either in terms of algorithms or organizational structure.

In Agrawal, Gans, and Goldfarb (2021), we formalized Bresnahan's insight, focusing on AI as a prediction technology. Prediction is useful because it improves decision-making. A system of decisions can involve multiple decision-makers who may have different information and whose incentives may not be aligned. Focusing on differences in information, our model showed that a productivity-enhancing AI might not be adopted if coordination between decision-makers is difficult. In other words, as a prediction technology, AI helps with decision-making. When there are multiple decisions and multiple decision-makers, AI can face resistance due to alignment. Even if it improves some decisions, if they cannot be coordinated with other decisions, then adopting AI could make things worse. We, therefore, hypothesize that co-invention for AI will require the development of systems to overcome coordination challenges.

2.4 Coordination of Decisions in Medical Care: An Application of AI as a GPT

In this section, we provide an example of an AI that improves medical diagnosis and discuss the necessary coordination of decisions that would lead to a substantial productivity boost. Specifically, we take the AI for heart attack diagnosis in Mullainathan and Obermeyer (2021) and examine what changes the hospital would need to undertake in order to get substantial value out of the tool.

When a patient arrives in the emergency department of a hospital, the medical staff assesses the likelihood of various ailments and recommends further testing. Mullainathan and Obermeyer focus on physician decisions to recommend testing for a heart attack. This testing can be invasive and costly. At the same time, a missed heart attack has severe consequences for the patient, as well as bottom line implications for the hospital. Using information available to physicians at the time they make a decision about testing, Mullainathan and Obermeyer developed an AI that performed substantially better than the doctors. The AI is built from data on 246,265 emergency visits at a large top-ranked hospital. Approximately 15 percent of patients required treatment. The paper documents that the AI predicted better than doctors. Doctors sometimes overtested, providing invasive tests to patients who were unlikely to be having a heart attack. Doctors also undertested, failing to order tests to many patients who were likely to need treatment. If the number of tests were fixed, the AI could re-allocate them from low risk to high risk patients, leading to better outcomes. It could also achieve the same outcomes with fewer tests. The focus of their paper as published is on understanding the nature of physician mistakes, showing that physicians use an overly simplistic model of the heart attacks.

The paper also contains an online appendix that explores how hospitals might change their processes in response to the algorithm. Next, we take the results of that appendix and build on them to model the potential for disagreement between physicians and hospital administrators. Specifically, in appendix 3, they discuss two different tests for heart attacks. The definitive test is cardiac catheterization. This involves a cardiologist inserting an instrument into the coronary arteries. If a blockage is found, a stent is inserted during the same procedure. Alternatively, physicians can recommend that the patient first receive a stress test. These tests are less expensive and less invasive, but also less accurate. Furthermore, if positive, the patient still needs to have the catheterization in order to insert the stent.

While the main paper does not distinguish between stress tests and testing through catheterization, it is an important decision that can cost the hospital thousands of dollars and can affect the patient's long-term outcomes. They estimate that the cost of catheterization is about $28,000 while the cost of a stress test is about $4,000. Patient outcomes and hospital profits are largely aligned. If hospitals identify patients who are having a heart attack, then the patient's life is saved and the hospital generates substantial revenue from caring for the patient.[3] Mullainathan and Obermeyer (appendix page 6)

3. Details in the appendix are supplemented by an interview of Ziad Obermeyer on January 25, 2022.

note, "it is intuitive and efficient for physicians to begin with stress testing for lower-risk patients . . . Higher-risk patients, on the other hand, should go straight to catheterization without incurring the additional cost and likelihood of false negative from stress testing."

Currently, stress testing serves a useful purpose. While Mullainathan and Obermeyer note that there is an active medical debate about whether stress tests should be used at all, stress tests continue to be used. They give doctors an outlet when they are highly uncertain whether a patient is at risk.

The question we explore next is what happens as the AI prediction gets better. Better prediction means less uncertainty. The risk will be more accurately measured. More patients will be clearly high risk, and more patients will be clearly such low risk that even a stress test is not cost effective. The simulations in Mullainathan and Obermeyer use their predictions of risk and demonstrate that stress tests should be used less when those predictions are more accurate.

Health economics often emphasizes differences in incentives between different players in the healthcare system, whether patients, doctors, insurers, or hospital administrators. For example, Bhattacharya, Hyde, and Tu's (2014) textbook, *Health Economics*, discusses the model in Harris (1977) that hospitals should be thought of as two separate economic actors: physicians and administration. The physicians decide on testing and diagnosis for each patient. The administration decides on which inputs should be available to physicians. With this division of decision-making, doctors have little incentive to control hospital costs (p. 103). In terms of testing, in other contexts widespread screening leads to better patient outcomes but at higher cost (p. 281). Doctors and administrators may be at odds as to which tests to do.

Table 2.2 provides back-of-the-envelope estimates of the benefits of allowing stress testing to doctors and to administrators with today's 15 percent rate of diagnosis accuracy upon arrival into the emergency department, an improved AI with 50 percent accuracy, and an almost-perfect AI with 99 percent accuracy. While loosely based on the values in Mullainathan and Obermeyer's appendix and elsewhere in the medical literature, these numbers are for demonstration purposes only.[4]

The second column shows that under a reasonable set of assumptions, doctors and administration are currently aligned. If a patient is predicted as having a 15 percent chance of a heart attack, both doctors and administrators will first send that patient for a stress test. If that stress test is positive, both doctors and administrators will move to catheterization.

The first and fourth columns show that the doctors and administration will also be aligned with a very accurate AI. The first column shows that if a

4. Estimates of revenue and profit vary. We use $100,000 in revenue and $20,000 in margin, based on Urbich et al's (2020) two-year revenue estimates meta-analysis and a 20 percent margin (RANGE 20k to 200k).

Table 2.2 **Estimates of the benefits of stress testing**

AI accuracy if positive	1%	15%	50%	99%
Doctor payoff				
Send patient home	$148,500	$127,500	$75,000	$1,500
Stress test first	$140,101	$135,915	$125,450	$110,799
Direct to catheterization	$122,000	$122,000	$122,000	$122,000
Administrative payoff				
Send patient home	$0	$0	$0	$0
Stress test first	$−892.15	$1,807.75	$8,557.5	$18,007.15
Direct to catheterization	$−1285	$1,725	$9250	$19,785

Calculations: Doctor: Benefit to doctor/patient of a healthy patient $150,000; cost of stress test to doctor $4,000; Cost of catheterization $28,000; false positive stress test 20 percent; false negative stress test 5 percent. Administration: Profit from detecting heart attack $20,000; profit from sending home $0; loss from stress test $800; loss from unnecessary catheterization $1,500; false positive stress test 20 percent; false negative stress test 5 percent. Numbers are back-of-the envelope and are not meant to represent accurate doctor or administration values.

patient has a 1 percent chance of having a heart attack or less, then the doctors and administrators agree that the patient should be sent home untested. The downside of the test is too high relative to the benefit of detecting the heart attack. The fourth column shows that if a patient is predicted as 99 percent likely to be having a heart attack, both doctors and administrators agree that the stress test should be skipped and the patient should go direct to catheterization.

However, the third column shows that if a patient is predicted to have a 50 percent chance of having a heart attack, then doctors and administrators might disagree. The source of disagreement relates to different estimates of the downside of an unnecessary catheterization, and to different estimates of the cost of undertaking a stress test. We have assumed that administrators perceive a larger cost to unnecessary testing than doctors.

Given the allocation of decision rights, as long as stress tests are available, doctors will choose to do a stress test first if they predict the patient has a 50 percent chance of having a heart attack. While the administration would prefer that the patient go straight to catheterization, the decision is the doctor's. The administrator, however, has the choice of whether to allow stress testing at all. If the administration provides a doctor with an AI that allocates patients to, say, either a 0.1 percent chance of having a heart attack or a 50 percent chance of having a heart attack, the doctor will then provide stress tests to anyone that the AI predicts at 50 percent. The administration should then decide that stress tests are not an option. And so the doctor would need to either send patients home, or to catheterization. The doctor will choose catheterization.

As modeled, the solution is straightforward. The administration should not offer the stress test. The doctor will choose catheterization. As practiced, however, it is unlikely to be so straightforward. The doctor will push back. A regulatory body may be called in. Patients' rights will be discussed. When the decision-makers are no longer aligned, then the structure of the game as modeled may change. In other words, the system as described has administration making a take-it-or-leave-it offer to the doctors, and then the doctors making the best decision given the circumstances. The doctors, however, can change the game. If the administration wants the doctors on board, it may need to change how doctors perceive the payoffs of unnecessary testing. This might involve new billing procedures, different liability protection, or other changes that suggest a change to the way the hospital operates.

This, in turn, might make the administrator hesitant to adopt the AI in the first place. The AI changes the decision alignment. The organization then needs to be more specific about its objective function and coordinate on whose payoffs determine the decision. Even though the AI improves patient outcomes, it creates conflict. Depending on the costs of that conflict, the administration might decide to forgo the benefits of better prediction.[5] Predictions can change decision alignment, and this lack of alignment becomes a barrier to AI adoption.[6]

We provide this example to demonstrate how AI can improve outcomes, but the specific nature of AI as prediction technology also generates challenges to its adoption. As noted in the previous section, our goal in this paper is to connect the literature on co-invention to an understanding of the particular benefits of each GPT. For AI, these are connected. The benefits relate to improved decision-making. Most organizations, however, have multiple decision-makers. The technology can lead to misalignment. Successful adoption may require negotiation, new processes, and a change in how payoffs are allocated.

2.5 Conclusion

This paper has connected two different streams in the literature on the diffusion and consequences of GPTs. One stream focuses on the barriers to adoption, and the need for co-invention to enable productivity growth. A second stream focuses on the benefits of each generation of technology. Using the examples of the internet and artificial intelligence, we show that understanding the consequences of GPT diffusion, and its associated challenges, requires understanding commonalities with prior GPTs in terms of co-invention, while recognizing that each technology brings with it specific

5. Another point is that if the AI isn't deployed early, then it may never gather enough data in order to improve the predictions to the point where the doctors and the administration are aligned give the predictions.

6. Gans (2022) provides a general treatment of when internal conflicts can make the adoption of radical technologies more difficult.

benefits that suggest which firms will adopt and the direction of the necessary co-invention.

Acknowledgments

We thank the editors for helpful comments and Yan Zhou for research assistance. For acknowledgments, sources of research support, and disclosure of the authors' material financial relationships, if any, please see https://www.nber.org/books-and-chapters/technology-productivity-and-economic-growth/similarities-and-differences-adoption-general-purpose-technologies.

References

Agrawal, Ajay, Joshua Gans, and Avi Goldfarb. 2018. *Prediction Machines: The Simple Economics of Artificial Intelligence*. Boston, MA: Harvard Business Review Press.

Agrawal, Ajay, Joshua Gans, and Avi Goldfarb. 2019. "Artificial Intelligence: The Ambiguous Labor Market Impact of Automating Prediction." *Journal of Economic Perspectives* 33 (2): 31–50.

Agrawal, Ajay, Joshua Gans, and Avi Goldfarb. 2021. "AI Adoption and System-Wide Change." NBER Working Paper No. 28811. Cambridge, MA: National Bureau of Economic Research. DOI: 10.3386/w28811.

Aral, Sinan, Erik Brynjolfsson, and Lynn Wu. 2012. "Three-Way Complementarities: Performance Pay, Human Resource Analytics, and Information Technology." *Management Science* 58 (5): 913–31.

Bhattacharya, Hyde, and Tu. 2014. *Health Economics. New York*: Red Globe Press.

Bloom, Nicholas, Marcela Carvalho, Tarek Hassan, Josh Lerner, Aakash Kalyani, and Ahmed Tahoun. 2021. The Diffusion of New Technologies. Working paper, Stanford University.

Bresnahan, T. 2020. "Artificial Intelligence Technologies and Aggregate Growth Prospects." Working paper, Stanford University.

Bresnahan, Timothy. 2010. "General Purpose Technologies." In *Handbook of the Economics of Innovation*, edited by Bronwyn Hall and Nathan Rosenberg. Chapter 18, 761–91.

Bresnahan, Timothy, Erik Brynjolfsson, and Lorin Hitt. 2002. "Information Technology, Workplace Organization, and the Demand for Skilled Labor: Firm-Level Evidence." *Quarterly Journal of Economics* 117 (1): 339–76.

Bresnahan, T., and S. Greenstein. 1996. "Technical Progress and Co-invention in Computing and in the Uses of Computers." *Brookings Papers on Economic Activity, Microeconomics* 1996: 1–83.

Bresnahan, T., and M. Trajtenberg. 1995. "General Purpose Technologies 'Engines of Growth'?" *Journal of Econometrics* 65: 83–108.

Brynjolfsson, Erik, and Lorin M. Hitt. 2003. "Computing Productivity: Firm-Level Evidence." *Review of Economics and Statistics* 85 (4): 793–808.

Brynjolfsson, Erik, Daniel Rock, and Chad Syverson. 2019. "Artificial Intelligence and the Modern Productivity Paradox: A Clash of Expectations and Statistics."

In *The Economics of Artificial Intelligence: An Agenda*, edited by Ajay Agrawal, Joshua Gans, and Avi Goldfarb, 23–57. Chicago, IL: University of Chicago Press.

Brynjolfsson, Erik, Daniel Rock, and Chad Syverson. 2021. "The Productivity J Curve: How Intangibles Complement General Purpose Technologies." *American Economic Journal: Macroeconomics* 13 (1): 333–72.

Catalini, Christian, and Joshua S. Gans. 2020. "Some Simple Economics of the Blockchain." *Communications of the ACM* 63 (7): 80–90.

Cockburn, Iain, Rebecca Henderson, and Scott Stern. 2019. "The Impact of Artificial Intelligence on Innovation." In *The Economics of Artificial Intelligence: An Agenda*, edited by Ajay Agrawal, Joshua Gans, and Avi Goldfarb, 115–46. Chicago, IL: University of Chicago Press.

David, Paul. 1990. "The Dynamo and the Computer: An Historical Perspective on the Modern Productivity Paradox." *American Economic Review Papers & Proceedings* 80 (2): 355–61.

Dranove, David, Chris Forman, Avi Goldfarb, and Shane Greenstein. 2014. "The Trillion Dollar Conundrum: Complementarities and Health Information Technology." *American Economic Journal: Economic Policy* 6 (4): 239–270.

Forman, Chris, Avi Goldfarb, and Shane Greenstein. 2005. "How Did Location Affect Adoption of the Commercial Internet: Global Village vs. Urban Leadership." *Journal of Urban Economics* 58 (3): 389–420.

Forman, Chris, Avi Goldfarb, and Shane Greenstein. 2008. "Understanding the Inputs into Innovation: Do Cities Substitute for Internal Firm Resources?" *Journal of Economics and Management Strategy* 17 (2): 295–316.

Forman, Chris, Avi Goldfarb, and Shane Greenstein. 2012. "The Internet and Local Wages: A Puzzle." *American Economic Review* 102 (1): 556–75.

Forman, Chris, and Anne Gron. 2011. "Vertical Integration and Information Technology Investment in the Insurance Industry." *Journal of Law, Economics, and Organization* 27 (1): 180–218.

Forman, C., and N. van Zeebroeck. 2012. "From Wires to Partners: How the Internet Has Fostered R&D Collaborations within Firms." *Management Science* 58 (8): 1549–1568.

Forman, C., and N. van Zeebroeck. 2019. "Digital Technology Adoption and Knowledge Flows within Firms: Can the Internet Overcome Geographic and Technological Distance?" *Research Policy* 48 (8): 103697.

Gans, Joshua S. 1995. "Inside the Black Box: A Look at the Container." *Prometheus* 13 (2): 169–83.

Gans, Joshua S. 2022. "A Theory of Visionary Disruption." *Mimeo*. Toronto.

Goldfarb, Avi, Bledi Taska, and Florenta Teodoridis. 2021. "Could Machine Learning Be a General Purpose Technology? Evidence from Online Job Postings." Working paper, University of Toronto.

Goldfarb, Avi, and Catherine Tucker. 2019. "Digital Economics." *Journal of Economic Literature* 57 (1): 3–43.

Harris, J. E. 1977. "The Internal Organization of Hospitals: Some Economic Implications." *Bell Journal of Economics* 8 (2): 467–482.

Jovanovic, Boyan, and Peter Rousseau. 2005. "General Purpose Technologies." In *Handbook of Economic Growth*, volume 1B, edited by Philippe Aghion and Steven N. Durlauf, chapter 18, 1181–224.

Lipsey, Richard, Kenneth Carlaw, and Clifford Bekar. 2005. *Economic Transformations: General Purpose Technologies and Economic Growth*. Oxford, UK: Oxford University Press.

Langer, N., C. Forman, S. Kekre, and B. Sun. 2012. "Ushering Buyers into Electronic Channels: An Empirical Analysis." *Information Systems Research* 23 (4): 1212–1231.

Mokyr, Joel. 1990. *The Lever of Riches*. Oxford University Press.

Moser, Petra, and Tom Nicholas. 2004. "Was Electricity a General Purpose Technology? Evidence from Historical Patent Citations." *American Economic Review Papers & Proceedings* 94 (2): 388–94.

Mullainathan, Sendhil, and Ziad Obermeyer. 2021. "Diagnosing Physician Error: A Machine Learning Approach to Low-Value Health Care." *Quarterly Journal of Economics* 137 (2): 679–727.

Nordhaus, W. D. 2007. "Two centuries of productivity growth in computing." *Journal of Economic History* 67 (1): 128–159.

Rosenberg, Nathan. 1963. "Technological Change in the Machine Tool Industry, 1840–1910." *Journal of Economic History* 23 (4): 414–43.

Shapiro, Carl, and Hal Varian. 1999. *Information Rules: A Strategic Guide to the Network Economy*. Harvard Business Review Press.

Urbich, M., G. Globe, K. Pantiri, et al. 2020. "A Systematic Review of Medical Costs Associated with Heart Failure in the USA (2014–2020)." *Pharmacoeconomics* 38 (11): 1219–1236.

3

Firm Investments in Artificial Intelligence Technologies and Changes in Workforce Composition

Tania Babina, Anastassia Fedyk, Alex He, and James Hodson

The arrival of new general purpose technologies (GPT) is a key driver of economic growth (Romer 1990; Aghion and Howitt 1992; Kogan et al. 2019, 2017). Yet as firms adapt their production processes and organization in response to technological changes, this shift raises major concerns about the impact on workers. For example, computer software and robots have displaced low- and medium-skilled workers (Autor et al. 2003; Acemoglu and Restrepo 2020), while the arrival of cotton-spinning machinery and electricity led to a complete re-organization of production processes within firms (Fizsbein et al. 2020; Juhász et al. 2024). In recent years, the focus has shifted to a new technological wave: artificial intelligence and related "big data" technologies. AI is a prediction technology, and predictions are at the heart of decision-making under uncertainty (Agrawal et al. 2019), making AI applicable to solve a variety of business problems with different potential effects on labor. On the one hand, firms might use AI to automate high-skilled tasks (Webb 2020).[1] On the other hand, investments in AI so far have been primarily associated with product innovation (Babina et al.

Tania Babina is an associate professor at the University of Maryland, an affiliate of the Centre for Economic Policy Research, and a faculty research fellow of the National Bureau of Economic Research.

Anastassia Fedyk is an assistant professor of finance at the Haas School of Business at the University of California, Berkeley.

Alex He is an assistant professor of finance at the University of Maryland.

James Hodson is the chief executive officer of the AI for Good Foundation and a scientific advisor at Cognism.

1. For theoretical treatments of the impact of artificial intelligence technologies on labor displacement, see Korinek and Stiglitz (2019), Acemoglu and Restrepo (2019b), and Agrawal et al. (2019).

2024), which can require complementary investments and more educated workforces. Indeed, Babina et al. (2024) document that AI-investing firms experience increases in their overall employment—and it is an open question whether (and how) this employment growth is associated with changes in labor composition.

In this paper, we examine whether firms that invest more heavily in AI technologies experience changes in labor composition and workforce organization. To date, in-depth empirical understanding of the relationship between firms' investments in new AI technologies and firms' labor composition has remained elusive due to two key challenges: the difficulty of measuring firm-level AI investments and the lack of granular data on firms' labor composition and labor organization (Seamans and Raj 2018; Frank et al. 2019). Several recent papers make progress in overcoming the first challenge by using firms' job postings and worker resumes to identify the hiring and stock of AI-skilled labor (Acemoglu et al. 2022a; Babina et al. 2024; Alekseeva et al. 2020; Abis and Veldkamp 2024).[2] The main contribution of this paper lies in overcoming the second challenge. We use matched employer-employee US data based on worker resumes, including detailed information on both individual jobs and employees' educational backgrounds. Using these data, we construct firm-level measures of labor composition and workforce organization, including employees' educational backgrounds and hierarchical positions, and link them to firm-level AI investments.

We find that firms that invest more in AI significantly shift toward more educated workforces, with greater emphasis on STEM degrees. At the same time, AI-investing firms become less top-heavy in terms of their organizational structure, with increasing shares of junior employees and less emphasis on middle-management and senior roles. Overall, our findings suggest that investments in AI are associated with major changes in firms' labor composition and organization, translating into a broader shift toward more junior employees with high educational attainment and technical expertise.

To construct workforce composition measures and assess their relationships to firms' AI investments, we leverage a unique combination of data sets that capture both the *stock* of current employees and the *demand* for new employees among US firms. The stock of current employees at each point in time comes from a resume data set provided by Cognism Inc., which offers job histories for 535 million individuals globally. Cognism resume data offer a complementary perspective to granular administrative firm-worker matched US data, which contain individual workers' wages but do not feature comprehensive information on individual workers' educational backgrounds or job characteristics. Cognism resume data, while representing more than 63 percent of full-time US employment as of 2018, offer detailed

2. These measures are complementary to surveys of AI use by firms (Zolas et al. 2020; Acemoglu et al. 2022b) and data on AI-related patents (Alderucci et al. 2020).

job titles and descriptions (from which Cognism infers hierarchical positions) and educational backgrounds including degree-granting institutions and majors. We complement the resume data with information on firms' demand for new workers from the job postings data provided by Burning Glass, which capture 180 million online job vacancies. While job postings data have been instrumental in understanding how firms target their new hiring, the resume data provide a full picture of what happens to the overall workforce within firms—including new hires and potential displacement. Since our goal is to study the impact of AI on AI-using firms rather than AI-producing firms, we exclude firms in the tech sectors, which are likely to be producers of new AI tools.

We begin our analysis by describing how firm ex-ante labor composition predicts future growth in firms' AI investments. We adopt the novel measure of AI investments proposed by Babina et al. (2024), based on firms' AI-skilled human capital. The human-capital-based approach is motivated by the heavy reliance of AI implementation on human expertise. The method first identifies skills that are empirically related to principal AI technologies (machine learning, computer vision, and natural language processing) from the Burning Glass job postings data and then uses the identified highly AI-related skills to classify AI-related workers in the Cognism resume data. At the firm level, growth in AI investments is more pronounced among firms that initially have more workers with doctoral degrees and STEM majors. This is in line with the evidence in Babina et al. (2024), who find that firms with more technical workers and more educated workers are able to attract AI talent more easily. The hierarchical structure of firms' labor organization—as measured by the shares of employees in junior, middle-management, and senior roles—does not significantly predict growth in AI investments.

We next address our main question: whether AI investments are associated with changes in labor composition and workforce organization. We consider three sets of outcomes related to firms' workforce composition and organization. First, motivated by the literature on technologies and firm organization (Acemoglu et al. 2007), we examine changes in firms' organizational structure using measures of organizational structure from the resume data. The relationship between technological investments and the relative weights of different hierarchical levels is ex ante ambiguous. As highlighted by theoretical work (Garicano and Rossi-Hansberg 2006; Bloom et al. 2014), different types of technologies can have opposing effects on the need for managerial layers. Second, we look at both workers' education levels in the resume data and educational requirements in the job postings data to test whether AI facilitates skill-biased technological change (Autor et al. 1998; Machin and Van Reenen 1998) or replaces high-skilled labor as predicted by Webb (2020). Here, too, the predicted effect of AI is ex ante ambiguous, and we provide the first systematic evidence of its direction. The shifts in labor composition are likely to go hand-in-hand with changes to organizational structure, as Caroli and Van Reenen (2001) point out that flattening hierarchical structures require higher human capital from each individual employee. Finally, we use detailed information on workers' majors and required skills to study how AI changes firms' demand for different types of labor.

Our main empirical specification is a long-differences regression of changes in labor outcomes from 2010 to 2018 on changes in the firm-level share of AI workers during the same period, following the standard approach in settings with slow-moving processes like technological change (e.g., Acemoglu and Restrepo 2020). As shown in Babina et al. (2024), AI investments accumulate gradually over time and generate effects that are not immediate, making the long-differences strategy well suited for our setting. Furthermore, by taking first differences in independent and dependent variables, the long-differences specification ensures that time-invariant firm characteristics do not drive the results. To bolster the causal interpretations of the results, we include a rich set of controls featuring industry fixed effects and firm-, industry-, and commuting-zone-level characteristics in 2010. All of our coefficient estimates are remarkably consistent across specifications with and without these detailed controls. Moreover, none of our results are driven mechanically by the hiring of AI workers, and excluding those workers from the calculation of dependent variables produces similar results. Finally, we show that our results are robust to using an instrumental variable strategy based on an instrument that isolates the variation in firms' AI investments that is driven by the supply of AI-skilled labor.

In terms of hierarchical structure, we provide evidence that AI investments are associated with firms becoming flatter, with higher shares of employees in entry-level or single-contributor roles and fewer employees in either middle-management or senior roles. Specifically, a one-standard-deviation change in the share of AI workers at a firm is associated with a 1.6 percent increase in the share of junior employees from 2010 to 2018, while middle management declines by 0.8 percent and senior management by 0.7 percent. This result is consistent with the channel suggested by Garicano and Rossi-Hansberg (2006) and explored by Bloom et al. (2014), where reductions in costs of accessing knowledge through improved data processing, such as AI technology, result in increased problem-solving ability of employees at all levels, leading to increased span of control and less reliance on top-heavy hierarchical structures.

In terms of labor composition, we observe a general upskilling trend associated with larger AI investments. Firms that invest more in AI tend to increase their shares of workers with bachelor's, master's, and doctoral degrees (correspondingly decreasing the share of workers without college education). A one-standard-deviation increase in the firm's share of AI workers translates into a 3.7 percent increase in the share of workers whose maximal educational attainment is an associate or bachelor's degree, a 2.9 percent increase in the share of workers whose maximal educational attainment is a master's degree, and a 0.6 percent increase in doctoral degrees. These increases in educated workers correspond to a 7.2 percent decline in the share of workers without college education. The upskilling shifts in education are also observed in the firms' explicit labor demand in the Burning Glass job postings, which feature both required education and required number of years of prior experience for prospective job applicants. For example, a one-standard-deviation increase in the share of AI workers is associated with a 0.5 additional year of required education in the firm's new job openings.

The additional demand for educated workers in AI-investing firms tends to concentrate in technical fields. Leveraging the information on majors of the most recent degree for each individual employee in the resume data, we observe that AI investments are associated with a significant increase in the share of employees with majors in STEM degrees and a corresponding decline in the share of employees with degrees in social science fields. Similarly, the skill requirements in Burning Glass job postings reveal that AI-investing firms experience a significant increase in demand for employees with skills in data analysis and IT, while decreasing their search for employees with skills in traditional operational fields such as finance and maintenance.

Our work contributes to the recent literature on the impact of AI technologies on the labor market. Previous literature has conjectured that AI has the potential to displace some human tasks, including high-skilled tasks (Acemoglu and Restrepo 2019a; Webb 2020; Frank et al. 2019; Mihet and Philippon 2019). Empirically, prior work made progress in measuring exposure to AI at the occupation level (Felten et al. 2018; Brynjolfsson et al. 2018; Webb 2020) and the impact of AI on overall labor demand and employment at the firm level (Alderucci et al. 2020; Rock 2019; Babina et al. 2024). Several papers look at the impact of AI on labor in specific settings, such as financial analysts and startups (Abis and Veldkamp 2024; Cao et al. 2021; Gofman and Jin 2022; Grennan and Michaely 2022).[3] Our work is closest to Acemoglu et al. (2022a), who use firms' occupational structure to proxy for *exposure* to potential displacement by AI and explore how this exposure relates to firms' labor demand. By contrast, we study the effect of firms' overall AI *investments*—including applications of AI that aim to displace workers and those that do not (e.g., AI-fueled product innovation in Babina et al. 2024). Furthermore, we complement prior work that looks at labor demand by examining changes in actual worker composition, including new hires and departures.

3. Relatedly, other papers compare decision-making of humans and AI algorithms in various settings (e.g., D'Acunto et al. 2019; Fuster et al. 2020; Jansen et al. 2023; Erel et al. 2021; Lyonnet and Stern 2022).

Our paper is the first to document the relationship between the use of AI technologies and workforce composition at the firm level. While Babina et al. (2024) show that AI investments increase total firm employment, our evidence further shows that this increase is concentrated in highly educated workers and high-skill workers with STEM backgrounds and IT skills. A potential explanation for our findings is that AI-fueled product innovation—the main channel through which AI investments power firm growth (Babina et al. 2024)—increases firms' demand for complementary skilled labor. These results contribute to the literature on the labor market effects of general purpose technologies, which shows that technologies like IT and electricity favor high-skilled labor but displace medium-skilled workers (Autor et al. 1998, 2003; Fizsbein et al. 2020; Zator 2019; Acemoglu and Restrepo 2022). Bessen et al. (2022) find that IT investments are associated with an increase in the returns to skill at the firm level. We show that AI investments are associated with an overall increase in firms' hiring of skilled labor, but these effects are heterogeneous. Demand for some high-skilled labor (e.g., STEM majors, IT skills) rises, while demand for other medium-skilled or high-skilled labor (e.g., finance, maintenance) declines.

Our evidence on firms' hierarchical structures also contributes to the literature on technology adoption and firm organization (Hitt 1999; Acemoglu et al. 2007; Bloom et al. 2014; McElheran and Forman 2019). We find that firms investing in AI technologies become less top-heavy, which is similar to the previously documented effect of IT but opposite to the effect of communication technologies. The combination of our results linking AI to flatter organizational structure and increased demand for skilled labor echoes the finding in Caroli and Van Reenen (2001) that there are complementarities between organizational change and skilled employees. Our results therefore support the notion that new technologies such as AI can be an important driver of skill-biased organizational change.

Methodologically, we provide a new measure of firms' organizational structure based on text descriptions of jobs in worker resumes. This measure can be applied to all firms across all industries and complements previous survey-based measures of firm hierarchy (e.g., Rajan and Wulf 2006; Bloom et al. 2012). More broadly, our method contributes to the growing literature that uses textual analysis to measure job tasks and skills (Kogan et al. 2019; Fedyk and Hodson 2023; Jiang et al. 2024; Hansen et al. 2021).[4]

The remainder of the paper is organized as follows. We introduce our data in section 3.1 and detail our methodology for measuring AI investments and

4. Our methodology also contributes to the literature that uses information about firms' employees to proxy for intangible capital. See Eisfeldt and Papanikolaou (2013); Crouzet and Eberly (2018); Peters and Taylor (2017) for recent examples of papers on intangible capital.

workforce composition in section 3.2. Section 3.3 explores how firms' initial workforce composition predicts AI investments, while section 3.4 presents our main results on the relationship between AI investments and changes in workforce composition and organization. Section 3.5 concludes.

3.1 Data

To investigate how the composition and structure of firms' workforces changes in firms that invest more heavily in AI, we bring together two data sets. First, we take advantage of a unique matched employer-employee data set built from resumes and featuring individual employees' detailed job descriptions and educational backgrounds. Second, we supplement the resume data with a comprehensive data set of job postings revealing firms' demand for education and skills.

3.1.1 Employment profiles from Cognism

We leverage the employment profile (resume) data set from Cognism, which offers matched employer-employee data covering approximately 535 million individuals globally. These data are introduced in detail in Fedyk and Hodson (2023) and Babina et al. (2024) and bring several key advantages that complement existing administrative data. First, Cognism offers broad coverage in the United States. Appendix figure A.1 compares the coverage of US full-time employment in the Cognism data against official numbers from the Bureau of Labor Statistics.[5] Cognism captures 42 percent of all US employment in 2010 (the beginning of our sample), and the coverage steadily increases to 63 percent in 2018 (the end of our sample), with the average coverage being 53 percent across these years.[6]

Second, while Cognism does not have information on wages (as would be included, for example, in the US Census Bureau's Longitudinal Employer-Household Dynamics program), the Cognism data provide detailed information on individual workers' occupations, job tasks, and educational backgrounds—the kind of information that is not available in administrative data. Specifically, for each individual, we observe the start and end dates of each job, the job title (often along with a detailed job description), each job's company name and location, the individual's educational record (with university names, degrees, and majors), as well as any patents, awards, or publications that the individual chooses to include on the resume. This allows us to examine how firms' investments in new technologies, such as AI, interplay

5. See http://www.nber.org/data-appendix/c14753/appendix.pdf.

6. Although our Cognism data snapshot is from July 2021, we follow Tambe et al. (2020) and Babina et al. (2024) and only use the years through 2018 to avoid potential noise from workers updating their resumes with a delay.

with granular changes in their workforce composition, including employee educational attainment, specialization, and seniority.

Finally, the Cognism data also bring advantages relative to the job postings data that have been previously used to understand the impact of AI on the labor markets (e.g., Alekseeva et al. 2020; Acemoglu et al. 2022a). Working directly with employee resumes enables us to see who is actually working at each firm, rather than only firms' demand for employees. As a result, we are able to capture changes in workforce composition that occur outside of new hiring (e.g., promotions, onboarding of new employees through acquisitions, or layoffs of existing employees).

Cognism's AI Research department leverages techniques from machine learning and natural language processing, including named entity disambiguation and graph-based modeling methods, to further enrich the resume data by normalizing job titles and occupations, associating employees with functional divisions and teams within each firm, and identifying institutions, degrees, and majors from education records. We match employer names in the Cognism data to the names of publicly traded firms in the Compustat data set using the approach developed in Fedyk and Hodson (2023). The matching of individual resumes to firm entities is performed dynamically to account for acquisitions and divestitures. We limit our attention to public firms with data in Compustat in order to link individual employees to firms and include detailed controls for other firm characteristics (e.g., sales, cash reserves, R&D expenditures, and markups). The data cover 657 million US-based person-firm-year observations between 2007 and 2018, of which 120 million (18 percent) are matched to US public firms. This is consistent with prior statistics showing that publicly listed firms account for approximately 26 percent of overall US employment (Davis et al. 2006). The sample of 120 million person-firm-years matched to US public firms corresponds to 19 million distinct individual employees.

We benchmark the resulting sample of Cognism employees at public firms against these firms' employment in the Compustat database. Appendix figure A.2 presents the median and interquartile range of firm-level coverage rates for each year from 2010 to 2018.[7] It is important to note that our analyses are performed on US-based employees in the Cognism data; however, US public firms do not report the number of US-based employees and instead only report their global employment numbers. Therefore, the coverage rate in appendix figure A.2 is lower than that in appendix figure A.1, where the denominator consists of US-based employment numbers. The coverage rate in appendix figure A.2 is stable throughout our sample period, with the median firm having around 30 percent of its global employment captured in the Cognism data set, and the interquartile range being 15–70 percent.

7. See http://www.nber.org/data-appendix/c14753/appendix.pdf.

Furthermore, appendix table A.1 reports the median coverage rate in each industry sector for our Compustat-Cognism matched data. The industry median coverage rates range from 18 percent (Health Care) to 52 percent (Finance and Insurance).

3.1.2 Job Postings from Burning Glass

The second data set we use covers over 180 million job postings in the United States in 2007 and 2010–2018. The data set is provided by Burning Glass Technologies (BG), which examines over 40,000 online job boards and company websites, collects the job postings data, parses them into a machine-readable form, and uses the data to construct labor market analytics products. BG employs a sophisticated deduplication algorithm to avoid double-counting vacancies that post on multiple job boards. BG data are quite comprehensive, covering approximately 60–70 percent of all vacancies posted in the United States, either online or offline.[8] The data contain detailed information for each job posting, including the job title, location, occupation, and employer name. Most importantly for our paper, the job postings are tagged with (i) thousands of specific skills standardized from the open text in each job opening, and (ii) specific requirements such as years of education and experience.

We focus on jobs with non-missing employer names (approximately 65 percent of all job postings) and at least one required skill (which corresponds to 93 percent of all job postings). Since we are interested in the composition of a firm's core workforce, we drop job postings that are internships. We match the employer firms in the remaining job postings to Compustat firms using fuzzy matching after stripping out common endings such as "Inc." and "L.P." For observations that do not match exactly on firm name, we manually assess the top ten potential fuzzy matches based on the firm name, industry, and location. Out of 112 million job postings with non-missing employer names and skills, 42 million (38 percent) are matched to Compustat firms. This slightly over-represents employees of publicly listed firms, which constitute just over one-fourth of US employment in the nonfarm business sector (Davis et al. 2006).

3.1.3 Additional Data Sources

We merge the Cognism resume data and the Burning Glass job postings data to several additional data sources. We collect commuting-zone-level wage and education data from the Census American Community Surveys (ACS) and industry-level wages and employment data from the Census Quarterly Workforce Indicators (QWI). Firm-level operational variables (e.g., sales, cash, assets) come from Compustat.

8. See Hershbein and Kahn (2018) for a detailed description of the BG data, including their representativeness, which is stable over time at the occupation level.

3.2 Methodology and Descriptive Statistics

3.2.1 AI Investments

We leverage the methodology proposed by Babina et al. (2024) to measure firms' investments in AI based on their intensity of AI-skilled hiring. The intuition is that successful implementation and use of AI technologies by firms requires employees with expertise in AI methods. Since other inputs to AI, such as data and computing infrastructure, are complementary to AI-skilled labor, our human-capital based measure allows us to capture the relative intensity of AI investments across firms.[9]

In order to identify AI expertise, we take advantage of (i) the detailed information on required skills in the job postings data and (ii) new, data-driven methodology for identifying AI-related jobs. Previous methods for classifying job postings based on the presence of key terms from a pre-specified list (e.g., Hershbein and Kahn 2018; Alekseeva et al. 2020) are likely to suffer from both Type I (incorrectly labeling tangentially related employees as AI-related) and Type II (missing real AI skills that did not make the initial dictionary) errors due to the arbitrariness of the list of keywords. This is especially relevant in a quickly evolving domain such as AI, where new emerging skills can be easily missed. The methodology from Babina et al. (2024) circumvents these challenges by learning the AI-relatedness of each of approximately 15,000 unique skills directly from the job postings data, based on their empirical co-occurrence (within required lists of skills across job postings) with unambiguous core AI skills. We then take the skills that are empirically most related to the core AI skills and search for those in our resume data. Finally, we aggregate the worker-level data to the firm-year level by calculating the share of the firm's employees who are AI-skilled.

More precisely, we start by measuring the AI-relatedness of each skill in the job postings data by calculating that skill's co-occurrence with Artificial Intelligence (AI) and its three main sub-fields: machine learning (ML), natural language processing (NLP), and computer vision (CV):

$$w_s^{AI} = \frac{\begin{matrix}\#\ \textit{of jobs requiring skill s and}\\ (\textit{ML, NLP, CV, or AI in required skills or in job title})\end{matrix}}{\#\ \textit{of jobs requiring skill s}}$$

Intuitively, this measure captures how correlated each skill s is with the core AI skills. For example, the skill "Recurrent Neural Network" has a value of 0.965, which means that 96.5 percent of job postings that list "Recurrent Neural Network" as a required skill also require one of the core AI skills or contain one of the core AI skills in the job title. Thus, a "Recurrent Neu-

9. It is possible that external AI software and solutions (e.g., IPSoft Amelia) may substitute for the hiring of AI-skilled labor. However, Babina et al. (2024) show that the use of external AI software solutions tends to be complementary to internal AI hiring and incorporating those in the measure of AI investments yields similar results.

ral Network" requirement in a job posting is highly indicative of that job being AI-related. On the other hand, the AI-relatedness measure of the skill "Microsoft Office" is only 0.003. In appendix table A.2, we list the skills with the highest AI-relatedness measures—namely, the skills that co-occur with the core AI skills in at least 70 percent of all job posting.[10]

In the Cognism resume data, we identify AI-skilled employees as those whose job positions directly involve AI. We begin with the set of 67 keywords in table A.2, which have the highest skill-level AI-relatedness measures in the job postings data. We then consider every employment record of each individual in the resume data and identify whether any of these AI-related terms appear in: (i) the job title or description; (ii) any patents obtained during the year of interest or the two following years (to account for the time lag between the work and the patent grant); (iii) any publications during the year of interest or the following year; or (iv) any awards received during the year of interest or the following year. If any of these conditions are met, then we classify that employee at that firm in that year as AI-skilled. For example, jobs with titles such as "senior **machine learning** developer" or publications such as "A new cluster-aware regularization of **neural networks**" are identified as AI jobs.

To aggregate to the firm level, we use the number of AI-related employees and the number of total employees at each firm in each year and compute the fraction of employees of that firm in that year who are classified as AI-skilled. Given that our empirical analyses focus on US-listed firms, our firm-level measure focuses on the employees who are based in the United States. Babina et al. (2024) provide a detailed discussion of this measure, perform multiple validation exercises, and offer detailed case studies of AI investments by individual firms in our sample. For the sake of brevity, we do not reproduce that analysis in this paper.

3.2.2 Labor Composition

We use the resume data to examine three aspects of firms' workforces: (i) educational attainment in terms of college and post-graduate degrees; (ii) specialization in terms of college majors (e.g., STEM vs. humanities vs. social science); and (iii) hierarchical structure in terms of the composition of employees across different levels of seniority. We describe the construction of each of these variables in turn below.

3.2.2.1 Educational Attainment

Cognism uses the educational information from the resumes to classify each individual at each point in time based on that individual's highest educational attainment to date. The categories are: (i) no secondary education; (ii) associate's degree; (iii) bachelor's degree; (iv) master's degree other

10. Reproduced from Babina et al. 2024, http://www.nber.org/data-appendix/c14753/appendix.pdf.

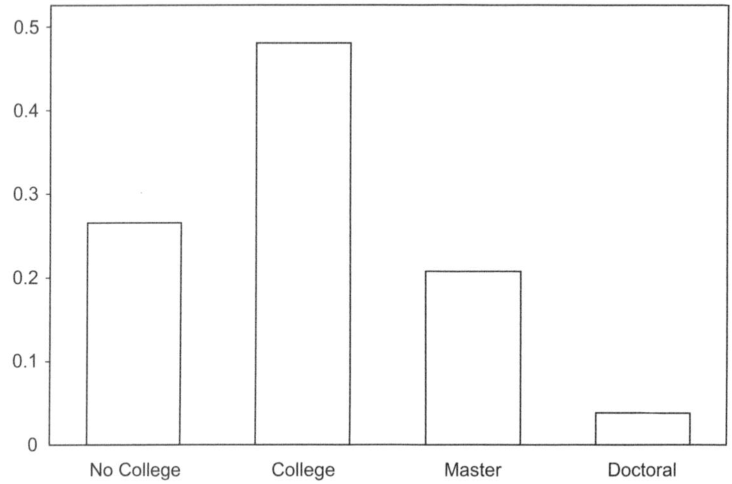

Fig. 3.1 Distribution of education levels in the Cognism resume data
This figure shows the fraction of workers in each education level (no college, college, master's, and doctoral) in the Cognism data. The four education levels are mutually exclusive and each worker is counted once for their highest level of education. The sample includes all workers in Compustat firms between 2010 and 2018.

than an MBA; (v) MBA; and (vi) doctoral degree (including Ph.D. and J.D. degrees). For each firm in our sample, we compute four educational attainment variables: (i) the share of employees in each year who have a college degree (either a bachelor's or an associate's); (ii) the share of employees who have at least a master's degree; (iii) the share of employees who have a doctoral degree; and (iv) the share of employees who do not have a college degree. Figure 3.1 plots the mean of these four shares in the resume data for the sample of Compustat firms.

3.2.2.2 Educational Specialization

Cognism extracts major information from individuals' education records and groups majors into broad categories of (i) Humanities, (ii) Social Sciences, (iii) Science, Technology, Engineering, and Mathematics (STEM), (iv) Fine Arts, and (v) Medicine. We take these broad categories and compute, for each firm in each year, the share of current employees whose most recent degrees fall in each category. Figure 3.2 plots the distribution of majors based on the most recent degree in the resume data for the sample of Compustat firms.

3.2.2.3 Seniority

The Cognism data are enriched with state-of-the-art machine learning techniques to identify employees' departments and seniority. First, over 20,000 individual job titles are classified manually based on markers of seniority and department. The remaining job titles are then classified into

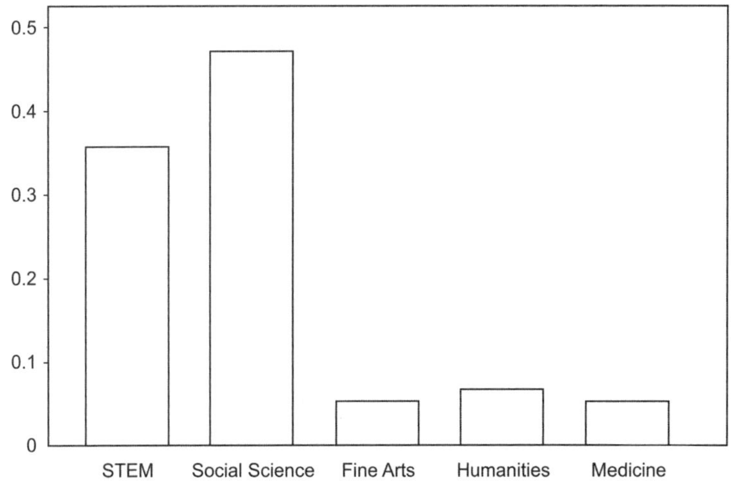

Fig. 3.2 Distribution of majors in the Cognism resume data

This figure shows the fraction of workers in each major (STEM, social science, fine arts, humanities, and medicine) in the Cognism data. STEM includes engineering (e.g., electrical, chemical, mechanical), physical sciences (e.g., math, physics, chemistry, computer science, statistics), and biological sciences (e.g., biology, pharmacology). The majors are mutually exclusive; for each worker, we record the major of the most recent degree earned. The sample includes all workers in Compustat firms between 2010 and 2018.

departments using a probabilistic language model and into seniority levels using an artificial neural network. There are six levels of seniority in total: (1) entry-level positions where individuals start straight out of undergraduate or high school education; (2) experienced staff in roles such as individual senior contributor but not managing others; (3) team leads who manage others but have little to no company-level decision-making responsibility; (4) middle management roles that oversee several smaller teams; (5) leadership positions that head larger departments or business segments; and (6) executive-level leadership such as the Chief Executive Officer and Chief Operating Officer. Fedyk et al. (2022) perform an evaluation of Cognism's seniority classification on the sample of accounting firms by assessing the model's output against a manually reviewed sample of over 10,000 positions. They find that Cognism's seniority classification has an accuracy rate of over 95 percent. In this paper, we group the seniority levels into three broader bands: low (consisting of entry-level positions and experienced individual contributors), medium (team leads and middle management), and high (leadership and the executive level). Figure 3.3 plots the shares of workers in each of these three seniority levels based on the resume data for the sample of Compustat firms. Overall, over 60 percent of employees are in junior-level or non-supervisory roles, with approximately 25 percent in mid-tier and 10–15 percent in senior management.

Other measures of firm organization structure, such as Rajan and Wulf

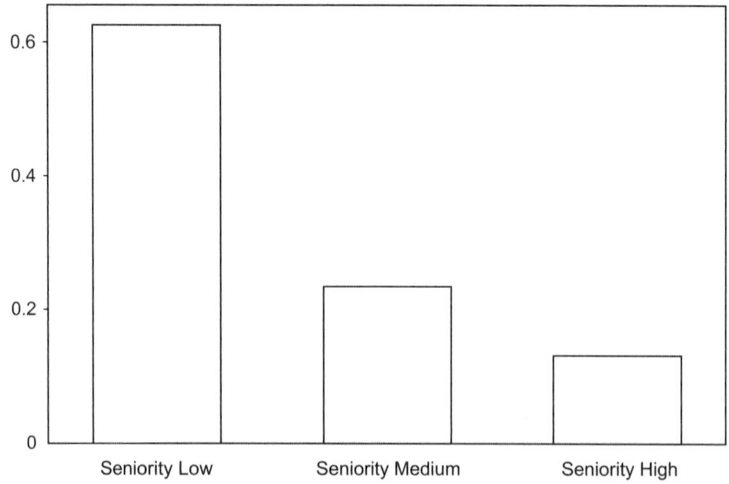

Fig. 3.3 Distribution of seniority levels in the Cognism resume data
This figure shows the fraction of workers in each seniority level (low, medium, and high) in the Cognism data. The seniority levels are described in text. The sample includes all workers in Compustat firms between 2010 and 2018.

(2006) and Guadalupe and Wulf (2010), are typically based on surveys of firm managers and focus on the breadth and depth of the hierarchy among managers. In particular, breadth is represented as the CEO's span of control, and depth is represented by the number of levels between the CEO and divisional managers.[11] Our measure is related to these measures: for example, flatter organizational hierarchy (i.e., more entry-level workers and fewer senior managers) is associated with more breadth and less depth. In addition, our measure offers several advantages. First, it is based on the actual organizational structure of the firm, complementing survey-based measures. Second, our measure captures the composition of workers across all hierarchical levels, which provides a more holistic picture of the firm's organizational structure than the number of levels between the CEO and lower-level managers or workers.

3.2.3 Labor Demand

We use the job postings data from Burning Glass to measure two aspects of firms' labor demand: (1) required education and experience and (2) required skills. Since these measures are calculated from firms' job postings, they only measure firms' labor demand—the types of workers firms wish to hire—instead of the types of workers working at each firm.

11. Other surveys, such as the World Management Survey (https://worldmanagementsurvey.org/), also measure the number of levels between the CEO and entry-level workers.

3.2.3.1 *Required Education and Experience*

For each job posting, Burning Glass codes the minimum years of required education and the minimum years of required experience. 59 percent of job postings specify an educational requirement, which averages 14.5 years of school. 52 percent of job postings specify a requirement for prior work experience in related fields, which averages 4 years. Figure 3.4 plots the distribution of the number of years of minimum education required and the number of years of minimum experience required (using job postings that specify a given requirement). Hershbein and Kahn (2018) show that average educational requirements in Burning Glass align well with the education levels of employed workers at the occupation and MSA levels.

3.2.3.2 *Skill Clusters*

Burning Glass groups all skills into one of 28 skill clusters. Skill clusters are groupings of skills that have similar functionality, can be trained together, and/or frequently appear together in job postings. For example, the skill "Python" belongs to the "Information Technology" skill cluster, and the skill "Machine Learning" belongs to the "Analysis" skill cluster. Table 3.1 presents the top five skills (i.e., skills appearing in the largest number of job postings) for each skill cluster.

For each job posting, we calculate the share of required skills that fall within each skill cluster. For example, if a job posting requires "Python" and "Machine Learning," then the share of the "Information Technology" skill cluster and the share of the "Analysis" skill cluster are both 50 percent. We then average these shares across all job postings of a given firm in a given year. This results in a weighted share of job postings that require skills in each skill cluster.[12] The shares of all 28 skill clusters add up to one.

3.2.4 Descriptive Statistics

We present summary statistics for each of our measures of worker composition. We start by showing the evolution of education levels and specialization of workers over time. Figure 3.5 plots the share of workers in four education levels (undergraduate, master's, doctoral, and less than college) based on the Cognism resume data over time. Figure 3.6 plots the share of workers in five major fields (STEM, social science, fine arts, humanities, and medicine) based on the Cognism resume data over time. For comparison, we also plot the distribution of education levels and majors of US workers in the Census American Community Survey (ACS), which is a 1 percent random sample of the US population, in each year between 2010

12. This is equivalent to weighting each skill required by a job posting by the inverse of the total number of skills required by the job posting. We do not directly compute the share of job postings requiring skills in a skill cluster, because generic skills like "communication" are required by most job postings, although they constitute a small part of the job requirements for each job posting.

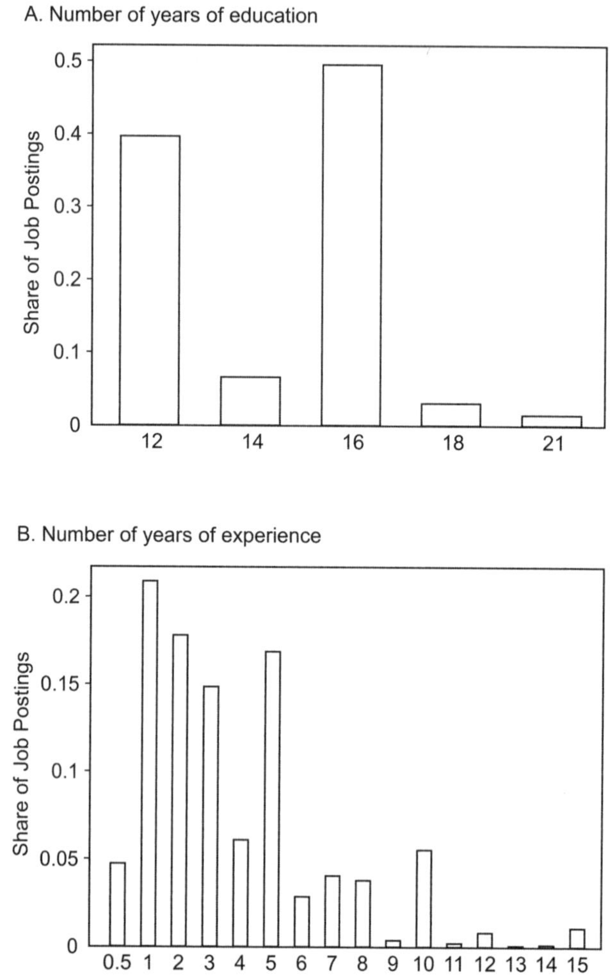

Fig. 3.4 Distribution of required years of education and experience in the Burning Glass job postings data

This figure shows the fraction of job postings with the number of years of required education (Panel A) or the number of years of required work experience (Panel B) in the Burning Glass job postings data. The sample includes all job postings of Compustat firms between 2010 and 2018.

and 2018 in appendix figures A.3 and A.4.[13] In both Cognism and ACS, the share of workers in each education level is mostly flat over time, with an intuitive slight upward trend in the share of workers with bachelor's or master's degrees and slight downward trend in the share of workers with no post-secondary education. In both data sets, there is a small increase in

13. See http://www.nber.org/data-appendix/c14753/appendix.pdf.

Table 3.1 **Top skills in each skill cluster in the Burning Glass job posting data**

This table reports the top five skills required by the largest number of job postings in each skill cluster in the Burning Glass job posting data.

Administration	Analysis	Business	Customer Service	Engineering	Finance	Health Care
Scheduling	Data Analysis	Project Management	Customer Service	Mechanical Engineering	Budgeting	Patient Care
Administrative Support	Data Collection	Staff Management	Customer Contact	AutoCAD	Accounting	Cardiopulmonary Resuscitation (CPR)
Data Entry	Business Intelligence	Quality Assurance and Control	Basic Mathematics	Computer Engineering	Customer Billing	Lifting Ability
Appointment Setting	SAS	Supervisory Skills	Cash Handling	Simulation	Financial Analysis	Treatment Planning
Record Keeping	Statistics	Business Process	Customer Checkout	Civil Engineering	Financial Reporting	Advanced Cardiac Life Support
Human Resources	**Information Technology**	**Legal**	**Marketing**	**Sales**	**Science**	**Supply Chain**
Occupational Health and Safety	Microsoft Office	Legal Compliance	Marketing	Sales	Chemistry	Store Management
Onboarding	Microsoft PowerPoint	Litigation	Social Media	Product Sales	Biology	Purchasing
Recruiting	SQL	Government Regulations	Packaging	Merchandising	Physics	Forklift Operation
Employee Training	Java	Legal Documentation	Client Base Retention	Business Development	Experiments	Procurement
Personal Protective Equipment	Software Development	Criminal Justice	Facebook	Sales Goals	Laboratory Testing	Inventory Management

(*continued*)

Table 3.1 (cont.)

Administration	Analysis	Business	Customer Service	Engineering	Finance	Health Care
Agriculture	**Construction**	**Design**	**Economics**	**Education**	**Utilities**	**Environment**
Snow Removal	Estimating	Adobe Photoshop	Economics	Teaching	Natural Gas	HAZMAT
Lawn Care	Carpentry	Microsoft Visio	Public administration	Training Programs	Energy Management	Hazardous Waste
Fertilizers	Cost Estimation	Graphic Design	Economic Development	Training Materials	Power Distribution	Environmental Science
Agronomy	Construction Management	Adobe InDesign	Social Studies	Technical Training	Power Generation	Water Treatment
Agribusiness	Interior Design	Adobe Acrobat	Policy Analysis	Special Education	Energy Efficiency	Natural Resources
Industry Knowledge	**Maintenance**	**Manufacturing**	**Media**	**Personal Care**	**Public Safety**	**Religion**
Retail Industry Knowledge	Hand Tools	Product Development	Journalism	Cooking	Asset Protection	Youth Ministry
Information Technology Industry Knowledge	Plumbing	Machinery	Music	Food Safety	Surveillance	Student Ministry
Biotechnology	Predictive/ Preventative Maintenance	Welding	Preparing Proposals	Child Care	Loss Control/ Prevention	Children's Ministry
Industrial Engineering Industry Expertise	HVAC	Six Sigma	Proposal Writing	Food Preparation	Handling of Crisis	Family Ministry
Asset Management Industry Knowledge	Schematic Diagrams	Manufacturing Processes	Content Management	Food Service Experience	Emergency Services	Religious Education

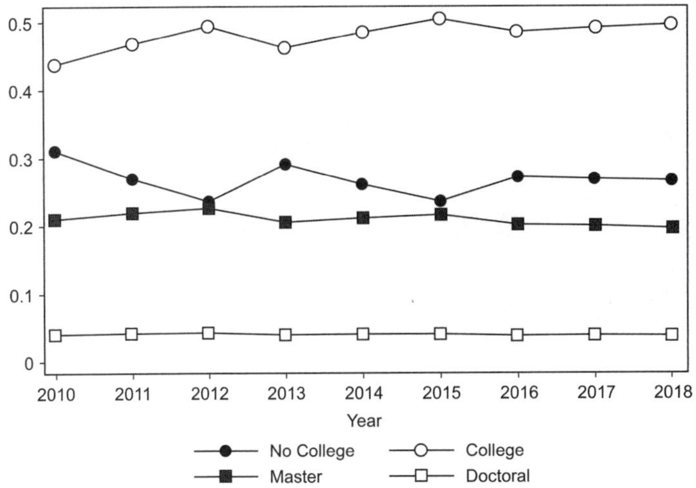

Fig. 3.5 Time series of workers' education levels in the Cognism resume data

This figure shows the time series of workers' education levels. Each line is the fraction of all employees (across all public firms) with each highest education level (no college, college, master's, or doctoral) in the Cognism resume data in a given year from 2010 to 2018.

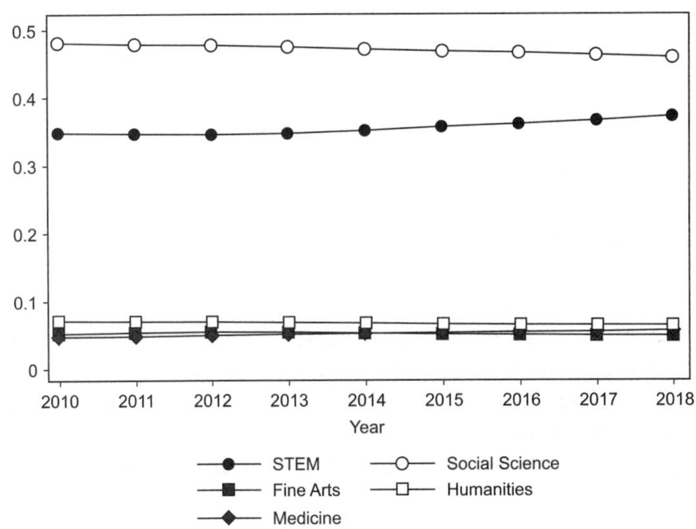

Fig. 3.6 Time series of workers' majors in the Cognism resume data

This figure shows the distribution of workers' majors over time. Each line is the fraction of all employees (across all public firms) in each major (STEM, social science, fine arts, humanities, and medicine) in the Cognism resume data in a given year from 2010 to 2018. STEM includes engineering (e.g., electrical, chemical, mechanical), physical sciences (e.g., math, physics, chemistry, computer science, statistics), and biological sciences (e.g., biology, pharmacology). The majors are mutually exclusive; for each worker, we record the major of the most recent degree earned.

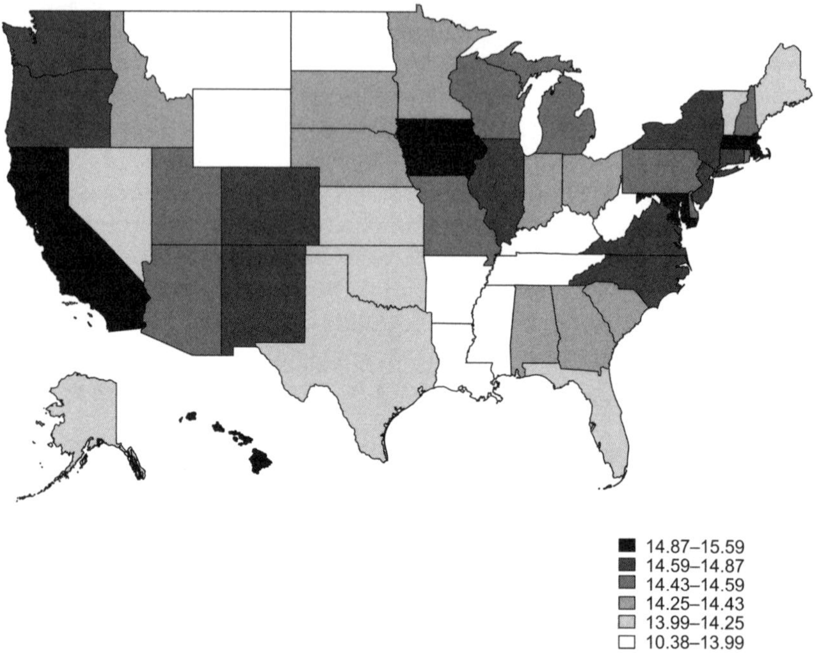

Fig. 3.7 Map of average required years of education in the Burning Glass job postings data

This figure shows a heat map of the average required years of education across U.S. states. It plots the average required years of education of job postings of public firms in each state from 2010 to 2018.

the share of workers with STEM majors and a small decrease in the share of workers with social science majors. While Cognism offers slightly more comprehensive coverage of more educated workers and workers in STEM fields, our benchmarking exercises suggest stable representativeness of the Cognism resume data across education categories and majors. Importantly, there is no differential over-representation of highly educated workers in some periods versus others.

Next, we document the variation of workers' education levels across geographic areas. Figure 3.7 considers the job postings data and shows the average required number of years of education in each state. Intuitively, states such as Massachusetts and California have the highest demand for educated workers.

We then look at the distribution of workers' education levels and specialization across industries. Figure 3.8 plots the average share of workers with undergraduate, master's, and doctoral degrees in the Cognism resume data for public firms in each of the 2-digit NAICS sectors. Firms in the "Education Services" sector and the "Professional and Business Services"

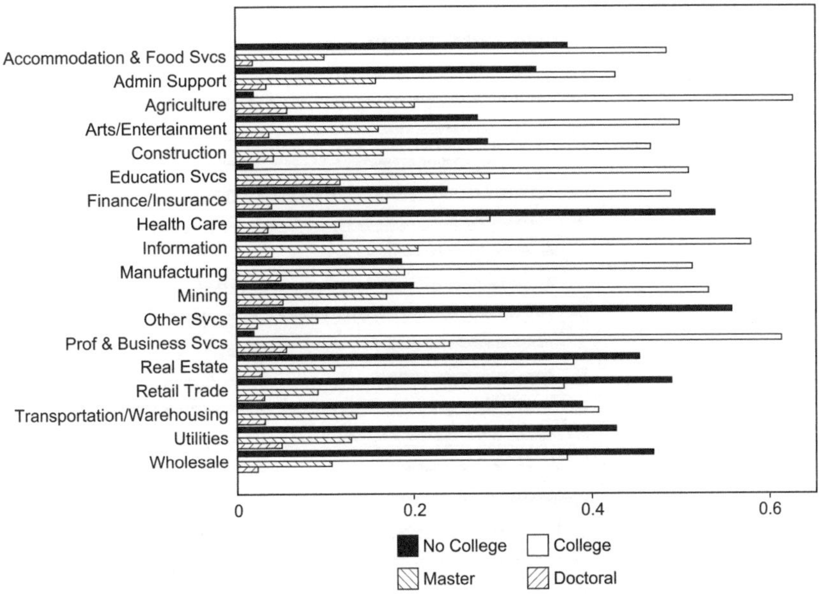

Fig. 3.8 Education level by industry sector in the Cognism resume data

This figure presents the share of workers in each highest level of education at the industry level, based on the sample of public firms. For each sector (based on NAICS 2-digit industry codes), we compute the share of workers with the highest level of education being less than college, college, master's, or doctoral in the Cognism resume data between 2010 and 2018.

sector have the highest shares of workers with undergraduate degrees, master's degrees, and doctoral degrees. Figure 3.9 considers the distribution of workers' educational majors across industries. We see intuitive trends that help validate Cognism's classification of educational majors: the tech sectors ("Professional and Business Services" and "Information") and the "Manufacturing" sector have high shares of workers with STEM majors, "Finance/Insurance" and "Real Estate" have the highest shares of workers with social science majors (which include all business school degrees such as MBAs), and the "Health Care" sector has the highest share of workers with degrees in medicine fields.

Finally, figure 3.10 considers the distribution of workers' seniority levels across industries. We observe that all industries have a pyramid structure, with the majority of workers in low-seniority levels and a small percentage of workers in high-seniority levels. The only exceptions are "Arts/Entertainment" and "Health Care," which are top-heavy with more workers in senior positions than in mid-level positions. Given the relative homogeneity of hierarchical structures across diverse industry sectors, even small changes in the proportion of employees in different levels is a meaningful indicator of shifts in a firm's organizational structure.

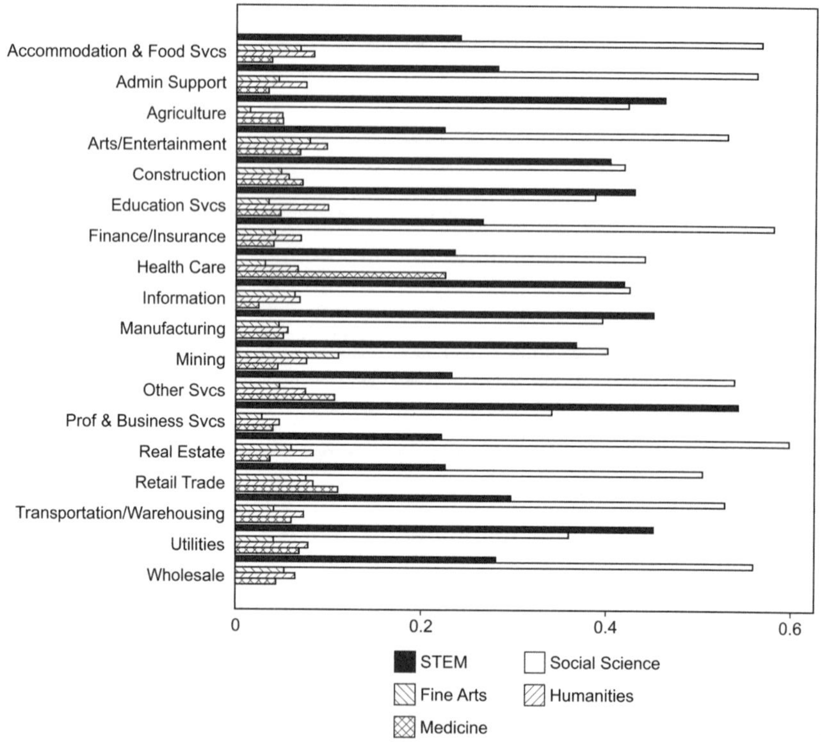

Fig. 3.9 Distribution of majors by industry sector in the Cognism resume data
This figure presents the share of workers in each major, based on the sample of public firms. For each sector (based on NAICS 2-digit industry codes), we compute the share of workers in each major (STEM, social science, fine arts, humanities, and medicine) in the Cognism resume data between 2010 and 2018. STEM includes engineering (e.g., electrical, chemical, mechanical), physical sciences (e.g., math, physics, chemistry, computer science, statistics), and biological sciences (e.g., biology, pharmacology). The majors are mutually exclusive; for each worker, we record the major of the most recent degree earned.

3.3 Does Ex Ante Labor Composition Predict Growth in AI Investments?

We consider the determinants of firms' investments in AI technologies and whether firms' initial labor composition can predict future AI investments. Theoretically, firms' initial labor composition could affect both their demand for AI investments and their ability to invest in AI by attracting AI talent. For example, Bresnahan (2019) and Agrawal et al. (2024) argue that the degree of modularity in the organizational structure of a firm could impact the firm's ease of AI adoption. When modularity is high, tasks are more independent, and there is less need for coordination; as a result, it is easier to implement AI and change decision-making in one part of the organization, as it does not require changes elsewhere. In terms of employee specialization, Acemoglu et al. (2022a) show that establishments with occu-

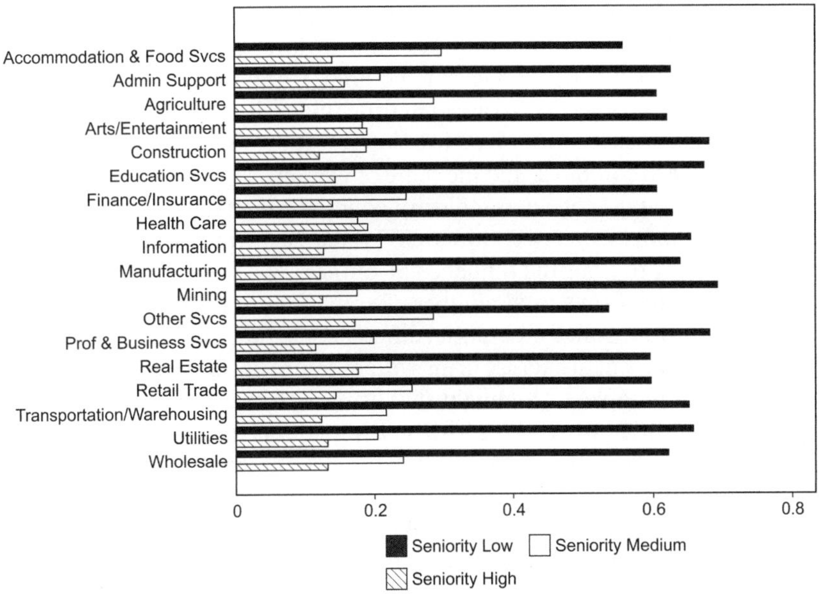

Fig. 3.10 Seniority level by industry sector in the Cognism resume data

This figure presents the share of workers in each seniority level at the industry level, based on the sample of public firms. For each sector (based on NAICS 2-digit industry codes), we compute the share of workers in each seniority level (low, medium, or high) in the Cognism resume data between 2010 and 2018.

pations that are more exposed to AI technologies have a higher demand for AI workers. And in terms of firms' workforce education, Babina et al. (2024) document that firms with alumni connections to universities that are historically strong in AI research invest more in AI by being able to attract AI-trained students from those universities.

We are interested in understanding the *use* of AI technologies by a wide range of firms. In order to not conflate this with the invention of new AI tools, we exclude firms in the tech sector (2-digit NAICS 51 or 54) from our empirical analyses. In table 3.2, we examine how ex ante worker composition predicts future growth in firm-level AI investments by estimating the following cross-sectional specification:

$$(1) \qquad \Delta\, ShareAIWorkers_{i,[2010,2018]} = \beta\, WorkerComposition_{i,2010} + IndustryFE + \epsilon_i ,$$

where $\Delta ShareAIWorkers_{i,[2010,2018]}$ denotes the change in the share of firm i's AI-skilled employees from 2010 to 2018, standardized to mean zero and standard deviation one to streamline the economic interpretation. All regressions include 2-digit NAICS industry fixed effects. The explanatory variables include the following measures of ex ante worker composition measured as of 2010: the shares of workers in each seniority level in column 1, the shares of workers in each education level in column 2, and the shares of workers in each major in column 3. To avoid multi-collinearity, we omit the share of workers in the high seniority level in column 1, the share of workers with no college degree in column 2, and the share of workers with medicine majors in column 3. Column 4 considers seniority, educational attainment, and college majors simultaneously. All continuous variables are winsorized at 1 percent and 99 percent to limit the influence of outliers. We weight the estimating equation by each firm's total number of employees in the Cognism resume data in 2010 to account for potential differences in precision in the measurement of AI investments across firms with different coverage.[14]

The results in table 3.2 highlight that firms with more workers with doctoral degrees and more workers with STEM majors invest more in AI going forward. This is broadly consistent with the evidence in Babina et al. (2024) that firms with more educated workforces and alumni connections to AI-strong universities are able to attract AI talent more easily. The hierarchical structure of the firm does not significantly predict AI investments.

3.4 Firms' AI Investments and Changes in Labor Composition

We explore how the key aspects of firms' labor composition change with firms' investments in AI. Firms that invest more in AI shift toward more educated workforces, with more emphasis on STEM degrees and skills in analysis and IT. At the same time, AI-investing firms become less top-heavy in terms of their hierarchies, with increasing shares of junior employees and less emphasis on middle-management and senior roles.

3.4.1 AI Investments and Employee Seniority

We begin the analysis by examining whether firms that invest in AI become more top-heavy or bottom-heavy in terms of their hierarchical structure. The direction of this shift is ex ante ambiguous and an open empirical question. On the one hand, AI contributes to firm growth (Babina et al. 2024), and as enterprises have grown in size over the 20th century, the share of employees in managerial positions has risen dramatically (Radner 1992). Thus, AI-fueled growth may result in the continuation of this trend toward increased organizational complexity and increased need for middle- and top-level managerial positions. For example, Caliendo et al. (2015) show that many firms expand by adding layers of management. On the other hand, Garicano and Rossi-Hansberg (2006) present a theoretical model where reductions in costs of accessing knowledge through improved data

14. Since the numbers of worker resumes are correlated with firm size, this weighting scheme also roughly weights firms in accordance with their contribution to the economy. Our results are also robust to weighting by Cognism's coverage rate of Compustat employment in 2010.

Table 3.2 Initial worker composition and AI investments

	Δ Share of AI Workers 2010–2018			
	(1)	(2)	(3)	(4)
Share of Workers with Low Seniority, 2010	−0.211			−0.394
	(0.393)			(0.414)
Share of Workers with Medium Seniority, 2010	−0.443			−0.152
	(0.407)			(0.425)
Share of Workers with College Degree, 2010		−0.489**		−0.457*
		(0.232)		(0.245)
Share of Workers with Master's Degree, 2010		0.891**		0.590*
		(0.402)		(0.310)
Share of Workers with Doctoral Degree, 2010		1.766**		2.933***
		(0.819)		(0.906)
Share of Workers with STEM Major, 2010			0.741**	1.238***
			(0.326)	(0.447)
Share of Workers with Social Science Major, 2010			−0.219	0.563**
			(0.286)	(0.232)
Share of Workers with Fine Arts Major, 2010			0.185	1.021
			(0.661)	(0.734)
Share of Workers with Humanities Major, 2010			1.321*	0.979
			(0.694)	(0.675)
Industry Sector FE	Y	Y	Y	Y
Adj R-Squared	0.096	0.134	0.125	0.158
Observations	1,218	1,218	1,216	1,216

Note: This table reports the coefficients from regressions of cross-sectional changes in AI investments by US public firms (in non-tech sectors) from 2010 to 2018 on the following ex ante firm characteristics measured in 2010: share of workers in each seniority level in column 1, share of workers in each education level in column 2, and share of workers in each major (based on the highest degree earned) in column 3. Column 4 includes all firm characteristics from columns 1 to 3. The dependent variable is the growth in the share of AI workers from 2010 to 2018 using the resume data from Cognism. Regressions are weighted by the number of Cognism resumes in 2010. All specifications control for industry sector fixed effects. The dependent variable is normalized to have a mean of zero and a standard deviation of one. Standard errors are clustered at the 5-digit NAICS industry level and reported in parentheses. *, **, and *** denote statistical significance at the 10 percent, 5 percent, and 1 percent levels, respectively.

processing (which is arguably the main effect of AI technology) result in increases in the problem-solving ability of employees at all levels, leading to increased span of control and less reliance on top-heavy hierarchical levels.

Previous technologies also had differing impacts on firm organization. Acemoglu et al. (2007) show that firms investing in new information technologies are more likely to favor decentralization. Bloom et al. (2014) find that information technology and communication technology have opposing effects on firm organization: information technology is a decentralizing force allowing workers and lower-level managers to handle more problems, while communication technology decreases autonomy and is associated with more centralization.

Empirically, we measure hierarchical flatness as the share of a firm's overall employees who are in more junior versus more senior positions: if firms become more top-heavy, increasing their middle-management and senior roles, then the share of employees in senior positions will rise, and vice versa. We link the changes in the shares of employees across levels to firms' AI investments using long-differences regressions, which are standard in settings analyzing slow-moving processes like technological progress (Acemoglu and Restrepo 2020) and especially well suited to study AI investments, which are gradual over time and have non-immediate effects (Babina et al. 2024). Specifically, we regress firm-level changes in the share of junior, middle-ranked, and senior employees from 2010 to 2018 on changes in AI investments proxied by the growth in the share of AI workers. By taking first differences in independent and dependent variables, the long-differences specification ensures that time-invariant firm characteristics do not drive the results. In table 3.3, we report the estimates from the following regression:

$$(2) \quad \Delta SeniorityLevel_{i,[2010,2018]} = \beta \Delta ShareAIWorkers_{i,[2010,2018]} + Controls'_{i,2010}\gamma + IndustryFE + \epsilon_i,$$

where the main independent variable, $\Delta ShareAIWorkers_{i,[2010,2018]}$, captures the change in the share of AI workers in firm i from 2010 to 2018, standardized to mean zero and standard deviation of one as in table 3.2. *IndustryFE* are 2-digit NAICS fixed effects. As in section 3.2.4, we focus on firms in non-tech sectors, and weigh the estimating equation by each firm's total number of employees in the Cognism resume data in 2010. In columns 1, 3, and 5 we include only industry fixed effects to examine the unconditional relationship between changes in AI investments and employee seniority. In columns 2, 4, and 6, we add a rich set of controls proposed by Babina et al. (2024) and measured at the start of the sample period in 2010: (i) firm-level characteristics (log sales, cash/assets, R&D/Sales, log markup, and the log of the firm's total number of jobs); (ii) characteristics of the commuting zones (CZ) where each firm is located (the share of workers in IT-related occupations, the share of college-educated workers, log average wage, the share of foreign-born workers, the share of routine workers, the share of workers in finance and manufacturing industries, and the share of female workers); and (iii) the log industry-average wage.[15] Summary statistics on key variables for the regression sample are provided in appendix table A.3.[16]

In columns 1 and 2 of table 3.3, the dependent variable is the firm-level change in the share of junior employees (i.e., employees in entry-level and single-contributor positions) from 2010 to 2018. In columns 3 and 4, the

15. When firms span multiple commuting zones, we calculate commuting-zone-level variables as the weighted average, using numbers of Burning Glass job postings in each commuting zone as weights.

16. See http://www.nber.org/data-appendix/c14753/appendix.pdf.

Table 3.3 **AI investments and workers' seniority levels**

	Δ Share Seniority Low		Δ Share Seniority Middle		Δ Share Seniority High	
	(1)	(2)	(3)	(4)	(5)	(6)
Δ Share AI Workers	0.015***	0.016***	−0.007***	−0.008***	−0.007**	−0.008**
	(0.004)	(0.004)	(0.002)	(0.002)	(0.003)	(0.003)
Industry Sector FE	Y	Y	Y	Y	Y	Y
Controls	N	Y	N	Y	N	Y
Adj R−Squared	0.175	0.334	0.170	0.232	0.170	0.314
Observations	1,218	1,218	1,218	1,218	1,218	1,218

Note: This table reports the coefficients from long-differences regressions of the change in the share of workers in each seniority level from 2010 to 2018 on the contemporaneous firm-level changes in AI investments among US public firms (in non-tech sectors). The independent variable is the growth in the share of AI workers from 2010 to 2018 based on the Cognism resume data, standardized to mean zero and standard deviation of one. The dependent variables are the changes in the share of workers in each seniority level (low in columns 1 and 2; medium in columns 2 and 4; and high in columns 5 and 6) in the Cognism resume data. Regressions are weighted by the number of Cognism resumes in 2010. All specifications control for industry sector fixed effects. Columns 2, 4, and 6 also include the baseline controls all measured as of 2010: firm-level characteristics (log sales, cash/assets, R&D/sales, log markup, and log number of jobs), log industry wage, and characteristics of the commuting zones where the firms are located (the share of workers in IT-related occupations, the share of college-educated workers, log average wage, the share of foreign-born workers, the share of routine workers, the share of workers in finance and manufacturing industries, and the share of female workers). Standard errors are clustered at the 5-digit NAICS industry level and reported in parentheses. *, **, and *** denote statistical significance at the 10 percent, 5 percent, and 1 percent levels, respectively.

dependent variable is the firm-level change in mid-level employees (i.e., team leads and middle managers), and columns 5 and 6 consider the firm-level change in senior employees (department heads and top-level leadership). The results reveal that AI-investing firms become flatter (or, more precisely, more bottom-heavy and less top-heavy). A one-standard-deviation increase in AI investments is associated with a 1.6 percent increase in the share of junior employees, accompanied by a 0.8 percent decline in both mid-level employees and senior management. Importantly, the results are almost identical with and without the inclusion of detailed ex ante firm-level, location-level, and industry-level controls in even columns, despite the adjusted *R-Squared* rising significantly (nearly doubling for both the share of junior employees and the share of senior employees). This makes it unlikely that the results are driven by ex ante omitted firm characteristics (Altonji et al. 2005; Oster 2019). In appendix table A.4, we alternatively weight the regressions by the coverage rate in 2010 and find similar results.[17]

One concern is that firms' hierarchical structure may change as a result of firm growth and not AI investments per se. For example, if the adjustment costs of hiring junior workers are lower, fast-growing firms will likely expand

17. See http://www.nber.org/data-appendix/c14753/appendix.pdf.

by hiring junior employees. In appendix table A.5, we directly control for firms' sales growth from 2010 to 2018 in the regressions.[18] While faster firm growth is indeed correlated with an increase in the share of junior workers and a decrease in the share of senior workers, the effects of AI investments remain unchanged conditional on firm growth. This suggests that the effects are not mechanically driven by firm growth.

The magnitude of the results in table 3.3 is economically meaningful, given that the cross-sectional average change in the share of junior employees over the sample period is only 0.18 percent (see table A.3), and there has been no overall trend toward more junior employees across the cross-section of US public firms. AI-investing firms experience fast shifts toward more junior employees and reductions in the share of senior-level employees. This is consistent with the theoretical prediction of Garicano and Rossi-Hansberg (2006) and empirical evidence in Bloom et al. (2014) that technologies that improve prediction and decision-making, such as AI, will give lower-level workers more autonomy and require fewer managerial layers in firms.

3.4.2 AI Investments and Employee Educational Attainment

We leverage the detailed individual-level information in the resumes to study the association between changes in firm-level AI investments and the upskilling of the firms' workforces in terms of the employees' educational attainment. Educational attainment is a particularly relevant trend to investigate in the context of firms' AI investments, given the extensive labor economics literature on skill-biased technological change (Autor et al. 1998; Acemoglu and Autor 2011; Autor et al. 2003; Katz and Murphy 1992). On the one hand, previous technologies such as IT have increased the relative demand for college graduates. In the case of AI, Babina et al. (2024) show that AI-investing firms engage in more product innovation, which may further increase firms' demand for skilled labor (Bresnahan et al. 2002). On the other hand, Webb (2020) predicts that AI is more likely to replace high-skilled tasks performed by highly educated workers than previous technologies such as software and robots. Grennan and Michaely (2022) study the impact of AI on a particular group of high-skilled workers—financial analysts—and find that AI replaces some technical tasks but increases the importance of soft skills. Furthermore, changes to organizational hierarchies may induce shifts in labor composition, as flatter hierarchical structures could require higher human capital from each individual employee (Caroli and Van Reenen 2001).

In table 3.4, we investigate the extent to which AI, as a technology, is associated with labor shifts toward more educated workers. To do this, we estimate the regression in equation 2 using the same independent variable and controls as in table 3.3, but looking at the changes in the share of

18. See http://www.nber.org/data-appendix/c14753/appendix.pdf.

Table 3.4 **AI investments and workers' education levels**

	Δ Share College		Δ Share Master's		Δ Share Doctoral		Δ Share No College	
	(1)	(2)	(3)	(4)	(5)	(6)	(7)	(8)
Δ Share AI Workers	0.033***	0.037***	0.027***	0.029***	0.007***	0.006***	−0.068***	−0.073***
	(0.012)	(0.010)	(0.004)	(0.004)	(0.001)	(0.001)	(0.014)	(0.014)
Industry Sector FE	Y	Y	Y	Y	Y	Y	Y	Y
Controls	N	Y	N	Y	N	Y	N	Y
Adj R-Squared	0.099	0.199	0.107	0.216	0.155	0.211	0.115	0.215
Observations	1,218	1,218	1,218	1,218	1,218	1,218	1,218	1,218

Note: This table reports the coefficients from long-differences regressions of the change from 2010 to 2018 in the share of workers in each highest education level on the contemporaneous firm-level changes in AI investments among US public firms (in non-tech sectors). The independent variable is the growth in the share of AI workers from 2010 to 2018 based on the Cognism resume data, standardized to mean zero and standard deviation of one. The dependent variables are measured using the Cognism resume data and represent the changes in the share of workers whose maximal attainment is a college degree in columns 1 and 2, the share of employees whose maximal attainment is a master's degree in columns 3 and 4, the share of employees with doctoral degrees in columns 5 and 6, and the share of employees with no college degree in columns 7 and 8. Regressions are weighted by the number of Cognism resumes in 2010. All specifications control for industry sector fixed effects. Columns 2, 4, 6, and 8 also include the baseline controls all measured as of 2010: firm-level characteristics (log sales, cash/assets, R&D/sales, log markup, and log number of jobs), log industry wage, and characteristics of the commuting zones where the firms are located (the share of workers in IT-related occupations, the share of college-educated workers, log average wage, the share of foreign-born workers, the share of routine workers, the share of workers in finance and manufacturing industries, and the share of female workers). Standard errors are clustered at the 5-digit NAICS industry level and reported in parentheses. *, **, and *** denote statistical significance at the 10 percent, 5 percent, and 1 percent levels, respectively.

workers in each education level as the outcome variable. To motivate our regression specification for examining changes in firms' low versus high-skilled workers, suppose that firms' production function takes the following form: $Q = AF(L^H, L^L, AI, X)$, where Q is output, A is productivity, L^H and L^L are high-skilled and low-skilled labor, respectively, AI is AI capital, and X is other inputs, including physical capital. Assume that labor input $L^j (j = H, L)$ is supplied flexibly at wage W^J, and other inputs are quasi-fixed. Following Caroli and Van Reenen (2001), we consider a translog short-run cost function, and Shepard's Lemma implies that the share of high-skilled labor in total labor costs is: $SHARE^H = \alpha \ln(W^H/W^L) + \beta AI + \gamma \ln Q$. Assuming that the production function is homothetic (which can be relaxed), after taking the differences, we get: $\Delta SHARE_{it}^H = \beta \Delta AI_{it} + X_i + \Delta u_{it}$.[19] Therefore, our long-differences specification approximately corresponds to the factor demand function, with a positive (or negative) coefficient β in a regression of high-skilled workers on AI investment indicating that AI and high-skilled labor are complements (or substitutes).

The results in table 3.4 show that larger AI investments are associated with educational upskilling of the workforce. Based on estimates from even columns when all controls are included, a one-standard-deviation increase in AI investments is associated with a 3.7 percent increase in the share of college-educated workers, a 2.9 percent increase in employees with master's degrees, and a 0.6 percent increase in employees with doctoral degrees. Correspondingly, the share of employees with no college education declines by a substantial 7.3 percent. Therefore, our results suggest that AI investments and high-skilled labor are complements. As with the results on seniority, the results on educational attainment are nearly identical with (even columns) and without (odd columns) the inclusion of detailed firm-level, location-level, and industry-level controls, indicating that these findings are likely not driven by omitted firm, industry, or geographic characteristics. The results are also interesting in light of relatively slow shifts in the educational makeup of the workforce in general, as shown earlier in figure 3.5. The share of workers with advanced degrees (master's and doctoral) has remained practically flat from 2010 to 2018 in the overall workforce. By contrast, the share of employees with advanced degrees (both master's and doctoral degrees) has risen significantly in firms that have been investing in AI, suggesting that there is a reallocation of highly educated workers away from non-AI investing firms and toward firms that invest more heavily in AI.

The reason for the shift toward more educated workforces in AI-investing firms appears to be, at least in part, increasing *demand* for educated and experienced employees on the firms' side. In table 3.5, we complement the results from the Cognism resume data with an analysis of labor-related outcomes measured using job postings data from Burning Glass. We estimate

19. We can write the relative wages lnWH/WL as composed of industry-year dummies, firm fixed effects, and idiosyncratic shocks.

Table 3.5 **AI investments and required education and experience in the job postings data**

	Δ Years of Education		Δ Years of Experience	
	(1)	(2)	(3)	(4)
Δ Share AI Workers	0.476**	0.516**	0.137*	0.061
	(0.204)	(0.217)	(0.072)	(0.078)
Industry Sector FE	Y	Y	Y	Y
Controls	N	Y	N	Y
Adj R-Squared	0.397	0.458	0.161	0.235
Observations	1,060	1,060	1,059	1,059

Note: This table reports the coefficients from long-differences regressions of the change from 2010 to 2018 in the average required education and experience on the contemporaneous firm-level changes in AI investments among US public firms (in non-tech sectors). The independent variable is the growth in the share of AI workers from 2010 to 2018 based on the Cognism resume data, standardized to mean zero and standard deviation of one. The dependent variables are the average required years of education in the Burning Glass job postings data in columns 1 and 2, and average required years of experience in the Burning Glass job postings data in columns 3 and 4. Regressions are weighted by the number of Cognism resumes in 2010. All specifications control for industry sector fixed effects. Columns 2 and 4 also include the baseline controls all measured as of 2010: firm-level characteristics (log sales, cash/assets, R&D/sales, log markup, and log number of jobs), log industry wage, and characteristics of the commuting zones where the firms are located (the share of workers in IT-related occupations, the share of college-educated workers, log average wage, the share of foreign-born workers, the share of routine workers, the share of workers in finance and manufacturing industries, and the share of female workers). Standard errors are clustered at the 5-digit NAICS industry level and reported in parentheses. *, **, and *** denote statistical significance at the 10 percent, 5 percent, and 1 percent levels, respectively.

equation 2 using the same independent variable and controls as in tables 3.3 and 3.4, but with the dependent variables being: (i) the change in the average number of years of education required in the firm's job postings from 2010 to 2018 (columns 1 and 2), and (ii) the change in the average number of years of experience required in the firm's job postings from 2010 to 2018 (columns 3 and 4).[20] We observe that firms that invest more in AI look for more educated and more experienced workforces. For example, a one-standard-deviation increase in the share of AI workers from 2010 to 2018 is associated with additional 0.52 years of educational experience (column 2), reinforcing the increased educational attainment of actual workers that we observe in table 3.4.

We perform a series of robustness tests in the appendix. First, in appendix table A.6, we exclude AI workers when calculating the share of workers in each education level (columns 1–6).[21] This has little impact on the results, suggesting that the educational upskilling is not mechanically due to the

20. The sample size is smaller than in table 3.4, because not all firms in the Cognism resume data are matched to job postings in Burning Glass data.

21. See http://www.nber.org/data-appendix/c14753/appendix.pdf.

hiring of AI workers. Second, appendix table A.7 shows that the results are robust when we alternatively weight the regressions by our Cognism data coverage rate in 2010. Finally, to account for potential non-homotheticity of the production function (i.e., the ratio of high-skilled to low-skilled labor changes as firm expands), we control for firm sales growth from 2010 to 2018 in appendix table A.8 and find similar results.

3.4.3 AI Investments and Employee Specialization and Skills

We consider one additional aspect of the changing workforce of firms and its relationship to AI investments: the importance of technical and non-technical skills. A number of recent studies point out that technical employee skills are uniquely important to modern firms. For example, Agrawal et al. (2021b) document that engineers and scientists are among the employees whose net flows (arrivals and departures) are most predictive of the firm's stock returns. Fedyk and Hodson (2023) show that technologies such as IT in the early 2000s and data analysis in 2010s can even be overvalued by corporate investors.

We use the resume data to observe whether AI investments are associated with broader changes in the technical specialization of AI-investing firms. Specifically, in table 3.6, we re-estimate equation 2 using the same independent variable and controls as in tables 3.3 and 3.4, but with dependent variables being: (i) the change in the share of employees whose most recent degree was in a STEM field in columns 1 and 2; (ii) the change in the share of employees whose most recent degree was in social science in columns 3 and 4; (iii) the change in the share of employees whose most recent degree was in fine arts in columns 5 and 6; (iv) the change in the share of employees whose most recent degree was in humanities in columns 7 and 8; and (v) the change in the share of employees whose most recent degree was in medicine in columns 9 and 10.

The results reveal that increased AI investments are associated with a general trend toward more technically skilled employees at the firm level. When all controls are included, a one-standard-deviation increase in the share of AI workers at the firm is associated with a 1.9 percent increase in the share of employees whose most recent degree is in STEM.[22] This increase is offset by declines in the shares of employees with backgrounds in social science (a decline of 1.1 percent), and medicine (a smaller decline of 0.4 percent).

Once again, we supplement our resume-based results with firms' demand from Burning Glass to see whether firms that invest more in AI start increasing their demand for technical skills more generally. AI has been highlighted as a technology that can shift the skill requirements of the workforce by Acemoglu et al. (2022a), who also consider job postings and find that estab-

22. This increase is not driven by the hiring of AI workers, who account for a small fraction of firms' employees. In appendix table A.6 columns 7 and 8 (http://www.nber.org/data-appendix/c14753/appendix.pdf), we exclude AI workers and find a similar increase in the share of workers in STEM fields.

Table 3.6 **AI investments and workers' majors**

	Δ Share STEM		Δ Share Social Science		Δ Share Fine Arts		Δ Share Humanities		Δ Share Medicine	
	(1)	(2)	(3)	(4)	(5)	(6)	(7)	(8)	(9)	(10)
Δ Share AI Workers	0.019***	0.019***	−0.011***	−0.011***	−0.004	−0.003	−0.000	−0.001	−0.003***	−0.004***
	(0.007)	(0.006)	(0.003)	(0.003)	(0.005)	(0.003)	(0.002)	(0.001)	(0.001)	(0.001)
Industry Sector FE	Y	Y	Y	Y	Y	Y	Y	Y	Y	Y
Controls	N	Y	N	Y	N	Y	N	Y	N	Y
Adj R−Squared	0.122	0.216	0.092	0.208	0.127	0.206	0.218	0.258	0.110	0.148
Observations	1,216	1,216	1,216	1,216	1,216	1,216	1,216	1,216	1,216	1,216

Note: This table reports the coefficients from long-differences regressions of the change in the share of workers in each major from 2010 to 2018 on the contemporaneous firm-level changes in AI investments among US public firms (in non-tech sectors). The dependent variables are the share of employees whose most recent degree was in a STEM field in columns 1 and 2, the share of employees whose most recent degree was in social science in columns 3 and 4, the share of employees whose most recent degree was in fine arts in columns 5 and 6, the share of employees whose most recent degree was in humanities in columns 7 and 8, and the share of employees whose most recent degree was in medicine in columns 9 and 10. The majors are mutually exclusive; for each worker, we record the major of the most recent degree earned. STEM includes engineering (e.g., electrical, chemical, mechanical), physical sciences (e.g., math, physics, chemistry, computer science, statistics), and biological sciences (e.g., biology, pharmacology). The independent variable is the growth in the share of AI workers from 2010 to 2018 based on the Cognism resume data, standardized to mean zero and standard deviation of one. Regressions are weighted by the number of Cognism resumes in 2010. All specifications control for industry sector fixed effects. Columns 2, 4, 6, 8, and 10 also include the baseline controls all measured as of 2010: firm-level characteristics (log sales, cash/assets, R&D/sales, log markup, and log number of jobs), log industry wage, and characteristics of the commuting zones where the firms are located (the share of workers in IT-related occupations, the share of college-educated workers, log average wage, the share of foreign-born workers, the share of routine workers, the share of workers in finance and manufacturing industries, and the share of female workers). Standard errors are clustered at the 5-digit NAICS industry level and reported in parentheses. *, **, and *** denote statistical significance at the 10 percent, 5 percent, and 1 percent levels, respectively.

lishments with more occupations that are highly exposed to AI are associated with both increased redundancies in existing skills and more requirements of new skills. We focus on skill clusters, and for each skill cluster in Burning Glass, we estimate equation 2 with the same independent variable and controls as in tables 3.3–3.6, but with the dependent variable being the share of job postings within each specific skill cluster. The results, reported in table 3.7, show that the main skill shifts associated with firms' AI investments are (i) increased demand for data analysis skills, (ii) increased demand for IT skills, and (iii) lower demand for maintenance skills. For example, a one-standard-deviation increase in the share of AI workers at a given firm from 2010 to 2018 corresponds to that firm increasing the share of its job postings requiring IT skills by 1.2 percent. These results suggest that AI skills are complementary to IT skills and can substitute for maintenance skills. Interestingly, firms that invest more heavily in AI do not reduce their demand for some of the skill groups that are most often predicted to be replaced by AI, such as customer service, HR, and legal skills.[23]

Overall, we find that firms' AI investments are associated with changing workforces and increased importance of technical skills. Babina et al. (2024) find that AI-fueled innovation is the main channel through which AI investments seem to power firm growth to date. Our findings are consistent with AI-fueled product innovation increasing firms' demand for complementary skilled labor in STEM and IT jobs, which are necessary to structure, store, and process data—a crucial input for AI applications.

3.4.4 Instrumental Variable Estimates

In this section, we use an instrumental variable strategy based on firms' ex ante exposure to universities' supply of AI graduates. The instrument was first used in Babina et al. (2024). The instrument isolates variation in firms' AI investments driven by the supply of AI-skilled labor, which is a key input to AI. This mitigates concerns regarding reverse causality and potential bias from unobserved demand shocks driving both firms' AI investments and changes in firm organization or workforce composition. The estimates are informative about the effects on firm organization or workforce composition if firms invest more in AI due to increased access to AI-skilled labor. In particular, we instrument firm AI investments using the variation in firms' ex ante exposure to the supply of AI talent from universities that are historically strong in AI research. As argued in Babina et al. (2024), academic research in AI has been ongoing for much longer than the commercial interest in AI, and universities that are historically strong in AI research have been able to train more AI-skilled graduates in recent years. As a result, firms' preexisting

23. This may be due to challenges in adopting AI for these tasks. For example, Tambe et al. (2019) identify complexity of HR phenomena, small data sets, and fairness and legal constraints as the main challenges in using AI techniques for HR tasks.

Table 3.7 **AI investments and required skills in the job postings data**

	Δ Share of Jobs w/ Administration Skill		Δ Share of Jobs w/ Analysis Skill		Δ Share of Jobs w/ Business Skill		Δ Share of Jobs w/ Customer Service Skill		Δ Share of Jobs w/ Engineering Skill		Δ Share of Jobs w/ Finance Skill		Δ Share of Jobs w/ Healthcare Skill	
	(1)	(2)	(3)	(4)	(5)	(6)	(7)	(8)	(9)	(10)	(11)	(12)	(13)	(14)
Δ Share AI Workers	−0.001	−0.000	0.005***	0.004***	0.001	−0.003	−0.006	0.004	−0.000	−0.002	−0.007	−0.011**	−0.003	−0.002
	(0.001)	(0.002)	(0.001)	(0.001)	(0.003)	(0.004)	(0.005)	(0.006)	(0.002)	(0.002)	(0.005)	(0.005)	(0.003)	(0.004)
Industry Sector FE	Y	Y	Y	Y	Y	Y	Y	Y	Y	Y	Y	Y	Y	Y
Controls	N	Y	N	Y	N	Y	N	Y	N	Y	N	Y	N	Y
Adj R-Squared	0.062	0.094	0.264	0.306	0.094	0.146	0.222	0.349	0.038	0.123	0.059	0.178	0.046	0.100
Observations	1,099	1,099	1,099	1,099	1,099	1,099	1,099	1,099	1,099	1,099	1,099	1,099	1,099	1,099
	Δ Share of Jobs w/ HR Skill		Δ Share of Jobs w/ IT Skill		Δ Share of Jobs w/ Legal Skill		Δ Share of Jobs w/ Marketing Skill		Δ Share of Jobs w/ Sales Skill		Δ Share of Jobs w/ Science Skill		Δ Share of Jobs w/ Supply Chain Skill	
	(1)	(2)	(3)	(4)	(5)	(6)	(7)	(8)	(9)	(10)	(11)	(12)	(13)	(14)
Δ Share AI Workers	0.001	−0.000	0.016**	0.012*	−0.001	−0.000	0.003*	0.001	0.004	0.008	−0.000	−0.001	−0.006***	−0.002
	(0.001)	(0.002)	(0.007)	(0.007)	(0.001)	(0.001)	(0.002)	(0.003)	(0.005)	(0.006)	(0.001)	(0.001)	(0.002)	(0.003)
Industry Sector FE	Y	Y	Y	Y	Y	Y	Y	Y	Y	Y	Y	Y	Y	Y
Controls	N	Y	N	Y	N	Y	N	Y	N	Y	N	Y	N	Y
Adj R-Squared	0.057	0.105	0.227	0.271	0.034	0.119	0.016	0.066	0.332	0.386	0.107	0.141	0.069	0.145
Observations	1,099	1,099	1,099	1,099	1,099	1,099	1,099	1,099	1,099	1,099	1,099	1,099	1,099	1,099

(continued)

Table 3.7 (cont.)

	Δ Share of Jobs w/ Agriculture Skill		Δ Share of Jobs w/ Construction Skill		Δ Share of Jobs w/ Design Skill		Δ Share of Jobs w/ Economics Skill		Δ Share of Jobs w/ Education Skill		Δ Share of Jobs w/ Utilities Skill		Δ Share of Jobs w/ Environment Skill	
	(1)	(2)	(3)	(4)	(5)	(6)	(7)	(8)	(9)	(10)	(11)	(12)	(13)	(14)
Δ Share AI Workers	−0.000	−0.000*	−0.001	−0.000	−0.001	−0.002	0.000	0.000	−0.001	−0.002*	−0.001	−0.000	0.001	0.001
	(0.000)	(0.000)	(0.000)	(0.001)	(0.001)	(0.001)	(0.001)	(0.000)	(0.001)	(0.001)	(0.001)	(0.001)	(0.001)	(0.001)
Industry Sector FE	Y	Y	Y	Y	Y	Y	Y	Y	Y	Y	Y	Y	Y	Y
Controls	N	Y	N	Y	N	Y	N	Y	N	Y	N	Y	N	Y
Adj R-Squared	0.074	0.107	0.055	0.083	0.169	0.352	0.081	0.176	0.068	0.103	0.023	0.081	0.181	0.192
Observations	1,099	1,099	1,099	1,099	1,099	1,099	1,099	1,099	1,099	1,099	1,099	1,099	1,099	1,099

	Δ Share of Jobs w/ Industry Knowledge Skill		Δ Share of Jobs w/ Maintenance Skill		Δ Share of Jobs w/ Manufacturing Skill		Δ Share of Jobs w/ Media Skill		Δ Share of Jobs w/ Personal Care Skill		Δ Share of Jobs w/ Public Safety Skill	
	(1)	(2)	(3)	(4)	(5)	(6)	(7)	(8)	(9)	(10)	(11)	(12)
Δ Share AI Workers	−0.001	0.002	−0.007***	−0.006***	−0.002*	−0.002	0.001	0.001*	0.001	−0.000	−0.000	0.000
	(0.003)	(0.003)	(0.002)	(0.002)	(0.001)	(0.001)	(0.001)	(0.001)	(0.001)	(0.002)	(0.000)	(0.001)
Industry Sector FE	Y	Y	Y	Y	Y	Y	Y	Y	Y	Y	Y	Y
Controls	N	Y	N	Y	N	Y	N	Y	N	Y	N	Y
Adj R-Squared	0.117	0.166	0.121	0.168	−0.002	0.028	0.099	0.108	0.161	0.239	0.154	0.248
Observations	1,099	1,099	1,099	1,099	1,099	1,099	1,099	1,099	1,099	1,099	1,099	1,099

Note: This table reports the coefficients from long-differences regressions of the change in the share of job postings requiring each skill cluster from 2010 to 2018 on the contemporaneous firm-level changes in AI investments among US public firms (in non-tech sectors). The dependent variables are the change in the average share of required skills in each skill cluster across all the job postings of the firm. The independent variable is the growth in the share of AI workers from 2010 to 2018 based on the Cognism resume data, standardized to mean zero and standard deviation of one. Regressions are weighted by the number of Cognism resumes in 2010. All specifications control for industry sector fixed effects. All even-numbered columns also include the baseline controls all measured as of 2010: firm-level characteristics (log sales, cash/assets, R&D/sales, log markup, and log number of jobs), log industry wage, and characteristics of the commuting zones where the firms are located (the share of workers in IT-related occupations, the share of college-educated workers, log average wage, the share of foreign-born workers, the share of routine workers, the share of workers in finance and manufacturing industries, and the share of female workers). Standard errors are clustered at the 5-digit NAICS industry level and reported in parentheses. *, **, and *** denote statistical significance at the 10 percent, 5 percent, and 1 percent levels, respectively.

connections to AI-strong universities offer a plausibly exogenous source of variation in firms' access to the supply of AI talent during the 2010s boom in commercial interest in AI.

The instrument for firm i is: $IV_i = \sum_u s_{iu}^{2010} AIstrong_u$, where s_{iu}^{2010} is the share of STEM workers in firm i in 2010 who graduated from university u, and $AIstrong_u$ equals one if university u is identified as an AI-strong university based on pre-2010 publications.[24] Two key concerns with our instrument are that AI-strong universities may also be strong in computer science (CS) outside of AI or generally be strong (highly-ranked) universities, which might affect firm outcomes through channels other than AI investments. To address these concerns, we control for firms' ex ante exposure to CS-strong universities $\sum_u s_{iu}^{2010} CSstrong_u$ and top-ranked universities $\sum_u s_{iu}^{2010} Top10_u$, where $CSstrong_u$ is the average pre-2010 share of (non-AI) CS researchers at university u, and $Top10_u$ equals one if a university is among the top 10 universities ranked by the US News & World Report.

Appendix tables A.9, A.10, and A.11 present the IV estimates.[25] In each table, the odd columns control for industry fixed effects and exposure to CS-strong and top-10 universities, and the even columns additionally control for (i) baseline controls (firm-, industry-, and commuting-zone-level controls), (ii) pre-period firm sales and employment growth between 2000 and 2008 to address unobservable firm characteristics that might simultaneously drive firms' growth trajectories and their hiring of AI workers, and (iii) state fixed effects to control for local labor market characteristics that might drive both firms' AI hiring and their growth. In all specifications, the first-stage F-statistics are above 10. Consistent with our main results using the long-differences specification, we find that instrumented firm AI investments are associated with the flattening of organizational hierarchy and upskilling of firms' workforce.[26] We also find that AI-investing firms experience an increase in the share of STEM workers and a decrease in the share of workers in social sciences, although these IV estimates are not statistically significant (appendix table A.11). These results suggest that the patterns we document are not driven by unobserved demand shocks simultaneously affecting AI investments and firm organization or workforce, but rather reflect the effects of AI investments due to supply shocks.

3.5 Conclusion

In this paper, we study the relationship between the use of AI technologies and workforce composition and organization at the firm level. We find that firms that initially have a more educated workforce and higher emphasis on

24. Babina et al. (2024) describe the data used to construct the IV and perform validation exercises in more detail.

25. See http://www.nber.org/data-appendix/c14753/appendix.pdf.

26. Appendix tables A.9 and A.10, http://www.nber.org/data-appendix/c14753/appendix.pdf.

STEM workers are more likely to invest in AI. At the same time, firm-level growth in AI investments is associated with an increasingly flatter hierarchical structure, an increase in the share of workers with college degrees and advanced degrees, and a further increase in the share of workers with STEM majors. Data on job postings reveal that firms investing in AI technologies increase their demand for workers with more years of education and workers with data analysis and IT skills.

Our evidence of major changes in firms' workforce composition and organization accompanying AI investments contributes to our understanding of how AI can transform firms' organization and production processes. As a predictive technology, AI improves individual employees' ability to make predictions and decisions, which increases the autonomy of workers and reduces the demand for managerial positions. However, unlike previous automation technologies that displaced routine tasks, AI investments are not associated with the reduction in demand for high-skilled workers performing prediction tasks, instead increasing the share of high-skilled labor at the firm level. Further understanding the interactions between AI technology, production processes, and firm organization would be a fruitful area for future work.

Our evidence also helps to shed light on the impact of AI on the labor market. At the firm level, AI is associated with increased demand for skilled labor and does not seem to displace tasks that are commonly predicted to be replaced by AI, such as customer service, human resources, and legal jobs. However, it remains an open question how these effects aggregate to the labor market level, and it is possible that AI displaces jobs in non-AI-investing firms. Furthermore, our results imply that there is a reallocation of skilled labor from non-AI-investing firms to AI-investing firms, which might have important implications for sorting and between-firm inequality in the labor market.

Finally, while the research in this paper examines the impact of firms' AI use before the popularization of generative AI tools like DALL·E and ChatGPT, the upskilling of employees in AI-investing firms is likely to accelerate with the adoption of generative AI tools. This upskilling effect is associated with AI-powered product innovation (Babina et al. 2024), and many firms that have already invested heavily in AI technologies are starting to use tools like ChatGPT to further improve their products and services.[27] Alternatively, the spread of AI as a software via tools like ChatGPT could

27. For example, (https://www.theverge.com/2023/3/9/23632312/microsoft-azure-openai-chatgpt-feature-available) Microsoft makes ChatGPT available in its Azure OpenAI service. This allows developers and businesses to integrate OpenAI's ChatGPT model into their own services. A broad range of companies like Morningstar (https://newsroom.morningstar.com/newsroom/news-archive/press-release-details/2023/Mo-an-AI-Chatbot-Powered-by-Morningstar-Intelligence-Engine-Debuts-in-Morningstar-Platforms/default.aspx) and Mercedes-Benz (https://www.cnbc.com/2023/06/15/mercedes-benz-microsoft-to-test-chatgpt-in-vehicles.html) have already partnered with Microsoft to incorporate ChatGPT into their products and services.

expose more workers to automation from AI, especially those who are highly skilled (Eloundou et al. 2023, Felten et al. 2023, Eisfeldt et al. 2023). Finally, early evidence suggests that generative AI can improve worker productivity across the skill distribution (Brynjolfsson et al. 2023; Casal and Kessler 2023; Dell'Acqua et al. 2023; Agarwal et al. 2023; Noy and Zhang 2023), and Agrawal et al. (2023) suggest that AI advances can potentially open up employment opportunities for workers with generic skills. More work is needed to understand the evolving impacts of firms' AI use on workers and labor composition.

Acknowledgments

The authors are grateful to Lucy Eldridge, John Van Reenen (discussant), Janis Skrastins (discussant), Robert Seamans (discussant), Bryan Seegmiller (discussant), and participants at the AEA, Federal Reserve Digitization Collab Week, the Jozef Stefan Institute Artificial Intelligence Lab, the Labor and Finance Conference, Microsoft Research, the NBER CRIW Conference on Productivity, Technology and Economic Growth, the Organisation for Economic Co-operation and Development (OECD), Stanford University Digital Innovation Lab, the US Government Accountability Office (GAO), the WFA, and Yeshiva University for helpful suggestions. The authors thank Cognism Ltd. for providing the employment data and Burning Glass Technologies for providing the job postings data. Peter Tong and Derek Luan provided excellent research assistance. For acknowledgments, sources of research support, and disclosure of the authors' material financial relationships, if any, please see https://www.nber.org/books-and-chapters/technology-productivity-and-economic-growth/firm-investments-artificial-intelligence-technologies-and-changes-workforce-composition.

References

Abis, Simona, and Laura Veldkamp. 2024. "The Changing Economics of Knowledge Production." *Review of Financial Studies* 37 (1): 89–118. See https://doi.org/10.1093/rfs/hhad059.

Acemoglu, Daron, and David Autor. 2011. "Skills, Tasks and Technologies: Implications for Employment and Earnings," *Handbook of Labour Economics* 4: 1043–1171.

———, and Pascual Restrepo. 2019a. "Artificial Intelligence, Automation, and Work." University of Chicago Press.

———, and ———. 2019b. "Automation and New Tasks: How Technology Displaces and Reinstates Labor." *Journal of Economic Perspectives* 33 (2): 3–30.

———, and ———. 2020. "Robots and Jobs: Evidence from U.S. Labor Markets." *Journal of Political Economy* 128 (6): 2188–2244.

———, and ———. 2022. "Tasks, Automation, and the Rise in US Wage Inequality." *Econometrica* 90 (5). See https://doi.org/10.3982/ECTA1981.

———, David Autor, Jonathon Hazell, and Pascual Restrepo. 2022a. "Artificial Intelligence and Jobs: Evidence from Online Vacancies." *Journal of Labor Economics* 40 (S1): S293–S340.

———, Gary Anderson, David Beede, Catherine Buffington, Eric Childress, Emin Dinlersoz, Lucia Foster, Nathan Goldschlag, John Haltiwanger, Zachary Kroff et al. 2022b. "Automation and the Workforce: A Firm-Level View from the 2019 Annual Business Survey." Technical Report 2022.

———, Philippe Aghion, Claire Lelarge, John Van Reenen, and Fabrizio Zilibotti. 2007. "Technology, Information, and the Decentralization of the Firm. *Quarterly Journal of Economics* 122 (4): 1759–1799.

Agarwal, Nikhil, Alex Moehring, Pranav Rajpurkar, and Tobias Salz. 2023. "Combining Human Expertise with Artificial Intelligence: Experimental Evidence from Radiology," NBER Working Paper 31422. Cambridge, MA: National Bureau of Economic Research.

Aghion, Philippe and Peter Howitt. 1992. "A Model of Growth through Creative Destruction." *Econometrica* 60: 323–51.

Agrawal, Ajay K., Joshua S. Gans, and Avi Goldfarb. 2019. "Artificial Intelligence: The Ambiguous Labor Market Impact of Automating Prediction." *Journal of Economic Perspectives* 33 (2): 31–50.

———, Joshua S. Gans, and Avi Goldfarb. 2024. "AI Adoption and System-Wide Change." *Journal of Economics and Management Strategy* 33(2): 327–337.

———, Joshua S. Gans, and Avi Goldfarb. 2023. "The Turing Transformation: Artificial Intelligence, Intelligence Augmentation, and Skill Premiums." NBER Working Paper 31767. Cambridge, MA: National Bureau of Economic Research.

Agrawal, Ashwini, Isaac Hacamo, and Zhongchen Hu. 2021. "Information Dispersion across Employees and Stock Returns." *Review of Financial Studies* 34 (10): 4785–4831.

Alderucci, Dean, Lee Branstetter, Eduard Hovy, Andrew Runge, and Nikolas Zolas. 2020. "Quantifying the Impact of AI on Productivity and Labor Demand: Evidence from U.S. Census Microdata." *Allied Social Science Associations.*

Alekseeva, Liudmila, José Azar, Mireia Gine, Sampsa Samila, and Bledi Taska. 2020. "The Demand for AI skills in the Labor Market" CEPR Discussion Paper No. DP14320.

Altonji, Joseph, Todd Elder, and Christopher Taber. 2005. "Selection on Observed and Unobserved Variables: Assessing the Effectiveness of Catholic Schools." *Journal of Political Economy* 113 (1), 151–84.

Autor, David H., Frank Levy, and Richard J. Murnane. 2003. "The Skill Content of Recent Technological Change: An Empirical Exploration." *Quarterly Journal of Economics* 118 (4): 1279–1333.

———, Lawrence Katz, and Alan Krueger. 1998. "Computing Inequality: Have Computers Changed the Labor Market?" *Quarterly Journal of Economics* 113 (4): 1169–213.

Babina, Tania, Anastassia Fedyk, Alex He, and James Hodson. 2024. "Artificial Intelligence, Firm Growth, and Product Innovation." *Journal of Financial Economics* 151: 103745.

Bessen, James E., Erich Denk, and Chen Meng. 2022. "The Remainder Effect: How Automation Complements Labor Quality." SSRN Scholarly Paper ID 4042317, Social Science Research Network, Rochester, NY, February.

Bloom, Nicholas, Luis Garicano, Raffaella Sadun, and John Van Reenen. 2014. "The Distinct Effects of Information Technology and Communication Technology on Firm Organization." *Management Science* 60 (12): 2859–2885. Publisher: INFORMS.

———, Raffaella Sadun, and John Van Reenen. 2012. "The Organization of Firms Across Countries." *Quarterly Journal of Economics* 127 (4): 1663–1705.

Bresnahan, Timothy F. 2019. "Artificial Intelligence Technologies and Aggregate Growth Prospects." *Prospects for Economic Growth in the United States*, edited by John W. Diamond and George R. Zodrow. Cambridge University Press.

———, Erik Brynjolfsson, and Lorin M. Hitt. 2002. "Information Technology, Workplace Organization, and the Demand for Skilled Labor: Firm-Level Evidence." *Quarterly Journal of Economics* 117 (1): 339–76.

Brynjolfsson, Erik, Danielle Li, and Lindsey R Raymond. 2023. "Generative AI at Work." NBER Working Paper 31161. Cambridge, MA: National Bureau of Economic Research.

———, Tom Mitchell, and Daniel Rock. 2018. "What Can Machines Learn, and What Does It Mean for Occupations and the Economy?" *AEA Papers and Proceedings* 108.

Caliendo, Lorenzo, Ferdinando Monte, and Esteban Rossi-Hansberg. 2015. "The Anatomy of French Production Hierarchies." *Journal of Political Economy* 123 (4): 809–52.

Cao, Sean, Wei Jiang, Junbo L Wang, and Baozhong Yang. 2021. "From Man vs. Machine to Man + Machine: The Art and AI of Stock Analyses." *Journal of Financial Economics* 160: 103910

Caroli, Eve, and John Van Reenen. 2001. "Skill-Biased Organizational Change? Evidence from A Panel of British and French Establishments." *Quarterly Journal of Economics* 116 (4): 1449–1492.

Casal, J. Elliott, and Matthew Kessler. 2023. "Can Linguists Distinguish between ChatGPT/AI and Human Writing? A Study of Research Ethics and Academic Publishing." *Research Methods in Applied Linguistics* 2 (3): 100068.

Crouzet, Nicolas, and Janice C Eberly. 2018. "Understanding Weak Capital Investment: The Role of Market Concentration and Intangibles." *AEA Papers and Proceedings* 2018: 426–31.

D'Acunto, Francesco, Nagpurnanand Prabhala, and Alberto G Rossi. 2019. "The Promises and Pitfalls of Robo-advising." *Review of Financial Studies* 32 (5): 1983–2020.

Davis, Steven J., John Haltiwanger, Ron Jarmin, Javier Miranda, Christopher Foote, and Eva Nagypal. 2006. "Volatility and Dispersion in Business Growth Rates: Publicly Traded versus Privately Held Firms." *NBER Macroeconomics Annual 2006* 21: 107–79.

Dell'Acqua, Fabrizio, Edward McFowland, Ethan R Mollick, Hila Lifshitz-Assaf, Katherine Kellogg, Saran Rajendran, Lisa Krayer, François Candelon, and Karim R Lakhani. 2023. "Navigating the Jagged Technological Frontier: Field Experimental Evidence of the Effects of AI on Knowledge Worker Productivity and Quality." Harvard Business School Technology & Operations Mgt. Unit Working Paper 24–013.

Eisfeldt, Andrea L., and Dimitris Papanikolaou. 2013. "Organization Capital and the Cross-section of Expected Returns." *Journal of Finance* 68: 1365–1406.

———, Gregor Schubert, and Miao Ben Zhang. 2023. "Generative AI and Firm Values." NBER Working Paper 31222. Cambridge, MA: National Bureau of Economic Research.

Eloundou, Tyna, Sam Manning, Pamela Mishkin, and Daniel Rock. 2023. "GPTs Are GPTs: An Early Look at the Labor Market Impact Potential of Large Language Models." *arXiv preprint arXiv:2303.10130*.

Erel, Isil, Léa H. Stern, Chenhao Tan, and Michael S Weisbach. 2021. "Selecting

Directors Using Machine Learning." *Review of Financial Studies* 34 (7): 3226–3264.

Fedyk, Anastassia, and James Hodson. 2023. "Trading on Talent: Human Capital and Firm Performance." *Review of Finance* 27: 1659–1698.

———, James Hodson, Natalya Khimich, and Tatiana Fedyk. 2022. "Is Artificial Intelligence Improving the Audit Process?" *Review of Accounting Studies* 27: 938–85.

Felten, Edward W., Manav Raj, and Robert Seamans. 2018. "A Method to Link Advances in Artificial Intelligence to Occupational Abilities." *AEA Papers and Proceedings* 108: 1–4.

———, Manav Raj, and Robert Seamans. 2023. "Occupational Heterogeneity in Exposure to Generative AI." Available at SSRN 4414065.

Fizsbein, Martin, Jeanne Lafortune, Ethan Lewis, and Jose Tessada. 2020. "Electrifying? How New Technologies Impact Productivity and Jobs." Working Paper 28076.

Frank, Morgan R., David Autor, James E. Bessen, Erik Brynjolfsson, Manuel Cebrian, David J. Deming, Maryann Feldman, Matthew Groh, João Lobo, Esteban Moro, Dashun Wang, Hyejin Youn, and Iyad Rahwan. 2019. "Toward Understanding the Impact of Artificial Intelligence on Labor." *Proceedings of the National Academy of Sciences* 116 (14): 6531–6539.

Fuster, Andreas, Paul Goldsmith-Pinkham, Tarun Ramadorai, and Ansgar Walther. 2022. "Predictably Unequal? The Effects of Machine Learning on Credit Markets." *Journal of Finance* 77 (1): 5–47.

Garicano, Luis, and Esteban Rossi-Hansberg. 2006. "Organization and Inequality in a Knowledge Economy." *Quarterly Journal of Economics* 121 (4): 1383–1435.

Gofman, Michael, and Zhao Jin. 2022. "Artificial Intelligence, Education, and Entrepreneurship." *Journal of Finance*, Forthcoming.

Grennan, Jillian, and Roni Michaely. 2022. "Artificial Intelligence and High-Skilled Work: Evidence from Analysts." Available at SSRN.

Guadalupe, Maria, and Julie Wulf. 2010. "The Flattening Firm and Product Market Competition: The Effect of Trade Liberalization on Corporate Hierarchies." *American Economic Journal: Applied Economics* 2 (4): 105–27.

Hansen, Stephen, Tejas Ramdas, Raffaella Sadun, and Joe Fuller. 2021. "The Demand for Executive Skills." NBER Working Paper 28959. Cambridge, MA: National Bureau of Economic Research.

Hershbein, Brad, and Lisa B. Kahn. 2018. "Do Recessions Accelerate Routine-Biased Technological Change? Evidence from Vacancy Postings." *American Economic Review* 108 (7): 1737–72.

Hitt, Lorin M. 1999. "Information Technology and Firm Boundaries: Evidence from Panel Data." *Information Systems Research* 10 (2): 134–49. Publisher: INFORMS.

Jansen, Mark, Hieu Nguyen, and Amin Shams. 2023. "Rise of the Machines: The Impact of Automated Underwriting." *Management Science*, Forthcoming.

Jiang, Wei, Yuehua Tang, Rachel (Jiqiu) Xiao, and Vincent Yao. 2024. "Surviving the Fintech Disruption." *Journal of Financial Economics* (forthcoming).

Juhász, Réka, Mara Squicciarini, and Nico Voigtländer. 2024. "Technology Adoption and Productivity Growth: Evidence from Industrialization in France." *Journal of Political Economy* 132(10).

Katz, Lawrence F., and Kevin M. Murphy. 1992. "Changes in Relative Wages, 1963–1987: Supply and Demand Factors." *Quarterly Journal of Economics* 107 (1): 35–78.

Kogan, Leonid, Dimitris Papanikolaou, Amit Seru, and Noah Stoffman. 2017.

"Technological Innovation, Resource Allocation and Growth." *Quarterly Journal of Economics* 132: 665–712.

———, ———, Lawrence Schmidt, and Bryan Seegmiller. 2019. "Technological Change and Occupations over the Long Run," Available at SSRN 3585676.

Korinek, Anton, and Joseph E. Stiglitz. 2019. "Artificial Intelligence and Its Implications for Income Distribution and Unemployment." *The Economics of Artificial Intelligence: An Agenda*. University of Chicago Press.

Lyonnet, Victor, and Léa H. Stern. 2022. "Venture Capital (Mis)Allocation in the Age of AI." SSRN Working Paper #4260882.

Machin, Stephen, and John Van Reenen. 1998. "Technology and Changes in Skill Structure: Evidence from Seven OECD Countries." *Quarterly Journal of Economics* 113 (4): 1215–1244.

McElheran, Kristina, and Chris Forman. 2019. "Firm Organization in the Digital Age: IT Use and Vertical Transactions in U.S. Manufacturing." SSRN Working Paper 3396116.

Mihet, Roxana, and Thomas Philippon. 2019. "The Economics of Big Data and Artificial Intelligence." *Disruptive Innovation in Business and Finance in the Digital World (International Finance Review)* 20: 29–43.

Noy, Shakked, and Whitney Zhang. 2023. "Experimental Evidence on the Productivity Effects of Generative Artificial Intelligence." *Science* 381 (6654): 187–92.

Oster, Emily. 2019. "Unobservable Selection and Coefficient Stability: Theory and Evidence." *Journal of Business & Economic Statistics* 37 (2): 187–204.

Peters, Ryan, and Lucien A. Taylor. 2017. "Intangible Capital and the Investment-q Relation." *Journal of Financial Economics* 123: 251–72.

Radner, Roy. 1992. "Hierarchy: The Economics of Managing." *Journal of Economic Perspectives* 30 (5): 1382–1415.

Rajan, Raghuram G., and Julie Wulf. 2006. "The Flattening Firm: Evidence from Panel Data on the Changing Nature of Corporate Hierarchies." *Review of Economics and Statistics* 88 (4): 759–73.

Rock, Daniel. 2019. "Engineering Value: The Returns to Technological Talent and Investments in Artificial Intelligence." Available at SSRN 3427412.

Romer, Paul M. 1990. "Endogenous Technological Change." *Journal of Political Economy* 98 (5, Part 2): S71–S102.

Seamans, Robert, and Manav Raj. 2018. "AI, Labor, Productivity and the Need for Firm-Level Data." NBER Working Paper No. 24239. Cambridge, MA: National Bureau of Economic Research.

Tambe, Prassana, Lorin Hitt, Daniel Rock, and Erik Brynjolfsson. 2020. "Digital Capital and Superstar Firms." NBER Working Paper No. 28285. Cambridge, MA: National Bureau of Economic Research.

———, Peter Cappelli, and Valery Yakubovich. 2019. "Artificial Intelligence in Human Re- sources Management: Challenges and a Path Forward." *California Management Review* 61 (4): 15–42. SAGE Publications Inc.

Webb, Michael. 2020. "The Impact of Artificial Intelligence on the Labor Market." SSRN Working Paper 3482150.

Zator, Michal. 2019. "Digitization and Automation: Firm Investment and Labor Outcomes." SSRN Working Paper 3444966.

Zolas, Nikolas, Zachary Kroff, Erik Brynjolfsson, Kristina McElheran, David N. Beede, Cathy Buffington, Nathan Goldschlag, Lucia Foster, and Emin Dinlersoz. 2020. "Advanced Technologies Adoption and Use by U.S. Firms: Evidence from the Annual Business Survey." NBER Working Paper 28290. Cambridge, MA: National Bureau of Economic Research.

4

The Strange and Awful Path of Productivity in the US Construction Sector

Austan Goolsbee and Chad Syverson

Aggregate productivity growth is the prime determinant of long-run growth in income per capita, and an economy's productivity growth reflects the productivity growth rates of the industries and sectors within it.

Yet despite decided growth in aggregate productivity for the US economy as a whole, the US construction sector has diverged considerably. Indeed, for decades now, measures of labor and total factor productivity (TFP) in the sector have trended downward. To be clear, the raw BEA data suggest that the sector has become *less* productive over time. A lot less productive: value added per worker in the sector was about 40 percent lower in 2020 than it was in 1970.

Economic researchers have remarked on these troubling patterns before; see, e.g., Stokes (1981), Allen (1985), Schriver and Bowlby (1985), Sveikauskas et al. (2016, 2018), and contemporaneous work by Garcia and Molloy (2023). The problem has also attracted the attention of broader analysts and audiences; see Changali et al. (2015), Economist (2017), Potter (2021), and Smith (2021) for examples. A great deal of attention has gone to the issue of whether measurement problems explain the sector's disappointing performance.

In this paper, we update some of this previous work and extend it to some new data sources and hypotheses. Together, these new approaches seem to reinforce the view that the poor performance is not just a figment of measurement error. We see similar stagnation using physical measures of

Austan Goolsbee is the Robert P. Gwinn Professor of Economics at the Booth School of Business at the University of Chicago.

Chad Syverson is the George C. Tiao Distinguished Service Professor of Economics at the Booth School of Business at the University of Chicago, and a research associate of the National Bureau of Economic Research.

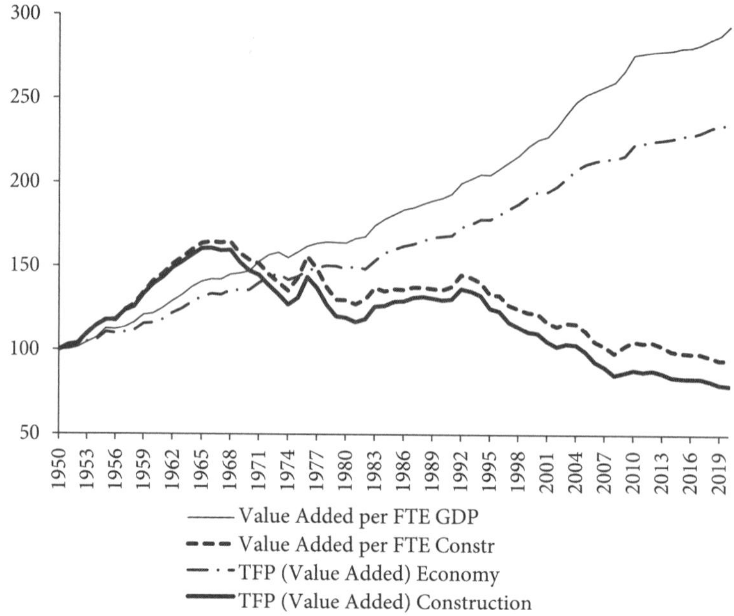

Fig. 4.1 Indexes of value added per worker and TFP, overall US and construction sector (BEA data)

productivity that are not dependent on price deflators. We also see that firms' abilities to turn materials into output has deteriorated and we document real issues with the sector's adjustment mechanisms; there is little reallocation from low productivity places to high-productivity places.

4.1 The Core Issue with Construction Productivity

Figure 4.1 shows indexes of US construction sector labor productivity and TFP from 1950 to 2020. For comparison, it also plots the same indexes for the overall economy.[1]

1. We compute productivity using the Bureau of Economic Analysis national and industry accounts data. Labor productivity is real value added divided by full-time-equivalent (FTE) employees. The change in total factor productivity (which we convert to an index level) is the growth rate in value added minus a weighted sum of the growth rates of labor and capital. The weights in a given year are the cost shares of the factor inputs, averaged across the current and prior year in the usual Divisia fashion. Labor costs are total labor compensation plus 67 percent of proprietor's income. (We base the 0.67 multiplier on labor's historical share of income being roughly two-thirds.) Capital costs are the sum of depreciation, the product of the real interest rate and the current value of installed capital, and 33 percent of proprietor's income. Analogous productivity series computed using gross output rather than value added (and in the case of TFP, subtracting the implied contribution of intermediate inputs) show similar patterns. We explore the trends in gross output, value added, and intermediate materials in the construction sector in more detail below.

Throughout the 1950s and well into the 1960s, both measures of construction sector productivity grew steadily. Indeed, they outpaced their whole-economy counterparts during that period. By 1970, however, the construction sector's labor productivity and TFP had both begun to fall. This downturn was not temporary; the decline has continued for the past half century.

This downturn did not mirror the economy-wide productivity pattern. Productivity in the entire economy grew throughout the period (albeit with some well-documented accelerations and decelerations). By 2020, while aggregate labor productivity and TFP were 290 percent and 230 percent higher than in 1950, both measures of construction productivity had fallen *below* their 1950 values.

This is stunningly bad productivity performance for a major sector. It is brought into special relief when compared to the over nine-fold increase in labor productivity the manufacturing sector experienced during the same period. Manufacturing, like construction, deals with the configuration and assembly of physical objects in preparation for use as either inputs into production or final consumption. Yet the two sectors experienced totally different productivity trajectories over the past 50 years.

Construction's poor performance might be just a curiosity if it were a trivial fraction of economic activity, but it is not. The sector's value added averaged 4.3 percent of GDP between 1950 and 2020. This share, while experiencing fluctuations, has remained fairly steady over the long run. Construction is a sizable share of aggregate output. It is large enough that its poor productivity performance noticeably drags down aggregate productivity growth. Construction labor productivity fell at an average rate of about 1 percent per year from 1970–2020. Had it instead *grown* at the (relatively modest) rate of 1 percent per year, annual aggregate labor productivity growth would have been roughly 0.18 percent higher.[2] This would have resulted in current aggregate labor productivity (and plausibly, income per capita) being about 10 percent higher than it actually was.

While we focus in this paper on US construction sector, the problem of laggard construction productivity growth appears more widespread. In the 29 countries for which the OECD reports construction sector value added per employee growth data over 1996–2019, 16 of the countries—as well as the EU-27 area as a whole—saw negative average labor productivity growth in their construction sectors over that 25-year period.[3]

Even in countries that saw positive construction productivity growth, it

2. This is calculated by multiplying the notional 2 percentage point increase in construction labor productivity growth by its average Domar weight (the sector's gross output as a share of GDP) of 0.090. This weight—see Domar (1961)—is the first-order approximation of the contribution of a sector or industry's productivity growth to aggregate productivity growth.

3. We use the "Productivity and ULC by Main Economic Activity" data from the OECD for these computations.

typically substantially lagged overall productivity growth in their economies. Average labor productivity growth across all 29 countries was 0.4 percent per year, in contrast to those countries' average overall labor productivity growth rates of 1.6 percent over the same period. The phenomena we explore at a detailed level within the United States may well apply more broadly. Their full international extent is worthy of future inquiry.

4.2 The Failure of Capital-Based Explanations for the Decline

First, we address perhaps the most obvious potential source of poor productivity growth, a lack of capital investment. If laggard investment led to lower capital-to-labor ratios, it would directly affect labor productivity. This could also influence TFP, if TFP were partially capital-embodied (Hulten 1992).

At first glance, though, this does not seem consistent with data for the construction industry. Figure 4.2 compares changes in the construction sector's current-value capital stock to that of the entire economy. While capital in construction did not grow as steadily as capital in the wider economy, construction's total capital stock growth since 1950 has actually been a bit larger, rising 7.8-fold as opposed to the 6.5-fold increase for total capital in the economy. There was no noticeable slowdown in capital growth after 1970, when sector productivity started to fall. Moreover, capital intensity—capital stock per FTE employee—did not fall in the sector relative to the overall economy. To the contrary, it actually rose a bit faster.

A more nuanced view of capital's role in construction productivity would

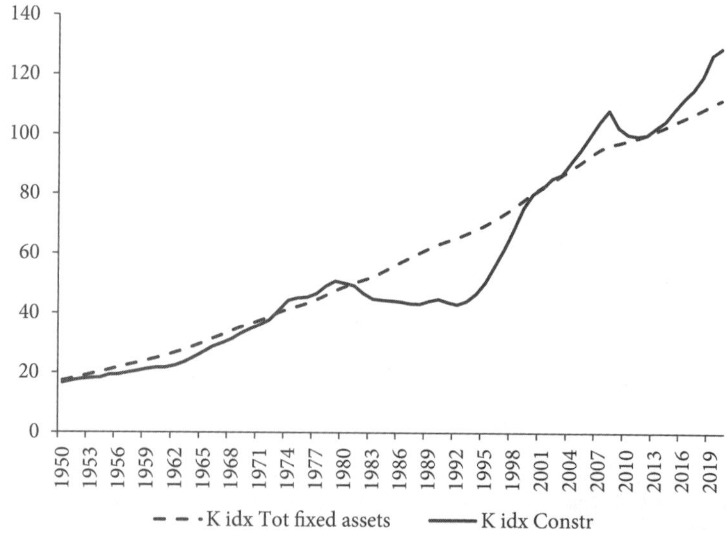

Fig. 4.2 Capital stocks (2012 = 100), total economy and construction sector

include intangible capital, which by definition is not contained in the capital series above. We can look, however, at what the BEA terms the capital stock of intellectual property (IP) products in the industry. The BEA defines this category of capital assets as including the capitalized value of R&D, software purchases, and—perhaps less relevant to construction—artistic originals. Following work like Brynjolfsson, Rock, and Syverson (2021), we can use IP capital stock as a proxy for intangible capital in the industry (which would include things like know-how, organizational strength, trade secrets, buyer-supplier relationships, sector-specific human capital, and so on).

The US construction sector is less IP-capital-intensive than the economy overall. For instance, in 2020 IP capital accounted for 4.0 percent of the sector's total capital stock, while the same ratio for the broader economy was 7.4 percent. On a per-employee basis, IP intensity in construction is an order of magnitude smaller than in the rest of the economy.[4]

However, the IP capital data in the construction sector are not really consistent with intangible capital driving the path of construction productivity, either. The sector had *no* recorded IP capital in the national accounts until 1970. Thus, throughout the 1950–1970 period when the sector's productivity growth kept up with or even exceeded aggregate productivity growth, there was no strong indication that the sector was putting into place large intangible investments. Only after the productivity slowdown had begun did the sector begin to invest in IP capital, and despite accumulating such capital at a rate exceeding that in the overall economy, the sector's productivity level continued to diverge from aggregate productivity growth.

4.3 The Traditional Confound: Measurement Problems

Because productivity is a residual—the variation in output unexplained by variation in measured inputs—mismeasurement of either output or inputs will be labeled productivity, even if unrelated to the actual efficiency of the production process. Understatements of output or overstatements of inputs would cause measured productivity to be lower than true productivity, so it is important to think about whether such issues might explain the patterns in construction.

We start from the observation in Syverson (2017) that attributing a *change* in productivity to mismeasurement requires not just establishing the presence of mismeasurement, but also a change in the *amount* of mismeasurement in the necessary direction at the same time as the measured productivity change. If we are to explain the reversal in productivity growth in construction in the late 1960s as resulting from measurement problems, we

4. Though part of this enormous difference is accounted for by the inclusion of the residential housing stock in economy-wide capital, which is limited in its market-activity marginal product.

need to demonstrate that some combination of growth in the understatement of output or overstatement of input occurred in the late 1960s.

We first consider labor input measurement. There are several plausible channels for labor measurement difficulties in construction, including a higher than average frequency of employees working irregular hours, contractor labor that may be misclassified by survey respondents, and, especially in more recent decades, labor supplied by undocumented workers.

Figure 4.3 plots three series for labor inputs in the construction sector: the sum of full-time and part-time employees (from the BEA), FTE employees (also from the BEA), and total employment (from the Current Employment Statistics of the BLS). These series capture different elements of labor inputs, such as the implied differential treatment of hours per worker when comparing summed full-time and part-time employees with FTE employees.

None of the series shows an obvious kink in the late 1960s. Moreover, they track one another closely, with no divergence at the time construction productivity started falling. The average pairwise correlations among the three series before 1970 is 0.983 and is 0.999 from 1970 on. In addition, the average annual growth rates of all three series were *lower* after 1970 than before. A mismeasurement-driven productivity slowdown would imply inputs that are growing misstatedly fast—that measured labor accelerated rather than decelerated as the data seem to show.

Given our earlier discussion about the trajectory of the construction industry's capital stock, mismeasurement of capital also seems unlikely to explain the measured productivity declines. Moreover, capital measurement

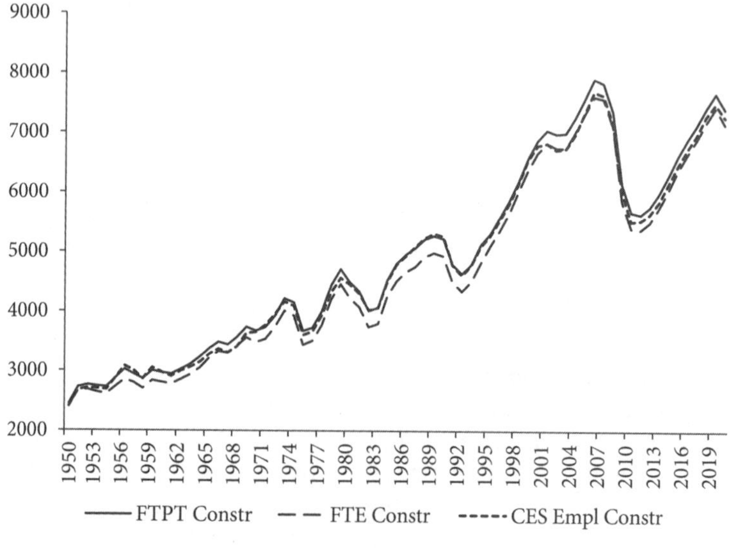

Fig. 4.3 Construction sector labor inputs, three measures

problems cannot be responsible for labor productivity mismeasurements, and labor productivity in construction exhibits the same broad pattern as does TFP (and likewise for intermediate/materials inputs).

Given the lack of obvious issues with measured inputs, much of the attention in the literature has centered on problems with measuring output.

As noted above, construction's value added share of GDP exhibited no long run trend over 1950–2020, so *nominal* construction value added grew at a similar rate to the overall economy. The components of this ratio are both nominal values, so the measured slowdown must, mechanically, be coming from differences in the output price deflators.[5]

Indeed, the construction sector's output deflator and the aggregate GDP deflator clearly start to diverge after the late 1960s. From 1950–69, the average annual growth rates of the construction and GDP deflators were almost identical—2.40 percent and 2.42 percent. From 1970 on, however, the GDP deflator averaged annual growth of 3.37 percent, while the construction value added deflator grew 5.47 percent per year. This sustained 2.1 percentage point annual difference means that even if nominal construction value added grows at a similar rate to GDP, real construction value added would grow much more slowly, and perhaps even fall.

This kink in the construction price deflator is also perhaps large enough to quantitatively explain the observed downturn in construction productivity. Figure 4.4 repeats the plot of figure 4.1, except it computes real construction output by deflating nominal construction value added with the GDP deflator rather than the deflator for the construction sector. The difference is striking. Now construction sector productivity grows throughout the entire 1950–2020 period, nearly matching the pace of overall productivity growth.

Clearly, the construction sector price deflator is, mechanically speaking, a key source of the downturn in measured construction productivity. Computing productivity by deflating nominal construction activity with the whole-economy deflator makes the construction productivity series look like overall productivity.

Note, however, that this is not evidence that we should use the aggregate GDP deflator for the construction industry or that the construction deflator is *wrong*. It could well be right and true construction productivity has, indeed, fallen for 50 years. However, the fact that it matters so much puts onus on those interested in understanding construction productivity to check the deflator's accuracy.

This is why some of the most important work on construction productivity in the existing literature, like Sveikauskas et al. (2016, 2018) and Garcia and Molloy (2023), focuses on subsets of the construction industry where

5. The potential role of price deflators in real construction output measurement in earlier decades was taken up by Gordon (1968) and Pieper (1991).

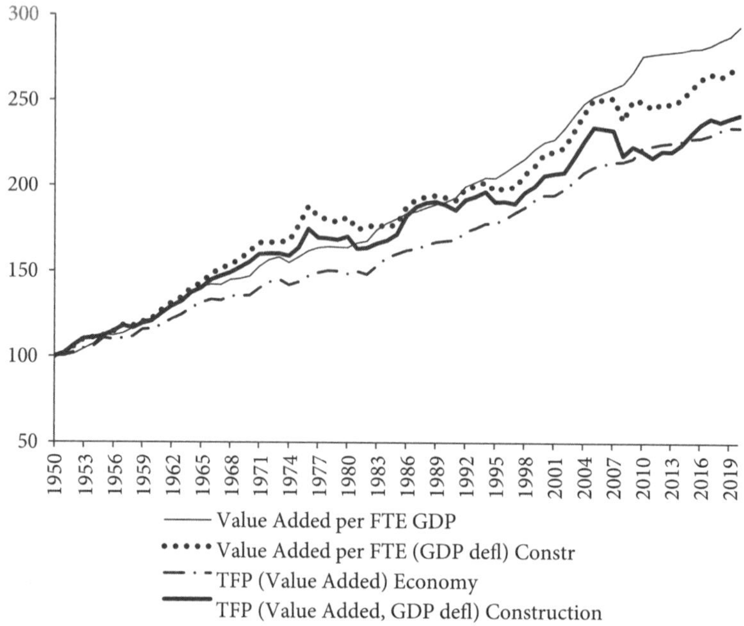

Fig. 4.4 Indexes of value added per worker and TFP, overall US and construction sector (BEA data)

they can build more accurate output price deflators to explore productivity growth dynamics. This work has found that in such cases, productivity declines are not as extreme in the last 30 years as suggested in the aggregate data, and in some cases productivity was in fact growing (albeit modestly). It is this idea that brings us to search for settings where we can potentially get around the output deflator issues, as we do in section 4.4 below.

4.3.1 Potential Sources of Growth in Construction Output Prices

Given that the construction sector output deflator is rising considerably faster than prices in the rest of the economy, it is worth exploring whether there are visible sources of this relative price increase.

A logical place to look is at construction input prices. If these are also rising faster than the overall price level after 1970, it would be a clue as to the origin of the fast-rising prices and declining real output of the sector.

We first look at construction's intermediate inputs prices, using the sector's intermediate inputs deflator from the BEA's KLEMS database. Figure 4.5 plots this deflator and its change since 1950, along with the construction sector output and GDP deflators for comparison. It is readily apparent that construction intermediates price growth has been on the order of price growth in the overall economy rather than the faster growth measured in

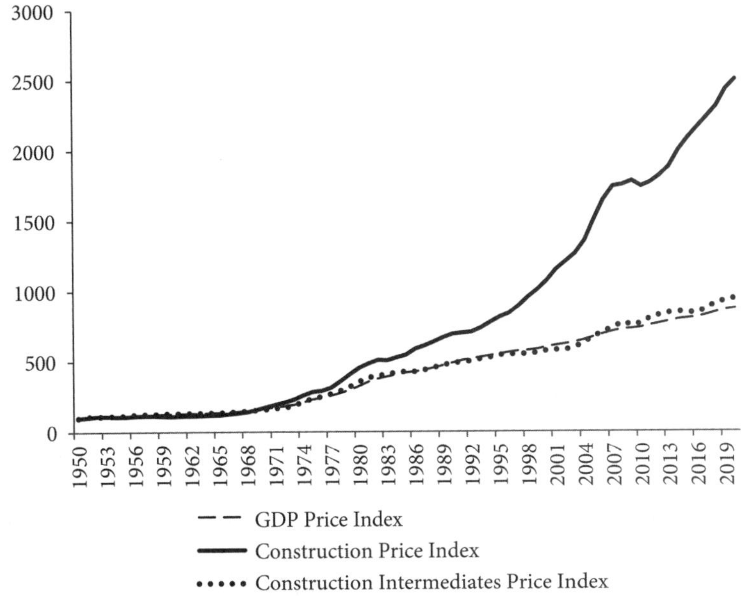

Fig. 4.5 Construction and GDP output price index compared to construction intermediates price index

construction output prices. Its time path overlaps considerably with the GDP deflator and lags the construction output deflator.[6]

We next look at relative labor prices by computing the nominal implied salary per worker for the sector and comparing its trajectory to that for the overall economy. We compute the implied salary as total labor compensation plus 0.67 times sole proprietor income, divided by the sum of employees and self-employed. The construction and overall-economy series track each other quite closely throughout 1950–2020. Construction salary growth is higher, but only slightly so (a difference of 0.14 percent in average annual growth rates). Moreover, there is no obvious divergence after 1970. Given the 2.1 percentage point average annual difference in construction and GDP deflators, this difference in relative labor prices is less than a tenth of that. Thus it may explain a part of the divergence in relative output prices, but this part is very small.

Direct measures of industry-specific capital prices are not readily available, but a prominent component of capital user costs is the depreciation rate. We compute depreciation rates for both the overall economy and the

6. In separate work, we have looked at the PPIs of 10 major construction sector inputs over the sample period. These are conceptual components of the intermediates deflator above. While there is variation in the average growth rate of these inputs' prices, their mean tracks the GDP deflator, just as the intermediates deflator does.

construction sector using BEA data on depreciation and capital stocks. While annual depreciation rates are higher in construction than for the overall economy, averaging 3.7 percent overall and 13.6 percent for construction over 1950–2020, there is no sign that *changes* in depreciation rates imply the relative user costs of construction capital are rising. In fact, the gap between construction and overall depreciation rates fell during the period, implying that this major element of capital costs was becoming relatively cheaper in construction. For the first five years of the period, the average difference between the overall and construction depreciation rates was 13.5 percent. For the last five years, it was 9.3 percent.

In sum, there is no obvious sign that changes in the relative prices of the construction sector's major inputs—intermediates, labor, and capital—drove the observed growth of relative construction output prices.

If relative unit input prices do not account for the increase in construction's relative output price, perhaps markups rose instead. To explore this possibility, we construct an approximation for markups by comparing sector revenues to its total measured input costs. Construction input costs include expenditures on intermediates (which we observe directly in the KLEMS data), total payments to labor (the numerator in the average salary calculation above), and payments to capital (depreciation plus the real interest rate multiplied by the industry capital stock plus 0.33 times proprietor's income). We divide revenues by the sum of these input expenditures as a proxy for markups.

The average of this markup ratio over 1950–2020 is 1.016, indicating a modest average margin of 1.6 percent in the construction sector. This margin has a slightly increasing trend of 0.024 percent per year. This corresponds to growth in the average margin of 1.7 percent over the entire 70-year period. To the extent this higher accounting margin reflects larger markups over costs, some of the increase in construction's relative output price came from growing markups.

However, there are two important caveats to this interpretation. First, this overall change is minuscule compared to the overall growth in construction prices observed during the period. It is two orders of magnitude smaller than the 2.1 percentage point annual growth in the relative price of construction output after 1970. Second, this is an increase in construction's absolute markup. If markups are also increasing in the economy overall (see De Loecker, Eeckhout, and Unger 2020 for evidence of this, at least since 1980), then there may be no increase in construction's *relative* markup and hence relative prices.

In sum, our analysis to this point indicates that only a small part of the large increase in relative output prices of the construction sector may come from increased relative wages and (perhaps) higher markups. The vast majority of the increase in construction's price deflator relative to average overall prices cannot be explained by increasing relative prices of construction inputs or markups.

This leaves a few possibilities to explain the divergence of the construction output and GDP deflators. One is that construction sector productivity did indeed fall, raising unit input requirements. Even though prices per unit of inputs did not rise (or rise faster than other prices outside the construction sector), the unit costs of output would increase because construction firms would need to buy more inputs than before to build a unit of output.

Another possibility is that construction output price mismeasurement became worse in the late 1960s. If, say, the quality of construction output accelerated as did prices along with it, but the deflator does not properly account for that quality difference, the increase in output quality would have to occur in a way that was not correlated with increases in construction input prices. But increased output quality from using more expensive inputs (better materials, much more skilled labor, etc.) is not consistent with the input price evidence above that input prices have not moved together with output prices.

4.4 Measuring Productivity in Physical Units

We next turn to methods that do not rely on output price measurement. Our approach is to focus on a setting where output and productivity can be measured in physical units rather than expenditure requiring a deflator. Researchers have applied this approach in the broader productivity literature, especially the part dealing with producer microdata, but of course doing so relies on having a setting where individual units are measured and there is reasonable homogeneity.[7] In this section we consider a part of the construction industry where those conditions might hold (loosely): home construction.

Output data are available for the US housing construction industry not just in value but in *number of housing units* as well. Exploring the evolution of the industry's productivity measured in houses per unit input, rather than deflated house value per unit input, lets us track a measure of the efficiency of the industry's production process that does not rely on a price index.

This advantage does come at an obvious cost, however. If the physical housing units change in quality over time, then a given number of housing units in one period will not be the same "real" quantity of housing as in another period. And we know that the average attributes of houses have changed over time; for instance, they have trended toward larger floor areas. Given the amount of data available on homes, however, we can also explore

7. A few recent examples include De Loecker et al. (2016), de Roux et al. (2021), and Orr (2022).

whether such changes materially affect the conclusions from using housing-unit-based productivity measures.

Our output data come from annual housing completions reported by the US Census Bureau. These begin in 1968 and are broken out by number of units per building: 1 unit, 2–4 units, and 5+ units. We combine this with CES employment data for the housing construction industry. After 1990, the employment data are reported separately by single-family and multi-family housing construction sub-industries. An older employment series for all residential construction activity extends from 1972–2002. It unfortunately precludes a breakout into single- and multi-family construction and also includes employment in repair and remodeling that is not reflected in the Census housing construction output data. Nevertheless, it is instructive to compare the (combined single- and multi-family housing construction) results from this older series to the more precise values starting in 1990, and we do so below.

Figure 4.6 shows the resulting annual productivity series, measured in housing units per employee. Looking first at the two post-1990 series, while there are some notably large swings in the average number of housing units built per employee in both the single-family and multi-family housing sub-industries (the largest in each being troughs during the Great Recession), there is no discernable upward trend over the three decades. Linear time trends fit to both series have statistically significant and negative slopes. For single-family housing, it is –0.023 (s.e. = 0.007) per year, and for multi-unit housing the slope is –0.081 (s.e. = 0.037) per year. Average productivity in

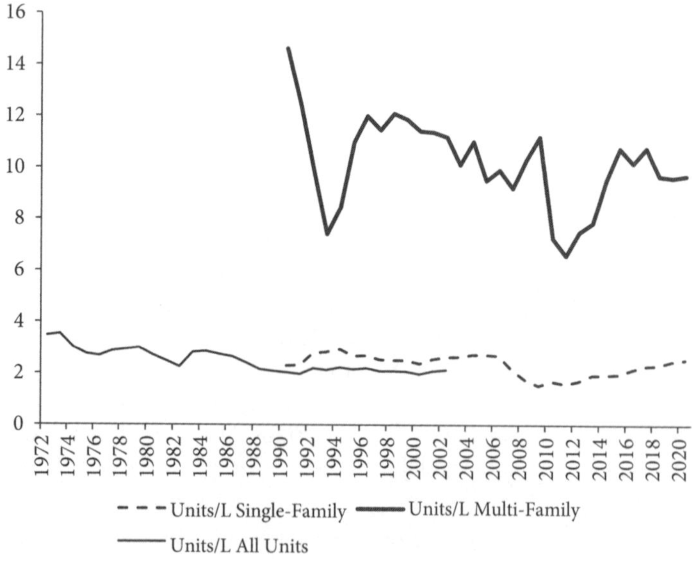

Fig. 4.6 Housing units per employee, housing industry

the first five years of the single-family (multi-unit) series is 2.63 (10.6) units per employee and in the last five years is 2.35 (10.0) units per employee.[8] Comparing the magnitudes of the negative trend estimates to the levels of these productivity measures, housing productivity measured in units per employee is declining at a rate of roughly –1 percent per year. This is about the same as seen above in the broader construction sector and using deflated value to measure output.

The older, 1972–2002 series exhibits, if anything, a stronger downward trend than the other two series.[9] The linear trend slope is –0.042 (s.e. = 0.005), and average units per worker in the first and last five years of the period are respectively 3.1 and 2.1. Though it is worth noting that during the 1990–2002 period of overlap, this productivity measure is basically level.

These data offer a complementary view into stagnant or declining construction productivity uninfluenced by price mismeasurement. The new residential construction industry, at least, does not seem to be becoming more efficient at building housing units.

As noted, however, the usefulness of physical-quantity-based productivity measures depends on the homogeneity of the units across settings and time. If housing units are getting better, the industry may be becoming more productive in terms of *housing quality* produced with a unit of input, even if the number of housing units per input has not increased.

One of the more obvious changes in housing units over the past several decades has been the increase in floor space per unit. Houses have been getting bigger. Data on the average square footage of completed single-family housing units is available from 1973–2020, and it rose from 1,660 ft^2 to 2,480 ft^2 over that period. The average size of multi-family units rose as well, but more moderately, from 1,021 ft^2 to 1,121 ft^2.

Recomputing our unit productivity series for residential construction as square footage of housing per employee, of course, exhibits more positive trends than do the housing-unit-based productivity values above (because the floor area has been trending up). The question is how much, and whether the prior significantly negative trends remain so.

The three series are in figure 4.7. The significant downward trend seen in the old series remains (the series now spans 1974–2002, as no average square footage per unit for multi-family buildings was available before 1974). The linear yearly trend coefficient is –30.8 ft^2 per employee (s.e. = 9.4).

The newer series do see some changes relative to their units per employee

8. As seen in the figure, since the Great Recession, houses per worker recovered to roughly their pre-Great Recession levels. Time will tell if this growth extends beyond the prior level or instead merely returns to the long-run average.

9. Because the employment data for this series includes not just single- and multi-family housing employment but repair and remodeling employment as well, this extra employment not generally dedicated to new home construction will cause the level of this productivity series to be lower than either of the other two.

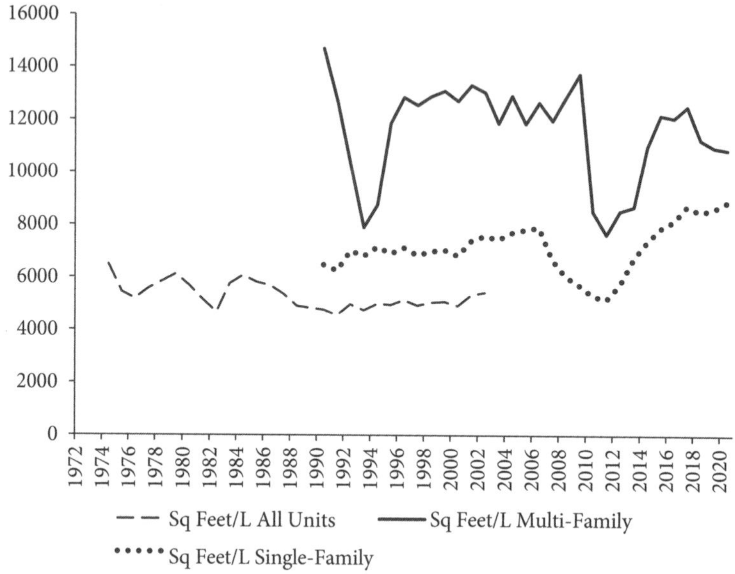

Fig. 4.7 Square footage of housing per employee, housing industry

patterns. For multi-family housing, which had a negative and significant trend in units per employee, the trend for square footage still has a negative point estimate (–42.6) but is now insignificant (s.e. = 37.9). Single-family housing now has a *positive* and significant annual trend growth of 37.4 ft^2 per employee (s.e. = 16.0).

The magnitudes are instructive, however. Average square footage built per employee in single-family housing construction over 1990–2020 is 7,120 ft^2. An annual trend growth of 37.4 ft^2 per employee off that base is 0.5 percent per year. So even in the most optimistic case, this is one-quarter of the 2.0 percent annual labor productivity growth in the overall economy during the period.[10]

4.5 Deteriorating Materials Productivity

Setting aside measurement problems, in this section we document a new type of productivity slowdown in the construction sector involving trends in the way which the sector converts intermediate inputs into outputs.

One summary measure of this process is the ratio of the sector's value

10. Recent work by Garcia and Molloy (2023) makes more elaborate corrections for housing quality changes and similarly find only modest deflator-driven understatement in official measures of the sector's productivity growth. Schmitz (2020) has proposed that lack of competition, perhaps structurally supported by industry trade associations, could explain poor productivity growth in housing construction.

added to gross output. The difference between these two is expenditures on intermediate inputs. Their ratio captures how much of the sector's final revenues are created through the application of value-added factors (labor and capital) as opposed to purchased from outside the sector.

Value added as a share of gross output in construction rose over the 1950–2020 period, from a level just below 0.4 in the early years to just above 0.5. The period of highest growth is circa 1985 to 2000, after which the series levels off. The sector has therefore shifted a greater portion of its final output production to activities inside the sector, done by its own labor and capital. As noted in Sveikauskas et al. (2018), specialized subcontractor labor is treated as a purchased service (a type of intermediate input) in standard KLEMS accounting. A shift toward less intensive use of subcontractors could account for some of the sector's shift toward a greater share of value added in gross output.

We break down this pattern further by looking at the separate trajectories of the revenue shares of each of the three major inputs into gross output (i.e., revenues): labor, capital, and intermediates.[11] Intermediate inputs' share fell throughout 1950–2020, from an average of 60.5 percent during the first five-year period (1950–54) to 48.9 percent over the last five years. About two-thirds of this 11.6 percentage point drop was recovered by labor inputs taking a larger share (growing from 33.6 to 41.9 percent) and another third by an increase in capital's share (5.9 to 9.3 percent).

We can also look at intermediate input efficiency by computing the relative growth of real gross output and real intermediates use. This growth in "materials productivity"—output obtained per unit of intermediate input—is an analog to the more commonly measured labor productivity.

Materials productivity for both all industries and the construction sector show an interesting pattern in figure 4.8. Materials productivity in construction looks much like labor productivity does, rising until the late 1960s, at which time the series turns downward and begins a half century of decline. All industries materials productivity, on the other hand, has a slow positive trend throughout the entire 1950–2020 period.

This turnaround is curious, especially when paired with the result that the sector's value added as a share of its gross output is growing. Given that the difference between these two values is intermediates purchases, this implies that over time the sector has been spending less on inputs to produce a given amount of gross output production. These productivity figures indicate this reduction in input spending is not because the sector has become more adept at converting intermediates into output (which would reduce the quantity of intermediates required). Instead, it seems to embody a substitution effect: as the industry became worse at converting intermediates into output, thereby

11. Results reported here are similar if we use inputs' shares of sector costs instead of revenues, which is not surprising given the low and slow-changing markups we estimated above.

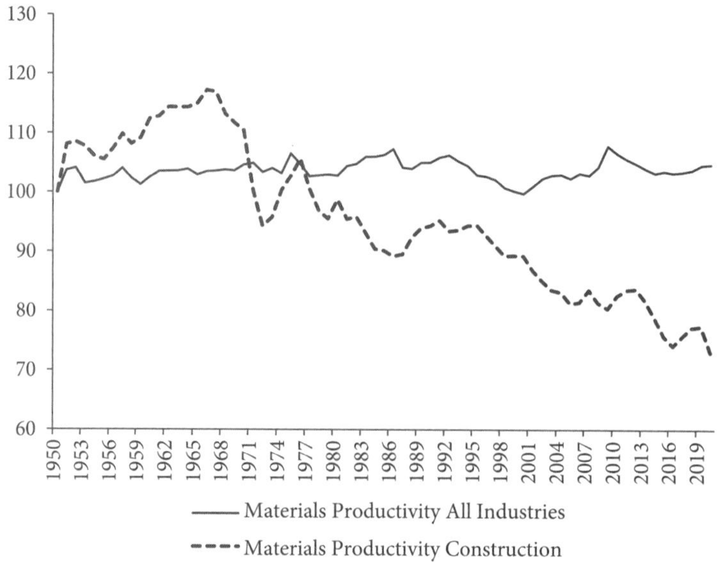

Fig. 4.8 Materials productivity (1950 = 100)

raising the implied (output) unit costs of intermediates, the industry has shifted toward a more value-added-intensive production process.

4.6 Productivity and Reallocation in Disaggregated Data

In this section we drill down below the sectoral aggregate data and investigate patterns in the disaggregated numbers. Specifically, we test whether, when there are producers with heterogeneous productivity levels, the market reallocates activity away from lower-productivity producers and toward higher-productivity producers. This would be consistent with efficiently operating input and output markets in the sector. The productivity literature has documented this reallocation mechanism as one way in which aggregate productivity growth can rise (indeed, it would facilitate aggregate productivity to grow even if no single producer's productivity rises).[12]

We employ the state-level output and employment data from the Census of Construction conducted every five years from 1972 to 2017. Our analysis assumes that construction inputs' marginal products are positively correlated with their average products. This would be the case, for example, if the production function were Cobb-Douglas, though this property holds for many other production functions as well.

12. This is sometimes referred to as the "between" mechanism (De Loecker and Syverson 2021).

Table 4.1 **Change in state's share of US construction value on initial labor productivity level**

	Change in state's share of US net construction, year t to $t + 5$ (percent) (1)	Change in state's share of US net construction, 1972–2017 (percent) (2)
ln(state's real net construction value per employee)$_t$	−2.92 (0.48)	−2.40 (3.01)
Year FE	Yes	No
State FE	Yes	No
N	459	51

The testable empirical prediction of efficient reallocation is that states or firms with higher construction productivity today should, all else equal, see construction activity grow faster in the future, as additional resources are moved to production in that setting.[13]

Using the state-level output and employment data from the Census of Construction, we first compute the labor productivity level (real net construction value per employee) of the construction sector in each state and census year. We then regress the future change in the state's share of all US net construction value on the labor productivity level in the baseline period. With allocative efficiency, we should see a positive coefficient: states with construction sectors that are initially higher productivity see an increase in their share of total construction value.

We run this regression using data computed at two different timings. The first uses a state-by-census-year panel that regresses the five-year change in share of US construction value from year t to year $t + 5$ on the state's construction labor productivity in year t. We include year and state fixed effects in this specification. We have data for nine inter-census changes from 1972 to 2017. The second specification is similar, but uses only a single long-difference of a state's share spanning 1972 to 2017 and regresses it on the state's 1972 construction labor productivity level.

The results are in table 4.1. Column 1 shows the results from the panel; column 2 reports the outcome of the long-difference specification. Neither indicates the hypothesized positive relationship between initial productivity and future growth. Both coefficients are negative, significantly so in the panel regression.

Thus at best there is no clear relationship between the productivity of a state's construction sector and the amount of construction activity that state

13. This is akin to the "dynamic allocation" test done for US hospitals in Chandra et al. (2016).

should expect to gain, be it the near or distant future. If anything, resources seem to move away from the more productive states.

This result may indicate the presence of market frictions that limit the ability of the construction sector's input and output markets to reallocate activity toward higher-productivity uses. The failure of this market mechanism blocks one of the two major channels through which productivity in an industry can grow, and may be a partial explanation of the aggregate productivity problems facing the industry.

4.7 Conclusion

Measured productivity performance in the construction sector has been unusually awful for 50 years. This has caught economic researchers' attention before but has gained increasing attention in broader policy-related circles in recent years. In this paper, we have updated some of this earlier work to show that measurement problems alone likely cannot explain all of the decline and that there are some problems facing productivity in the industry that have not been documented previously.

First, from a purely accounting perspective, input-based explanations simply cannot account for the half-century decline in productivity. Most of the observed productivity decline results from the divergence between the construction sector's output price deflator from average price growth in the economy. This is summarized by the fact that if nominal construction activity is deflated by the GDP deflator instead of the sector-specific deflator, the path of implied productivity in the sector is much closer to that observed in economy-wide productivity. This importance of the deflator to the measured decline is not itself evidence that the construction sector output deflator is wrong, however.

Further exploring the deflator's growth, we find that increases in input unit prices do not seem to be driving its divergence. Either construction productivity truly is declining, raising unit input requirements, or there is some form of mismeasurement that is uncorrelated with higher input prices (i.e., ruling out quality-based explanations where the sector shifts to higher-quality and more expensive inputs).

Several pieces of evidence suggest that measurement errors in the deflator are not the sole cause of poor productivity performance in the sector. When we measure productivity performance in physical units in a key industry in the sector—residential housing construction—it also shows declining or stagnant productivity.

The sector's ability to transform intermediates into finished products has deteriorated.

We also document evidence that something keeps producers in areas where the sector is more productive from growing. Rather than construction inputs flowing to areas where they are more productive, the activity share of these areas either stagnates or even falls. This problem with allocative efficiency may be accentuating the aggregate productivity problem for the industry.

The productivity struggle is not just a figment of the data. It is real. Further research is needed to test between competing explanations and sharpen the picture of what has been happening in the sector. Certainly construction is an important enough component of total economic activity to warrant attention.

Acknowledgments

We would like to thank Pengyu Ren, Nicole Bei Luo, and Rebecca Goldgof for their outstanding research assistance and conference participants at the Hutchins Center at Brookings and the Conference on Research in Income and Wealth for comments. We thank the Initiative on Global Markets at the University of Chicago's Booth School for financial assistance. For acknowledgments, sources of research support, and disclosure of the authors' material financial relationships, if any, please see https://www.nber.org/books-and-chapters/technology-productivity-and-economic-growth/strange-and-awful-path-productivity-us-construction-sector.

References

Allen, Steven G. 1985. "Why Construction Industry Productivity Is Declining." *Review of Economics and Statistics* 67 (4): 661–9.

Brynjolfsson, Erik, Daniel Rock, and Chad Syverson. 2021. "The Productivity J-Curve: How Intangibles Complement General Purpose Technologies." *American Economic Journal: Macroeconomics* 13 (1): 333–72.

Chandra, Amitabh, Amy Finkelstein, Adam Sacarny, and Chad Syverson. 2016. "Health Care Exceptionalism? Performance and Allocation in the US Health Care Sector." *American Economic Review* 106 (8): 2110–44.

Changali, Sriram, Azam Mohammad, and Mark van Nieuwland. 2015. "The Construction Productivity Imperative." McKinsey Productivity Sciences Center.

De Loecker, Jan, Jan Eeckhout, and Gabriel Unger. 2020. "The Rise of Market Power and the Macroeconomic Implications." *Quarterly Journal of Economics* 135 (2): 561–644.

De Loecker, Jan, Pinelopi K. Goldberg, Amit K. Khandelwal, and Nina Pavcnik. 2016. "Prices, Markups, and Trade Reform." *Econometrica* 84 (2): 445–510.

De Loecker, Jan, and Chad Syverson. 2021. "An Industrial Organization Perspective on Productivity." In *Handbook of Industrial Organization*, Volume 4, edited by Kate Ho, Ali Hortaçsu, and Alessandro Lizzeri. Amsterdam: North Holland.

de Roux, Nicolás, Marcela Eslava, Santiago Franco & Eric Verhoogen. 2021. "Estimating Production Functions in Differentiated-Product Industries with Quantity Information and External Instruments." NBER Working Paper No. 28323. Cambridge, MA: National Bureau of Economic Research.

Domar, Evsey D. 1961. "On the Measurement of Technological Change." *Economic Journal* 71 (284): 709–29.

Economist. 2017. "Efficiency Eludes the Construction Industry." *Economist* August 19.

Garcia, Daniel, and Raven Molloy. 2023. "Can Measurement Error Explain Slow Productivity Growth in Construction?" Finance and Economics Discussion Series 2023-052. Washington: Board of Governors of the Federal Reserve System.

Gordon, Robert J. 1968. "A New View of Real Investment in Structures, 1919–1966." *Review of Economics and Statistics* 50 (4): 417–28.

Hulten, Charles R. 1992. "Growth Accounting When Technical Change is Embodied in Capital." *American Economic Review* 82 (4): 964–80.

Pieper, Paul E. 1991. "The Measurement of Construction Prices: Retrospect and Prospect." In *Fifty Years of Economic Measurement: The Jubilee of the Conference on Research in Income and Wealth*, edited by Ernst R. Berndt and Jack E. Triplett. Chicago, IL: University of Chicago Press.

Orr, Scott. 2022. "Within-Firm Productivity Dispersion: Estimates and Implications." *Journal of Political Economy* 130 (11): 2771–2828.

Potter, Brian. 2021. "Measuring Construction Efficiency." *Construction Physics*, October 22. https://constructionphysics.substack.com/p/measuring-construction-efficiency.

Schmitz, James A. Jr. 2020. "Solving the Housing Crisis Will Require Fighting Monopolies in Construction." Federal Reserve Bank of Minneapolis Working Paper No. 773.

Schriver, William R., and Roger L. Bowlby. 1985. "Changes in Productivity and Composition of Output in Building Construction, 1972–1982." *Review of Economics and Statistics* 67 (2): 318–22.

Smith, Noah. 2021. "What Happened to Construction Productivity?" Blog post, *Noahpinion*, September 29. https://noahpinion.substack.com/p/what-happened-to-construction-productivity.

Stokes, H. Kemble Jr. 1981. "An Examination of the Productivity Decline in the Construction Industry." *Review of Economics and Statistics* 63 (4): 495–502.

Sveikauskas, Leo, Samuel Rowe, James Mildenberger, Jennifer Price, and Arthur Young. 2016. "Productivity Growth in Construction." *Journal of Construction Engineering and Management* 142 (10): 04016045-1-8.

Sveikauskas, Leo, Samuel Rowe, James Mildenberger, Jennifer Price, and Arthur Young. 2018. "Measuring Productivity Growth in Construction." *Monthly Labor Review* January: 1–33.

Syverson, Chad. 2017. "Challenges to Mismeasurement Explanations for the US Productivity Slowdown." *Journal of Economic Perspectives* 31 (2): 165–86.

5

Digital Concrete
Productivity in Infrastructure Construction

Diane Coyle and Rehema Msulwa

5.1 Introduction

The construction industry accounts for 6–7 percent of nominal annual GDP in the United Kingdom (as in the United States), and its measured labor productivity growth has been close to zero for many years (compared to declining productivity in the United States). This is consistent with the popular image of construction sites as low-tech environments. Yet Griliches (1994) designated construction as a "hard-to-measure" sector, and indeed the disappointing aggregate performance is puzzling to industry observers, who note there have been increases in the productivity of specific activities, including a significant increase in the use of digital tools (Goodrum, Haas, and Glover 2002). Work by the US Bureau of Labor Statistics to improve deflators for some parts of the sector went some way to resolve the puzzle in US data, involving more detailed deflators for different activities (Sveikauskas et al. 2016; see also Goolsbee and Syverson 2022 on residential construction); but did not consider either activity shifts within the sector or the implications for (quality-adjusted) deflators of the ongoing digitization of construction.

In this paper, we explore the ongoing impact of digitization on the structure and productivity of the UK's civil construction sector. Our focus will be major projects and civil engineering rather than residential construction; civil construction has experienced, and likely will continue to see, more

Diane Coyle is the Bennett Professor of Public Policy and codirector of the Bennett Institute at the University of Cambridge, a research associate of the Economic Statistics Centre of Excellence, and a director of The Productivity Institute.

Rehema Msulwa is an associate professor in Major Programme Management at Saïd Business School at the University of Oxford.

digitization, and there are fewer complexities related to land use and land values than is the case with housing construction. In the infrastructure subsector there has also been substantial change in market structure since 1980, along with accelerating technical change. Among these changes, designs and materials used have seen innovation, particularly to bring about environmental improvements in construction and use. The use of building information modelling (BIM) tools has steadily commoditized the design stage, leading to considerable outsourcing to countries such as Brazil, India, and Poland. On sites, much construction activity is contracted out to specialist subcontractors. In between, both consultants and major contracting firms seek to capture value through digitally enabled project and program management using integrated 3D software models that capture data through time from design through construction to operation (sometimes known as "digital twins"). For example, sensors embedded in concrete or steel can be monitored in real time allowing reduced maintenance costs or averting structural failures. Thus, operational costs for clients may be reduced over time. In addition, parts of large structures are increasingly built offsite for on-site assembly, a process enabled by BIM, whose major benefit is reduced construction time and improved component standardization and quality. Some major firms are building vertically integrated off-site factories to produce these parts for their construction projects. Finally, the incorporation of digital sensors is enabling provision of related maintenance services following completion of a project. There is therefore apparently ample potential for productivity improvements.

While all these developments are widely recognized in the industry, these changes are seemingly not yet well reflected in output, price, and productivity statistics. We consider whether this could be due either to only gradual implementation of the technologies across the sector, or alternatively to measurement issues such as failure to quality-adjust deflators (although there may well be other reasons for productivity headwinds, such as planning restrictions, not discussed here). The former, often described as a productivity J-curve effect (Brynjolfsson, Rock, and Syverson 2021), would imply delay in seeing the productivity benefits of digitization. Issues with output or input price deflators, which would imply some mismeasurement of productivity, could arise from the absence of relevant quality adjustments (e.g., enhanced asset lives or performance), or from the failure to capture well some price changes (e.g., lower-cost outsourced services). There have also been activity shifts across SIC 2007 classifications, which could have led to some mismeasurement of relevant input volumes and deflators.

In this paper, we first set the scene by describing the productivity performance of the infrastructure sector in the United Kingdom as captured in official statistics. We describe the evolution of its market structure, touching on sector classification issues. We summarize the digital technologies being implemented across the infrastructure sector, and the way these are shifting value added across the supply chain. Drawing the threads together, we then discuss the challenges for productivity measurement raised by: changing input prices; a shifting pattern of value added and output prices; depreciation and measurement of capital services; productivity impacts in adjacent sectors.

5.2 Measured Productivity Performance in UK Infrastructure

Flat or negative productivity growth in construction has been experienced in many countries. There has not been much progress across Europe, while labor productivity in the sector in the United States is lower today than it was in 1964 (WEF 2018). Those countries that have experienced rapid productivity growth, such as China and South Africa, started from a low base level. Blanco et al. (2017) identified several common challenges: regulation, contracting barriers, inefficient design and engineering processes, poor procurement and supply chain management, failure to improve workforce skills, and failure to deploy new digital and materials technologies. This lackluster performance characterizes many countries despite the substantial differences in funding and governance mechanisms for major projects. In comparison to some other countries, including the United States, the flat productivity record of the UK industry is relatively good.

Our focus is on SIC 2007 Section F, Division 42, covering roads, rail, utilities, and other civil engineering projects, although as discussed further below, some parts of other sectors (Division 71, Architectural and Engineering Services, and Section C Manufacturing) are closely linked. This division accounts for about 19 percent of the whole construction sector (at current prices) in recent figures, although with substantial variation at different periods. However, according to the most recent official figures, all sectors of construction saw their productivity grow more slowly than the rest of the economy up to the pandemic (figure 5.1), and over a long period its labor productivity has been flat and its total factor productivity (TFP) declining (figure 5.2). Infrastructure assets have become relatively more expensive over time (WEF 2018).

The intermediate expenditures used to calculate nominal value added in infrastructure construction have shifted over time from materials to services (mainly architectural, engineering, and technical services). Office for National Statistics (ONS) figures show that in 2018, compared with 1997, the share of the sector's intermediate spending on computer services had risen by 1.3 percentage points and on architectural, engineering, technical and testing services by 2.7 percentage points, while the shares of other categories in total intermediates expenditure declined (by 4 percentage points in the case of mining and quarrying products) (all figures ONS 2021, Table 7). The shift can be summarized as more intangibles and less material being used, in this most material of industries. This is reflective of the progression

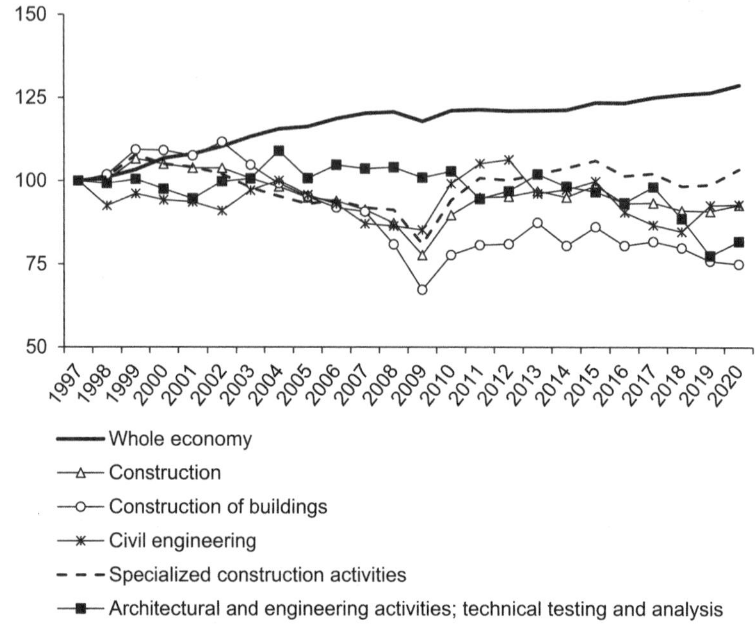

Fig. 5.1 UK productivity (GVA per hour worked), whole economy and construction, 1997–2020, 1997 = 100
Source: ONS (2021).

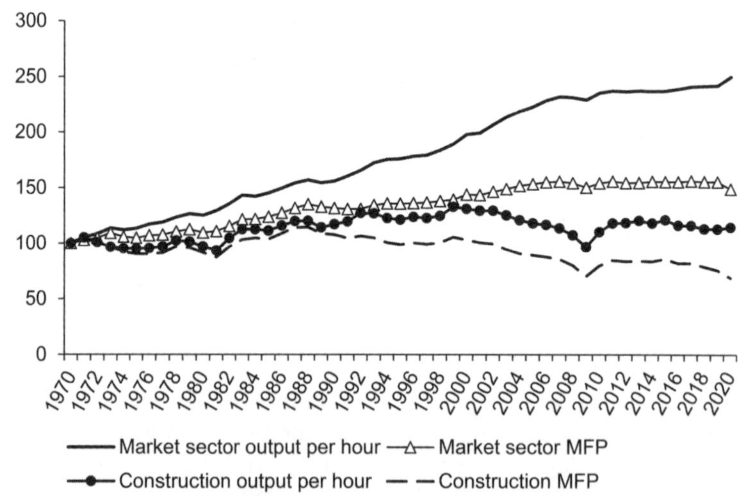

Fig. 5.2 Total factor productivity, 1997–2020, Index 1997=100
Note: MFP, multifactor productivity, is used by ONS as the term for TFP.
Source: ONS (2021).

of digitization and the way this is changing the structure of the industry, as we detail below.

Real value added in construction as a whole and the infrastructure sector in particular has increased more slowly than for the whole economy; for infrastructure the volume terms index has trended upward since the late 1990s, with a dip in the post-financial crisis period, but more slowly than constant price GDP. The output price index for this segment of construction has increased faster than the GDP deflator: if this output price had risen by the same as the GDP deflator, the counterfactual real volume index would have increased by over 11 percent more between 1997 and 2021 than its recorded growth. Output prices for the infrastructure sector are also more volatile than for construction as a whole while following the same profile. The published index has shown an acceleration recently, although less so than for all output prices (figure 5.3).

There are additional questions about input prices. The index used may not fully reflect the price of the services taking a growing share of purchases

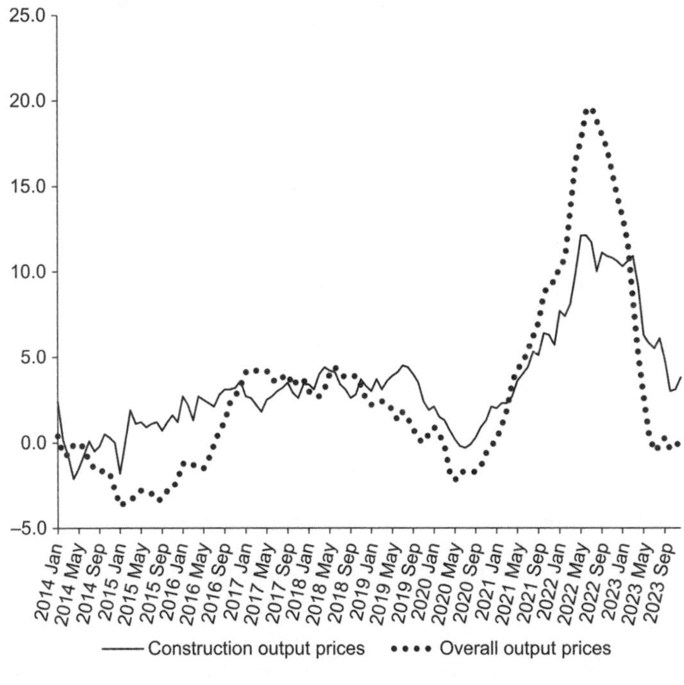

Fig. 5.3 Output prices, 12 m % change, infrastructure construction and overall PPI

Source: ONS. Construction output price indices, https://www.ons.gov.uk/businessindustryandtrade/constructionindustry/datasets/interimconstructionoutputpriceindices and Growth rates of output and input producer price inflation (PPI), https://www.ons.gov.uk/economy/inflationandpriceindices/datasets/growthratesofoutputandinputproducerpriceinflation.

of intermediates, as compared to materials inputs, so as noted above there may be an increasing "mismeasurement" challenge in double deflating sector value added. We return to this below. Data for the volume of labor and capital services used are also required to calculate TFP. ONS (2021) figures show that there has been a gradual upskilling in the construction labor force (although around two-fifths have no qualifications or GCSE only), so hours worked can be quality adjusted to reflect the higher average qualification level; the share of hours worked by the most highly educated has increased over two decades (from 1 percent to 4.7 percent), albeit remaining lower than the share of this group in whole economy hours worked. This upskilling could be linked to the increasing technological sophistication of the sector, but we do not consider it further here. Capital stock measures include the usual tangible assets, software, and R&D but not data or other intangibles; capital services used have grown quickly over time. The proportion of the sector's capital stock in the form of IT hardware and recorded intangibles has increased significantly from 6 percent in 1997 to 14 percent in 2020 (ONS 2021). There has been a sharp increase in capital services used in the sector over that period.

While civil engineering has not been the worst performing part of the sector in terms of productivity performance, it is nevertheless surprising that its productivity record has been flat for decades, given the downward pressures on costs through the bidding process and the technological changes the industry has already experienced (for example in areas such as tunnelling or engineering design) as well as the digital transformation that is now under way. While productivity stagnation might be attributed to the extreme fragmentation and decentralized project organization that still categorizes the broader architecture, engineering, and construction industry today (Hall 2018), there are several areas where it is worth exploring reasons for delayed productivity effects or measurement challenges. These areas include the changing structure of the industry, as well as the shift in intermediates purchased, due in large part to implementation of digital technologies.

5.3 A Brief History of the UK Infrastructure Sector[1]

The origins and market structure of the industry today can be traced back to the Industrial Revolution, and the building of canals in the second half of the 18th century. The development of the infrastructure and construction industry was driven by the rapid growth in Britain's urban population, the accumulation of wealth, and the emergence of new materials and new tech-

1. Unless otherwise stated, this and the next section draw from Murray (2021) presented at the University of Cambridge Digital Economics & Policy Online Workshop on Construction and Infrastructure.

nologies like cast iron and steam power, which created a need for increased specialization in design and construction. The development of Britain's railways in the 19th century, and the introduction of the Joint Stock Companies Act of 1844, were pivotal as the opportunity to invest extended from a few wealthy individuals to the broader middle class.

The Institution of Civil Engineers (ICE), created in 1818, began to formalize the roles of consulting engineers and contractors and to encourage standard practices in construction. At the time there was a focus on rail. Given the risks associated with railway construction, contractors relied on banks to provide their working capital and to cover their losses on projects. By the early 20th century, companies would engage in bidding and tender processes dominated mostly by consulting engineers. Most consulting engineering firms were unlimited liability partnerships; the fees they could charge were fixed by the ICE, and companies were forbidden from advertising their services or competing on price. Instead, contractors competed on reputation. Profit came from firms delivering a final project for a lower cost than the project price for which they had tendered.

The war and the postwar government brought nationalization, with the creation of large publicly owned enterprises like British Railways and the Central Electricity Generating Board. The investments that governments made through such entities in motorways, civil aviation, power generation and telecommunications enabled the consultants and contractors to grow and specialize. These nationalized infrastructure companies developed their own technical capabilities and invested in research in universities and in their own laboratories. Computers began to be used in engineering design and construction planning, and the rate at which the construction industry accumulated know-how accelerated. By the early 1970s, British contractors were recognized around the world for their capabilities.

This process went into reverse in the late 20th century. Following the 1979 election of the Conservative Government, the UK government privatized national infrastructure companies, deregulated engineering consultancy, and sold or outsourced many technical functions that had developed within the public sector. Firms involved in construction of big projects increasingly competed on low price for government-funded contracts and contracts in the privatized infrastructure industry. As governments outsourced more of the services that had been provided from within the public sector, some contractors reinvented themselves as facilities managers and service providers. For example, in 2001, Tilbury Douglas—a respected construction company founded in the 19th century—rebranded itself as Interserve plc and diversified into maintenance and facilities management through a series of acquisitions. It became one of the largest contractors in Britain before it issued a series of profit warnings and went into administration in 2019. In March 2021 what remained of the company changed its name back to Tilbury Douglas.

Table 5.1 **Top five UK project managers, total UK staff, annual UK fees, 2015 & 2021**

	Staff 2015*	Staff 2021	% Change	Annual UK fees £m 2014/2015	Annual UK fees £m 2020/2021
Mott MacDonald	5,933	7,059	19%	394.5	868
Turner & Townsend	1,897	2,907	53%	183.5	273
Arcadis	3,700	3,881	5%	309	462
Aecom	7,423	6,679	−10%	644	—
Gardiner & Theobald	672	867	26%	103	161
Total	19,640	21,393	9%	1,634	1,764 (excl. Aecom)

*Mott Macdonald figures reflect acquisition of JN Bentley, and include Franklin + Andrews Limited.

Turner & Townsend figures reflect acquisition of Thinc Group Holdings Pty Limited.

Arcadis figures reflect acquisition of Hyder Consulting in October 2014 and incorporation of EC Harris surveyors; Aecom figures reflect merger with URS in October 2014.

Source: Building UK.

5.4 Current Structure of UK Infrastructure Industry

There are almost 25,000 companies making up the civil engineering construction sector in Britain, the vast majority with fewer than 25 employees (ONS 2020).[2] The sector is composed of some large companies (table 5.1) and a patchwork of SMEs and micro-businesses. This market structure is changing thanks to digitization and automation as described below (Orstavik 2014; Whyte 2019), with the innovations integrating and optimizing processes but involving higher fixed costs (Pittman 2018; Cao and Hall 2019; Griffin et al. 2019). The continuous deployment of technology in the industry is recognized as critical for continuing innovation (WEF 2018; Barbosa et al. 2017; Oti-Sarpong 2019). One important change is that industrialized construction increasingly includes off-site manufacturing, namely the use of prefabricated components, or kits-of-parts, made in a factory to high and consistent quality for subsequent installation in their final positions in a structure on site (Goodier and Gibb 2007; Dunlop Taylor 2020). The present-day use of off-site manufacturing has been embedded in applications of digital technologies (Jin et al. 2018). Another important change is the progressive outsourcing of engineering design, often overseas, through the use of digital design and information tools, known as Building Information Management (BIM). These and other digitally enabled innovations are described further below.

The changing character of major construction projects has had implica-

2. These are GB, not UK figures, i.e. Northern Ireland is excluded.

tions for the industry structure, the companies involved, the environment and for people (Oesterreich and Teuteberg 2016). Through companies like those listed in table 5.1, new services have emerged including project management, construction taxation and legal support services, value and risk management consultancy, and specification and design management. Contractors charge separate fees for these services, whereas they were provided previously as part of a total fee. As engineering consultancies have moved into program and project management and delivery, so too have major contractors, whose profitability has also been squeezed despite their practice of contracting out substantial parts of the on-site work to a large number of subcontractors.

The changing structure of the industry has also involved more internationalization. The Engineering News Record, a source of industry statistics, reports that the leading 225 companies globally generated $71.88 billion in design revenue in 2018 from projects outside their home countries, up 11.3 percent from $64.59 billion in 2017. This is a significant increase from 2002 when the top 200 firms generated $18.9 billion in revenue from projects outside their home countries. Thus, as an example, project design has become highly commoditized, the use of outsourcing to countries such as Brazil, India, and Poland widespread, and the price of these services has reportedly fallen. The latter is consistent with the considerable reported variation in median salary among project professionals from country to country. Relative to the UK, Brazil, India, and Poland provide lower (labor) cost alternatives.

An important defining characteristic of the UK industry today is its organizational separation from clients. This contrasts with some other industries where continuing services are becoming a more significant part of value creation in the "servitization" process, although this is also starting to change. Contractors and their supply chain still tend to have limited involvement with clients upfront in the feasibility stage of a project. The lack of integration along (sometimes global) supply chains is manifested in a wide-scale use of on-site subcontracting and multiple tiered interfaces and significant transaction costs. These include large overhead costs in contracting and coordination, and (often inappropriate) risk transfer to subcontractors. This structure in turn has led to an industry that tends to be focused solely on cutting costs rather than adding value. As described by Farmer (2016: 17), "[T]hose tiers of the industry closest to clients or indeed forming parts of clients' organizations themselves have effectively become process managers for a wider cascaded supply chain rather than having direct delivery control by employing their own workforce."

The intensified competition in the industry has seen many contractors reduce their overheads by selling off their plant (capital assets), reducing their technical staff and subcontracting much of the work they had done themselves. Today, it is still common for 80 percent of the value of an infra-

Table 5.2 Annualized project management salary (in USD) by country

Country	N=	Median Salary USD
United States	34,430	$120,000
Australia	1,011	$103,789
Germany	1,280	$99,512
UK	849	$87,993
Singapore	664	$79,464
Canada	2,083	$73,761
UAE	406	$71,345
France	1,138	$68,222
South Korea	130	$65,363
Saudia Arabia	297	$62,400
Japan	886	$62,331
South Africa	588	$54,688
Mexico	1,115	$43,674
Brazil	969	$35,489
Indonesia	73	$35,360
Peru	588	$32,363
China	1,664	$28,932
India	622	$26,917
Colombia	942	$25,560
Nigeria	221	$23,370
Egypt	170	$11,765

Source: Project Management Institute (2023); market exchange rates https://www.pmi.org/-/media/pmi/documents/public/pdf/learning/salary-survey-thirteenth-edition-non-members.pdf?rev=16bd8bb399034b588bdb59631c7cc97d.

structure project to be subcontracted to specialist suppliers and contractors. And many of the engineers, estimators, and construction managers that previously used to enable these companies to deliver complex projects have been replaced by vertically integrated commercial managers and experts in contracting (Murray 2021). As described below, digitization opportunities are causing new shifts in the sector. But today the UK construction industry is dominated by a few large international consulting firms with more than 50,000 staff and more than $10bn in revenues and a long tail of smaller firms. The larger firms are publicly quoted or owned by private investors. These companies provide technical, professional, and construction services, including project managing construction and contracting with construction firms. In 2019 there were four UK-based construction companies with an annual turnover exceeding £3 billion (table 5.3). The turnover of the UK's largest construction firm, Balfour Beatty, was almost twice that of competitor Kier Group in 2019 and was £600 million up from 2018. Balfour Beatty's revenue was significantly bigger than other companies on the market, including having a revenue three times that of Amey UK.

Large firms contract with a multitude of smaller contractors under what are sometimes described as adversarial circumstances. Small firms will have

Table 5.3 **UK top five construction firms by 2021 turnover (in millions of British pounds), 2014 to 2021**

Firm	2014	2015	2016	2017	2018	2019	2021
Balfour Beatty	8,793.00	8,444.00	8,215.00	8,234.00	7,802.00	8,405.00	8,263.0
Kier Group	2,954.30	3,275.90	4,082.30	4,282.30	4,512.80	4,479.40	3,328.5
Morgan Sindall Group	2,219.80	2,384.70	2,562.00	2,792.70	2,972.00	3,071.00	3,212.8
Amey UK	2,167.90	2,531.90	2,591.00	2,581.30	2,581.30	2,667.80	2,406.8
Interserve Grp	2,913.00	3,204.60	3,244.60	3,666.90	3,666.90	3,225.70	2,263.7

Source: The Construction Index, https://www.theconstructionindex.co.uk/market-data/top-100-construction-companies/2022.

awareness of digital construction-related tools but lack familiarity with the software systems (Vidalakis et al. 2020). The resulting structure of the construction industry is thus characterized by extreme fragmentation in three dimensions: horizontal, vertical, and longitudinal (Fergusson 1993). Horizonal fragmentation is the result of an intensive project-based, trade-by-trade competitive bidding environment of traditional project deliveries. In the context of lump-sum bids, for example, clients will tend to choose the "lowest qualified bidder" from those qualifying general contractors. In turn, these bidders solicit lump-sum bids from multiple specialized subcontractors, either at large, or from a list of approved prequalified subcontractors. Processes happen sequentially and are not coordinated. And since subcontractors tend to be less digitized than contractors, the system benefit across the supply chain of technology adoption is diluted.

As a result, the industry delivers bespoke products and is thus unable to deliver process efficiencies resulting from learning and repetition. Vertical fragmentation occurs because each project stage requires a different set of stakeholders, decision-makers, and values. The decoupling of different stages can give rise to self-interested behavior and project participants passing costs on to participants in subsequent stages. Longitudinal fragmentation occurs because project teams disband at the end of individual projects and are selected on future projects by fresh competitive bidding. Taken together, this means that there are significant transaction costs in all infrastructure projects, with substantial fragmentation of work on-site in particular among the many subcontractors. Furthermore, the lowest price continues to drive tendering processes. Procurement methods can therefore exacerbate segregated, adversarial, and competition-based approaches over integrated, collaborative, and partnership-based based methods (Hall et al. 2018). Integrated project delivery, an emerging form of project organization, attempts to address this shortcoming (Hall and Scott 2019).

It follows that the procurement and commercial arrangements in the current industry structure are entrenched with unusually high levels self-employment and unaligned contractual and incentive structures coupled with distrust, a lack of transparency, and inefficiencies. This structure acts as a barrier to investment (ORR 2019). Further, years of downward output price pressure and rising input costs have disincentivized long-term capital investments and ingrained low-risk behaviors. As Lewis and Offer (2022) observe, while technological innovations mainly originate in the private sector, commercial finance is often too risk averse or has too short an investment horizon to implement costly new technologies in long-lived infrastructure projects whose externalities (such as network effects or spillovers between supply chain participants) cannot be internalized. In the next section we first describe the digital changes under way.

5.5 Digitizing Concrete: Technology and Future Productivity Trends

As noted, digitization has spread significantly at the design and build stage, with building information modelling (BIM), but industry participants agree that there is a lot of remaining scope in terms of adopting digital technologies. Major companies such as Crossrail, Ferrovial/Heathrow Airport, Mott MacDonald, Anglian Water, Highways England, and Sellafield among others have pioneered a range of other digital innovations. Despite the success of these companies in creating their own production systems or restructuring their supply chains to deliver their desired outcomes, there has been limited wider adoption across the construction industry. Nevertheless, different elements of digitization offer the promise of some productivity gains. Figure 5.4 illustrates the points in the value chain at which digitization can operate. Although presented as a linear sequence here, stages can take place simultaneously or with a different order and involve a mix of processes and actors in different parts of the world (Oesterreich and Teuteberg 2016).

5.5.1 Building Information Modelling

Building Information Modelling (BIM) is defined as the use of a shared digital representation of a built asset to facilitate design, construction, and operation processes to form a reliable basis for decisions (ISO 2018). It is used as a broad term describing the process of creating and managing digital information about a built asset such as a building, bridge, highway, or tunnel (HM Government 2012). For example, the Infrastructure Project Authority defines BIM as: "A combination of process, standards, and technology through which it is possible to generate, visualize, exchange, assure and subsequently use and re-use information, including data, to form a trustworthy foundation for decision-making to the benefit of all those involved in any part of an asset's lifecycle. This includes inception, capital phase procurement and delivery, asset and facility management, maintenance, refurbishment, and ultimately an asset's disposal or re-use" (IPA 2021: 56). BIM also facilitates more collaborative ways of working by allowing for more efficient methods of designing, creating, and maintaining assets. Increas-

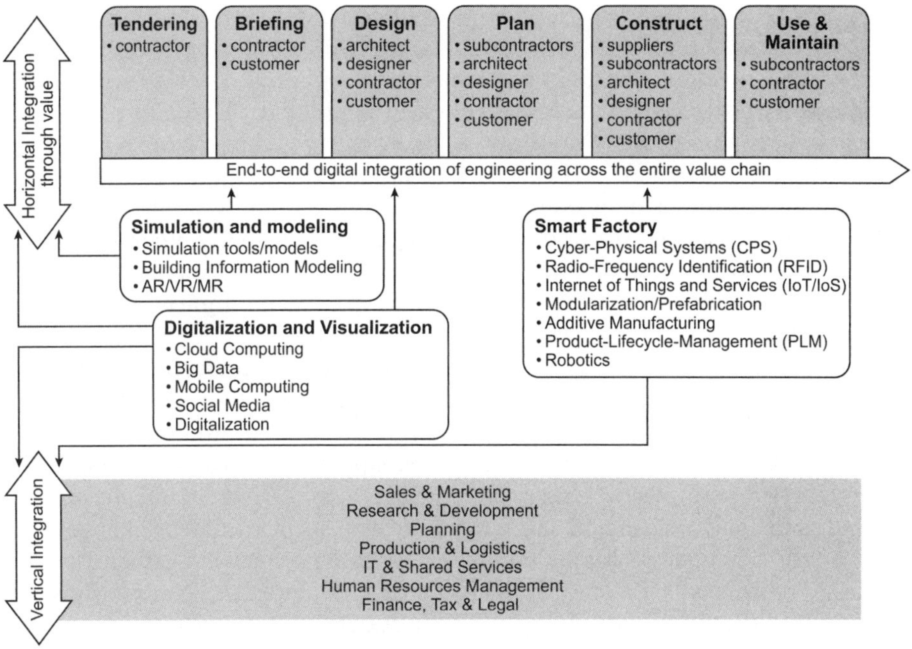

Fig. 5.4 Impact of digital technologies on the construction value chain
Source: Oesterreich and Teuteberg, 2016.

ingly it underpins information management processes (PWC 2018). BIM is now widely used across the sector (figure 5.6).

5.5.2 Design for Manufacture and Assembly (DfMA) and Off-Site Manufacture

DfMA is a design approach that focuses on ease of manufacture and efficiency of assembly by standardization of components. Traditionally, DfMA has been applied to sectors such as the design of automotive and consumer products, both of which need to efficiently produce high-quality products in large numbers. The large construction contractors have begun to adopt DfMA for the off-site prefabrication of construction components such as concrete floor slabs, structural columns, and beams. The use of prefabrication and other off-site construction methods on infrastructure projects "offers an alternative to this current construction status-quo by promising transformative improvements across the asset lifecycle in time, cost, quality and health and safety," KPMG (2016: 3). In addition, the implementation of DfMA for project delivery is considered to hold the potential for significant productivity improvement by reducing problems of cost overruns, delays and safety concerns, among others (Hall et al. 2018).

5.5.3 Digital Twins

A digital twin is a digital representation of a physical asset, system, or process, which receives data from its physical counterpart. The data are used to simulate the impact of an action virtually before making changes in the real world (UK Parliament POST 2021). The term *Digital Twin* is commonly associated with smart manufacturing and Industry 4.0, with the "twin" part dating back at least to the 1960s. As part of the Apollo program, for instance, NASA created "twins" of the Command Module, Lunar Module, and Lunar Rover. The twins all stayed on the ground but were used extensively for maintenance, support, and troubleshooting (SCCANZ 2020). In construction, digital twins jointly owned by engineers, construction majors, and customers can in principle be used as a means of optimizing the operation and maintenance of physical assets, systems, and processes (Sacks et al. 2020). By analyzing the virtual model, opportunities can be exploited and actual problems prevented in the physical twin. Artificial intelligence (AI) and analytics can update the digital twin as its physical twin changes. "Smart" components connected to a cloud-based system can gather data using sensors which allows analysis of real-time status and comparisons with historical data. For example, if sensors detected a queue of traffic on a road, the digital twin would be updated to reflect this and might signal to traffic lights in the physical world to alter their operation, improving traffic flow. Likewise, digital twins can be used for urban planning, as in Singapore, Glasgow, Boston, and Jaipur, and to assess the impacts of proposed changes such as how much additional energy demand a new development might generate. The UK's National Digital Twin Programme is exploring the potential to create a national model, which would connect digital twins of separate elements of national infrastructure. As part of this, the Centre for the Protection of National Infrastructure is developing an Information Management Framework to allow secure and consistent data sharing between digital twins (UK Parliament POST 2021).

5.5.4 Sensors in Infrastructure Assets

Both during construction of new infrastructure assets and for existing infrastructure there is an increasing use of sensors. Examples include fiber optics, wireless sensor networks, low power sensors based on micro electromechanical systems, and computer vision enabling data harvesting. This can lead to considerably enhanced efficiencies, cost reductions, resilience, and adaptability with benefits for the construction industry during the construction stage, and subsequently for the operator served by the infrastructure and their customers. The subsequent gains will include for instance reduced delays and downtime, and lower maintenance costs. For example, the Centre for Smart Infrastructure and Construction at the University of Cambridge has developed fiber optic sensor technologies that enable continuous strain measurements, a key element of materials testing that captures the impact of external forces on stationary objects, for lengths of up to 10 km. This technology has been used to monitor a 100-year-old former Royal Mail Railway tunnel during construction of Crossrail's Liverpool Street Station tunnels very close beneath. It has also been used to monitor the performance of deep shafts and retaining walls at other Crossrail sites.[3]

5.5.5 Data

The adoption of digital technologies entails a huge increase in data generation. In addition to use of cloud capacity, platforms that enable both the gathering and distribution of data from different sources in one place are required (Sategna et al. 2019). Their adoption enables users across the project value chain to coordinate better and achieve process improvements. Improved methods of data collection, storage, and sharing would address a persistent challenge of poor coordination within the construction industry. Data is also at the heart of BIM, digital twins, and digital construction more generally. However, currently the data sets available during and at the conclusion of construction projects are usually of low quality. There is largely paper-based reporting, poor documentation practices, unprioritized and unorganized data, low reliability repetitive reporting, multiple data and metadata standards, and a lack of system connectivity. Hence when a project moves from construction to operation, the operations team is generally tasked with reconstructing a vast amount of the "as-built" or "as-is" BIM at great time and expense (Hunhevicz et al. 2022). The productivity potential lies in enabling sharing data and digital models through information management systems (CDBB 2021). Collecting, storing, and sharing complete, high-quality data sets at the end of the project requires that data gathering should take place from as early in the project as possible. Doing so calls for both technological and process related innovations. Blockchain has been proposed as potentially transformative (Hunhevicz et al. 2022). But in any case, standardization and governance around data sharing will be essential.

5.5.6 Implementation of Digital Tools

A key aspect of improving construction productivity using digital tools is improving the information flow between the complex interfaces of various supply chain participants, systems, and also across the total lifecycle of assets. Multiple obstacles will have to be overcome for the industry-wide adoption. These include foundational BIM, common data standards and environment, asset information management, design automation, and digital platforms for end-to-end delivery. Nevertheless, the industry perceives a major opportunity to create value or to reduce inefficiency through data and information sharing. This includes common data standards and the

3. Crossrail has been opened as the Elizabeth Line.

Box 5.1 Examples of digital technology deployment

Anglian Water

Anglian Water is the largest water and wastewater company in England and Wales geographically, covering 20 percent of the land area. It has been trialing new technology to find and measure leaks in water mains. Sensors measure the variation of electricity passing through the pipe walls, as current does not pass through non-metallic pipe walls but will pass through a defect or leak. Therefore, the bigger the defect the larger the electricity flow. The technology can detect any holes as small as a centimeter in diameter as well as estimating how much water is lost in liters per second, meaning the company can prioritize repairs accordingly. According to the company, the adoption of these and other digital developments, including advanced analytics through a Digital Business Twin saved £1.4 million in operating costs in 2021.

National Highways (Highways England)

National Highways aims to develop a virtual twin of England's motorways and major road network to predict the time and location of maintenance issues, replacing drawings and static 3D models with dynamic and data-rich digital twins, pdf documents with databases, and file exchange with shared cloud exchange. National Highways also aims to introduce smart materials able to partly automate manual routine maintenance. For instance, it will be easier to identify when and where potholes occur, and integrate live data from sensors on the road surface with a digital twin.

creation of a common understanding of the digital environment. It also includes the development of basic tools that enable data sharing so that all stakeholders can work with a consistent set of data models. Fundamentally reducing the friction in data sharing is something that needs to be addressed, given the structure of the supply chain and subcontracts described earlier. In addition to technological applications, this will require the development of commercial relationships between parties in the supply chain, based on a mutual interest to share data, and may require policy intervention to enable or coordinate. An understanding of the data value chain, and valuing digital assets, would be helpful in improving performance. Digital twins, data, and related information are intangibles that are challenging to capture in traditional financial reporting, or in national accounts. Yet the examples of productivity gains achieved by companies deploying digital twins or using data purposively have been impressive (see Box 5.1).

Laing O'Rourke DFMA Modern Methods of Construction

Laing O'Rourke is a pioneer in modern methods of construction (MMC). The company has invested in DfMA aiming for 70 percent of the construction be taken off-site, claiming big gains (60 percent) in process efficiency, and time needed (30 percent). Apart from efficiency and speed, 'DfMA 70:60:30' is also aimed at improving product quality, reducing material waste, and supporting the creation of a more digitally skilled workforce. Its £200M Centre of Excellence for Modern Construction in Nottinghamshire employs 400 people, who design and precision manufacture off-site a range of components for use in major building and infrastructure projects, such as twin walls, floor slabs, pillars, facades, and digital modular bridges to span roads and railways.

Jacobs' *Replica* Digital Twin Software

Jacobs' *Replica* digital twin software is a suite of object-oriented blocks and libraries developed since 2001. Models are assembled within a customizable interface to simulate numerous aspects of a system simultaneously. The software can simulate large, interconnected, multi-component resource systems from drinking water supply to energy generation. Capturing and visualizing results related to fluid dynamics, operations and controls, and process and water quality, for example, enables understanding of tradeoffs in the system.

Sources: Company documentation

Digitization is likely to change the structure of the industry further. Data science and related skills will be needed (and are scarce). There has been some upward trend in skill levels in the industry (ONS 2021); it seems likely that the new technologies could increase demand for both highly skilled workers (complementary to the technology) and low-skilled workers (to the extent some activities are routinized). As noted, the traditional engineering consultancies and design companies are seeing their activities being outsourced and commoditized. Equally, the current contractor model in construction is slowly changing. The traditional smaller (sub-) contractors are being gradually replaced by manufacturing companies making components off-site. The on-site contract is expected to increasingly become an assembly process, with certain specialists doing ground engineering to get the structure off the ground.

The potential for digitizing the industry is seen by participants as significant, albeit aspirational: "Perhaps as much as 50 percent of the cost of producing high-performing built assets can be eliminated" is a representative comment (Stacey 2021). Digitization should enable less costly and faster construction, higher and more consistent quality assets (as quality is easier to monitor in a factory than it is on-site with many subcontractors), and ongoing reductions in operational expenditures thanks to the sensors embedded in new infrastructure, cutting maintenance costs and downtime. However, achieving these elements of productivity gains may not be achievable within existing contractual relationships and business models; rather, there needs to a wider restructuring of business models and supply chain relationships, including data sharing among parties to major projects. Indeed, the industry lacks a consistent performance measurement framework that enables learning and better decision-making (Murguia et al. 2022).

This description of the way the benefits of using digital technology are related to the structure of contractual relationships in the sector makes it clear that—as in many other sectors—there is likely a "productivity J curve" (Brynjolfsson, Rock, and Syverson 2021). The effective use of digital technology even within a single firm requires organizational change and learning, such that productivity might even decline initially. The process of adoption is likely to be even slower when contracting between different firms is involved, particularly with regard to digital technology, as it may significantly shift the information asymmetries (Williamson 1985). While there is certainly industry hype about the potential of digital tools, there is productivity potential from the use of digital in infrastructure, as the use of different aspects of the technology continues to diffuse across the sector and as new assets are built and demonstrate the gains. However, in addition to the time lag for digital adoption to occur and to deliver productivity gains, there may be some considerations relating to productivity measurement.

5.6 Measurement Challenges

In this section we consider some measurement issues relating to classification, quality adjustment of input and output price indices, and maintenance and depreciation.

The industry has begun to collate, through the Infrastructure Projects Authority, more detailed statistics on revenues and costs. One of its key metrics is project revenue per hour of labor. For 55 projects started between 2017 and 2021, this figure (excluding two large defense outliers) averaged £183.50, but with a large standard deviation of £286. The projects include a large variety, from road and rail schemes to flood defenses and hospitals. Even within categories, the revenue per hour worked varies substantially, with no trend evident over the four years available; for example, figure 5.5 shows the revenue per hour for rail projects as an example.

The industry also uses the concept pre-manufactured value (PMV), which

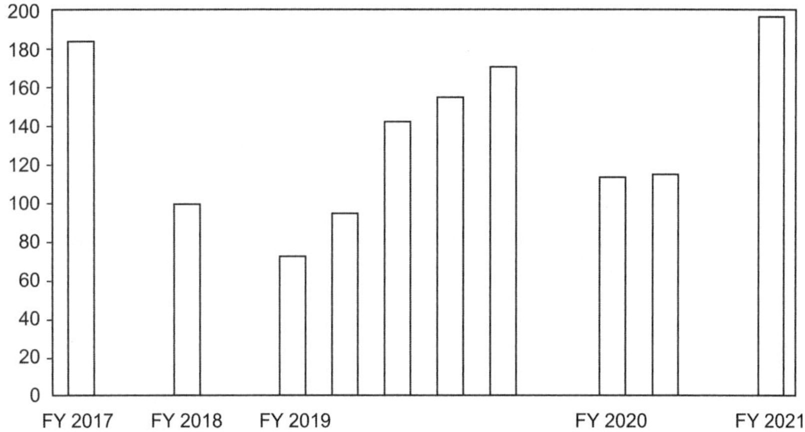

Fig. 5.5 Revenue/hour worked, £, rail infrastructure projects
Source: IPA; project level data; year indicates start date of project.

refers to the total costs incurred up to work starting on-site, excluding the design and consultancy stage, expressed as a percentage of gross costs. These costs include raw materials, components, off-site manufacture, assembly, and transportation. A higher PMV for a project is understood by those in the industry to reflect higher on-site productivity thanks to waste reduction, faster delivery speeds and better integration of activities. This figure varies considerably, even excluding lumpy defense projects, ranging from 10 percent to 88 percent. For example, for the rail projects shown in figure 5.5, the PMVs (where available) range from 20 percent to 77 percent, demonstrating the challenge of dealing with great heterogeneity and lumpiness of infrastructure projects for the purposes of economic measurement. What's more, the industry approach differs from the economic definition of productivity, not least as these figures are all in current prices. PMV is imperfect and has been criticized within the industry on the grounds that it does not necessarily measure (or result in) improved productivity of projects as a whole. Nor do these industry figures make it easy to draw any conclusions about changes over time, given the variation and lumpiness.

5.6.1 Sector Classification

In any case, productivity measures based on official statistics could potentially miss important changes in the structure of the construction industry because Section F, Division 42 in the Standard Industrial Classification does not account for construction-related activities such as architectural and engineering activities and off-site manufacturing. Architectural and engineering businesses sit in professional, scientific, and technical activities (division 71, Section M) while modern methods of construction, such as modular and off-site construction, are likely classified as manufacturing (Section C across several divisions). The performance of architectural and engineering services follows a very similar trend to the series for the construction industry in the statistics, however, with a slow productivity growth record. Expanding the scope of construction to include these activities would thus have little impact on current measures of productivity (ONS 2021). However, the fact that engineering and other services have a similarly lackluster productivity record is even more surprising than for the construction sector itself, as these are exactly the parts of the process that have most extensively digitized to date.

The transition to off-site manufacturing using DfMA is less extensive although increasingly implemented in major projects by some key firms. Of the small selection of the reported DfMA case studies, the reported benefits focus on the time savings (Davies 2013) followed by improved and more consistent quality and safety. Sinclair et al. (2016) found a 20–60 percent reduction in construction program time, and greater program certainty. Gao et al. (2020) also document significant time savings. There has been no consistent data collection although industry bodies are developing measurement frameworks (van Vuuren and Middleton 2020).

If the off-site manufacturing is carried out by a division of a firm whose principal activity is construction, such as Laing, the activity will be reported in the construction sector (Section F); published annual reports do not break the revenues associated with the activity out separately. Dunlop Taylor (2010, 2020) reports, based on industry and marketing databases combined with FAME data, that other off-site manufacturing is recorded in manufacturing (Section C) across several different sub-sectors (23, 24, 25). He found that about half the value added from off-site manufacture was due to large companies (over 1,200 employees). Using a random sample of the identified firms, he found that current price value added in 2018 was about £1.7bn, just under 6 percent of all value added by new UK construction. Even if off-site manufacture provides a substantial lift to the productivity of a major project, it would have to grow substantially to shift the overall sector-wide productivity figures. Dunlop Taylor's figures indicate that (in current price terms) the gross output of off-site manufacture has grown about 2 percent a year and valued added about 0.6 percent a year from 2000–2018.

We conclude that while the changing structure of the sector has some implications for interpreting productivity figures, these are not yet large.

5.6.2 Input Prices

Measurement of (output and input) prices in the infrastructure sector is inherently challenging as the projects are distinctive, and quality is hard to measure. These challenges will have larger implications for interpreting productivity statistics.

There is industry evidence that the use of BIM and outsourcing of the

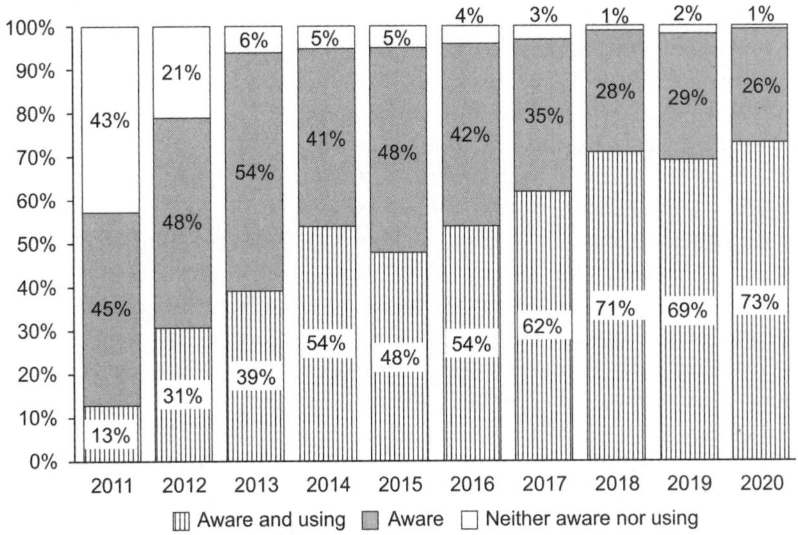

Fig. 5.6 BIM adoption in the UK 2011 to 2020
National Building Specification (NBS) (2020)

design stage are widespread (figure 5.6). Survey evidence of design and other construction professionals (NBS 10th National BIM Report) suggests nearly three-quarters of the construction industry uses BIM, which has been mandated in public sector projects since 2016. The NBS 2019 survey reported growth in BIM awareness and adoption, from 10 percent in 2011 to over 70 percent (NBS 2020). During this period, in 2015, the UK government reported that the delivery of the Level 2 BIM program enabled a 20 percent savings on CAPEX as recorded by Cabinet Office (now IPA) case studies against the 2009/2010 benchmarks (HM Government 2015). Moreover, a Cabinet Office Benchmarking Report in 2016 estimated that BIM enabled £3bn in capital savings between 2011 and 2015. Use of BIM can also improve safety and save time due to improved coordination. Incorporating reduced costs and improved quality in design would also affect the deflator and hence measured productivity of (upstream) Division 71. Anecdotal evidence in the industry suggests the price of these design services has in fact declined significantly in recent years. However, there remains variation in subcontractors' adoption and implementation of BIM, which are mostly related to company size.

Two potential factors influencing price declines for design, intermediate services, and off-site manufacturing include internationalization and standardization. Business, professional, and technical services have been among the most rapidly growing services sectors in developed countries (WTO 2021). At the same time, these services ranging from legal to management services, and from architectural to advertising services, became one of the main export sectors in certain developing economies, such as India and Brazil. In Brazil for example, in 2007 services accounted for 45 percent of Brazil's total commercial services exports, totaling US$10 billion, with architectural, engineering, and other technical consultancy services the largest subsectors, followed by legal services. Consistent with assertations made by Keune (2007), today, work is outsourced to countries in Asia, Central and South America, Eastern Europe, and beyond. As Ribeirinho et al. (2020) argue, "greater standardization will lower the barriers to operating across geographies. As scale becomes increasingly important to gaining competitive advantages, players will increase their global footprints—especially for low-volume projects in high-value segments such as infrastructure." This too will have an impact on prices as in the long term, increased competition could lead to price reductions and quality improvements.

Another consideration in terms of input costs is waste. The construction industry currently produces a huge amount of waste. "Construction, demolition and excavation accounted for an astonishing 62 percent of the United Kingdom's total waste in 2018," (Defra 2021; see also Osmani 2012). In both 2012 and 2016, construction and demolition waste in the United Kingdom was around 120 million tonnes per annum (GCB 2020; Osmani 2012). In 2012 this included an estimated 13 million tonnes of unused material (Osmani 2012). A large portion of the waste cannot be recycled. There are strong environmental pressures to reduce waste, through the use of digital tools such as BIM and DfMA improving coordination and reducing uncertainty about the on-site construction process (CDBB & CSIC 2020).

These shifts suggest that there is a case for looking in more depth at the revenue and price data to consider sampling (are prices for outsourced services being effectively captured?) and quality adjustment, including input price effects of the gradual shift toward off-site manufacture. One aspect of quality adjustment is the impact of higherquality construction on asset lives; if these lengthen, the capital stock will depreciate more slowly. Using firm-level detail to construct price indices could also affect intermediates prices used in double deflating value added. Price indices should be adjusted for the higher quality of BIM-enabled construction, and ONS is considering whether it can use proxies such as change orders, non-conformance reports, or accident reports.

5.6.3 Servitization, Output Quality, and Output Prices

Sensors are increasingly embedded in new infrastructure. Sensor technology is capable of producing vast amounts of data to help streamline operations and to monitor the health of infrastructure. Part of the change in industry structure being brought about by digitization is the increasing provision of ongoing services by the infrastructure companies to their customers subsequently operating services, a process of "servitization" familiar from parts of manufacturing. These include monitoring the condition of the asset and also embedded digital services such as signaling systems or information systems. The process is shifting value added along the supply chain. Monitoring of the condition of the asset brings benefits of reduced uncertainty, improved safety, and the averting of closures or service disruption and resulting time savings (compared to the counterfactual), all with corresponding cost savings (KPMG 2016; WPI Economics 2020).

To the extent that the servitization of infrastructure assets is carried out by construction companies, the benefits in terms of reduced operating costs and quality improvements will be reflected in the sector's revenues and value added. Yet there would also be downstream gains—for example, for train operating companies experiencing reduced delays and disruption, which are costly for them in terms of lost revenues, fines, and compensation, as well as repairs. It is also improving the quality of the sector's output: service providers and their users experience fewer delays, reduced maintenance needs, greater safety, and reduced risk of asset failure (or greater resilience). Work by the US BLS (Sveikauskas et al. 2016) to improve measurement of the construction sector through better price indices made little difference to the productivity performance of the highways sector, the closest sector to infrastructure they considered. However, this work did not account for potential quality change. A dramatic example of the potential is the sensor system operating on Japan's high-speed Shinkansen network: the sensors detected via seismometer the impending 2011 earthquake and automatically halted trains on the network in the affected area, likely saving many lives. The process of embedding sensors is incremental as relatively few infrastructure assets are built each year (although there is also considerable retrofitting, for instance of fiber optic monitoring of stresses in London's 100-year-old Tube tunnels (Soga and Schooling 2016), but there are nevertheless quality improvements over time that it would be desirable to capture in output prices. One type of quality indicator for example would be reductions in delays. Digitization in infrastructure construction will be reflected in economic gains in adjacent sectors. Train services and rail tracks are complements, and it is not clear that allocating productivity gains due to sensors on the track to the train operating company is the right way to measure the creation of economic value.

Setting this conceptual issue to one side, developing a quality-adjusted output price index will require collection of additional data from the industry and agreement about what quality characteristics might be included, for example in a hedonic output price index. The potentially useful data are held across a large number of client organizations, mainly public sector, and relate to projects that are quite distinctive. These can be divided into sectors that consist of somewhat more similar projects (communications, education, health, energy, transport, flood defense, etc.) and we are continuing to work with the Infrastructure Projects Authority to access the project data, which would include revenue per hour and input costs, with a view to developing an aggregate index.

Finally, a wider set of quality considerations concerns the environmental impact of built assets, an issue of intense discussion in the industry. Improved environmental performance might be linked to digital technology—for example, "smart" motorways that can reduce congestion and pollution—or to other factors such as the use of different materials (less concrete, more recyclable materials) in construction. Economic statistics are concerned with measurement of outputs, not outcomes, so we do not consider this further here; and yet from the user perspective these are also quality improvements.

5.6.4 Maintenance, Capital Stock, and Capital Services

The lifetime of infrastructure projects can be long. In the United Kingdom, Victorian bridges and sewers, and even Roman roads (albeit much maintained and upgraded) are still in use in the 21st century. Many infrastructure assets undergo upgrades or enlargement, significantly extending their lives. Many in the industry are arguing for measurement of its output in terms of the services delivered to end users on a whole lifetime basis, including environmental impacts. This outcome-based approach speaks to the debate about wider measures of the economy than are captured in current definitions of GDP (Heys et al. 2019; Foxton et al. 2018).[4] On the other hand, there has been much commentary on the depreciation of some infrastructure such as roads due to inadequate maintenance over time. Maintenance and appropriate depreciation affect calculation of capital stock and capital services for TFP measurement. In the standard growth accounting framework, (real) capital stocks are estimated using the perpetual inventory method, with assumed (geometric) depreciation rates applied and an assumption of constant asset life (Jorgenson and Stiroh 2000).

$$K_{jt} = K_{j(t-1)}(1 - \delta_j) + I_{jt}[(1 - \delta_j)/2] - O_{jt}$$

where:

K_{jt} = real net stock for year t for asset type j
δ_j = annual depreciation rate for asset type j
I_{jt} = real investment for year t for asset type j
O_{jt} = other changes in volume of assets for year t for type j (often assumed to be zero)

Equivalently,

4. There are three types of maintenance: corrective, preventative, and predictive. Corrective maintenance refers to repairs made after a problem or failure occurs; preventative maintenance refers to scheduled repairs made based on past experience of need; and predictive maintenance occurs because data for an asset indicate that a failure is imminent. While digital sensors aim to reduce total maintenance needs by replacing more costly corrective and preventive with predictive spend, this largely lies in the future.

$$K_{jt} = K_{j(t-1)} + I_{jt} - O_{jt} - M_{jt}$$

where:

$$M_{jt} = K_{j(t-1)}\delta_j + (I_{jt}\delta_j / 2),$$

real depreciation (consumption of fixed capital) year t for asset j.

Some portion of the infrastructure in use has been depreciated to near-zero and is delivering no measured capital service. This part of the capital stock is thus underestimated. On the other hand, some assets may be delivering lower than measured capital services due to inadequate maintenance. Recent work in the United States for the Bureau of Economic Analysis (BEA) (Bennett et al. 2020) highlighted the latter problem, reporting that investment in many types of infrastructure had not kept pace with depreciation, with rising average age of assets. They found variation between asset types and called for more research on maintenance spending, asset life, and appropriate depreciation rates. Another consideration will be the role of intangible assets as the sector digitizes, and particularly the measurement of data assets. Digital assets themselves are generally thought to have shorter lives, but in the case of infrastructure their introduction is likely to reduce maintenance requirements and lengthen the material, steel and concrete, asset lives. The appropriate choice for digital concrete is an open question and will vary considerably between types of asset. A further issue, which we do not pursue here, is how to assess productivity over the whole lifetime of infrastructure assets, taking into account reduced maintenance and down-time costs, and the environmental benefits of longer asset lives.

5.7 Conclusions

We have considered the puzzle of slow productivity growth in construction of infrastructure projects, in the face of evidence of rapid adoption of digital technologies, from two perspectives: the possibility that there are delays in the resulting productivity gains, and the possibility of mismeasurement. Both seem likely to contribute to the flat productivity performance of the sector—along with other factors we have not discussed here such as regulatory burden or low skills. In terms of the productivity lag, the current fragmented structure of the industry in the United Kingdom involves high transactions costs. Digital technology and information management could considerably reduce these, but this will require far greater coordination and data sharing, along with changes to business models and contracting. In terms of the measurement challenges, quality-adjusted input prices seem likely to have declined by more than implied by the current index given the considerable digitization and outsourcing that has already occurred upstream, while output quality gains and the impact on productivity of adjacent sectors are statistical issues needing further investigation.

The UK sector's flat productivity performance to date is perhaps not so puzzling in the light of the issues we have discussed here. But it is important to note that productivity J-curve implementation delays and the measurement questions with regard to price indices, quality adjustment, or sectoral shifts are interrelated: the further the digitally enabled restructuring of the infrastructure sector that is under way proceeds, the more acute the potential productivity mismeasurement will become.

Acknowledgments

We gratefully acknowledge funding from Office for National Statistics (ONS) as part of the research program of the Economic Statistics Centre of Excellence (ESCoE), and from The Productivity Institute funded by UKRI (grant number ES/V002740/1). Our thanks to participants in workshops at the University of Cambridge, NBER and the Productivity Institute, and to the many industry participants we interviewed, particularly Mark Enzer, Simon Murray, John Pelton, Kevin Reeves, and Melissa Zanocco. We are also grateful for comments from Kevin Fox, Sanjiv Mahajan, Josh Martin, Sam Stacey and Bart Van Ark, from anonymous ESCoE reviewers, as well as from University of Cambridge engineering colleagues Qian Chen, Campbell Middleton, Danny Murguia, and Jennifer Schooling. Finally, we thank Jennifer Charlson and Adam Livingstone of the UK Infrastructure Projects Authority for their assistance with understanding project data. For acknowledgments, sources of research support, and disclosure of the authors' material financial relationships, if any, please see https://www.nber.org/books-and-chapters/technology-productivity-and-economic-growth/digital-concrete-productivity-infrastructure-construction.

References

Barbosa, F., J. Woetzel, J. Mischke, M. Ribeirinho, M. Sridhar, M. Parsons, N. Bertram, and S. Brown. 2017. "Reinventing Construction through a Productivity Revolution." Executive summary, February. McKinsey Global Institute. https://www.mckinsey.com/~/media/mckinsey/business%20functions/operations/our%20insights/reinventing%20construction%20through%20a%20productivity%20revolution/mgi-reinventing-construction-executive-summary.pdf.

Bennett, J., R. Kornfeld., D. Sichel, and D. Wasshausen. 2020. "Measuring Infrastructure in the Bureau of Economic Analysis National Economic Accounts." BEA Working Paper Series, WP2020–12. Suitland, MD: Bureau of Economic Analysis. https://www.bea.gov/system/files/papers/BEA-WP2020–12.pdf.

Blanco, J., A. Mullin, K. Pandya, and M. Sridhar. 2017. "The New Age of Engineering and Construction Technology." Capital Projects and Infrastructure, July. McKinsey & Company. https://www.mckinsey.com/~/media/McKinsey/Industries/Capital%20Projects%20and%20Infrastructure/Our%20Insights/The

%20new%20age%20of%20engineering%20and%20construction%20technology/The-new-age-of-engineering-and-construction-technology.pdf.

Brynjolfsson, E., D. Rock, and C. Syverson. 2021. "The Productivity J-Curve: How Intangibles Complement General Purpose Technologies." *American Economic Journal: Macroeconomics* 13 (1): 333–72.

Cao, J., and D. Hall. 2019. "An Overview of Configurations for Industrialized Construction: Typologies, Customer Requirements, and Technical Approaches." In *Proceedings of the 2019 European Conference on Computing in Construction* 1: 295–303.

CDBB & CSIC. 2020. "Flourishing Systems: Re-envisioning Infrastructure as a Platform for Human Flourishing." https://www.cdbb.cam.ac.uk/files/flourishing-systems_revised_200908.pdf.

CDBB. 2021. "The Value of Information Management in the Construction and Infrastructure Sector." Report, June. KPMG. https://www.cdbb.cam.ac.uk/files/cdbb_econ_value_of_im_report.pdf.

Chen, K., and W. Lu. 2018. "Design for Manufacture and Assembly Oriented Design Approach to a Curtain Wall System: A Case Study of a Commercial Building in Wuhan, China." *Sustainability* 10 (7): 2211.

Davies, G. 2013. "The Future of DfMA is the Future of Construction." *Engineering Excellence Journal* 77: 44–73.

Defra. 2021. UK Statistics on Waste, Governmental Statistical Service, London, Department for Environment, Food and Rural Affairs. https://assets.publishing.service.gov.uk/government/uploads/system/uploads/attachment_data/file/1002246/UK_stats_on_waste_statistical_notice_July2021_accessible_FINAL.pdf.

Dunlop Taylor, Mark. 2010. "A Definition and Valuation of the UK Offsite Construction Sector." *Construction Management and Economics* 28 (8): 885–96. DOI: 10.1080/01446193.2010.480976.

Dunlop Taylor, Mark. 2020. "A Definition and Valuation of the UK Offsite Construction Sector: Ten Years On." *International Journal of Construction Management* 22 (15): 2877–2885. DOI: 10.1080/15623599.2020.1829783.

Farmer, M. 2016. "The Farmer Review of the UK Construction Labour Model: Modernise or Die. Time to Decide the Industry's Future." London, Construction Leadership Council. https://www.constructionleadershipcouncil.co.uk/wp-content/uploads/2016/10/Farmer-Review.pdf.

Fergusson, K. J. 1993. *Impact of Integration on Industrial Facility Quality*. Unpublished Ph.D. thesis, Stanford University, Palo Alto, CA.

Foxton, F., J. Grice, R. Heys, and J. Lewis. 2018. "The Welfare Implications of Public Goods: Lessons from 10 Years of Atkinson in the UK." In *6th IMF Statistical Forum*. https://www.imf.org/~/media/Files/Conferences/2018/6th-stats-forum/session-4-richard-heys-the-measurement-of-the-impact-of-public-sector-paper.ashx.

Gao, S., R. Jin, and W. Lu. 2020. "Design for Manufacture and Assembly in Construction: A Review." *Building Research and Information* 48 (5): 538–50.

GCB. 2020. "Zero Avoidable Waste in Construction: What Do We Mean By It and How Best To Interpret It." Technical Author: K. Adams, editors: R. Pearce and J. Thornback. Construction Products Association, February. https://www.constructionleadershipcouncil.co.uk/wp-content/uploads/2016/05/ZAW-Report-Final-Draft-25-February-2020.pdf.

Goodier, C., and A. Gibb. 2007. "Future Opportunities for Offsite in the UK." *Construction Management and Economics* 25 (6): 585–95.

Goodrum, P. M., C. T. Haas, and R. W. Glover. 2002. "The Divergence in Aggregate and Activity Estimates of US Construction Productivity." *Construction Management and Economics* 20 (5): 415–23.

Goolsbee, A., and C. Syverson. 2022. "The Strange and Awful Path of Productivity in US Construction." Presented at CRIW Conference on Technology, Productivity, and Economic Growth, March 17–18 2022, Washington, DC. https://conference.nber.org/conf_papers/f159268.pdf.

Griffin, A., R. Hughes, C. Freeman, J. Illingworth, T. Hodgson, M. Lewis, and E. Perez. 2019. "Using Advanced Manufacturing Technology for Smarter Construction." In *Proceedings of the Institution of Civil Engineers-Civil Engineering* 172 (6): 15–21.

Griliches, Z. 1994. "Productivity, R&D, and the Data Constraint." In *R&D and Productivity: The Econometric Evidence*, edited by Zvi Griliches, 347–74. Chicago, IL: University of Chicago Press.

Hall, D. M., J. K. Whyte, and J. Lessing. 2020. "Mirror-Breaking Strategies to Enable Digital Manufacturing in Silicon Valley Construction Firms: A Comparative Case Study." *Construction Management and Economics* 38 (4): 322–39.

Hall, D. M., and W. R. Scott. 2019. "Early Stages in the Institutionalization of Integrated Project Delivery." *Project Management Journal* 50 (2): 128–43.

Hall, D. M., A. Algiers, and R. E. Levitt. 2018. "Identifying the Role of Supply Chain Integration Practices in the Adoption of Systemic Innovations." *Journal of Management in Engineering* 34 (6): 04018030/1–04018030/14.

Hall, D. 2018. "Cracks in the Mirror: Conceptualizing the Ongoing AEC Industry Re-organization." In *Proceedings of the 16th Engineering Project Organization Conference*, 458–77.

Heys, R., J. Martin, and W. Mkandawire. 2019. "GDP and Welfare: A Spectrum of Opportunity." ESCoE Discussion Paper No. 2019–16, Economic Statistics Centre of Excellence (ESCoE) and Office for National Statistics.

Heys, R. 2018. "Challenges in Measuring the Modern Economy." Presentation at the ESCoE Conference, May 16–17, Bank of England, London.

HM Government. 2015. Digital Built Britain: Level 3 Building Information Modelling—Strategic Plan, HM Government. https://assets.publishing.service.gov.uk/government/uploads/system/uploads/attachment_data/file/410096/bis-15-155-digital-built-britain-level-3-strategy.pdf.

HM Government. 2012. "Industrial Strategy: Government and Industry in Partnership, Building Information Modeling (BIM)." HM Government. https://assets.publishing.service.gov.uk/government/uploads/system/uploads/attachment_data/file/34710/12-1327-building-information-modelling.pdf.

Hunhevicz, J. J., M. Motie, and D. M. Hall. 2022. "Digital Building Twins and Blockchain for Performance-Based (Smart) Contracts." *Automation in Construction* 133: 103981.

IPA. 2021. "Transforming Infrastructure Performance: Roadmap to 2030." London, Infrastructure and Projects Authority. https://assets.publishing.service.gov.uk/government/uploads/system/uploads/attachment_data/file/1016726/IPA_TIP_Roadmap_to_2030_v6__1_.pdf.

ISO. 2018. ISO 19650–1:2018-Organization and Digitization of Information about Buildings and Civil Engineering Works, including Building Information Modelling (BIM)—Information Management Using Building Information Modelling—Part 1: Concepts and Principles. https://www.iso.org/standard/68078.html.

Jin, R., S. Gao, A. Cheshmehzangi, and E. Aboagye-Nimo. 2018. "A Holistic Review of Off-Site Construction Literature Published between 2008 and 2018." *Journal of Cleaner Production* 202: 1202–1219.

Jorgenson, D. W., and K. J. Stiroh. 2000. "US Economic Growth at the Industry Level." *American Economic Review* 90 (2): 161–67.

Keune, R. 2007. "Architectural Services in Global Trade in Professional Services." In Sixth Services Experts Meeting Domestic Regulation and Trade in Professional Services, 15–16 February 2007. Paris: OECD and World Bank. https://www.oecd.org/site/tadstri/40778733.pdf.

KPMG. 2016. "Smart Construction: How Offsite Manufacturing Can Transform Our Industry, UK." April. KPMG. https://home.kpmg/content/dam/kpmg/pdf/2016/04/smart-construction-report-2016.pdf.

Lewis, O., and A. Offer. 2022. "Railways as Patient Capital." *Oxford Review of Economic Policy* 38 (2): 260–77.

Murguia, D., Q. Chen, T. Jansen van Vuuren, A. Rathnayake, V. Vilde, and C. Middleton. 2022. "Digital Measurement of Construction Performance: Data-to-dashboard strategy." Proceedings of the 22nd CIB World Building Congress, 1–10.

Murray, S. 2021. "Evolution of the UK Construction Sector." Applied Digital Economics & Policy Online Workshop on Construction and Infrastructure, July 21, 2021, University of Cambridge, Cambridge.

NBS. 2020. "NBS' 10th National BIM Report." May 26. https://www.thenbs.com/knowledge/national-bim-report-2020.

Oesterreich, T. D., and F. Teuteberg. 2016. "Understanding the Implications of Digitisation and Automation in the Context of Industry 4.0: A Triangulation Approach and Elements of a Research Agenda for the Construction Industry." *Computers in Industry* 83: 121–39.

ONS. 2020. Construction statistics, Great Britain: 2020, Office for National Statistics. https://www.ons.gov.uk/businessindustryandtrade/constructionindustry/articles/constructionstatistics/2020.

ONS. 2021. "Productivity in the Construction Industry, UK: 2021, An Investigation into Productivity Growth and Its Drivers in the UK Construction Industry." Office for National Statistics (ONS). https://www.ons.gov.uk/economy/economicoutputandproductivity/productivitymeasures/articles/productivityintheconstructionindustryuk2021/2021-10-19.

ORR. 2019. "Review of Construction Sector Productivity Work Relevant to Highways England's Performance and Efficiency." March 11, 2020. Office of Rail and Road. https://www.orr.gov.uk/media/10561.

Osmani, M. 2012. "Construction Waste Minimization in the UK: Current Pressures for Change and Approaches." *Procedia—Social and Behavioral Sciences* 40: 37–40.

Orstavik, F. 2014. "Innovation as Re-institutionalization: A Case Study of Technological Change in Housebuilding in Norway." *Construction Management and Economics* 32 (9): 857–73.

Oti-Sarpong, K. 2019. "Offsite Manufacturing, Construction and Digitalisation in the UK. Construction Industry—State of the Nation Report." December. Cambridge Centre for Housing & Planning Research. https://www.cchpr.landecon.cam.ac.uk/system/files/documents/state_of_the_nation_osm.pdf.

Paschou, T., M. Rapaccini, F. Adrodegari, and N. Saccani. 2020. "Digital Servitization in Manufacturing: A Systematic Literature Review and Research Agenda." *Industrial Marketing Management* 89: 278–92.

Pittman, J. 2018. "Reimaging the Future of Making: Automation Helps People Live and Work Better." Redshift by Autodesk. https://redshift.autodesk.com/future-of-automation/.

PWC. 2018. "BIM Level 2 Benefits Measurement Methodology." PwC BIM Benefits Methodology and Report, Centre for Digital Built Britain, University of Cambridge. https://www.cdbb.cam.ac.uk/news/2018JuneBIMBenefits.

Ribeirinho, M. J., J. Mischke, G. Strube, E. Sjödin, J. L. Blanco, R. Palter, J. Biörck, D. Rockhill, and T. Andersson. 2020. "The Next Normal in Construction." Executive summary, June. McKinsey & Company. https://www.mckinsey.com/~/media/McKinsey/Industries/Capital%20Projects%20and%20Infrastructure/Our%20Insights/The%20next%20normal%20in%20construction/executive-summary_the-next-normal-in-construction.pdf.

Sacks R., I. Brilakis, E. Pikas, H. S. Xie, M. Girolami. 2020. "Construction with digital twin information systems." *Data-Centric Engineering* 1:e14. doi:10.1017/dce.2020.16.

Sategna, L.G., D. Meinero, and V. Marco. 2019. "Digitalising the Construction Sector: Unlocking the Potential of Data with a Value Chain Approach." Committee for European Construction Equipment (CECE). https://www.cece.eu/publications/digital-reports.

SCCANZ. 2020. "Data Leadership Guidance Note: Digital Twin." April. Smart Cities Council, Australia New Zealand. https://www.smartcitiescouncil.com/sites/default/files/anz_smartcitiescouncil_com/public_resources/guidance_note_digital_twin_issue_0.pdf.

Sinclair, D., J. Johnson, I. Heptonstall, R. Francis, N. Fraser, S. McCarthy, K. Davie, N. Magdani, and S. Stacey. 2016. "RIBA Plan of Work 2013 Designing for Manufacture and Assembly." London: Royal Institute of British Architects (RIBA). http://consig.org/wp-content/uploads/2018/10/RIBAPlanofWorkDfMAOverlay pdf.pdf.

Soga, K., and J. Schooling. 2016. "Infrastructure Sensing." *Interface Focus* 6: 20160023.

Stacey, S. 2021. "Disruption Is Coming—Let's Rise to the Challenge It Brings." Building website, Comment, June 28. https://www.building.co.uk/comment/disruption-is-coming-lets-rise-to-the-challenge-it-brings/5112411.article.

Sveikauskas, L., S. Rowe, J. Mildenberger, J. Price, and A. Young. 2016. "Productivity Growth in Construction." *Journal of Construction Engineering and Management* 142 (10): 04016045.

UK Parliament POST. 2021. "Smart Cities." Postnote No. 656, September. London: The Parliamentary Office of Science and Technology. https://researchbriefings.files.parliament.uk/documents/POST-PN-0656/POST-PN-0656.pdf.

Van Vuuren, T., and C. Middleton. 2020. *Methodology for Quantifying the Benefits of Offsite Construction*. C792, February. London, UK: CIRIA. www.ciria.org/c792.

Vidalakis, C., F. H. Abanda, and A. H. Oti. 2020. "BIM adoption and implementation: focusing on SMEs." *Construction Innovation* 20 (1): 128–147. https://doi.org/10.1108/CI-09-2018-0076.

WEF. 2018. "Shaping the Future of Construction: An Action Plan to Accelerate Building Information Modelling (BIM) Adoption." February. Cologny/Geneva, Switzerland: World Economic Forum. https://www3.weforum.org/docs/WEF_Accelerating_BIM_Adoption_Action_Plan.pdf.

WPI Economics. 2020. "Cellular-Connected Drones." January. http://wpieconomics.com/site/wp-content/uploads/2020/01/Final_Vodafone-Drone-Report-Web-Spreads.pdf.

Whyte, J. 2019. "How Digital Information Transforms Project Delivery Models." *Project Management Journal* 50 (2): 177–94.

Williamson, O. E. 1985. *The Economic Institutions of Capitalism: Firms, Markets, Rational Contracting*. New York: The Free Press.

WTO. 2021. International Trade Statistics 2021. World Trade Organization.

6 After Redefinition TFP Accounting

Jon D. Samuels

6.1 Introduction

Economic measurement issues related to the computer and electronics sector are a useful lens to examine the overall state of economic statistics because this sector often highlights broader measurement issues that are important for other sectors and for the economy as a whole. The Solow paradox and productivity puzzle encouraged important economic research that helped pave the way to official industry-level production accounts that show how innovation in the computer and electronics sector made a significant contribution to economic growth during the information technology (IT) boom of the late 1990s and early 2000s (Jorgenson, Ho, and Stiroh 2005). The slowdown in measured productivity growth after 2004 led to a reexamination of measurement challenges encountered by growth analysts, again with a focus on IT-related industries. Byrne, Fernald, and Reinsdorf (2016) conclude that mismeasurement of IT is not a likely source of the measured productivity slowdown.

This paper does not assert that there is a measurement problem in the IT sector but does use the computer and electronics sector as another important example of an issue that can complicate analysis of the sources of aggregate productivity growth. We examine the role of secondary production in understanding the sources of growth. In the BEA-BLS integrated industry-level production account, which provides the bottom-up sources of gross domestic product (GDP) and aggregate TFP growth, the economic accounting is done based on the concept of establishments. If an establishment produces more than one output, the total value of all output is typically grouped with

Jon D. Samuels is a senior research economist and chief of the National Accounts Research Group at the US Bureau of Economic Analysis.

other establishments to which this output is primary. For example, according to BEA data, about 6.2 percent of the gross output of the computer and electronics sector in 1987 was research and development and own account software because these activities are conducted within the same establishments that produce computer hardware. This share increased to 21.5 percent in 2019. Obviously, there are good reasons that R&D and own account software are included in the output of the computer and electronic sector because the production of computer and semiconductor hardware is intertwined with the production of R&D and own account software. But there are also good reasons why analysts would want to separate the activities. The production of R&D and own account software is very different in nature from the physical production of computers and semiconductor hardware. If the computer and electronics sector devotes an increasing amount of resources to the production of R&D, measured productivity in the combined sector reflects this composition shift. This is potentially important in assessing the sources of aggregate productivity change if productivity change in the production of hardware is different from the productivity change in the production of R&D and own account software.

The purpose of this paper is to present a new industry-level productivity account that reorganizes secondary production to align with the BEA's After Redefinition tables and uses this account to measure the sources of US economic growth. BEA's After Redefinition input-output tables reorganize outputs and inputs when the production process of the secondary output significantly differs from an industry's primary product. For example, all construction activity is moved to the Construction sector in the After Redefinition tables. An advantage of this new organization is that this allows for a bottom-up analysis of the contribution of productivity growth that avoids confounding compositional change between primary and secondary products with changes in measured TFP growth for industries that embed secondary output. It is important to note that there are other ways to approach handling of secondary production in industry accounting. For example, it may be of interest to move all secondary production to the industry in which it is primary. This would result in an account that approaches the concept of commodities instead of industries, but the objective of this paper is to construct an account that aligns with BEA's After Redefinition tables.

In addition to providing a potentially cleaner view of the sources of productivity growth, the realignment of the productivity accounts has two other major benefits from an analytical perspective. The first is related to measuring international competitiveness at the industry level. Jorgenson, Nomura, and Samuels (2016) show how to measure industry price and productivity gaps at the industry level to assess competitiveness on international markets. But, the constructs in that paper may suffer from the same basic issue: price and productivity gaps may reflect the composition of secondary production and thus obscure the true economic competitiveness of certain products. For example, Jorgenson, Nomura, and Samuels (2018) find that the chemicals sector in Japan surpassed the chemicals sector in the United States in its productivity level. Suppose that chemicals sector in the United States does significantly more R&D than the same sector in Japan. If this were true, then the measured productivity gap could reflect the composition of R&D and not the gap in actual production of chemical products. In assessing competitiveness on international markets, it is the latter concept that is of primary interest. This basic issue is also relevant in efforts to reconceptualize from national to global economic accounting, such as the proposal in Samuels and Strassner (2019) for the same reason: establishment-based price and productivity gap measures embed composition differences due to secondary production.

Another major benefit of productivity accounts that are more closely aligned to products is the analysis of global value chains (GVCs) and measuring trade in value added (TiVA). TiVA measures are based on answering the following question using input-output tables: For a given export, how much of the value of the export is composed of domestic value added (including from all upstream industries that contribute to that export), and how much of the value of that gross export is embedded value from foreign producers? Because of this, TiVA estimates are (ideally) based on narrow products instead of broad industries to avoid including (mostly) irrelevant value. For example, using the before redefinition industry concept to construct TiVA, estimates would impose that every time the United States exported a computer more R&D had to be done to support that export. To avoid that, using after redefinition input-output tables is preferable, and BEA uses this approach in its recent TiVA work.[1] But, suppose one wanted to take it one step further and estimate the worker skill composition embedded in TiVA. Without a corresponding production account that is matched to the relevant input-output tables, it is not possible to consistently estimate this value. This paper presents such an account.

The importance of distinguishing between products and industries has a long history in input-output accounting and has been addressed in the context of productivity accounting as well. Raa and Wolff (1991) find that the distinction between commodities and industries matters for certain sectors, but not for the overall economy under a certain set of assumptions and the data available at the time. While the premise of this paper is basically the same, it is worth revisiting. First, the BEA now produces official after redefinition input-output tables that address this basic issue that are data driven and avoid some of the stronger assumptions of Raa and Wolff (1991). Second, the national accounts have since recognized research and

1. Recent discussion: Single Country TiVA, https://www.bea.gov/system/files/2021-11/Trade-in-Value-Added-Update-on-Work-with-NSF.pdf.

development and own account software as a capital asset, which necessitates including this in gross industry output in the establishment-based industry accounts. Third, KLEMS (Capital, Labor, Energy, Materials, Services) productivity accounts have advanced so that there is now price data for detailed inputs. This allows for a cleaner mapping between inputs used in primary and secondary production.

At the outset, it is important to note that the new production account presented in this paper does involve assumptions to translate measured data into estimates of output and input that can be assigned between primary and secondary industries, and there are certainly other ways to implement such an account.[2] The sections below will enumerate those assumptions, but how far these assumptions are from economic reality in comparison to the many other assumptions used to measure industry growth and (total factor) productivity is not obvious, nor is it the focus of this paper. Therefore, the estimates presented in this paper should be considered in the context of the other broad sets of assumptions that are used to assemble economic estimates of TFP growth.

We find that distinguishing between primary and secondary production is important for measuring TFP growth, but only for a small subset of industries for the sample period for which data is available to make the adjustment between primary and secondary production. The major impacts are in the computer and electronic products and data processing, internet publishing, and other information services sectors. Another noteworthy finding is that the manufacturing sector has a smaller share in GDP when nonmanufacturing secondary production is moved out of the sector.

The paper proceeds by first describing the construction of an industry-level production account that adjusts for secondary production, first by focusing on the nominal production account including industry outputs and inputs in sections 6.2.1 and 6.2.2. The second component of this is linking prices to these output and inputs to construct a real account for measuring industry TFP and this is described in section 6.2.3. Section 6.3 presents the sources of economic growth when secondary production is moved out of its primary industry. Section 6.4 concludes.

6.2 Constructing After Redefinition KLEMS Accounts

This section discusses the steps and economic assumptions employed to construct the production account that adjusts for secondary production. The nomenclature used to refer to this new account is "after redefinitions" to follow the terminology used by BEA in constructing its input-output tables. The point of comparison for this account is the BEA-BLS Integrated

2. See the appendix (http://www.nber.org/data-appendix/c14749/appendix.pdf) for additional discussion.

Industry-Level Production Account, which is built with the "before redefinition" input-output tables. For brevity, and because there is a large accompanying literature, the methods and economic assumptions of BEA-BLS integrated industry-level production account are not covered in this paper.[3]

6.2.1 After Redefinition Output and Input in Current Dollars

Assembling after redefinition KLEMS (capital, labor, energy, materials, services) accounts requires constructing industry output, intermediate input, capital, and labor services in current and constant dollars. The basic approach is to distinguish primary and secondary production where secondary production is defined as production of goods and services that use a substantially different input pattern. Because it is often difficult to analyze input patterns systematically based on available source data, choosing what to redefine likely involves analyst judgment based on product line information like that from the economic census. The starting point for after redefinition KLEMS in this paper is the official data produced by BEA on after redefinition input-output tables as this provides a consistent measure of output and intermediate input (EMS) in current dollars that sums to the official GDP. The basic method for translating the before redefinition tables to after redefinition is given in Horowitz and Planting (2006) so this paper provides only a broad overview to convey the important ideas. In the extreme case, every industry produces only one commodity (so that the make table is diagonal) but this is not the approach in the official after redefinition tables produced by BEA. The after redefinition KLEMS productivity account presented in this paper follows the official BEA data on redefinitions, though alternatives with other assumptions around reclassification may be worth considering.[4,5]

The basic motivation for after redefinition input-output tables is that grouping disparate outputs within the same industry complicates input-output analysis. Consider a stylized case where an accommodations (hotel) establishment also produces restaurant meals that are served to both hotel and non-hotel guests. A typical input-output approach to figuring out how many more inputs would be required to expand the number of rooms offered by the hotel (while keeping the number of restaurant meals to outsiders held constant) wouldn't be possible when meal sales are included in the input and output measures of the industry. At the same time, if one wanted to answer

3. See Garner et al. (2020) for a more recent discussion of the BEA-BLS data and Jorgenson, Ho, and Stiroh (2005) for a comprehensive description of the general concepts and methods.

4. A simpler approach that could be implemented with publicly available summary level data is to use the published Make table. Some notes on this approach and its caveats are discussed in the appendix, http://www.nber.org/data-appendix/c14749/appendix.pdf.

5. It is worth noting that this paper follows BEA's approach for reallocating output that is for own use in addition to output that is for sale. While it would be of interest to construct an alternative account that redefines only output that is sold on the market, this would require a new time series of input-output tables and would not match BEA's published after redefinition tables.

a question about how many more inputs would be required to produce both more hotel rooms and more meals to outsiders, having the output grouped together is useful.

The first step BEA takes in constructing the after redefinition input-output tables is to decide which industries have secondary production to be redefined. In these cases, the value of output of the secondary product is moved to the industry in which it is primary. For example, construction activities performed in any industry are moved to the construction sector in the after redefinition tables.

The second step is to reallocate the accompanying intermediate inputs from the primary to the secondary industry. For example, when margin sales on shampoo in a salon are redefined to the retail trade industry, the corresponding intermediate inputs need to be moved as well. The basic assumption employed BEA's after redefinition tables is to impose that the intermediate input composition (across detailed commodities) for the output being redefined corresponds to the intermediate input composition of the secondary industry. Therefore, if output is being moved from beauty salons to retail trade, the basic assumption is that the accompanying intermediate inputs that are moved have the same composition as those in the retail trade sector. The proportion of output that is not reallocated to intermediate input is reallocated to value added. The starting point for the estimates presented in this paper is these official after redefinition use tables that are published by BEA.

6.2.2 After Redefinition Capital and Labor Services in Current Dollars

The after redefinition production account requires estimates of nominal capital and labor services for the redefined industries. BEA's published after redefinition input-output tables include information on employee compensation, gross operating surplus (GOS), and taxes on production and imports, but the gross operating surplus includes mixed income for self-employed so this cannot be directly mapped to capital and labor services in the redefined industries. Furthermore, it is imperative to capture heterogeneity within the capital and labor inputs (think differences in information technology and structures capital input and highly educated experienced workers and less educated inexperienced workers) in the after redefinition accounts to match the categories used in the before redefinitions BEA-BLS integrated industry level production account.

The primary reason for recognizing this heterogeneity is that it is necessary to distinguish between changes in input composition from changes in total factor productivity growth. Measures that fail to account for this heterogeneity will confound shifts to higher quality inputs and growth in TFP (Jorgenson and Griliches 1967). Unfortunately, there is not reliable source data on which detailed capital and labor inputs are used to produce which outputs within establishments. For example, the beauty salon that sells beauty products is likely to employ the same worker to undertake both tasks, but the skill mix and capital composition of running the production line in pharmaceutical manufacturing may be very different from the skill mix and capital composition in producing R&D on pharmaceuticals.

The nominal capital and labor estimates presented in this paper are constructed using the following method. Total employee labor compensation is reallocated using the same assumption and data that are used in the official after redefinition tables; the value of labor compensation that is moved into an industry reflects the share of employee labor compensation in value added in the secondary industry. For example, if meat processing value added is reallocated from the wholesale sector to the manufacturing sector, the portion of this that is attributed to employee labor compensation is determined by the share of employee labor compensation in value added in the manufacturing sector. This reproduces the official after redefinition estimate of employee compensation.

Gross operating surplus is reallocated in a similar fashion, but an adjustment is made to split mixed income into labor and capital income. Specifically, for all reallocations of gross operating surplus, unpublished BEA data are used to link the reallocation of gross operating surplus to its industry of origin. The industry of origin is used to split the reallocated GOS into self-employed labor compensation and a remainder that gets allocated to capital income based on this same share in the BEA-BLS integrated industry level production account. For example, if meat processing value added is reallocated from the wholesale sector to the manufacturing sector, the portion of this that is attributed to GOS is determined by the share of GOS in value added in the manufacturing sector. But the share of GOS that is allocated to self-employed labor compensation is determined by the share of self-employed workers in GOS in the wholesale sector. The reason why the allocation between self-employed labor and GOS is not based on the share in the manufacturing sector will be discussed below.

Finally, taxes on production and imports are reallocated to secondary industries using the same approach as employee compensation but are assigned to capital income. Including taxes on production and imports in capital income is also the approach the BEA-BLS integrated industry-level production account, though work is underway at BEA to revisit this.

The above describes the estimates of total nominal capital and labor services by industry, but additional steps are needed to determine the composition of capital and labor. There is no information on this in the official after redefinition tables. This prototype account considers two categories of labor: workers with a BA degree and above and other workers (those with less education), and five types of capital assets (IT equipment, software, R&D, entertainment originals, and other capital). The assumption used to determine this allocation is that the composition of capital and labor being reallocated reflects the *primary* industry from which it is being reallocated. Thus, if employee labor compensation from the meat processing industry is reallocated from the wholesale sector to the manufacturing sector, then the share of this labor compensation that is attributed to workers with a BA degree in the redefined manufacturing sector reflects the share of labor compensation paid to workers with a BA degree in the wholesale meat processing industry. This approach is employed for two basic reasons. The first reason is based on the idea that much of what is being reallocated is produced under a joint production technology. For example, if the process of wholesaling meat is fundamentally inseparable from the process of meat processing within an establishment (e.g., due to feedback loops in the process), then the composition of inputs used in meat processing must be the same as the composition of inputs used in meat wholesaling. Another example is that it may be the case that conducting R&D (and returns from R&D) in medical sector is fundamentally inseparable from the provision of medical care. In the case of only two input types, this assumption can be represented with a generalized production function of the form $F(Y_1, Y_2) = G(LC, LN)$ where Y_1 and Y_2 are meat wholesaling and meat processing and LC and LN are workers with a BA or higher degree and others. This specification can be compared to separable production functions of the form $Y_1 = G(LC_1, LN_1)$ and $Y_2 = G(LC_2, LN_2)$ where inputs can be separated and allocated across meat processing and meat wholesaling. It is important to reemphasize that the source data are establishment based so that splitting inputs between meat wholesaling and meat processing and imposing separate production functions, which may be more intuitive, likely involves stronger economic assumptions than the assumption employed in this paper that the two outputs are produced jointly.

The second reason that the composition of the inputs is assumed to match that of the primary industry is practical. If the composition of inputs is assumed to be the same as the destination industry, when inputs are reallocated, the reallocation may result in negative inputs in the primary industry. For example, if college labor compensation is to be moved between the chemicals sector and the professional, scientific, and technical services industry sector and the professional, scientific, and technical services industry is much more intensive in college labor than the chemicals sector, then so much college labor could be taken out of the chemicals sector that negative labor compensation for college workers in this sector is left as a residual. This causes obvious problems in the chemicals sector. Furthermore, any attempt to address this would likely have to include an entire rebalancing of the input-output tables.

The same basic approach is used to allocate capital across the five types of capital. The GOS being reallocated (after adjusting for self-employed workers) is allocated to the five types of capital based on shares in the primary industry. Similarly, the taxes on production and imports that are reallocated to capital are assumed to have the same capital composition as capital in the primary industry. Importantly, all the redefinitions and reallocations result in no changes to nominal GDP.

6.2.3 Prices for After Redefinition Capital and Labor Services

Each component of nominal output, intermediate input, capital, and labor that is reallocated needs to be associated with a price index to construct KLEMS quantity indexes and measure TFP growth. Due to the way that BEA constructs its industry accounts, associating each component of output and intermediate input with a price index is straightforward. BEA constructs its industry accounts at an unpublished level of detail called the item level. When these items are moved in the redefinition of output and reallocation of intermediate input, the accompanying price index can easily be attached to each new component of output and intermediate input. For the account presented in this paper, these items are then aggregated up to a new after redefinition estimate of the price and quantity of industry output and intermediate input.

Constructing after redefinition capital and labor prices is significantly more complicated due to the underlying assumptions discussed above that allow for jointly produced secondary production. Joint production implies that the composition of the capital and labor services being reallocated matches the composition of the primary industry and therefore necessitates tracking all the flows across industries, not just the final allocation of capital and labor. The intuition behind this method is that capital and labor prices reflect production conditions in the primary industry because returns to capital and labor are inextricably linked to the primary production process. For example, the price of R&D capital in the computer and electronics sector reflects the rate of return in that sector and this is the price that is relevant for measuring the input and output of R&D. Unpublished details on the flows of labor compensation and gross operating surplus allow for tracing gross flows of capital and labor inputs for each industry. To construct a price index for each primary input for each industry, each component of capital and labor is linked to a price index from its industry of origin and weighted by the value contributed by each industry of origin. For example, the miscellaneous professional, scientific, and technical services sector after redefinition industry has labor compensation added to it that originates from both the chemicals sector and the computer and electronic products sector. The price index for college-educated labor in the redefined miscellaneous professional, scientific, and technical services sector is constructed as the weighted price change of the college labor prices in these two sectors where the weights capture the relative importance of these in comparison to the college educated labor that was measured in the Miscellaneous professional, scientific, and technical services sector before redefinitions. Of course, because labor compensation may move out of the Miscellaneous professional, scientific, and technical services sector, the weights reflect these net flows.

6.3 The Sources of Economic Growth After Redefinitions

This section presents a bottom-up accounting of the sources of economic growth using the after redefinitions industry-level production account. The results are divided into two basic sections; the first provides the sources of growth at the industry level after redefinitions in comparison to before redefinitions, and the second section compares the aggregate sources of growth using the two concepts.

6.3.1 Industry Sources of Growth Adjusting for Secondary Production

The results show that the broad industry trends are similar between the after and before redefinitions production account but there are some noteworthy differences. Tables 6.1–6.3 show the industry sources of growth after redefinition, before redefinition, and the differences between the two. As expected, based on the motivation for this paper presented above, the computer and electronic products sector has faster measured TFP growth after secondary production has been moved. Table 6.3 indicates that this is mostly driven by faster value added growth in the redefined sector (faster output growth and a smaller contribution of intermediate input). Underlying detail (not published) shows that the output difference mostly is driven by the movement of research and development and own account software output from the computer and electronic products sector. Because the research and development and own account software are associated with a price index that grows faster than the computer and electronic product equipment price, moving this output from the sector results in faster real output growth. Table 6.3 also demonstrates the importance of the complete production account in understanding the differences in measured TFP growth. While the redefinitions did not have a significant impact on the measured contributions of capital and labor in this sector, the redefinitions had a large impact on the measured contribution of intermediate input. After redefinitions, the contribution of intermediate was lower than the contribution before redefinition and this reflects the intermediate product mix used in producing research and development and own account software differs from the product mixing in producing computer and electronic equipment. It is important to note that neither of these measures is necessarily preferred over the other. If one is interested in understanding the narrower concept of productivity in the production of computer hardware, for example in comparison to other countries, then the after redefinition concept is likely more useful. If one is interested in the entire production process for computers and electronic components including all the R&D and own account software, then the before redefinition concept may be more appropriate. It is important to emphasize the even after redefinitions, the computer and electronics sector uses some R&D and own account software as a capital input, but no longer produces it as an output.

Table 6.1 **After redefinitions sources of industry output growth 1997–2019**

	Output Growth	Capital Contribution	Labor Contribution	Intermediate Contribution	TFP Growth
Farms	1.27	0.07	0.02	0.29	0.89
Forestry, fishing, and related activities	0.34	0.32	0.77	−0.74	0.00
Oil and gas extraction	3.23	−0.24	−0.46	1.47	2.47
Mining, except oil and gas	−1.33	0.26	−0.42	−0.41	−0.76
Support activities for mining	6.38	0.86	1.47	1.27	2.78
Utilities	0.51	0.65	0.01	−0.11	−0.04
Construction	0.40	0.22	0.53	0.55	−0.90
Wood products	0.02	0.08	−0.35	−0.29	0.58
Nonmetallic mineral products	−0.33	0.21	−0.14	−0.39	−0.01
Primary metals	−0.40	−0.03	−0.39	−0.81	0.83
Fabricated metal products	0.01	0.16	−0.07	0.08	−0.15
Machinery	0.18	0.14	−0.28	0.03	0.30
Computer and electronic products	4.71	0.61	−0.60	−1.68	6.37
Electrical equipment, appliances, and components	−0.82	0.08	−0.32	−0.91	0.33
Motor vehicles, bodies and trailers, and parts	2.17	0.18	−0.14	1.47	0.66
Other transportation equipment	2.13	0.34	0.16	1.10	0.52
Furniture and related products	−0.66	0.10	−0.50	−0.15	−0.10
Miscellaneous manufacturing	0.42	0.31	−0.16	−0.51	0.79
Food and beverage and tobacco products	0.44	0.20	0.08	0.38	−0.21
Textile mills and textile product mills	−4.00	−0.13	−1.07	−3.17	0.37
Apparel and leather and allied products	−7.42	−0.12	−1.66	−6.08	0.44
Paper products	−1.17	−0.10	−0.46	−0.59	−0.02
Printing and related support activities	−1.16	0.12	−1.00	−1.35	1.07
Petroleum and coal products	0.90	0.22	−0.01	0.46	0.23
Chemical products	0.34	1.09	−0.17	0.09	−0.67
Plastics and rubber products	−0.04	0.16	−0.19	−0.31	0.31
Wholesale trade	2.98	0.99	0.18	1.50	0.31
Retail trade	2.73	0.85	0.10	1.13	0.66
Air transportation	0.46	0.43	−0.39	−0.21	0.64
Rail transportation	0.58	0.13	−0.68	0.35	0.77
Water transportation	1.08	0.19	0.11	0.58	0.20
Truck transportation	1.52	0.44	0.32	1.16	−0.39
Transit and ground passenger transportation	3.98	0.56	0.98	2.12	0.31
Pipeline transportation	1.21	2.89	−0.23	−2.49	1.03
Other transportation and support activities	2.31	0.12	0.96	1.93	−0.70
Warehousing and storage	6.68	0.44	2.01	3.45	0.78
Publishing industries, except internet (includes software)	2.35	1.38	−0.24	−0.45	1.65

(continued)

Table 6.1 **(cont.)**

	Output Growth	Capital Contribution	Labor Contribution	Intermediate Contribution	TFP Growth
Motion picture and sound recording industries	2.50	0.77	0.36	0.22	1.15
Broadcasting and telecommunications	4.42	2.05	−0.22	1.66	0.94
Data processing, internet publishing, and other information services	9.65	3.32	0.08	3.87	2.39
Federal Reserve banks, credit intermediation, and related activities	1.59	1.48	0.37	0.38	−0.63
Securities, commodity contracts, and investments	3.61	0.19	0.74	2.72	−0.03
Insurance carriers and related activities	4.38	1.05	0.38	2.52	0.42
Funds, trusts, and other financial vehicles	1.73	0.02	0.02	1.28	0.41
Real estate	2.75	1.25	0.08	0.96	0.46
Rental and leasing services and lessors of intangible assets	2.66	2.66	−0.01	0.85	−0.83
Legal services	0.40	0.82	0.26	0.42	−1.11
Computer systems design and related services	7.10	0.42	2.88	0.85	2.95
Miscellaneous professional, scientific, and technical services	2.90	0.62	0.82	1.19	0.26
Management of companies and enterprises	3.16	0.18	1.43	1.76	−0.21
Administrative and support services	3.67	0.77	0.97	1.67	0.26
Waste management and remediation services	1.86	0.20	0.85	0.91	−0.10
Educational services	2.31	0.23	1.40	1.28	−0.60
Ambulatory health care services	3.12	0.28	1.56	0.81	0.47
Hospitals and Nursing and residential care	2.85	0.29	1.00	1.71	−0.15
Social assistance	3.31	0.04	1.84	1.76	−0.33
Performing arts, spectator sports, museums, and related activities	2.80	0.21	0.55	0.99	1.05
Amusements, gambling, and recreation industries	2.34	0.16	1.01	1.16	0.01
Accommodation	1.76	1.52	−0.17	0.76	−0.35
Food services and drinking places	2.06	0.38	0.54	1.09	0.05
Other services, except government	0.43	0.15	0.35	0.82	−0.89
Federal	1.18	0.32	0.04	0.72	0.09
State and local	1.61	0.48	0.48	0.60	0.04

Note: Average annual percentage growth. A contribution is a share-weighted growth rate.

Table 6.1 (cont.)

	Output Growth	Capital Contribution	Labor Contribution	Intermediate Contribution	TFP Growth
Motion picture and sound recording industries	2.50	0.77	0.36	0.22	1.15
Broadcasting and telecommunications	4.42	2.05	−0.22	1.66	0.94
Data processing, internet publishing, and other information services	9.65	3.32	0.08	3.87	2.39
Federal Reserve banks, credit intermediation, and related activities	1.59	1.48	0.37	0.38	−0.63
Securities, commodity contracts, and investments	3.61	0.19	0.74	2.72	−0.03
Insurance carriers and related activities	4.38	1.05	0.38	2.52	0.42
Funds, trusts, and other financial vehicles	1.73	0.02	0.02	1.28	0.41
Real estate	2.75	1.25	0.08	0.96	0.46
Rental and leasing services and lessors of intangible assets	2.66	2.66	−0.01	0.85	−0.83
Legal services	0.40	0.82	0.26	0.42	−1.11
Computer systems design and related services	7.10	0.42	2.88	0.85	2.95
Miscellaneous professional, scientific, and technical services	2.90	0.62	0.82	1.19	0.26
Management of companies and enterprises	3.16	0.18	1.43	1.76	−0.21
Administrative and support services	3.67	0.77	0.97	1.67	0.26
Waste management and remediation services	1.86	0.20	0.85	0.91	−0.10
Educational services	2.31	0.23	1.40	1.28	−0.60
Ambulatory health care services	3.12	0.28	1.56	0.81	0.47
Hospitals and Nursing and residential care	2.85	0.29	1.00	1.71	−0.15
Social assistance	3.31	0.04	1.84	1.76	−0.33
Performing arts, spectator sports, museums, and related activities	2.80	0.21	0.55	0.99	1.05
Amusements, gambling, and recreation industries	2.34	0.16	1.01	1.16	0.01
Accommodation	1.76	1.52	−0.17	0.76	−0.35
Food services and drinking places	2.06	0.38	0.54	1.09	0.05
Other services, except government	0.43	0.15	0.35	0.82	−0.89
Federal	1.18	0.32	0.04	0.72	0.09
State and local	1.61	0.48	0.48	0.60	0.04

Note: Average annual percentage growth. A contribution is a share-weighted growth rate.

Table 6.1 **After redefinitions sources of industry output growth 1997–2019**

	Output Growth	Capital Contribution	Labor Contribution	Intermediate Contribution	TFP Growth
Farms	1.27	0.07	0.02	0.29	0.89
Forestry, fishing, and related activities	0.34	0.32	0.77	−0.74	0.00
Oil and gas extraction	3.23	−0.24	−0.46	1.47	2.47
Mining, except oil and gas	−1.33	0.26	−0.42	−0.41	−0.76
Support activities for mining	6.38	0.86	1.47	1.27	2.78
Utilities	0.51	0.65	0.01	−0.11	−0.04
Construction	0.40	0.22	0.53	0.55	−0.90
Wood products	0.02	0.08	−0.35	−0.29	0.58
Nonmetallic mineral products	−0.33	0.21	−0.14	−0.39	−0.01
Primary metals	−0.40	−0.03	−0.39	−0.81	0.83
Fabricated metal products	0.01	0.16	−0.07	0.08	−0.15
Machinery	0.18	0.14	−0.28	0.03	0.30
Computer and electronic products	4.71	0.61	−0.60	−1.68	6.37
Electrical equipment, appliances, and components	−0.82	0.08	−0.32	−0.91	0.33
Motor vehicles, bodies and trailers, and parts	2.17	0.18	−0.14	1.47	0.66
Other transportation equipment	2.13	0.34	0.16	1.10	0.52
Furniture and related products	−0.66	0.10	−0.50	−0.15	−0.10
Miscellaneous manufacturing	0.42	0.31	−0.16	−0.51	0.79
Food and beverage and tobacco products	0.44	0.20	0.08	0.38	−0.21
Textile mills and textile product mills	−4.00	−0.13	−1.07	−3.17	0.37
Apparel and leather and allied products	−7.42	−0.12	−1.66	−6.08	0.44
Paper products	−1.17	−0.10	−0.46	−0.59	−0.02
Printing and related support activities	−1.16	0.12	−1.00	−1.35	1.07
Petroleum and coal products	0.90	0.22	−0.01	0.46	0.23
Chemical products	0.34	1.09	−0.17	0.09	−0.67
Plastics and rubber products	−0.04	0.16	−0.19	−0.31	0.31
Wholesale trade	2.98	0.99	0.18	1.50	0.31
Retail trade	2.73	0.85	0.10	1.13	0.66
Air transportation	0.46	0.43	−0.39	−0.21	0.64
Rail transportation	0.58	0.13	−0.68	0.35	0.77
Water transportation	1.08	0.19	0.11	0.58	0.20
Truck transportation	1.52	0.44	0.32	1.16	−0.39
Transit and ground passenger transportation	3.98	0.56	0.98	2.12	0.31
Pipeline transportation	1.21	2.89	−0.23	−2.49	1.03
Other transportation and support activities	2.31	0.12	0.96	1.93	−0.70
Warehousing and storage	6.68	0.44	2.01	3.45	0.78
Publishing industries, except internet (includes software)	2.35	1.38	−0.24	−0.45	1.65

(continued)

Table 6.2 **Before redefinitions sources of industry output growth 1997–2019**

	Output Growth	Capital Contribution	Labor Contribution	Intermediate Contribution	TFP Growth
Farms	1.27	0.07	0.02	0.29	0.89
Forestry, fishing, and related activities	0.27	0.39	0.77	−0.83	−0.06
Oil and gas extraction	3.52	−0.07	−0.10	1.39	2.30
Mining, except oil and gas	−0.78	0.50	−0.18	−0.33	−0.77
Support activities for mining	5.22	0.26	0.80	1.55	2.60
Utilities	0.54	0.77	−0.02	−0.11	−0.10
Construction	0.48	0.28	0.53	0.59	−0.92
Wood products	0.04	0.07	−0.34	−0.29	0.61
Nonmetallic mineral products	−0.30	0.20	−0.14	−0.37	0.01
Primary metals	−0.40	−0.03	−0.40	−0.80	0.83
Fabricated metal products	0.00	0.18	−0.10	0.08	−0.16
Machinery	0.22	0.19	−0.28	0.05	0.26
Computer and electronic products	4.41	0.54	−0.61	−1.34	5.83
Electrical equipment, appliances, and components	−0.75	0.11	−0.35	−0.87	0.36
Motor vehicles, bodies and trailers, and parts	2.11	0.19	−0.15	1.43	0.65
Other transportation equipment	2.01	0.30	0.03	1.10	0.57
Furniture and related products	−0.63	0.13	−0.52	−0.13	−0.11
Miscellaneous manufacturing	0.67	0.37	−0.06	−0.37	0.73
Food and beverage and tobacco products	0.47	0.19	0.09	0.38	−0.19
Textile mills and textile product mills	−3.97	−0.16	−1.07	−3.11	0.37
Apparel and leather and allied products	−7.74	−0.04	−2.14	−5.85	0.30
Paper products	−1.18	−0.09	−0.47	−0.60	−0.02
Printing and related support activities	−1.34	−0.07	−1.01	−1.37	1.12
Petroleum and coal products	0.90	0.26	−0.03	0.46	0.21
Chemical products	0.51	1.04	−0.07	0.16	−0.62
Plastics and rubber products	−0.01	0.17	−0.19	−0.30	0.30
Wholesale trade	2.95	1.02	0.26	1.50	0.17
Retail trade	2.48	0.85	0.11	1.06	0.45
Air transportation	0.45	0.41	−0.42	−0.21	0.67
Rail transportation	0.52	0.06	−0.70	0.34	0.82
Water transportation	1.19	0.17	0.20	0.56	0.26
Truck transportation	1.53	0.42	0.31	1.14	−0.35
Transit and ground passenger transportation	3.94	0.54	0.95	2.12	0.33
Pipeline transportation	0.90	1.75	0.09	−2.58	1.64
Other transportation and support activities	2.21	0.09	0.91	1.96	−0.74
Warehousing and storage	6.68	0.39	2.03	3.55	0.71
Publishing industries, except internet (includes software)	2.67	1.49	−0.15	−0.32	1.65

(continued)

Table 6.2 (cont.)

	Output Growth	Capital Contribution	Labor Contribution	Intermediate Contribution	TFP Growth
Motion picture and sound recording industries	2.57	0.78	0.42	0.23	1.15
Broadcasting and telecommunications	4.37	2.09	−0.23	1.62	0.89
Data processing, internet publishing, and other information services	10.28	4.44	0.75	4.15	0.93
Federal Reserve banks, credit intermediation, and related activities	1.61	1.46	0.38	0.38	−0.61
Securities, commodity contracts, and investments	3.61	0.17	0.74	2.71	−0.02
Insurance carriers and related activities	4.39	1.04	0.40	2.51	0.43
Funds, trusts, and other financial vehicles	2.00	0.05	0.08	1.60	0.27
Real estate	2.67	1.19	0.08	0.95	0.44
Rental and leasing services and lessors of intangible assets	2.72	3.08	0.07	0.92	−1.34
Legal services	0.40	0.81	0.26	0.42	−1.10
Computer systems design and related services	6.83	0.24	2.73	0.98	2.88
Miscellaneous professional, scientific, and technical services	2.95	0.76	1.19	1.20	−0.19
Management of companies and enterprises	3.21	0.18	1.46	1.71	−0.15
Administrative and support services	3.72	0.81	1.00	1.66	0.25
Waste management and remediation services	1.86	0.20	0.84	0.91	−0.09
Educational services	2.64	0.52	1.35	1.25	−0.48
Ambulatory health care services	3.12	0.27	1.54	0.82	0.49
Hospitals and Nursing and residential care	2.89	0.31	1.03	1.70	−0.14
Social assistance	3.30	0.09	1.83	1.75	−0.36
Performing arts, spectator sports, museums, and related activities	2.84	0.18	0.37	0.88	1.41
Amusements, gambling, and recreation industries	1.85	0.74	0.43	1.19	−0.51
Accommodation	1.67	0.86	0.18	0.79	−0.15
Food services and drinking places	2.10	0.06	0.65	1.16	0.24
Other services, except government	0.74	0.31	0.36	0.94	−0.87
Federal	1.18	0.32	0.04	0.72	0.09
State and local	1.61	0.48	0.48	0.60	0.04

Note: Average annual percentage growth. A contribution is a share-weighted growth rate.

Table 6.3 **Difference after and before redefinitions sources of growth, 1997–2019**

	Output Growth	Capital Contribution	Labor Contribution	Intermediate Contribution	TFP Growth
Farms	0.00	0.00	0.00	0.00	0.00
Forestry, fishing, and related activities	0.07	−0.07	0.00	0.09	0.06
Oil and gas extraction	−0.29	−0.17	−0.37	0.08	0.17
Mining, except oil and gas	−0.55	−0.24	−0.24	−0.08	0.01
Support activities for mining	1.16	0.60	0.66	−0.28	0.17
Utilities	−0.03	−0.11	0.03	0.00	0.06
Construction	−0.08	−0.06	0.00	−0.04	0.02
Wood products	−0.01	0.02	−0.01	0.00	−0.02
Nonmetallic mineral products	−0.04	0.00	0.00	−0.02	−0.02
Primary metals	0.00	0.00	0.01	−0.01	0.00
Fabricated metal products	0.01	−0.02	0.03	−0.01	0.01
Machinery	−0.04	−0.05	0.00	−0.02	0.03
Computer and electronic products	0.29	0.07	0.01	−0.33	0.54
Electrical equipment, appliances, and components	−0.07	−0.03	0.03	−0.04	−0.03
Motor vehicles, bodies and trailers, and parts	0.06	−0.01	0.01	0.04	0.01
Other transportation equipment	0.12	0.04	0.13	0.00	−0.05
Furniture and related products	−0.03	−0.03	0.01	−0.02	0.01
Miscellaneous manufacturing	−0.25	−0.06	−0.10	−0.14	0.06
Food and beverage and tobacco products	−0.02	0.01	−0.01	−0.01	−0.02
Textile mills and textile product mills	−0.03	0.03	−0.01	−0.06	0.01
Apparel and leather and allied products	0.32	−0.08	0.48	−0.22	0.14
Paper products	0.01	−0.01	0.01	0.00	0.00
Printing and related support activities	0.18	0.19	0.01	0.02	−0.04
Petroleum and coal products	0.00	−0.04	0.02	0.00	0.02
Chemical products	−0.17	0.06	−0.11	−0.07	−0.05
Plastics and rubber products	−0.02	−0.02	0.00	−0.01	0.01
Wholesale trade	0.03	−0.03	−0.08	0.00	0.14
Retail trade	0.25	0.00	−0.02	0.07	0.20
Air transportation	0.01	0.01	0.03	−0.01	−0.03
Rail transportation	0.06	0.07	0.02	0.01	−0.04
Water transportation	−0.11	0.02	−0.09	0.02	−0.05
Truck transportation	0.00	0.01	0.01	0.02	−0.04
Transit and ground passenger transportation	0.04	0.02	0.03	0.00	−0.02
Pipeline transportation	0.31	1.15	−0.32	0.10	−0.62
Other transportation and support activities	0.10	0.03	0.06	−0.03	0.04
Warehousing and storage	0.00	0.04	−0.02	−0.09	0.08
Publishing industries, except internet (includes software)	−0.32	−0.11	−0.09	−0.13	0.00

(*continued*)

Table 6.3 **(cont.)**

	Output Growth	Capital Contribution	Labor Contribution	Intermediate Contribution	TFP Growth
Motion picture and sound recording industries	−0.07	−0.01	−0.06	−0.01	0.01
Broadcasting and telecommunications	0.05	−0.04	0.00	0.03	0.05
Data processing, internet publishing, and other information services	−0.62	−1.13	−0.68	−0.28	1.47
Federal Reserve banks, credit intermediation, and related activities	−0.02	0.01	−0.01	0.00	−0.02
Securities, commodity contracts, and investments	0.00	0.01	0.00	0.00	−0.02
Insurance carriers and related activities	−0.01	0.01	−0.02	0.01	−0.01
Funds, trusts, and other financial vehicles	−0.26	−0.02	−0.06	−0.32	0.14
Real estate	0.08	0.06	0.00	0.01	0.01
Rental and leasing services and lessors of intangible assets	−0.06	−0.42	−0.08	−0.07	0.52
Legal services	0.00	0.01	0.00	0.00	−0.01
Computer systems design and related services	0.27	0.17	0.15	−0.12	0.07
Miscellaneous professional, scientific, and technical services	−0.06	−0.14	−0.36	−0.01	0.45
Management of companies and enterprises	−0.05	0.00	−0.03	0.04	−0.06
Administrative and support services	−0.05	−0.04	−0.03	0.01	0.01
Waste management and remediation services	0.00	0.00	0.00	0.00	−0.01
Educational services	−0.33	−0.28	0.05	0.03	−0.12
Ambulatory health care services	0.01	0.01	0.02	−0.01	−0.02
Hospitals and Nursing and residential care	−0.04	−0.02	−0.03	0.01	−0.01
Social assistance	0.01	−0.05	0.02	0.01	0.03
Performing arts, spectator sports, museums, and related activities	−0.04	0.03	0.17	0.12	−0.36
Amusements, gambling, and recreation industries	0.49	−0.57	0.58	−0.03	0.51
Accommodation	0.09	0.66	−0.34	−0.03	−0.21
Food services and drinking places	−0.04	0.32	−0.11	−0.06	−0.19
Other services, except government	−0.31	−0.16	−0.01	−0.12	−0.02
Federal	0.00	0.00	0.00	0.00	0.00
State and local	0.00	0.00	0.00	0.00	0.00

Note: Average annual percentage growth. A contribution is a share-weighted growth rate.

Interestingly, the miscellaneous professional, scientific, and technical services industry (the industry that produces R&D for sale) has significantly higher TFP growth after redefinitions; its measured productivity growth was slightly negative before redefinitions and slightly positive after redefinitions. Table 6.3 shows how this works out from an accounting perspective; this was mostly driven by differences in the labor contribution which was significantly lower after redefinitions. In practice what happens is that over the entire period about 20 percent more output is added to the sector each in each year. But the underlying data indicates that the industries that produce this output became more intensive in intermediate inputs over time relative to the labor and capital inputs that were also being reallocated to this sector. Once the linked prices are applied to this new composition of inputs, the resulting TFP growth is higher in the after redefinition industry. Regardless of the accounting explanation of the result, the basic premise is that the after redefinition estimate reflects something fundamentally different than the estimate before redefinition. The after redefinition estimate more closely captures the commodity concept of R&D while the before redefinition concept is aimed at measuring R&D production that is primarily for sale on the market. Of course, the differences in the TFP growth estimates reflect both these different concepts and the economic assumption that were used to translate between the two concepts.

Other industries where TFP growth was noticeably higher using the after redefinitions production account were the data processing, internet publishing, and other information services industry; rental and leasing services and lessors of intangible assets; and amusements, gambling, and recreation industries. Industries where TFP growth was noticeably lower using the after redefinitions production account include the pipeline transportation industry; performing arts, spectator sports, museums, and related activities; accommodation; and the food services and drinking places sector. Figure 6.1 shows that the TFP growth measured before and after redefinitions did not change the basic trends for most industries. Figure 6.2 shows how translating between the before redefinition production account and the after redefinition production account impacts TFP measures for each sector. The takeaway is that only for a few sectors did the long-term trend in TFP get impacted by the translation. Yet, for certain industries, the difference may be large enough to affect our understanding of industry trends.

Finally, the results show that there is not a major difference in the productivity slowdown in computer and electronic products sector using after redefinition concept even though R&D and own account software became a large share of industry output over the period. After redefinitions, TFP grew by about 8.8 percent per year from 1997 to 2007 and by about 3.5 percent per year from 2009 to 2019. This deceleration of about 4.8 percent per year is very similar to the TFP deceleration in measured TFP growth before redefinitions of 5.0 percent per year over the same periods. Results for the other sectors are given in table 6.4.

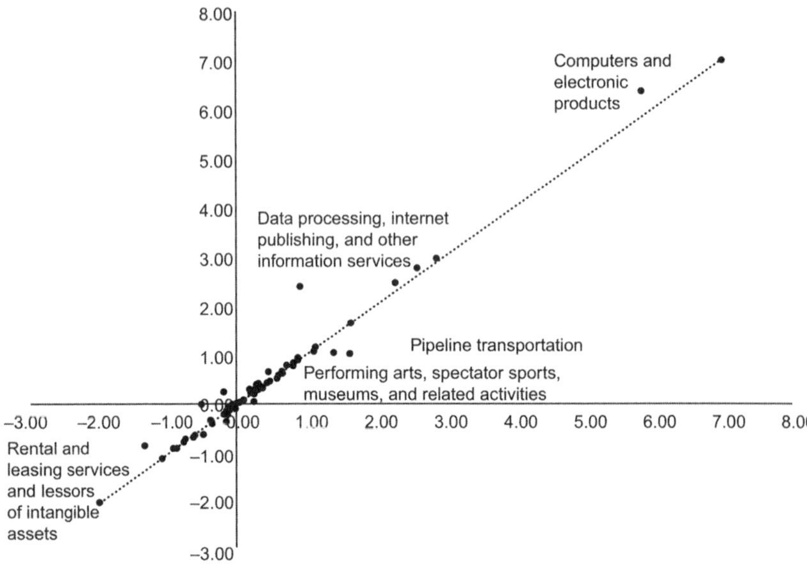

Fig. 6.1 TFP growth after redefinitions v. before redefinitions, 1997–2019

6.3.2 Aggregate Sources of Growth Adjusting for Secondary Production

This section compares the aggregate sources of growth using the after redefinition concept to the existing measures that are based on the before redefinition concept. Table 6.5 shows that within major sectors the most noticeable difference is the shift in the contribution and share of other services in growth, though even this is relatively small. The share of nominal GDP that is attributed to other services is somewhat higher after redefinitions. The bottom portion of the table also shows that both manufacturing and trade are smaller after redefinitions while construction is larger.

Table 6.6 shows that aggregate TFP growth is measured to be slightly higher over the 1997–2019 period using the after redefinition production account. Since aggregate nominal GDP, capital, and labor are unchanged between the two concepts, this result reflects the prices applied to the detailed components of capital and labor that are linked to their primary industries and the composition of intermediate inputs after redefinition.[6] The largest contributor to the aggregate TFP difference is the other services industry which likely reflects its higher nominal weight in the after redefinitions production account. Overall, the contributions of both capital and labor to aggregate value-added growth are slightly smaller in the after redefinitions production account, but these differences are not large enough to change the basic story on the sources of economic growth.

6. The concept of aggregate productivity in this paper is based on the direct (Domar-weighted) aggregation of TFP growth across industries.

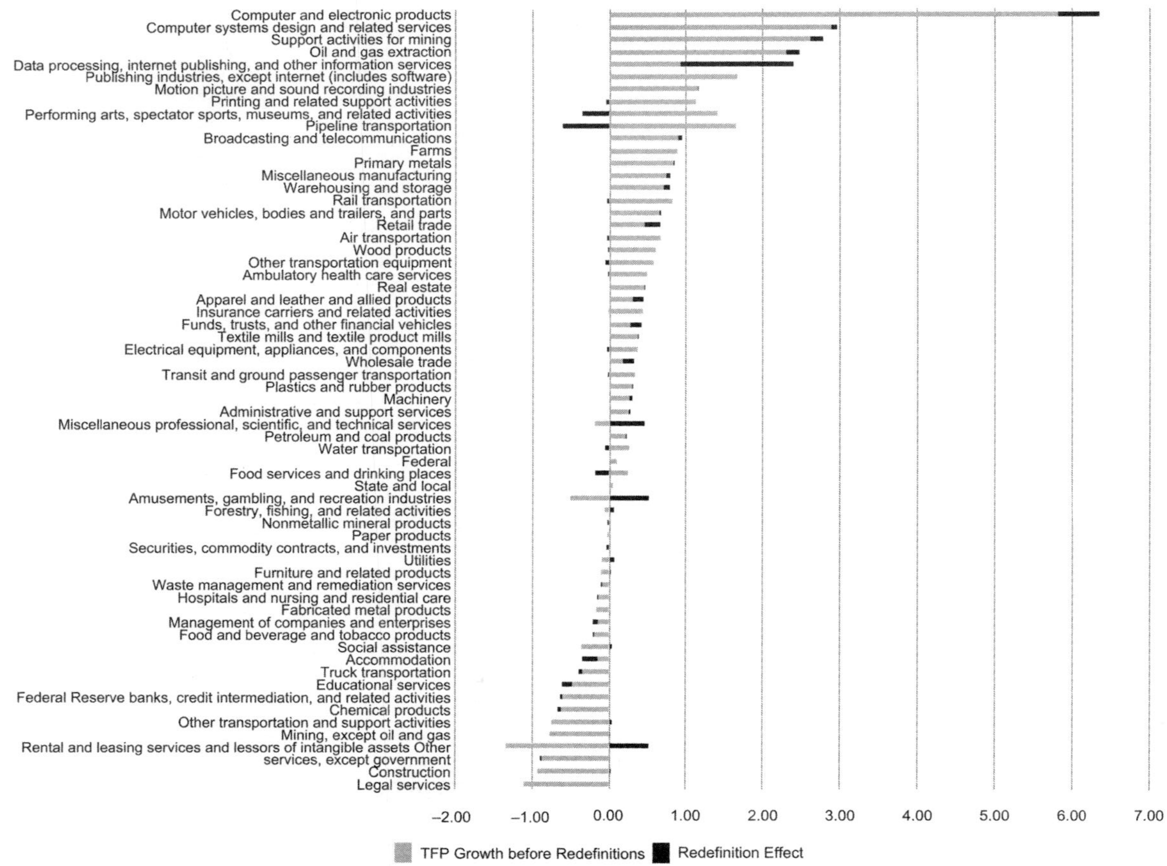

Fig. 6.2 TFP growth after redefinitions, 1997–2019

Table 6.4 **Differences in TFP growth by subperiod, 1997–2019**

	Before Redefinitions			After Redefinitions			
	1997–2007	2009–2019	Difference	1997–2007	2009–2019	Difference	Difference-in-Difference
Farms	0.65	0.49	−0.17	0.65	0.49	−0.17	0.00
Forestry, fishing, and related activities	0.37	−0.77	−1.14	0.49	−0.72	−1.21	−0.07
Oil and gas extraction	0.30	3.05	2.75	−0.15	3.61	3.76	1.00
Mining, except oil and gas	0.75	−1.48	−2.23	0.38	−0.92	−1.30	0.93
Support activities for mining	6.21	0.50	−5.71	6.57	0.45	−6.13	−0.41
Utilities	−0.03	0.08	0.11	0.07	0.12	0.05	−0.06
Construction	−1.28	−0.50	0.78	−1.22	−0.47	0.75	−0.03
Wood products	0.55	0.55	0.01	0.59	0.45	−0.14	−0.15
Nonmetallic mineral products	−0.22	0.79	1.01	−0.22	0.73	0.95	−0.06
Primary metals	0.72	0.88	0.15	0.70	0.87	0.17	0.02
Fabricated metal products	0.33	0.11	−0.22	0.35	0.11	−0.23	−0.01
Machinery	1.02	−0.04	−1.06	1.05	0.00	−1.05	0.01
Computer and electronic products	8.28	3.50	−4.78	8.88	3.92	−4.96	−0.18
Electrical equipment, appliances, and components	0.73	0.21	−0.52	0.69	0.21	−0.48	0.03
Motor vehicles, bodies and trailers, and parts	1.30	1.57	0.27	1.30	1.53	0.23	−0.04
Other transportation equipment	0.98	0.54	−0.44	0.85	0.60	−0.25	0.19
Furniture and related products	0.13	0.49	0.36	0.15	0.39	0.24	−0.12
Miscellaneous manufacturing	1.42	−0.26	−1.67	1.44	−0.07	−1.52	0.16
Food and beverage and tobacco products	0.19	−0.52	−0.71	0.18	−0.49	−0.67	0.04
Textile mills and textile product mills	1.03	0.11	−0.91	1.04	0.09	−0.95	−0.04
Apparel and leather and allied products	0.15	0.46	0.31	0.29	0.52	0.23	−0.07
Paper products	0.20	−0.34	−0.54	0.20	−0.33	−0.52	0.02
Printing and related support activities	1.78	0.83	−0.95	1.69	0.82	−0.87	0.08
Petroleum and coal products	1.06	−0.50	−1.55	1.05	−0.50	−1.55	0.00
Chemical products	0.32	−1.04	−1.36	0.28	−1.06	−1.34	0.02
Plastics and rubber products	0.68	0.01	−0.67	0.70	0.04	−0.66	0.01
Wholesale trade	0.81	0.16	−0.64	1.15	0.12	−1.03	−0.39
Retail trade	0.72	0.60	−0.12	0.95	0.73	−0.22	−0.10
Air transportation	−0.17	1.60	1.78	−0.21	1.59	1.80	0.03

Rail transportation	1.85	0.18	−1.66	1.78	0.16	−1.62	0.05
Water transportation	0.78	−1.32	−2.10	0.73	−1.44	−2.18	−0.07
Truck transportation	−0.30	−0.23	0.07	−0.33	−0.31	0.02	−0.05
Transit and ground passenger transportation	0.33	0.62	0.29	0.32	0.60	0.28	−0.01
Pipeline transportation	1.16	2.75	1.59	0.49	2.07	1.59	0.00
Other transportation and support activities	0.68	−2.12	−2.80	0.61	−1.93	−2.54	0.26
Warehousing and storage	1.04	0.42	−0.62	1.08	0.61	−0.47	0.15
Publishing industries, except internet (includes software)	1.26	2.84	1.58	1.18	2.95	1.77	0.18
Motion picture and sound recording industries	2.33	−0.71	−3.04	2.30	−0.67	−2.97	0.07
Broadcasting and telecommunications	1.67	0.41	−1.26	1.69	0.48	−1.21	0.05
Data processing, internet publishing, and other information services	0.74	−0.15	−0.88	3.16	0.57	−2.58	−1.70
Federal Reserve banks, credit intermediation, and related activities	−0.28	−1.92	−1.64	−0.28	−1.96	−1.68	−0.04
Securities, commodity contracts, and investments	0.13	−0.95	−1.09	0.13	−0.99	−1.12	−0.04
Insurance carriers and related activities	0.73	0.93	0.20	0.72	0.92	0.20	0.00
Funds, trusts, and other financial vehicles	0.78	0.75	−0.03	0.89	0.94	0.05	0.08
Real estate	−0.02	0.96	0.98	0.00	0.97	0.97	−0.02
Rental and leasing services and lessors of intangible assets	−3.33	0.83	4.16	−2.36	0.88	3.24	−0.93
Legal services	−0.53	−1.03	−0.49	−0.55	−1.03	−0.48	0.01
Computer systems design and related services	2.35	3.51	1.15	2.93	3.34	0.42	−0.74
Miscellaneous professional, scientific, and technical services	−0.95	0.40	1.34	−0.06	0.54	0.60	−0.74
Management of companies and enterprises	−1.31	1.90	3.21	−1.45	1.88	3.33	0.12
Administrative and support services	0.51	0.00	−0.51	0.50	0.02	−0.48	0.03
Waste management and remediation services	0.06	−0.32	−0.38	0.06	−0.33	−0.39	0.00
Educational services	−0.46	−1.10	−0.64	−0.70	−1.00	−0.30	0.34
Ambulatory health care services	0.54	0.22	−0.32	0.52	0.22	−0.31	0.01
Hospitals and Nursing and residential care	−0.06	−0.66	−0.60	−0.05	−0.66	−0.61	−0.01
Social assistance	−0.30	−0.47	−0.17	−0.32	−0.35	−0.03	0.14
Performing arts, spectator sports, museums, and related activities	1.33	1.12	−0.21	0.87	0.91	0.04	0.25
Amusements, gambling, and recreation industries	−0.92	0.15	1.06	−0.34	0.67	1.00	−0.06
Accommodation	−0.16	0.92	1.07	−0.25	0.48	0.73	−0.35
Food services and drinking places	0.80	0.13	−0.67	0.57	0.06	−0.50	0.17
Other services, except government	−1.17	−0.28	0.90	−1.08	−0.31	0.77	−0.13
Federal	0.26	0.05	−0.21	0.26	0.05	−0.21	0.00
State and local	0.13	0.06	−0.07	0.13	0.06	−0.07	0.00

Note: Average annual percentage growth. A contribution is a share-weighted growth rate.

Table 6.5 Sector sources of value added growth, 1997–2019

	After Redefinition	Before Redefinition
Contributions		
Value Added	2.19	2.20
Agriculture, Forestry, Fishing, Hunting, Mining	0.08	0.09
Transportation, Warehousing, Utilities	0.06	0.06
Construction	−0.02	−0.01
Manufacturing	0.25	0.26
Computer and electronic products	0.18	0.19
Trade	0.26	0.26
Information	0.25	0.27
Finance, Insurance, Real Estate, Rental and Leasing	0.48	0.47
Other Services	0.64	0.61
Government	0.19	0.19
Shares		
Shares in Nominal Value Added	100.0	100.0
Agriculture, Forestry, Fishing, Hunting, Mining	2.4	2.5
Transportation, Warehousing, Utilities	4.4	4.5
Construction	4.5	4.0
Manufacturing	11.1	12.1
Computer and electronic products	1.3	1.5
Trade	10.8	11.5
Information	4.4	4.7
Finance, Insurance, Real Estate, Rental and Leasing	19.0	19.1
Other Services	26.7	24.6
Government	16.7	16.8

Note: Average annual percentage growth. A contribution is a share-weighted growth rate.

6.4 Conclusions

There are some noteworthy differences in measured TFP growth across industries when the production account is adjusted to reallocate secondary production. Measured TFP growth of computers and electronic products and data processing, internet publishing, and other information services is significantly higher once secondary production is moved out of these industries. Because these industries are of particular focus in understanding the role of the information economy, it is worth considering these differences when analyzing the sources of economic growth. It is also noteworthy that in aggregate, the manufacturing share of GDP is somewhat smaller once non-manufacturing output produced by the manufacturing sector is moved out of manufacturing.

On the other hand, the approach to accounting for secondary production that is considered in this paper does not change major trends in estimated TFP growth over the 1997–2019 period. Therefore, it is unlikely that this adjustment would matter much for understanding the sources of economic

Table 6.6 Sector sources of value added growth, 1997–2019

	After Redefinition	Before Redefinition
Contribution		
Capital	1.15	1.18
Agriculture, Forestry, Fishing, Hunting, Mining	0.01	0.01
Transportation, Warehousing, Utilities	0.04	0.04
Construction	0.02	0.02
Manufacturing	0.11	0.11
Computer and electronic products	0.02	0.02
Trade	0.15	0.17
Information	0.17	0.19
Finance, Insurance, Real Estate, Rental and Leasing	0.36	0.36
Other Services	0.18	0.18
Government	0.10	0.10
Labor	0.57	0.60
Agriculture, Forestry, Fishing, Hunting, Mining	0.01	0.01
Transportation, Warehousing, Utilities	0.02	0.02
Construction	0.04	0.04
Manufacturing	−0.08	−0.08
Computer and electronic products	−0.02	−0.02
Trade	0.02	0.03
Information	−0.01	0.00
Finance, Insurance, Real Estate, Rental and Leasing	0.07	0.07
Other Services	0.42	0.42
Government	0.08	0.08
TFP	0.48	0.42
Agriculture, Forestry, Fishing, Hunting, Mining	0.07	0.07
Transportation, Warehousing, Utilities	0.00	0.00
Construction	−0.08	−0.08
Manufacturing	0.22	0.22
Computer and electronic products	0.19	0.19
Trade	0.08	0.06
Information	0.10	0.09
Finance, Insurance, Real Estate, Rental and Leasing	0.05	0.04
Other Services	0.04	0.01
Government	0.01	0.01

Note: Average annual percentage growth. A contribution is a share-weighted growth rate.

growth or international economic competitiveness. Nevertheless, it cannot be ruled out that a longer time series of after redefinition TFP measures using the method considered in this paper may have a more noteworthy impact on measured TFP growth, or that the application of different assumptions that refine the translation of outputs and inputs between industries may yield different estimates and a different conclusion.

Acknowledgments

The views expressed in this paper are those of the authors and do not necessarily represent the US Bureau of Economic Analysis or the US Department of Commerce. I am grateful to Michael Cortez of BEA for excellent research assistance and Connor Franks of BEA for his help in assembling the after redefinition output and intermediate input data. I thank John Fernald for his discussion of this paper at the March 2022 Conference on Research in Income and Wealth and Tom Howells for valuable comments. For acknowledgments, sources of research support, and disclosure of the author's material financial relationships, if any, please see https://www.nber.org/books-and-chapters/technology-productivity-and-economic-growth/after-redefinition-tfp-accounting.

References

Basu, S., J. Fernald, J. Fisher, and M. Kimball. 2013. "Sector-Specific Technical Change." Manuscript, Federal Reserve Bank of San Francisco.

Byrne, D., J. Fernald, and M. Reinsdorf. 2016. "Does the United States Have a Productivity Slowdown or a Measurement Problem?" *Brookings Papers on Economic Activity* 1: 109–182.

Garner, C., J. Harper, M. Russell, and J. Samuels. 2020. "Integrated Industry-Level Production Account for the United States and the Sources of U.S. Economic Growth Between 1987 and 2018." *Survey of Current Business* 100 (4).

Horowitz, K. J., and M. A. Planting. 2006. *Concepts and Methods of the U.S. Input-Output Accounts*. U.S. Department of Commerce.

Jorgenson, D., and Z. Griliches. 1967. "The Explanation of Productivity Change." *Review of Economic Studies* 34 (3): 249–83.

Jorgenson, D., M. Ho, and K. Stiroh. 2005. *Information Technology and the American Growth Resurgence*. MIT Press.

Jorgenson, D., K. Nomura, and J. Samuels. 2016. "A Half Century of Trans-Pacific Competition: Price Level Indices and Productivity Gaps for Japanese and U.S. Industries." In *The World Economy, Growth or Stagnation? edited by* D. Jorgenson, K. Fukao, and M. Timmer. Cambridge University Press.

Jorgenson, D., K. Nomura, and J. Samuels. 2018. "Progress on Measuring the Industry Origins of the Japan-U.S. Productivity Gap." Unpublished Manuscript.

Raa, T., and E. N. Wolff. 1991. "Secondary Products and the Measurement of Productivity Growth." *Regional Science and Urban Economics* 21 (4): 581–615.

Samuels, J., and E. Strassner. 2019. "Toward a Global Integrated Industry-Level Production Account: A Proposal." *International Productivity Monitor* 36: 7–33.

7

Data, Intangible Capital, and Productivity

Carol Corrado, Jonathan Haskel, Massimiliano Iommi, Cecilia Jona-Lasinio, and Filippo Bontadini

7.1 Introduction

A defining aspect of the digital age is the use of data, specifically large stores of digitized information referred to as "big data." Much popular work on big data appears in the business strategy literature. By a very long way, the best-selling book on the subject is *Big Data: A Revolution That Will Transform How We Live, Work, and Think*, by Mayer-Schönberger and Cukier (2013). The book makes several statistical claims, suggesting that data will be used to disprove much casually held causal intuition and reduce many measurement problems—in line with those who believe in the transformational promise of digital tools that adjust themselves to perform better as they are exposed to more and more data (e.g., Brynjolfsson and McAfee 2014) and assertions in the press that data are the new oil (e.g., *Economist* 2017).

These statements—some from a decade ago—would imply that data have had significant impacts on economic activity. But has it? Economic growth has slowed globally, and business productivity performance has been subpar. Though it is frequently suggested that business users face high adjustment costs in deploying the modern digital tools needed to derive knowledge from data, the very purpose of modern software and computing systems hosted in

Carol Corrado is a senior policy scholar at the Center for Business and Public Policy at the McDonough School of Business at Georgetown University.

Jonathan Haskel is a professor of economics at Imperial College Business School, Imperial College London, and an External Member of the Monetary Policy Committee at the Bank of England.

Massimiliano Iommi is a senior researcher at the Italian National Statistical Institute (ISTAT), and a research fellow at the Luiss Lab of European Economics.

Cecilia Jona-Lasinio is a professor of applied economics at Luiss Business School in Rome.

Filippo Bontadini is an assistant professor of applied economics at LUISS University.

the cloud is to reduce technical barriers to user engagement in data analysis. As it seems unlikely that there has been a failure in the inherent productivity of artificial intelligence (AI) and cloud-based technologies, this paper looks to the character of knowledge gained through data as a contributor to the slowdown in productivity growth.

Data is conceptualized as an intangible asset in this paper: a storable, nonrival (yet excludable) factor input that is only partially captured in existing macroeconomic and financial statistics. The paper introduces a framework for capturing asset creation based on the processing and transformation of digitized information into usable knowledge in an economy. This knowledge is referred to as "data capital," and the framework we introduced is amenable to measurement and quantitative analysis.

The first part of this paper (sections 7.2 through 7.4) addresses how the increased use of data affects intangible capital conceptually and empirically. New estimates of investment in data and data capital are developed and analyzed in relation to intangible capital. The second part of the paper (sections 7.5 through 7.7) models how data capital, innovation, and productivity are related and includes an analysis of how data capital affects intangible asset prices and potential labor productivity growth. An eighth section concludes.

This paper makes, we believe, three contributions. The first is its development and analysis of industry-level estimates of data capital consistent with concepts used by management strategists and technologists. We find that data assets, from stores of raw data to actionable intelligence derived via data analytic tools, are largely subsumed within intangible capital. A second contribution is the paper's modeling of the economic impacts of data capital, which finds that the efficiencies associated with modern data capital lowers intangible asset prices and strengthens the (partial) appropriability of the asset class. Third, the paper frames the likely macroeconomic impacts of these developments, using the recently issued EUKLEMS & INTANProd database (LLEE 2023). A feature of this database relative to its predecessors is that it includes estimates of intangible investment consistent with the intangible capital framework attributable to Corrado, Hulten, and Sichel (2005, 2009) for all European Union countries, Japan, the United Kingdom, and the United States.

The paper finds that that the increased data intensity of intangible capital boosts its productive efficiency and thereby labor productivity growth by as much as one-quarter percentage point per year currently and potentially more in the future. At the same time, the increased role of proprietary big data in production processes for intangible assets renders the asset class more appropriable. This implies fewer productivity spillovers to investments in intangible assets and slower growth in total factor productivity (TFP). All told we estimate that the appropriability effect has, so far, more than offset the efficiency effect and that the rise of modern data capital has contributed to the recent slowdown in productivity growth.

7.1.1 Relation to Recent Literature

Recent literature has advanced many models that focus on economic mechanisms affected by data and intangibles. How does our approach relate to these models?

At the micro level, data assets are usually assumed to have diminishing returns, e.g., Varian (2019) points out that there are diminishing returns to more and more training data fed to artificial intelligence (AI) algorithms. Jones and Tonetti (2020) formulate a model of an economy in which big data are an intermediate input with diminishing returns and analyze the welfare consequences of data and data sharing. Despite treating data as an intermediate (versus as an asset as we do in this paper), the Jones and Tonetti (2020) welfare analysis remains relevant. Their model, like ours, is based on the observation that firms hoard proprietary data for their own use and that this behavior stanches the reuse of data as a nonrival good, which is socially inefficient. The analysis of Arrieta-Ibarra et al. (2018) also focuses on the inefficiency of current data use in economies, highlighting the monopsony position of firms collecting consumer data and arguing that this depresses the value of personal data and the potential for productivity gains from its use.

Most descriptive models of data in the economics literature assume diminishing returns to data assets but also show how they can co-exist with firm-level cost advantages due to the scale effects in data-dependent production processes. This is the gist of *the Economist* (2017) article, which emphasized how data enable retail and social media giants to expand their customer base by exploiting network effects. *The Economist* also speculated that data hampers "creative destruction," noting that data enable giant firms to utilize surveillance systems to "see" when a new product or service gains traction and take action to avoid being blindsided by competition from new entrants (e.g., Facebook's acquisition of WhatsApp).

Business and management scholars frequently emphasize scale and scope economies created by data in business activities such as marketing, distribution, and after-market services. It should be noted, however, that there is little economy-level evidence for these effects. In fact, an econometric study of the global advertising and marketing services business found that scale efficiencies did not arise during the 1990's era of globalization (Silk and Berndt 2003).

The combined impact of scale and scope economies created by the use of big data, whether data-induced scale efficiencies in production processes or network externalities induced on the demand side, will manifest as a rise in market power if data assets (and intangibles in general) are not accounted for in competition indicators such as rates of returns, price markups, or productivity dispersion. Virtually all studies finding a rise in market power in recent decades (e.g., as reviewed in the IMF's April 2019 *World Economic*

Outlook, IMF 2019) rely on firm-level data sets that exclude or improperly account for intangibles. Official macrodata currently account for a portion of total intangible assets, and evidence using official macrodata to investigate whether markups are rising is less dispositive (Basu 2019). In fact, aggregate data adjusted to include all Corrado, Hulten, and Sichel (2005, 2009) intangibles suggest that abnormal rents have not, in fact, accrued to US private industries as a whole (see Corrado, Haskel, Jona-Lasinio, and Iommi 2022, figure 4 and its discussion).

But industry concentration measures have risen, and many attribute this to scale economies of intangible assets at the firm level (e.g., Haskel and Westlake 2018; Crouzet and Eberly 2019; De Ridder 2019). Economies due to data-driven intangible capital also could be driving the widening of within-industry productivity dispersion documented in Andrews, Criscuolo, and Gal (2016), and a study addressing whether the increase in within-industry productivity dispersion since 2000 can be attributed to intangibles found that it could (Corrado, Criscuolo, Haskel, Himbert, and Jona-Lasinio 2021). While this evidence was stronger at large firms, strictly speaking, economies of scale were not detected. Dispersion was rather explained by financial barriers to the accumulation of intangible assets—which affect some firms more than others—and by the complementarity of intangibles with expenditures on digitization.

Where does this leave us? First, the intangible capital framework is consistent with the welfare-enhancing processes of data sharing as theorized by Jones and Tonetti in that (a) data assets have diminishing returns in production, but (b) returns to data assets will only spill over to other firms to the extent data can be copied or shared within an industry or economy. Second, increased productivity dispersion between "leaders" and "laggards" hints at how *average* productivity growth in an economy can slow at the same time as innovative, competitive firms amass big data: a breakdown in the diffusion of data-derived knowledge from the leaders to the laggards. In this paper we suggest that productivity spillovers to intangible capital have in fact weakened as production processes—notably, production processes for intangible assets—have become dependent on proprietary big data.

In related work, Akcigit and Ates (2021) attribute slow productivity growth and declining business dynamism to a breakdown in knowledge diffusion. They give four reasons for this breakdown, three of which are supported by their R&D-inspired models of innovation and analysis of developments in patent protection by large firms. Their fourth reason for a breakdown in knowledge diffusion is attributed to the rise of proprietary big data used by productivity "leaders." Akcigit and Ates do not offer direct empirical support this proposition, but we believe the that the evidence advanced in this paper, combined with our previously mentioned microdata-based work on the determinants of productivity dispersion, provide a solid base of evidence for this view.

7.1.2 Rise of Proprietary Big Data

As background for the arguments that we develop in this paper, consider first some examples of exclusive (or rival) versus nonrival uses of data in modern economies. Though data are inherently nonrival, the degree to which owners share data with the public or other organizations in an industry (or the economy) depends upon both context and competitive factors, as illustrated by the range of examples listed in table 7.1.

The examples given on lines 1–5 of the table mainly reflect applications of big data using new digital technologies by firms, i.e., digital platform-based businesses and/or machine learning and other AI-based algorithms applied to massive data. Product-led growth strategies (line 6) refers to marketing innovations based on user feedback data (also enabled by new technologies). Customer lists and after-sales customer feedback data long have been inputs to brand development and the design of marketing and customer retention strategies (line 7) and are emerging as fertile ground for application of data technologies.

Examples of "nonrival" data use range from marketers of personal data for companies (line 8), to longer-standing examples of industry-level data sharing, e.g., financial records held by credit bureaus and shared across financial institutions (line 9), vehicle accident and major repair records shared by buyers and sellers in used car markets (line 10), personal medical records shared by medical care services providers (line 11), to newer cross-platform and cross-purpose uses (lines 12 and 13).

Table 7.1 Examples of data use

Rival
1. Product-level forecasting (e.g., Amazon)
2. A/B Internet testing and marketing (e.g., Google)
3. IoT factory systems (e.g., Siemens)
4. Targeted advertising on consumer content platforms
5. Fintech (e.g., algorithmic trading, digital lending, etc.)
6. Product-led growth strategies (e.g., Slack)
7. Customer lists/after sales services design
Nonrival
8. DaaS (Data as a Service) platforms (e.g., BDEX)
9. Financial records (FICO scores)
10. Vehicle records (CARFAX reports)
11. Personal medical records (across service providers)
12. Open-source data generated by web users (traffic patterns)
13. Private by-product data put to alternative uses (e.g., Zillow data used for economic research)
14. Genomic and other public biomedical research data
15. Official statistics (economic, demographic, social)

Note: Data are inherently nonrival. The grouping of examples in the table reflects the degree to which data owners share their data assets with other organizations or the public.

Finally, the table lists some examples of government open data. Governments generate rather vast stores of information and are working to make the data they collect more "open," i.e., freely available for anyone to download, modify, and distribute without legal or financial restriction. This suggests that government statistics are a public good externality—and possibly productivity enhancing. The UK Open Data Institute (ODI) estimates that the use of "core" public open data alone—data such as addresses, maps, weather, and land and property ownership records—currently contributes an additional 0.5 percent of the country's GDP in economic value every year (ODI 2016). A review of estimates and surveys of the value of US government data in business decision-making concluded that (a) the value of government data is increasing, and that (b) while companies are generating ever-increasing amounts of big data from their own operations, the combination of proprietary data with comprehensive government data often creates more strategic benefit (Hughes-Cromwick and Coronado 2019).

These examples suggest that while data have much potential for use and economic benefit when shared, many applications of big data involve proprietary use. Data-dependent business models are on the rise (Nguyen and Paczos 2020), as are regulations to protect consumer privacy, e.g., the General Data Protection Regulation (GDPR) in the European Union and the US equivalent, California Consumer Privacy Act (CCPA). These regulations limit third-party sales, even though certain cross-purpose uses of data (e.g., lifestyle data collected by marketers used in precision medicine solutions) have the potential to affect the pace of innovation. Conversely, policy interventions can facilitate data sharing and competitive entry, e.g., the data sharing environments facilitated by open banking policies in the United Kingdom and other countries.[1]

All told, the foregoing suggests that a conceptual framework for measuring and analyzing data needs to account for the fact that: (a) data are nonrival and capable of improving economic welfare when shared or replicated at low cost; but that (b) data, though nonrival, are frequently used exclusively.

7.2 A Framework for Data Value Creation

7.2.1 The Data Stack

Many economic models of data focus on data as a "free" by-product of economic activity, and observers focus on certain special features of data, such as how rapidly they accumulate. Data, in the sense of raw digitized records, may of course accumulate at an astonishing pace and be stored at

1. Open banking refers to a data sharing environment in which financial intermediaries—both incumbents and fintech entrants—can compete for customers. For an analysis of the impact of open banking regulations on financial innovation globally, see Babina, Buchak, and Gornall (2022).

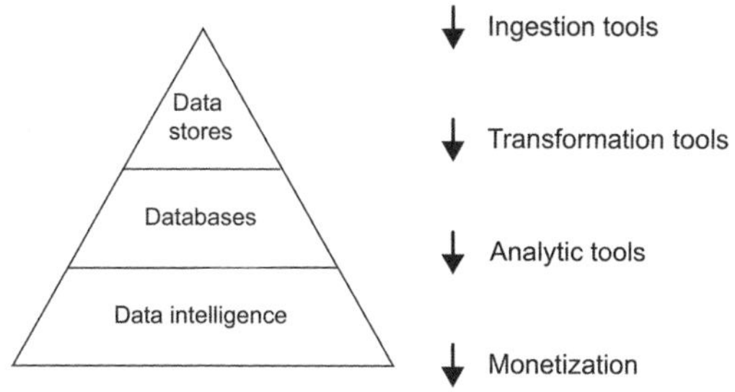

Fig. 7.1 The data asset value chain

Note: The stack to the left depicts the stages of data asset value creation based on applying layers of tools shown on the right.

little to no cost. But accumulation of raw bits and bytes does not imply that a flow of services is being provided to production processes in an economy.

Our approach to developing a framework for the analysis of data is thus based on the following observations/assumptions: (1) The accumulation of data has the potential to boost real output only when producers also invest in transforming such records into analytical insights and actionable business intelligence. (2) Knowledge-based assets gleaned from the application of data technologies to data (raw or transformed) are productive assets in an economy. (3) The appropriability of returns to these assets implies that business spending on data accumulation and transformation and on the conduct of data analytics are intangible capital investments.

Our specific approach to data value creation is illustrated in figure 7.1, which depicts a framework that embraces widely used approaches in both the technology and management literatures. Technologists characterize data according to a "data stack" that describes the transformation of raw data into usable data structures and intelligence. Business management strategists use a "value chain" construct that includes monetization, or market implementation, as a capability required for creating value from data assets.[2] Technologists usually depict a sequence of data forms and digital tools in a single pyramid (e.g., Roca 2021a). The data pyramid has deep roots in information science; it was used by Varian (2019) to depict the relationship between data, information, and knowledge in his analysis of AI.

Figure 7.1 separates data forms, i.e., types of data, from the tools used to create them. Three major types of data appear in the business-oriented data value creation literature. These types are depicted on the left in figure 7.1 and reflect the business strategists' notion of an information value chain, where greater value is produced as data is processed into usable intelligence. The digital technology tools that enable value creation from nondigitized

2. See again Mayer-Schönberger and Cukier (2013), also PriceWaterhouseCoopers LLP (2019).

records are depicted on the right. The sequence of data assets is horizontally aligned with the tools used in their formation on the left, i.e., ingestion tools are used to create data stores, etc.

The three layers of value in figure 7.1's data stack—data stores, databases, and data intelligence—correspond to an asset type amenable to measurement and analysis. The data asset types are defined as follows:

- *Data stores* are raw records that have been stored but not yet cleaned, formatted, or transformed for analysis, e.g., data scraped from the web or sensor and economic data captured from production or transactions activity. Raw records also cover the raw data collected from experiments, statistical surveys, or administrative records.
- *Databases* consist of transformed raw data, records that have been cleaned, formatted, and structured such that they are suitable for some form of data analytics or visualization.
- *Data intelligence* reflects the further integration of data with advanced analytic tools (e.g., machine learning training algorithms). Data intelligence is a set of quantitative inputs that provides actionable guidance for decision-makers and includes solutions to scientific and engineering problems.

The "modern" data stack is hosted in the cloud and, compared with legacy, on-premises data management systems, requires little technical configuration by users. According to technologists (e.g., Roca 2021b), "the modern data stack lowers the technical barrier to entry for data integration." And "components of the modern data stack are built with analysts and business users in mind, meaning that users of all backgrounds can not only easily use these tools, but also administer them without in-depth technical knowledge."

7.2.2 Data Capital as Intangible Capital

The data value chain framework, in which greater value added is created as raw data is processed and developed into insights and solutions, applies to data-driven development of engineering designs, customer platforms, and organizational practices, and data-driven R&D processes. This suggests that data assets are largely subsumed—though not explicitly identified—in measures of intangible capital covering the full range of assets. Let us then consider the definitional/conceptual overlap between the data assets in the data stack and activities covered by existing measures of intangible assets. For this we refer to the latest EUKLEMS & INTANProd database (LLEE 2023), which as previously mentioned incorporates all Corrado et al. (2005) intangible assets.

Identified intangible investment asset types are set out in table 7.2. Column 1 of the table shows that there are three major categories of intangible assets: digitized information, innovative property, and economic competen-

Table 7.2 **Intangible investment: major categories and asset types**

Categories (1)	Investment by Asset Type (2)	NA (3)	Examples of Assets and Property (4)
Digitized Information	1. Software	Yes	Digital capabilities, tools
	2. Databases	Yes	Trade secrets (data
Innovation Property	3. Research and Development (R&D)	Yes	Patents, licenses
	4. Mineral exploration	Yes	Mineral rights
	5. Artistic, entertainment, and literary originals	Yes	Copyrights, licenses
	6. Attributed designs (industrial)	No	Patents, trademarks
	7. Financial product development	No	Trademarks, software patents
Economic Competencies	8. Brand and market research	No	Brand equity, customer lists, market insights
	9. Business process and organizational practices	No	Operating models and platforms, supply chains and distribution networks, and management and employee practices
	10. Employer-provided training	No	Firm-specific human capital

Note. Column 3 indicates whether the asset type is currently included as investment in national accounts (NA). In national accounts, only databases generated by firms for their own internal use or embedded and sold as software products are included.

Source: Updated version Corrado, Hulten and Sichel (2005) as set out in Corrado (2024).

cies. Column 2 reports specific assets used to populate each major category, and column 3 reports whether the asset is covered in national accounts. As may be seen, only lines 1 through 5 are included in official measures of capital formation and GDP.

At first blush one might infer from column 1 of table 7.2 that the digitized information grouping of intangible assets includes the data stack's individual asset types, but as may be seen in the itemized list in column 2 of table 7.2, only databases appear. This implies that national accounts' estimates of the value of investment in databases exclude the cost of acquiring or ingesting the data stores they contain; in addition, as a matter of practice, outright purchases of data stores and databases are included only if they are embedded and sold as software products.

Consider now data intelligence, the most valuable, and final, stage of the data value chain per figure 7.1. This is where the utility of the intangible capital framework becomes especially apparent. The data stack pertains to all knowledge created from data, i.e., it encompasses all modern, data-driven services product development, marketing and business operations intelligence. Compared with national accounts, which may contain the software tools and databases used to produce this intelligence, intangible capital inherently contains the production of this intelligence from "soup to nuts" via, e.g., its inclusion of investments listed on lines 7, 8, and 9 of table 7.2—investments in new financial product development, marketing, and organization practices.

An increase in the use of data capital in R&D activities (line 3) will cover novel forms of data-derived scientific intelligence, including the development of new AI techniques and certain bio-engineered substances/formulas. It will exclude, however, many uses of modern data-driven engineering design that yield improved industrial production systems and business operations, solutions typically regarded as not sufficiently novel to be included in R&D. Investments in modern engineering design are covered in the intangible framework via line 6. Investments in business operations are a component of line 9, which includes outlays for the re-design of computer systems and network platforms to facilitate the ingestion and transformation of raw data.

The intangibles framework thus covers most, if not all, forms of data intelligence. Indeed, while virtually all assets in table 7.1 are potentially data driven, the intangible framework can be used to inform the development of empirical estimates of data—and especially data intelligence. Approaches that lack this perspective have missed key application areas of modern data science. For example, the Statistics Canada (2019a, b) implementation covered financial and marketing forms of data-derived intelligence but did not include engineering design and business operations.

Engineering design is generally recognized as a key factor in innovation. A meta-analysis of the joint evolution of engineering design and data science concluded that *data-driven* engineering design has become increasingly more prominent due to the developments in AI (Chiarello, Belingheri, and Fantoni 2021). The emergence of digital platforms that use big data to design cost-efficient routes/processes for manufacturing parts production is a related development (Mandel 2019).

In summary, the rise in use of data suggests that the composition of intangible investment is becoming more data intensive. This is especially true for investments in new financial products, industrial design, branding and marketing, and organizational processes, i.e., "data-intensive intangibles." Beyond this main message, key findings regarding the measurement of data capital are as follows:

- Data value creation involves the generation of data assets—data stores, databases, and data intelligence. This is in addition to the design and production of the digital tools used to create them.
- Data stores, purchased databases, and most forms of data intelligence are not currently captured in official statistics.
- Data intelligence is the most valuable, and final, stage of the data value chain as it pertains to investments in modern digital business practices and engineering design.

- Data intelligence has many forms—operations, marketing, engineering design, and scientific experimentation—and previous works have *not fully covered data intelligence* in their measurement schemes.

7.3 Measuring Data: Approaches and Methods

The economics literature has used diverse frameworks and approaches to measure the value of data. These frameworks and approaches are reviewed in Corrado, Haskel, Iommi, and Jona-Lasinio (2022a, 2022b). The reviews cover how concepts used in company financial accounts differ from national accounts and how methods used to measure data vary according to the scope, context, and economic sector of origin of the data to be valued (i.e., personal or institutional). After summarizing takeaways from these reviews, this section provides an overview of the methods and approach used to measure the value of data in this paper.

7.3.1 Takeaways from Prior Reviews

The economics literature has taken three main directions to develop estimates of the value of data. These include (1) approaches based on consumers' valuations, (2) approaches based on firm valuations and market transactions, and (3) approaches based on estimates of resource costs used to produce data assets.

The first takeaway from our prior reviews is that approaches aimed at valuing consumers' personal information will not encompass the full data value chain of figure 7.1, which includes data originating in business and government organizations. That said, because some of the largest and fastest growing tech companies are built mainly on the economics of transforming personal information into business and marketing intelligence, the valuation of personal data is viewed with keen interest. The World Economic Forum (WEF 2011) and OECD (2013) identified two broad categories of data—personal data and institutional data—based on the economic sector of origin of the information.

A "personal data" value chain can be thought of as a construct that sits within the figure 7.1 data value chain in which public open data and business-specific information also reside and contribute to value creation. Because the overall value of data in economies derives, at least in part, from the combination of personal data with institutional and public open data, the value of personal data *as an economic resource* cannot be readily disentangled from the value of other data records in an economy.

The second takeaway is that it is necessary to adopt a method that yields comprehensive coverage of data use in market activities. Ideally this implies using methods based on market prices and market valuations. Market prices paid and received in actual transactions are the best proxy for quantifying the value of data.

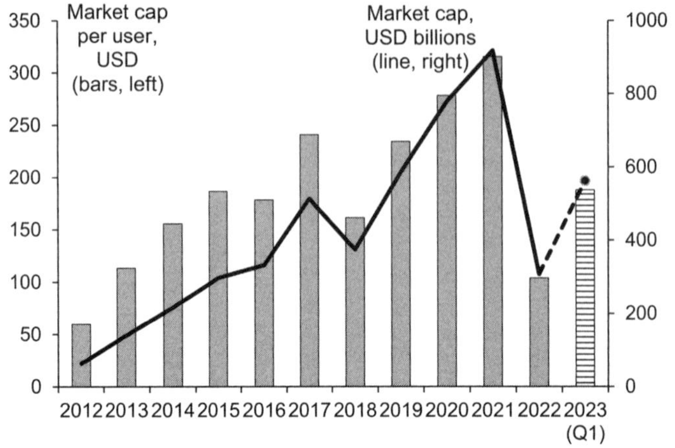

Fig. 7.2 Facebook/Meta market capitalization per active user, 2012 to 2023 (Q1)
Source: Number of Facebook monthly active users from Statistica, Q4 of each year. Market capitalization is Nasdaq value for December of each year (except as noted for 2023).

Adopting a market-based approach faces many obstacles, however. There is no well-defined market for most types of data, and when information on transactions is available, valuations are highly context dependent. Moreover, market transactions in unprocessed data will not capture the entire transformation chain necessary to generate values digitized information.[3] Studies of digital platform companies (e.g., Li, Norei, and Yamana 2019) underscore that the valuation of a company's data assets is highly dependent on the degree of vertical integration in a company's data value chain—consistent with the data stack in which only the monetization of data intelligence captures the value of the entire chain.

The examination of market capitalizations of companies that derive most (or all) of their income from advertising linked to personal data provides essential insights on measuring the value of data, but their methods are not very well suited to the development of comprehensive statistics. For example, figure 7.2 illustrates that the volatility in market capitalizations of individual companies is a major pitfall of using financial market indicators as a measurement tool. The figure plots the value of an individual (active) record at Facebook/Meta (the bars in the figure), which has fluctuated with the company's market capitalization (the line in the figure). As a result, the value of a typical Facebook user's data, which averaged nearly 200 USD from 2013 to 2023 (Q1), stood both well above, and well below, that average

3. Large-scale market transactions exist primarily for third-party data produced by data brokerage or data aggregator companies. These companies usually collect information from publicly available personal records and then aggregate, store, and sell it to different customers through licensing subscriptions or contractual arrangements. Third-party data sit near the beginning of the value chain and their valuation will not reflect the entire chain.

at times (e.g., more than 300 USD in Q4 of 2021 but only 100 USD in Q4 of 2022).

A third takeaway is that, absent comprehensive arms-length transactions, a resource cost approach offers the best method for valuing data in an economy. National accounts estimate investment by asset type based on a resource cost approach.[4] The aim of the approach is to consistently record investment flows and capital stocks for each industry (or institutional) sector. This involves estimating values for all sources of supply for each asset and deriving the asset valuations and quantities using information on prices for newly produced assets and how fast they lose value as they age (economic depreciation).

If firms purchased all or most data assets from market transactions, as they do with tangible assets, measuring the cost of data would be conceptually like measuring expenditures for a construction firm's purchase of excavators and concrete mixers. Instead, most digitized information used by businesses is not transacted on markets but produced in-house. Many of the components of intangible investment listed on table 7.2 also are produced, at least in part, in-house. For intangible assets, compilers must come up with two components of nominal investment for each asset type: own-account investment (when assets are produced and used in-house) and purchased investment (when assets are bought from producers in arm's length transactions).

Information on data products usually is missing in surveys of production or capital spending, and the national accountant's total supply approach is difficult to implement for valuing data as an asset. Statistics Canada (2019a, 2019b) pioneered a practical approach to valuing data assets using the sum-of-costs method national accountants employ for in-house investments, e.g., own-account software, to comprehensively measure data investments in an economy. This is the approach we use in this study.

7.3.2 Sum-of-Costs Method

The measurement of in-house investment using sum-of-costs methods is as follows: Imagine a firm having a "software factory" inside it, and your task is to estimate the gross output of this hypothetical factory based on the market value of the payments made to factors employed by it (labor, capital, and intermediates). This task begins by identifying the workers in the factory-within-the-factory. Based on knowledge of the compensation paid to these workers, the total payments made to all factors involved in the in-house production can be estimated.

As a practical matter, workers are identified by occupation, and consider-

4. Though the approach differs substantially in context and application from the cost-based valuation method used in financial accounting, the concepts do overlap. See the previously cited reviews for further elaboration.

ation is given to the likelihood they are not involved in producing new assets their entire workday. For example, the conventional approach to measuring in-house software production in national accounts is to assume that software developers spend 50 percent of their time working in their firm's "software factory" to produce original code. In-house production of data assets can be estimated in a similar fashion.

Statistics Canada (2019a, 2019b) prepared experimental estimates for Canada's total economy and major institutional sectors—nonfinancial corporations, financial corporations, nonprofit institutions serving households, and governments. Occupational groups were selected from among those generally associated with converting raw data into digital formats suitable for knowledge creation and monetization.

The Statistics Canada schema included three asset types that generally align with those in the data stack of figure 7.1, though Statistics Canada called the third category "data science" and viewed it as unmeasured R&D, e.g., spending to develop new AI algorithms. Data and AI data tools are inextricably bound via feedback training data used to develop and/or enhance the performance of AI tools, and the data stack/data value chain notion of how value is created from data does not end with the development of *new* algorithms. Section 7.2's discussion of the data stack and its overlap with intangible investment suggests that value creation due to data intelligence also occurs when existing AI tools or analytics are fine-tuned with data to obtain firm-specific solutions for product design, services development, marketing campaigns, and business organization processes.

Statistics Canada estimated bands for the value of investment in the three data types that ranged from 1.75 to 2.25 percent of the country's GDP in 2018. They further found that about 47 percent of the total was accounted for by nonfinancial corporations, 31 percent by financial corporations, 20 percent by governments, and 2 percent by nonprofit institutions serving households. Statistics Canada produced estimates in volume terms (i.e., adjusted to consider price changes) and used them to develop capital stock measures. Price indexes were based on weighted input costs (without a productivity adjustment). Service lives were assumed to be 25 years for data stores, 5 years for databases (the same as software), and 6 years for their data science category.

Goodridge, Haskel, and Edquist (2021) took essentially the same approach as Statistics Canada to estimate the value of investments in data capital for 16 EU countries. Their results suggest that including the Statistics Canada grouping of occupations engaged in producing data stores and data intelligence (which they refer to as data transformation and knowledge creation) raises own-account gross fixed capital formation by around 60 percent compared to own-account investment in software and databases measured in EU official national accounts. In GDP terms, their estimates are in line with the results for Canada.

Emerging work analyzes skill requirements and work activities (tasks) by detailed occupation to classify workers (Autor 2013), an approach thought to be well-suited for identifying workers engaged in own-account data asset production. In an early application, Squicciarini and Le Mouel (2012) used detailed task-level information on occupations from O*NET to measure own-account investment in organizational capital.[5] Babina, Fedyk, He, and Hodson (2022) used skills information from Burning Glass job postings and resumes from Cognism to estimate industry-level AI workers and AI investments at US publicly traded corporations.

Santiago-Calderón and Rassier (2022) also use skills information from Burning Glass but combine this with O*NET's detailed occupation descriptors, and employment and wage data by detailed occupation from the OEWS survey.[6] The authors employ a machine learning model to estimate the number of employees and employment time devoted to data asset production in the US economy. They estimate that data investment was about 1 percent of US business sector gross value added (GVA). Though less than the estimate for the business sector of Canada and market sector industries in European countries covered in Goodridge et al. (2021), the upshot of all three studies is that data investment is rather small.

7.4 Estimates of Data Investment in European Countries

The sum-of-costs method is used to develop estimates of data asset creation coherent with the value chain framework of section 7.2 and national accounts. Broadly speaking, the estimates are developed from occupation employment and wage share data from Labor Force Surveys conducted in nine European countries; these surveys use the International Standard Classification of Occupations (ISCO) system to define occupations.

7.4.1 Features of the Application

The identification of workers engaged in producing data includes workers engaged in the data-driven business functions of engineering design, business operations, and marketing. This is in line with the discussion of data assets and intangible capital in section 7.2 and a departure from prior works that excluded, or only partially included, workers in these business functions in their estimates of the value of data.

Our occupation identification procedure exploits information from four

5. O*NET is a database covering nearly 1000 standardized occupations and their descriptors; descriptors include job requirements (knowledge, skills, and abilities) and work activities and tasks. Information is updated annually to capture changes in occupations as they evolve over time.

6. OEWS refers to The Occupational Employment and Wage Statistics (OEWS) program of the US Bureau of Labor Statistics, which produces employment and wage estimates annually for approximately 830 occupations.

primary sources: (1) the results of the skills-based studies described above (Babina, Fedyk, He, and Hodson 2022; Santiago-Calderón and Rassier 2022); (2) the ISCO and detailed O*NET occupation descriptors; (3) detailed employment data by occupation from OEWS; and (4) a concordance of the ISCO system for classifying occupations in European economies and the SOC system used in North America. The skills-based studies and O*NET and OEWS data use the SOC system, for which more detailed information and estimates are available than for the for ISCO system.

In addition to data assets, we generate sum-of-costs estimates of investment in software assets. National accounts combine software and databases in a single published asset category using a total supply approach, and these estimates are incorporated in the measures of intangible investment that follow the schema of table 7.2, e.g., EUKLEMS & INTANProd. The four sum-of-costs investment series are generated for 14 NACE "letter" level nonagricultural market sector industries of nine European, mainly western, economies.[7] Estimates cover the years 2010 to 2019. An appendix to this paper provides further details on the procedures and data sources used to develop the data and software sum-of-costs estimates reported in this paper.[8]

The estimates generated in this paper capture values produced in the market sector regardless of whether the produced output is intended for own final use or final sale. The produced value of data is a good proxy for data capital investment in the market sector if data transactions between the government and the market sector are rather small.

Strictly speaking, estimating market sector investment requires adjusting the estimates of in-house production for imports and exports of data flows as well. Information on transactions in data stores and databases, whether in domestic sales or international trade, is not readily apparent in official statistics (Ker and Mazzini 2020). This is mainly because official statistics are focused on industry activity, and industry classifications generate inexact identification of data production activities, i.e., Zillow sells its data on home real estate valuations, Nielsen sells it consumer survey data, as do credit agencies such as Experian, but these firms engage in widely different primary production activities and classified accordingly.

7.4.2 Empirical Results

Our main results on the relative size and growth of market sector data asset production and intangible investment are shown in figures 7.3(a)–(d). Data asset production is shown according to the three segments in the data

7. NACE is the system for classification of industries used in Europe. Market sector industries exclude NACE sections L (real estate activities), O (public administration and defense; compulsory social security), P (education), Q (human health and social work activities), and T (activities of households as employers; undifferentiated goods- and services-producing activities of households for own use).

8. See http://www.nber.org/data-appendix/c14737/appendix.pdf.

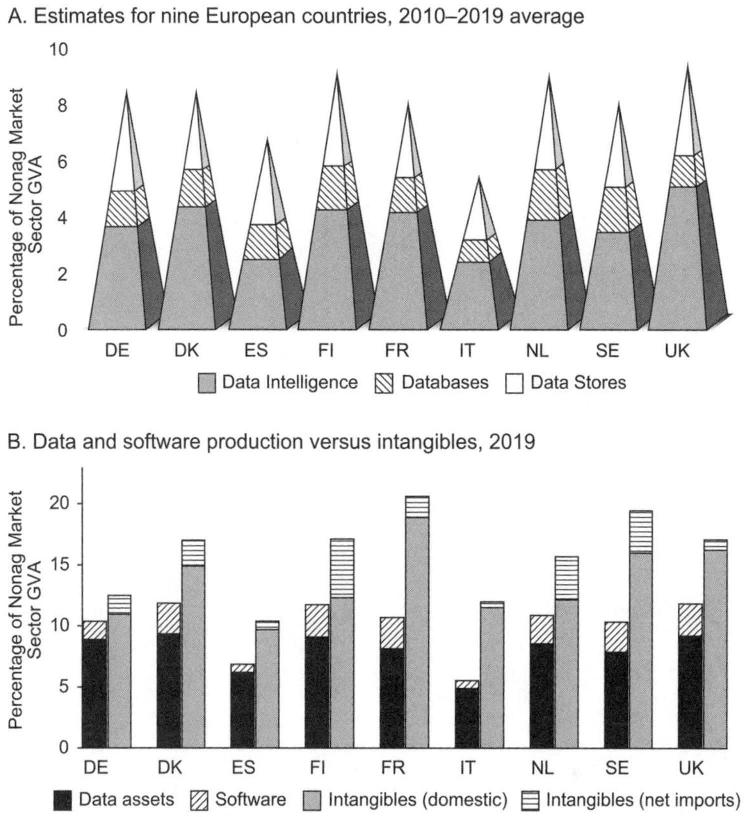

Fig. 7.3 Estimates of the data value chain

European country abbreviations are as follows: Denmark (DK), Germany (DE), Finland (FI), France (FR), Italy (IT), Netherlands (NL), Spain (ES), Sweden (SE), and the United Kingdom (UK).

value chain in the upper panel of the figure. The total data value chain averages 7.8 percent relative to nonagricultural market sector gross value added (GVA) in the covered countries and years. The United Kingdom is the most data intensive of the countries included (9.1 percent), and Italy and Spain are the least (5.2 and 6.5 percent, respectively).[9] Data intelligence is the largest segment in the data value chain, with databases the smallest.

The middle panel of figure 7.3 suggests that resources allocated to data

9. The authors have collaborated on work commissioned by the UK Department for Digital, Culture, Media (DCMS) to develop a business survey and assess the significance and value of data to industry and its impact on productivity in the United Kingdom. The resulting survey, the *Department for Science, Innovation and Technology (DSIT) Data Use and Productivity Longitudinal Survey*, provided time use estimates and implied values for spending on data in the United Kingdom that are broadly in line with the estimates reported in this paper. Reports detailing the survey's technical design, the survey's business microdata, and macroeconomic implications are forthcoming from DCMS.

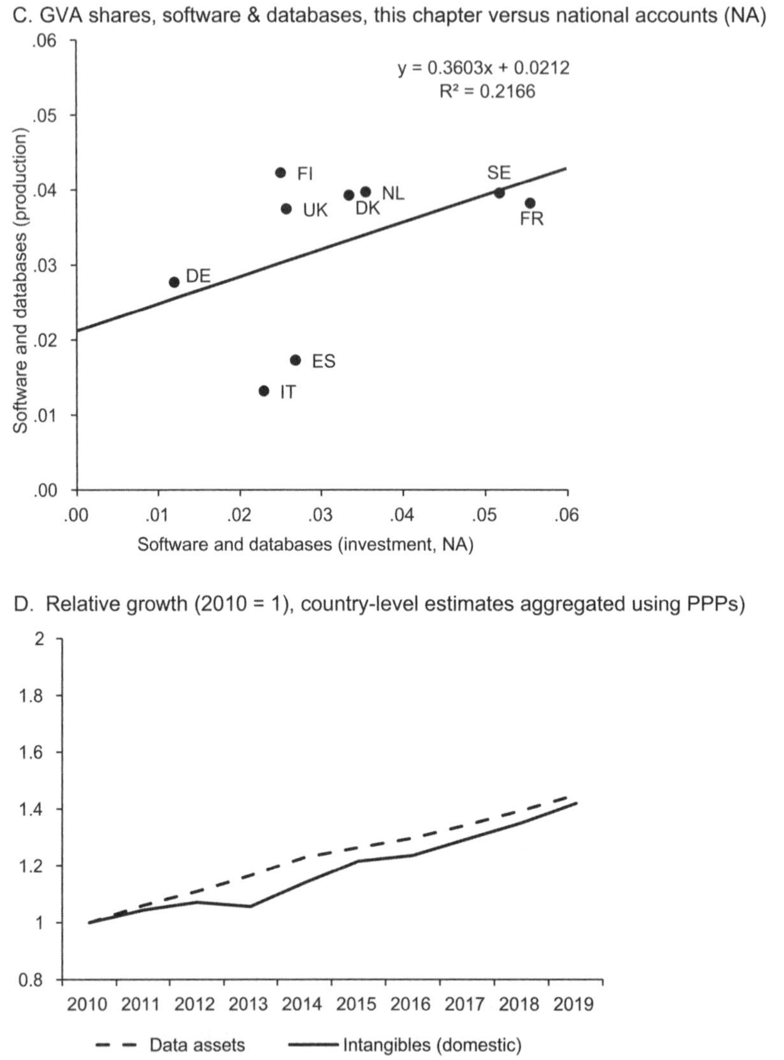

Fig. 7.3 (cont.)

asset production (the solid blue bars) were less than domestically produced intangible assets in 2019 (the solid gray bars). Averaged over countries (without regard to size of country), data asset production averaged 50 percent of intangible investment in 2019 and close to 50 percent of intangible asset domestic production. The panel also shows our estimates of the value of domestically produced software investment (the solid red bar stacked above the data asset production bar). The sum of data production and software production, which reflects in part the production of data tools, is 64 percent of intangible investment and 73 percent of domestic production of intangibles. Software production activity is found to be much smaller than production activity in the data value chain, reflecting the fact that a significant share (about one-half) of net imports of intangibles is software.

The GVA shares of our sum-of-costs production estimates for software and databases are compared with those for official investment estimates for the combined category in the bottom left panel of figure 7.3, in panel (c).[10] The correlation of our sum-of-costs estimates is not all that strong (R^2 of the simple regression line is .22), but there is a positive and significant intercept in the relationship shown on the figure, in line with the fact that that our sum-of-costs estimates miss net imports. Note further that even though methods used to develop our data and software production estimates are harmonized across countries (i.e., are the same; see appendix[11]), notable cross-country differences remain.[12]

The bottom right panel of figure 7.3, panel (d), illustrates that estimated nominal data production (aggregated over countries using PPPs) grew 5 percent faster than intangibles through 2015, but not thereafter. Cost efficiencies enabled by data-driven forms of intangible investment imply that the *real* growth of data assets may have eclipsed that of overall real intangible investment, however; we discuss the rationale for this thinking and evidence for it in the next section of this paper.

Table 7.3 shows the sectoral distribution of data capital investment (column 1) compared with intangible investment (column 2) for five groups of NACE letter industries. Average rates for all nonagricultural market sector industries are shown in the memo item (line 6).

The most data intensive industry groups are shown on lines 1 to 3. These consist of the professional, scientific, and technical activities; information and communication services; and finance and insurance activities sectors. Along with manufacturing (line 4), these sectors also post high rates of intangible, knowledge-based investments (column 2 of the table). The manufacturing sector invests disproportionately in R&D compared with other intangibles, however, suggesting that R&D processes (in manufacturing) are less data intensive than business functions such as marketing, and supply logistics that are more predominant in services industries.

10. Recall, national statistical agencies do not report software assets separate from database assets.

11. http://www.nber.org/data-appendix/c14737/appendix.pdf.

12. Many observers suggest that cross-country differences in measurement methods contribute to the differences seen in official data on software and database investment rates across EU countries (see discussions in Colecchia and Schreyer 2001, Timmer, Inklaar, O'Mahony, and van Ark 2011, and Goodridge et al. 2021). Though figure 7.3(c) mixes two concepts and shows that the range in investment rates across countries (.01 to .05) is larger than that for production shares (.01 to more than .03), the figure suggests that software and database investment rates do differ fundamentally across EU countries.

Table 7.3 **Sectoral distribution of investment in data and total intangibles, percentages of sector gross value added in nine European countries, 2010 to 2019**

	Selected industry sectors	Data investment (1)	Intangible investment (2)
1.	Professional, scientific & technical activities	16.3	27.0
2.	Information and Communication	14.2	28.2
3.	Financial and Insurance activities	14.5	14.2
4.	Manufacturing	7.3	21.6
5.	Administrative & support service activities	4.8	11.1
Memo:			
6.	Nonagricultural market sector	7.8	16.9

Note: Each cell represents the unweighted average of investment as a percentage of sector gross value added over time and countries. Industries shown correspond to NACE letter sectors M (row 1), J (row 2), K (row 3), C (row 4), N (row 5), and B to K, M, N, R, and S (row 6). European countries include Denmark (DK), Germany (DE), Finland (FI), France (FR), Italy (IT), Netherlands (NL), Spain (ES), Sweden (SE), and the United Kingdom (UK).

Data asset production by *type* of data also differs across industry sectors (not shown), but consistent with figure 7.3 (a), the most data-intensive sectors are those with high contributions from data intelligence. This underscores the reasoning from our analysis of the data stack, that data intelligence is the final and most valuable stage of the value chain.

7.4.3 Data Capital and Intangible Capital: How Much of an Overlap?

Our section 7.2 discussion suggested that measured data capital and intangible capital overlap significantly and that, conceptually, data capital is subsumed within intangible capital, especially in its "data-intensive" components: new financial products, industrial design, branding and marketing, and organizational processes. This idea is supported by simple correlation tests indicating that data capital and intangibles are moderately linked (correlation coefficient is 0.5) and that correlation is stronger with data-intensive intangibles (correlation coefficient increases to 0.6).[13]

To further explore this evidence, table 7.4 reports the results of a regression analysis of the relationship between labor productivity, data capital, and intangibles. The relationship is explored within a simple production function framework with controls for country, industry, and time fixed effects.

Column 1 is a benchmark specification showing that intangible and tangible capital are statistically significantly associated with labor productivity

13. Appendix table A2 (http://www.nber.org/data-appendix/c14737/appendix.pdf) reports a matrix of correlations between the major components of investment in data and major components of investment in intangibles (in both level and growth terms).

Table 7.4 **Regression model estimates of the contribution of the growth in data and intangible capital deepening to labor productivity growth**

	(1)	(2)	(3)	(4)	(5)
Intangible capital	.216***	.123***			
	(.027)	(.031)			
Tangible capital	.168***	.029	.166***	.034	.034
	(.029)	(.036)	(.029)	(.036)	(.036)
Data capital		.325***		.331***	
		(.05)		(.051)	
Data-intensive intangibles			.033**	.005	.007
			(.016)	(.016)	(.016)
National accounts intangibles			.073***	.05**	.049**
			(.02)	(.02)	(.02)
Training			.132***	.061**	.067**
			(.027)	(.029)	(.029)
Databases					−.006
					(.037)
Data stores					.005
					(.061)
Data intelligence					.316***
					(.065)
Observations	6,614	6,522	6,680	6,588	6,588

Note: Dependent variable is labor productivity computed as change in the natural log of value added per hour; value added is adjusted to include intangibles not currently capitalized in national accounts. All explanatory variables are in similar, i.e., per hour, delta natural log terms. Estimates are generalized least squares. All columns include time, industry and country fixed effects.

Standard errors are in parentheses. *** p<.01, ** p<.05, * p<.1.

growth. Adding data capital in column 2 reduces the coefficient of intangibles by 50 percent and renders tangible capital statistically insignificant. We next run a Wald test to check if data and intangible capital coefficients are equal. The Wald test indicates that the null hypothesis of perfect equality can be rejected at 0.05 significance statistical level, implying that both capitals contribute to explaining labor productivity growth.

Next, the overlap of data capital and intangible capital is examined in terms of components of intangibles: data-intensive intangibles, national accounts intangibles, and training; training is not included in the first two groupings. These results are reported in columns 3 and 4, which show that once we control for data assets, data-intensive intangibles lose their statistical significance. This suggests that the data-intensive grouping of intangibles and data capital capture similar factors affecting labor productivity growth. Finally, column 5 looks at the individual categories of data capital, which reveals that the high statistical significance of the relationship of data capital with labor productivity growth is mainly driven by data intelligence.

7.4.4 Data Intelligence and SNA Guidance

International guidelines for compiling GDP given by the 2008 System of National Accounts (SNA) will be soon superseded by the planned 2025 SNA. This new SNA is expected to expand the types of intangible investment in GDP to include data. Though not officially endorsed as of this writing, the guidance of the United Nations digitalization task team (DZTT) is to create a new asset category called "data" and to report it separate from current category of computer software (United Nations DZTT 2023). The guidance defines data in a manner generally consistent with the data stack of figure 7.1 and calls for a sum-of-costs approach be used for measuring investment in data.

The analysis in the SNA guidance depicts a data value chain with three stages where the final stage is termed "insights" (rather than "data intelligence"). Studies investigating the measurement of data in preparation for the 2025 SNA (e.g., Statistics Canada 2019a, 2019b; Santiago-Calderón and Rassier 2022) conceptually include something like what we have set out as investment in data stores and databases but not the full scope of the data value chain including data intelligence.

The omission of data intelligence seems to be the primary reason why prior studies produce estimates of data investments that are much smaller than those developed in this paper. In a value chain the output of final stage reflects the further processing of the output of earlier stages. It is possible that national account practitioners interpret the final stage output of the data value chain as another good or service entirely, rather than as a data asset as done in this paper. If so, the distinction they are making is semantic because the output of the data value chain is still capital to the extent its use in production is long-lasting.[14] The distinction seems to be reinforced elsewhere in the 2025 SNA deliberations. Guidance from the Joint Globalization task team (GZTT) suggests that marketing assets may also be included in investment if measuring them is determined to be feasible (United Nations GZTT 2023). This of course is coherent only if marketing assets do not overlap with data assets, which goes against the logic of the data stack as well as the empirical analysis in this paper (e.g., table 7.4 and the correlations reported in the appendix).[15]

The exclusion of data intelligence notwithstanding, the very small size of estimates generated by prior studies follows from the approach used to identify occupations for estimating the costs of data asset production—occupations with job and/or skill descriptors that include the word *data* in

14. This logic is of course symmetric with that used for tangible capital, e.g., an engine block made by a machine tool is still a capital good (despite its difference in character).

15. http://www.nber.org/data-appendix/c14737/appendix.pdf.

them (e.g., Customer Data Integration, Customer Service Database, Data Management, and Data Science to name just a few). Though we include these occupations in our analysis, we also allocate fractional amounts of the value of time of selected managers, professionals, and technicians to the production of data assets. To justify this approach, we appeal to both the data stack *and* the intangible capital framework—but note, the SNA guidance language also provides support.

The guidance by the United Nations Digitalisation Task Team (UN DZTT) for the 2025 SNA lists some specific costs that data asset investment should include, and these costs include more than the costs of digitizing and organizing records into databases for visualization and application of analytics. For example, the "costs of planning and developing a data production strategy" (UN DZTT 2023, page 8) are to be included, an activity sure to involve a company's C-suite as well as its computer and data professionals. The costs of "analyzing data for the purpose of drawing conclusions from it" (United Nations DZTT 2023, page 8) are also to be included, an ongoing activity that involves multiple types of managers and technical professionals that may, or more likely may not, have *data* in their job descriptions.

Finally, as previously discussed, modern data use fosters faster, more efficient experimentation and feedback in business processes. Existing SNA guidance does not address how the relative efficiency of data assets is to be captured in price statistics and thereby reflected in real GDP and productivity calculations. This is a major omission and a topic discussed in some depth in the next part of this paper.

7.5 Data Investment, Growth Accounting, and Innovation

The aggregate effects of the rise of data capital are analyzed using the upstream/downstream two-sector model summarized in Corrado et al (2022a). The model is based on Corrado, Hulten, Sichel (2005, 2009) as adapted and termed "upstream/downstream" in Corrado, Goodridge, and Haskel (2011).

As previously suggested, data affect innovation and productivity growth in divergent ways. On the one hand cutting-edge digital tools that exploit big data have the potential for making production and innovation processes more efficient. On the other hand, the data assets created by them may be inextricably bound with network externalities in customer demand that weaken competition and/or, due to the difficulty of replicating proprietary data assets, weaken knowledge diffusion in economies. This section investigates how these two forces—the "efficiency" promise of big data/AI versus the "appropriability effect" (that restrains TFP growth)—operate in a two-sector model with data/intangible capital.

Box 7.1 A Model of an Economy with Intangibles

A simplified model of the economy divides production into two broad sectors: (1) an "upstream" sector that produces new knowledge that can be commercialized; and (2) a "downstream" sector that uses the knowledge generated by the upstream sector to produce final output. For simplicity, the model assumes that there are no exports or imports of intangible assets and no intermediate purchases of other goods and services.

Sectoral activity is described and denoted as follows:

- Upstream output reflects the production of new commercial knowledge. This is also intangible investment, which in volume terms intangible investment is N and in nominal terms is $P^N N$, where P^N is a price index for intangible assets.
- Downstream output reflects the production of (tangible) investment and consumer goods, $P^Y Y$, or $P^I I + P^C C$, in nominal terms.
- The outstanding stock of commercially valuable knowledge reflects the accumulation of the upstream sector output after adjusting for losses due to economic depreciation (i.e., aging), i.e., the stock of intangible capital, R, is given by the perpetual inventory relationship, $R_t = N_t + \delta^R R_{t-1}$.
- Freely available basic knowledge, scientific or otherwise, is represented by R^{Basic}. It is an input to upstream production, e.g., open-source software, which we assume is produced outside the model. (This assumption can be relaxed with no major change in model implications.)
- The value of intangible capital, defined as its replacement cost, is given by $P^N R$. The payments made to the owners of R are denoted by $P^R R$, where P^R is the per period rental price equivalent of using intangible capital in production.
- The stock of tangible assets is denoted by K, its value by $P^I K$, and payments to owners by $P^K K$. Labor inputs and their price are L and P^L, respectively.

7.5.1 Upstream/Downstream Model of an Economy

A simplified model of an economy with data as an intangible asset divides production into two broad sectors: (1) an "upstream" sector that *produces new knowledge* that can be commercialized, e.g., a new or improved product design (or product formula), or a software program adapted to the needs of the organization; and (2) a "downstream" sector that *uses the knowledge* generated by the upstream sector to produce final output.

Box 7.1 sets out the upstream/downstream model in more detail, including

- Total factor productivity in the upstream and downstream production functions is given by *AN and AY*.

Regarding monopoly power:

- R is inherently nonrival and thus only partially appropriable. Appropriability lasts for the time the producer-innovator can sell or rent the knowledge to the downstream sector at a monopoly price.
- The downstream sector is assumed to be a price-taker for knowledge, i.e., monopoly power resides in the upstream sector. Final output prices for consumption and tangible investment are assumed to be competitive, as are factor input prices for labor and tangible capital.

The sectoral production and income flows in this economy are written as follows:

(B1–1) $N = A^N F^N(L^N, K^N, R^{Basic}); P^N N = P^L L^N + P^K K^N + \pi^N$

(B1–2) $Y = A^Y F^Y(L^Y, K^Y, R); P^Y Y = P^L L^Y + P^K K^Y + P^R R$

where π^N is the upstream sectors' pure rents from innovation—rents that are embedded in P^N and P^R.

In this model, the asset price of commercial knowledge P^N and the price of its $P^R = (r + \delta^R) P^N$ ignoring asset price inflation. The user cost of tangible capital is similarly linked to its asset price. The model is closed via arbitrage of returns (r) across sectors, i.e., returns to investments in innovation (that build intangible capital R) with returns to alternative long-term investments (that build tangible capital K).

The model allows for the existence of "abnormal" innovator profits for periods of time, but intertemporal arbitrage operates to constrain innovator profits to zero (i.e., $\pi^N = 0$) in long-term equilibrium. As a practical matter, with continuous entry of innovators (and waves of technological change), the model is consistent with varying degrees of market power continuously embedded in time series for intangible asset prices.

sectoral inputs and their payments, sectoral outputs and their prices, and sectoral productivity. Intangible investment is the value of the upstream sector's output in this model—the investment stream corresponding to data asset creation in our prior discussion. The outstanding stock of data assets is then the accumulation of upstream output after adjusting for losses due to ageing (economic depreciation).

The downstream production sector uses the stock of data-derived intelligence to produce final goods, and the upstream sector is remanded a portion of the income earned from the sale of final goods in return. Because knowledge producers demand (and earn) returns on their investments, the value of the data knowledge stock must be included in calculations of the realized return to capital, which is arbitraged across sectors and asset types in competitive equilibrium. As mentioned previously, not recognizing data and other forms of intangible capital in calculations of the realized return to capital can cause observers to mischaracterize the competitive intensity of markets and industries.

To the extent there are pure rents from innovation in this model, they create a wedge between asset prices for data capital (P^N) and its production cost; by extension (see box 7.1), they enter the per period remand paid by downstream producers for use of the data capital (P^R). The model thus allows for innovators/data capital owners to hold temporary market power, a common feature of many economic models of innovation, especially Schumpeterian-inspired models such as Aghion and Howitt (1992). In these models, innovation results from entrepreneurial investments motivated by prospects of monopoly rents.

The temporary nature of the market power is due to the inherent nonrival character of knowledge-based assets. As valuable commercial knowledge diffuses (is copied/replicated), innovator profits are competed away. This loss of revenue-generating capacity forms the conceptual basis for the relatively short service lives found for intangible capital in empirical studies (reviewed in De Rassenfosse and Jaffe 2017) and surveys (e.g., Awano et al. 2010).

7.5.2 Data Capital in GDP and Growth Accounting

Without the capitalization of data assets, GDP consists solely of downstream sector output Y, but when upstream investments in building data stores, databases and developing data intelligence are capitalized, aggregate value added Q reflects production in both sectors:

$$P^Q Q = P^Y Y + P^N N = P^C C + P^I I + P^N N \tag{1a}$$

$$\equiv P^L L + P^K K + P^R R. \tag{1b}$$

As seen in (1a) to the right, investment in final demand is expanded to include data value creation and thus GDP is larger. Factor income, the second line (1b), accounts explicitly for returns to intangible assets in total capital income. The term may contain monopolistic returns to innovation in the price element P^R as discussed above.

When Solow's sources-of-growth decomposition is applied to GDP with investment expanded to cover data value creation, the usual log differentiation cum constant returns yields:

$$dq = \sigma_Q^X dx + \sigma_Q^R dr + da \tag{2}$$

where σ_Q^X is the combined factor income share for conventional inputs L and K in total production and σ_Q^R is the factor income share attributed to owners of data/intangible capital.[16] This decomposition says that output growth consists of a contribution from conventional inputs $\sigma_Q^X dx$, a contribution from paid-for, commercially valuable knowledge $\sigma_Q^R dr$, plus total factor productivity (TFP) growth *da*. What is different in this model then is that the contribution of paid-for data capital has become a source of growth.

7.5.3 Data Capital and Knowledge Diffusion

The intangibles framework also helps explain the origins of TFP growth, and this is no less true when the framework is applied to data capital. Unappropriated returns that the economy enjoys when knowledge-based assets are copied and used at low-cost in production elsewhere in an economy are a source of growth in measured TFP. The costless diffusion (or "spread") of innovators' knowledge from one organization to another—a phenomenon termed "knowledge spillovers" by Griliches (1992) in the context of R&D—drives the increasing returns on investments in knowledge that play a central role in modern growth theory (Romer 1990, Jones 2005).

From this perspective, whether data are proprietary or freely available (per the range of examples given in table 7.1) becomes crucial for assessing the productivity implications of data assets. Consider how Lyft was able to duplicate and compete against Uber's innovative, data-enabled ridesharing business model. The idea of ridesharing as a business model was freely available once Uber became a fast-growing enterprise. So were the mapping and traffic data needed for ridesharing implementation because governments make this information freely available. But when data-enabled innovations are based on proprietary data (Amazon's very efficient delivery system, Google's targeted advertising systems, etc.), they operate more like trade secrets than patented technologies. After all, patented technologies are disclosed when filed and protected only for a time. Innovations stemming from trade secrets are not easily (or ever) duplicated, and first-mover advantage may be maintained.

So, when proprietary data-derived knowledge assets are a prevalent source of innovation, knowledge diffusion—and TFP growth—will weaken. This is the "appropriability" effect of data capital, i.e., unless offset by moves to promote industry data sharing, an increase in the share of data-derived intangible capital in total intangible capital will lead to lower measured growth of total factor productivity due to fewer spillovers from a given stream of investment.[17]

16. The decomposition is obtained via the usual log differentiation of (1b) assuming constant returns to scale and that factors are paid their marginal revenue product. The notation "dz" is the log change in "Z" where Z is any variable in the model. Conventional inputs K and L are combined as X and weighted appropriately.

17. A secondary aspect of this effect is that proprietary big data will create longer-lasting positions of competitive advantage (all else equal), which implies that data-derived knowledge stocks have longer service lives (i.e., lower values for R).

The "appropriability effect" is not the whole story of the impact of data on innovation but it has much potential for being very significant. Aggregate productivity in the upstream/downstream model can be expressed as

$$da = s_Q^Y da^Y + s_Q^N da^N, \tag{3}$$

i.e., the share-weighted sum of total factor productivity growth in each sector. To the extent proprietary data assets are like trade secrets and generate commercial knowledge that is not easily replicated at low cost, the appropriability effect operates largely via its impact on da^Y, the first term in (3). The production shares in figure 7.4b imply that the weight on downstream productivity s_Q^Y ranges anywhere from 80 to 90 percent, so even small changes in da^Y have significant impacts on aggregate (measured) productivity da.

7.5.4 Data Capital and Data Technologies

The efficiencies of modern data technologies are an opposing force to the diminishment of productivity spillovers to investments in intangible capital. To the extent the latest wave of AI-driven digital technologies cum data assets produces innovations more efficiently, the second term in (3), upstream total factor productivity da^N, is boosted. Though the impact will become larger as the production share of data capital in intangibles increases, it is also possible that data and data technologies create innovations and efficiencies that are impactful enough to offset the heavily weighted, diminished pace of da^Y.

As the composition of intangible capital becomes, in effect, data capital, the relative efficiency of data capital will be reflected in lower relative prices for intangible assets. The relative decline in prices of intangible assets due to use of data in their production is the "efficiency effect" of data capital. This is analogous to the situation with ICT capital, whose relative efficiency is a familiar theme in the productivity literature. In the initial phases of ICT innovations in the 1990s through the rapid adoption of mobile by the early 2000s, ICT capital asset prices fell very rapidly—between 10 and 20 percent annually.[18]

7.6 Intangible Asset Prices

Let us then look at prices of intangible assets to see what they may be signaling about the relative productivity of data capital.

7.6.1 Intangible Asset Price Change in the Upstream/Downstream Model

The change in intangible asset prices dp^N is obtained by log differentiation of the upstream factor payment equation (shown in box 7.1 as equation B1–1), yielding:

18. Byrne and Corrado (2017a, 2017b) develop and report these relative ICT prices and analyze their implications as measures of the relative productivity of the asset class.

$$dp^N = \sigma_N^L dp^L + \sigma_N^K dp^K + \sigma_N^\pi d\pi^N - da^N. \tag{4}$$

This equation expresses dp^N as a weighted average of changes in constant quality unit input costs (the first two terms) and innovator profits (the third), offset by changes in the efficiency of upstream production (the last term).

Consider now how changes in marginal productivities of factor inputs may offset changes in input costs. Let upstream input, L^N, be an aggregate of services provided by a range of worker types that differs from its "transactions unit" equivalent, hourly input H^N, by a composition effect, Θ. The composition effect accounts for differences in the marginal productivity of different worker types employed in production; thus, aggregate labor input may be expressed as $L^N = \Theta H^N$. A similar logic applies to capital inputs but, for simplicity, in what follows we ignore the role capital productivity by implicitly combining it with upstream TFP in a single term, denoted as *db*.

This simplifies the modeling of upstream production, i.e., upstream production may be represented as a function of multiple labor types and technology that is essentially free. "Free technology" includes all aspects of data technologies, e.g., open-source AI engines and other software that engender data production cost efficiencies; cloud technologies that enable computing and data processing efficiencies; and trends in the availability and use of public and/or open data.

This simplified data capital production model is rewritten as

$$dp^N = \sigma_N^L (dw - d\theta) + \sigma_N^\pi d\pi^N - db, \tag{4'}$$

where the impact of *upstream* labor input composition changes on data/intangible asset prices is explicit in the term $d\theta$. Grouping the terms in (4′) according to factors that positively influence price change versus those that exert a downward influence yields

$$dp^N = (\sigma_N^L dw + \sigma_N^\pi d\pi^N) - (\sigma_N^L d\theta + db). \tag{5}$$

The first group of terms includes increases in wages and innovator profits. The second group reflects improvements in the marginal productivity of the sector's average worker and the combined impact of embodied and disembodied technical change in the production of intangibles.

7.6.2 Relative Efficiency of Data Capital: Some Evidence

Equation (5) suggests how data and data technologies might affect intangible asset prices. Evidence that the impact of data technologies on intangible capital asset price change might be rather powerful include: (a) strong relative demand for skills used in the production of data capital, (b) stunning growth in the availability of open-source software based on data technologies, and (c) direct indicators of data production capital cost efficiencies, i.e., costs of algorithm design, cloud computing, and advertising/marketing media. These indicators are reviewed in turn below:

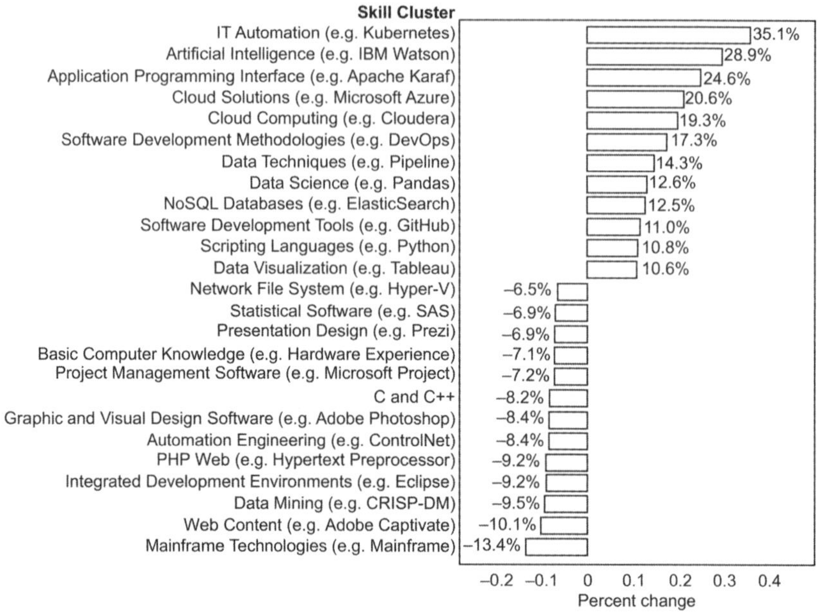

Fig. 7.4 Emerging skill clusters including artificial intelligence and cloud solutions relative to other tech occupations

Percent change in the share of selected skill cluster mentions in job ads for tech occupations from 2019 to the last 12 months ending in February 2021

Source: The Conference Board (2021) based on The Conference Board®-Burning Glass® Help Wanted OnLine® (HWOL) data series. © 2023 The Conference Board, Inc. Content reproduced with permission.

7.6.3 AI/Cloud Systems Skill Demand

Skills related to automation, AI, data connectivity, and cloud storage/computing are reshaping IT work. Direct evidence of employer demand for these skills—is suggested by figure 7.4, which shows that the demand for AI and cloud systems skills accelerated the fastest among IT roles during the pandemic. To the extent this shifted the composition of the upstream workforce, it boosts $d\theta$ and suggests that workforce composition changes associated with increased data use may have significantly offset wage pressures on asset prices for data capital.

The figure also underscores that upstream labor composition effects are moves *within* the usual grouping of workers termed "high-skilled" in measures of labor composition used in practical growth accounting. The latter are developed using broad groupings of employment by worker type, implying that the usual growth accounting understates the contribution of upstream labor composition to labor productivity growth and, consequently, thereby elevating da^N.

7.6.4 Open-Source Software

Studies that quantify the resource cost of open-source software (OSS) activity suggest significant value creation, much of which is arguably correlated with the production of data capital.

Robbins et al. (2021) set out a sectoral framework for measuring investments in OSS in GitHub repositories, where much cutting edge open-source software is held. They use software engineering metrics (lines of code and project complexity) to estimate OSS resource cost in terms of global person-months of effort, enumerating results by country from 2009 to 2019. For the United States, their person-months estimates translated to \$38 billion in new OSS investment activity in 2019, having grown nearly 20 percent per year from 2014 to 2019—and likely boosting da^N (though to an unquantified degree).[19] Their estimates of person-months of effort in value creation for the nine European countries for which data capital production estimates were reported in section 7.4 grew about 22 percent annually, moving the level of person months in these countries from 87 to 94 percent of US person-months from 2014 to 2019.

The very rapid growth in the value of OSS in GitHub repositories owes, at least in part, to the relative growth in AI applications in overall OSS software. AI application software ranges from general purpose algorithms to specific application-tuned systems, e.g., the software that runs industrial Internet-of-Things (IoT) installations and advanced robots. The OECD developed a classification algorithm to determine the fraction of AI GitHub repositories in all GitHub repositories and found very fast relative growth of AI open-source applications based on measures of "commits" (changes to code).[20] Despite their estimates of stunning growth of AI software in OSS repositories (a three-fold relative increase), the OECD also reports that the proportion of AI in the total is still rather small.

7.6.5 Cloud and Other Efficiencies

Many studies document improvements in the efficiency of modern cloud systems to ingest, store, process, and analyze large quantities of data (e.g., Byrne, Corrado, and Sichel 2021; Coyle and Nguyen 2018). The findings are consistent with a strong impetus to upstream productivity growth. But the effect will show through in productivity estimates only insofar as these

19. By contrast the US national accounts reports that gross fixed capital formation on software by private sector industries grew 7.5 percent per year from 2014 to 2019.

20. Barruffaldi et al. (2020, page 32) report, ". . . in 2010, there were 50 active AI GitHub repositories that had gathered 1,350 commits from contributors, making up 0.26 percent of total commits on GitHub that month. In June 2017, AI software activity had increased to 26,275 commits on 1,533 projects, making up 0.74 percent of total commits on GitHub . . . most of [the 2010 to 2017] growth [took] place since 2014. . . [from 2014 to 2017], AI open-source software grew about three times as much as the rest of open-source software."

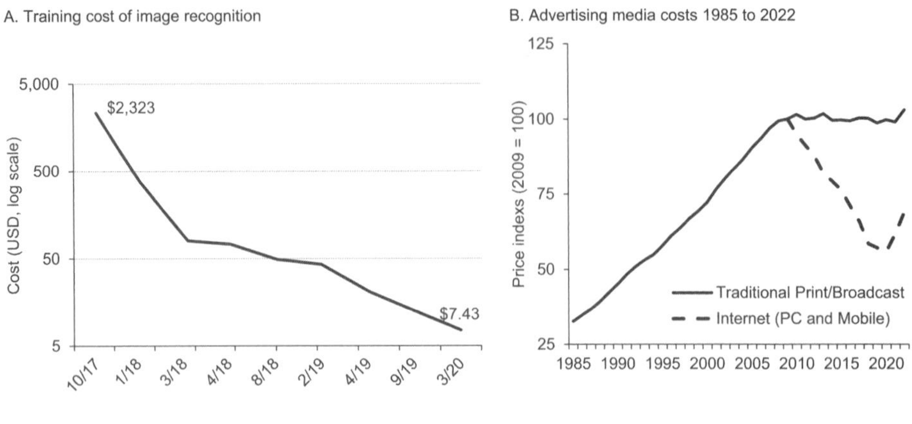

Fig.7.5 Data-driven cost efficiencies

Sources. Panel (a): AI Index Report (2021, page 49). Panel (b): Corrado (2024), figure 6.

changes in intangible/data capital production costs are captured in intangible asset prices.

Indicators of these cost efficiencies are shown in figure 7.5. According to tests shown in the AI Index Report (Zhang et al. 2021, 49), the costs of training a contemporary image recognition system was "a few dollars in 2020, down by around 150 times from costs in 2017" (figure 7.5, left panel). This dramatic reduction represents progress in both algorithm design and drops in the costs of cloud-computing resources. Similar factors have affected the accumulation of data on consumer buying patterns and tastes that have lowered (directly and indirectly) advertising media costs (figure 7.5, right panel), though note that internet advertising media costs reversed course and began to rise sharply in the aftermath of the pandemic (2021 and 2022).[21]

Hard-to-measure services price research typically does not address intangible asset-producing activities—R&D labs, marketing teams, engineering design projects—nor do assessments of productivity mismeasurement view these activities as hotbeds of rapid quality change missed by price collectors. That said, the digital transformation of economies, rise of digitally enabled business models, and increased use of data in business more generally is arguably driving down the production costs of intangible assets.

7.6.6 A New Intangible Asset Price Deflator

A price deflator for US intangible investment, reported in Corrado (2024), has been constructed using a brand and marketing investment price deflator

21. The media cost price indexes are developed from detailed BLS input cost indexes aggregated using information from the Census Bureau and industry sources. The appendix in Corrado (2024) provides additional details.

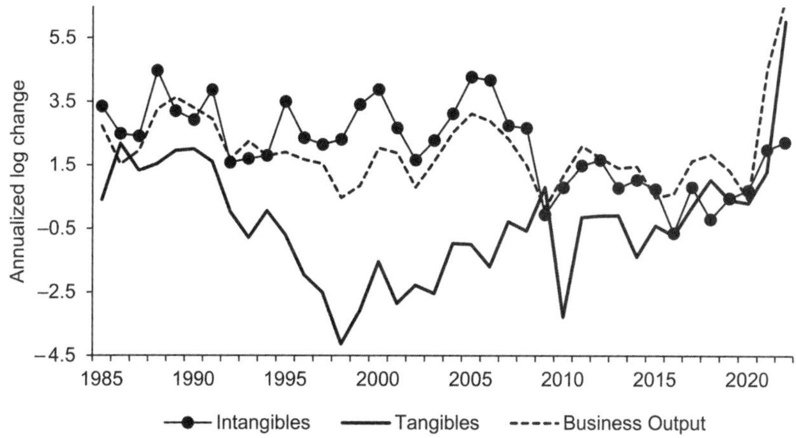

Fig. 7.6 US intangible and tangible asset price change, 1985 to 2022
Note. Private nonresidential assets. Natural log changes, annualized.
Source. Intangibles price, Corrado (2024); Tangible price, constructed from NIPA table 5.3.4, Business output price, NIPA table 1.3.4 (NIPA data accessed May 2023).

calculated using the media input cost price indexes shown in figure 7.5 (b) and a production/content creation cost price index based on the gross output price index for the advertising and public relations industry (NAICS 5418). Changes in the resulting price index for intangible assets are shown in figure 7.6 and table 7.5.

Figure 7.6 shows that prices for intangible assets exhibit a disinflationary trend beginning in 2009, in line with the prediction that increased data intensity of intangible capital improves its production efficiency and slows its price change. The slower pace of price change mainly reflects the net effects of sharply slower price change for investments in brand and marketing and in organizational capital (table 7.5, lines 5 and 6).

From 2009 to 2019, the relative price of total intangible assets fell 0.8 percent per year in the United States (table 7.5, line 7) and the relative price of the data-intensive components, investments in branding, marketing and organizational process change (lines 9 and 10), fell 2–1/4 percent per year. During the pandemic and subsequent global inflation (2019 to 2022, column 3), the relative prices of these assets fell even faster, primarily reflecting the sharp rise in overall business output prices (4.1 percent from 2019 to 2022, not shown on the table).

As advances in data technologies continue, the composition of intangibles will continue to shift toward data assets. This implies that declines in the relative price of intangible assets in the 1 to 2 percent range seem likely to persist for a time, which in turn implies a range for declines in the relative price of data-intensive intangible assets, i.e., data capital, of about 2 to 4 percent per year.

Table 7.5 US intangible and tangible asset price change, selected periods

	Asset group	1995 to 2009 (1)	2009 to 2019 (2)	2019 to 2022 (3)
1.	Intangibles	2.7	.7	1.6
2.	Tangibles	−1.7	−.4	2.5
Intangibles, selected components:				
3.	Software	−1.9	−1.6	−1.0
4.	R&D	2.2	1.8	3.4
5.	Brand and marketing investment	3.4	−.8	1.0
6.	Organization process investment	3.0	−.7	.8
Relative price change (asset price/business output price):				
7.	Intangibles, total	1.2	−.8	−2.5
8.	Software	−3.4	−3.1	−5.1
9.	Brand and marketing investment	1.9	−2.3	−3.1
10.	Organization process investment	1.4	−2.2	−3.3

Note: Private nonresidential assets. Natural log changes, annualized.

Sources. Lines 1 and 2 and denominator of lines 7 to 9, see figure 7.7; lines 3 and 4, NIPA table 5.3.4 (accessed May 2023); lines 5 and 6, Corrado (2024).

7.6.7 Relative Asset Prices and "Potential" Growth in Labor Productivity

The long-term growth-promoting potential of a capital input depends on the extent to which its volume rises more rapidly than its relative price falls (i.e., that the input shares continue to rise). In the context of data/AI, this is typically viewed as a question about the degree of substitutability between AI/data capital and human efforts, the limits to which are discussed in Nordhaus (2021).

We have argued in sections 7.3 and 7.4 that the rise of modern data capital is mainly a shift in the composition of intangible capital. This suggests data capital may then be viewed as improving the productivity of capital, i.e., it is an *efficiency* effect resulting from the substitution of data capital for other capitals (tangible or intangible). As a first step then, we can estimate the impact of data capital on labor productivity by making assumptions about data capital's relative productivity and income share, assuming labor's share is fixed.

The steady-state solution to the two-sector upstream/downstream model provides a starting point for calibrating estimates of the growth-promoting potential of data capital. To obtain a simple, closed-form steady state solution for this model, simplifying assumptions must be made, mainly, that the sectoral production functions (box 7.1 equations B1–1 and B1–2) exhibit constant returns and differ only by their "A" terms and that there is faster TFP growth in the data capital-producing sector, i.e., $da^N > da^Y$. For further details on this solution in similar models, see Oulton (2012) and Byrne and Corrado (2017a).

The contribution of data capital to the growth in labor productivity in this solution is the sum of a "use" or "investment" effect:

$$(6a) \qquad \frac{\underline{\sigma}^R}{\underline{\sigma}^L} \cdot \textit{productivity advantage}$$

plus a "production share" effect,

$$(6b) \qquad \underline{\omega}^D \cdot \textit{productivity advantage}.$$

The "underbar" notation in (6a) and (6b) denotes steady-state solution values. Thus, $\underline{\sigma}^R$ and $\underline{\sigma}^L$ represent steady state income shares of data capital and labor, respectively, and $\underline{\omega}^D$ is the steady state domestic production share of data investments.

"Productivity advantage" is the steady-state solution for the relative productivity of data capital. By assumption there is faster TFP growth in the data capital-producing sector, i.e., $da^N > da^Y$, and the solution for this productivity difference is (the negative of) data capital's relative price change. Thus, the relative productivity of data capital in steady growth is given by

$$(7) \qquad \textit{productivity advantage} = -(d \ln p^N - d \ln p^Y),$$

i.e., the rate of decline in the *relative* price of data assets (sign reversed).

Table 7.6 presents alternative scenarios for potential labor productivity growth using equations (6) and (7). The scenarios vary according to assumptions regarding the breadth of data capital use and production (the rows of the table) and the productivity advantage of data capital (the columns). The assumptions are drawn from measures developed and reviewed in this paper.

Table 7.6 **Productivity scenarios: contribution of data capital to potential labor productivity growth (percentage points)**

	Productivity advantage (Relative asset price growth differential)	
Income and production share	Narrow edge 2 percentage point	Large edge 5 percentage points
Broad use		
(and net exporter of data services)	0.51	1.26
10 percent capital income share		
11 percent production share		
Limited use		
(and net importer of data services)	0.23	0.58
5 percent capital income share		
4.5 percent production share		

Note: Contributions include the sum of the use and production effects of data capital.

The capital input shares of data capital are assumed to range from 5 to 10 percent, i.e., a bit above the approximate band about the estimates for the penetration of data capital in intangible capital as discussed in section 7.4. Production shares are assumed to be the capital income share +/– 10 percent, a rough estimate of the range for net exports of intangibles (excluding R&D and software, not shown but embedded in the share of intangible investment attributed to net imports in figure 7.4b).

The upper and lower bounds for the productivity advantage are drawn from the relative price differential implied by the data-intensive components of intangibles investment shown in table 7.5. They are set at 1 and 5 percent, respectively. This lower bound is a bit below the US historical experience, whereas the upper bound is higher. Deflators for data-intensive components of intangibles rely on national accounts prices, e.g., gross output deflators for industrial design and management consulting that are unlikely to incorporate efficiency gains due to increased application of AI or use of open-source content, and the upper bound incorporates these measurement realities.

For the upper bound, consider first the long-term price decline of conventionally defined IT capital, about 15 percent per year (based on the estimates reported in Byrne and Corrado 2017b). Our best estimates of price declines for two data-intensive intangibles are extremely modest by comparison, and an upper bound for the relative productivity of data capital at 5 percentage points per year is likewise very modest. All calculations assume labor's share of total income $\underline{\sigma}^L$ equals 0.7.

All told, our scenarios for the contribution of data capital to labor productivity growth range by more than a factor of 5—from 0.23 percentage point per year to 1.26 percentage point per year. The range highlights the synergies among data capital efficiency and an economy's capability for digital transformation of its production processes.

Having established that data capital has considerable potential for impacting labor productivity growth, let us now address how data capital affects measured total factor productivity *da*.

7.7 Data Capital and Total Factor Productivity

To calculate total factor productivity, we use the recently issued EUKLEMS & INTANProd database, which reports productivity data including investment streams for the intangible assets listed in table 7.2 for Europe, the United States, and Japan.[22] The investment and capital estimates for assets not regularly capitalized in national accounts are developed using national

22. This update/expansion of EUKLEMS was funded by the European Commission's Directorate General for Economic and Financial Affairs.

accounts-consistent methods, i.e., they are not calibrations of a model or developed from data in company financial reports.[23]

The EUKLEMS & INTANProd database covers the years 1995 to 2020 (as of June 2023). Below we report and analyze estimates of total factor productivity for the 9 European countries included in the empirical analysis of the data value chain in section 7.4 of this paper, as well as for the United States, for all years except the global pandemic year 2020. It should be noted that INTANProd includes estimates of total industry intangible investment for 25 EU countries; intangible investment for market sector industries for 19 EU countries (though histories for both are short for some). NACE "letter-level" TFP estimates are available for aggregation to total industry and to nonagricultural market sector industries for 9 EU countries beginning in 1995 and 11 countries beginning 2001. The limitation on EU countries available for analysis of total factor productivity change reflects the availability of sufficient years of consistent input and output data for industry-level growth accounting.

The EUKLEMS & INTANProd data used here are from the project's analytical module, accessed late February 2023.[24] For international comparability, the intangible capital estimates reflect the incorporation of price deflators for brand and marketing that are harmonized to include the drop in advertising media marketing costs shown in figure 7.5 (b); see Bontadini et al. (2023, pages 31–32). The quality change component of asset price deflators for computers, communications equipment, and software also are harmonized across countries, and net stocks of capital (intangible and tangible) are estimated using common rates of economic depreciation.

7.7.1 Growth Decompositions

The growth accounting reported below is in per hour terms, i.e., the growth in output per hour is decomposed into its proximate factors. The accounting for the European aggregate is developed at the country-industry level, where industries are aggregated to nonfarm "market" sector aggregates for each country and weighted using purchasing power parities to form the European aggregate. Nonfarm market sector aggregates used here exclude the public sector and most majority-public industries, resulting in coverage

23. Methods used to develop the harmonized estimates of intangible investment are documented in Bontadini et al (2023), available on the EUKLEMS & INTANProd portal at https://euklems-intanprod-llee.luiss.it. Compared with previous estimates issued via the INTANInvest database (at www.intaninvest.net), the figures in EUKLEMS & INTANProd reflect significant improvements to the own-account components of intangible investment and to intangible asset price deflators for non-national accounts components.

24. Compared with previous editions of EUKLEMS, the LUISS update presents productivity in two "modules": one with capital stock estimate issued by national statistical offices ("statistical" module) and another harmonized for international comparability ("analytical" module).

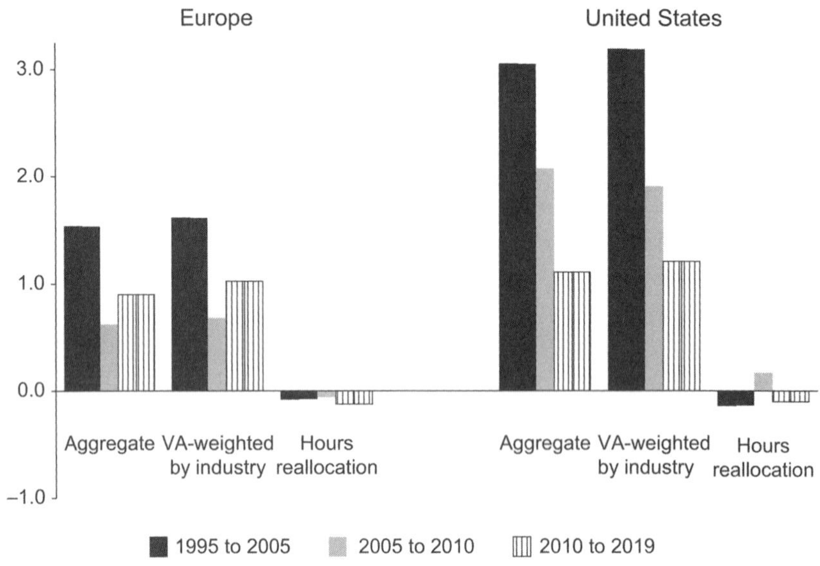

Fig. 7.7 Labor productivity and hours reallocation, percentage points per year
Source: EUKELMS & INTANProd. LLEE (2023).

that is broadly similar, though not identical, to the nonfarm business sector used for headline productivity statistics in the United States.[25]

As commonly understood, country-level output per hour reflects both "within" and "between" industry sector effects, with the reallocation of labor across sectors (the "between" effect), e.g., out of agriculture to manufacturing, being an important factor driving productivity change in some countries. Figure 7.7 shows that the reallocation of hours across market sector industries has had a negligible impact on broad changes in market sector output per hour in Europe and the United States in recent decades.[26]

The calculations reported in figure 7.7 follow Stiroh (2002). The first set of columns shows changes in aggregate labor productivity $d\ln(V/H)$, where H denotes aggregate hours and V real value-added output, and second two sets of bars display its decomposition into two terms, the impact of productivity growth in each industry (a "pure productivity" or "within" effect)—and a reallocation effect, the impact of hours worked moving from low- to high-productivity industries, i.e.,

$$d\ln\left(\frac{V}{H}\right) = \sum_i \sigma_i^{PV} d\ln\left(\frac{V_i}{H_i}\right) + \sum_i \sigma_i^{PV} d\ln H_i - d\ln H \tag{8}$$

25. The market sector aggregates are formed as described in footnote 7.

26. This statement excludes the global pandemic year 2020, where reallocation of hours jumped but was largely reversed thereafter; for further discussion and individual country results, see Bontadini et al. 2024).

where σ_i^{PV} denotes the value-added (Divisia) weight of industry *i* in (nominal) aggregate value added, and the second and third terms on the right-hand side (combined) capture reallocation. As explained in Stiroh (2002, 1572), aggregate hours growth, $d \ln H$, weights industries by their (lagged) share of aggregate hours, so aggregate productivity rises if industries with value-added shares above their hourly labor share experience growth in hours.

To analyze the drop in "pure" labor productivity growth in market sector industries in the aftermath of the global financial recession (GFR), period averages from 2010 to 2019 are compared with those from 1995 to 2005 for two reasons. First, the comparisons exclude the onset and initial recovery years of the GFR during which changes in factor utilization created sharp, temporary fluctuations in productivity that obscure underlying trends.[27] Second, our analysis of trends in big data pointed to 2009/2010 as a break date for the emergence of efficiency effects due to the increased use of data in the production of intangible assets such as marketing, industrial design, and organization practices/structure.

Figure 7.8 sets out decompositions of the within-industry change in labor productivity that account for the full range of intangibles per table 7.2. These decompositions are calculated as follows:

$$(9) \qquad \sum_i \sigma_i^{PV} d \ln\left(\frac{V_i}{H_i}\right) = \sum_i \sigma_i^{PL} d \ln\left(\frac{L}{H_i}\right) + \sum_i \sigma_i^{PK} d \ln\left(\frac{K_i}{H_i}\right) + \sum_i \sigma_i^{PR} d \ln\left(\frac{R_i}{H_i}\right) + d \ln a$$

where the first term is the contribution of labor composition, the second two are contributions of capital intensity (tangible and intangible), and the final term total factor productivity.[28] Comparing the first set of columns in figure 7.8 for each region with the last set (i.e., comparing average changes and contribution from 1995 to 2005 with 2010 to 2019), the drop in labor productivity growth is mainly accounted for by slowdowns in tangible capital deepening and total factor productivity (TFP) growth. In the United States, TFP growth is 0.9 percentage point less per year in the period after 2010. In Europe the drop is much less, about 0.2 percentage points, though it followed five years during which TFP posted a sharp negative average change (–0.5 percent per year). That said, the drops in labor productivity, contribution of tangible capital intensity, and TFP growth are rather more dramatic for the United States.[29]

27. This is not to imply that these temporary factors are similar for each region shown. Indeed, differences in labor market strategies, e.g., a greater emphasis on job retention strategies and job stability in the Euro area relative to the United States, appear to create very disparate short-run impacts on job levels in response to a common shock.

28. For simplicity, the superscript notation for the income shares on the right side of equation (10) do not indicate that the nominal values for each factor's income have their own price element.

29. These drops from the so-called "bubble" years may seem exaggerated compared to the 20 years of slow productivity growth that preceded them. But when the recent experience is

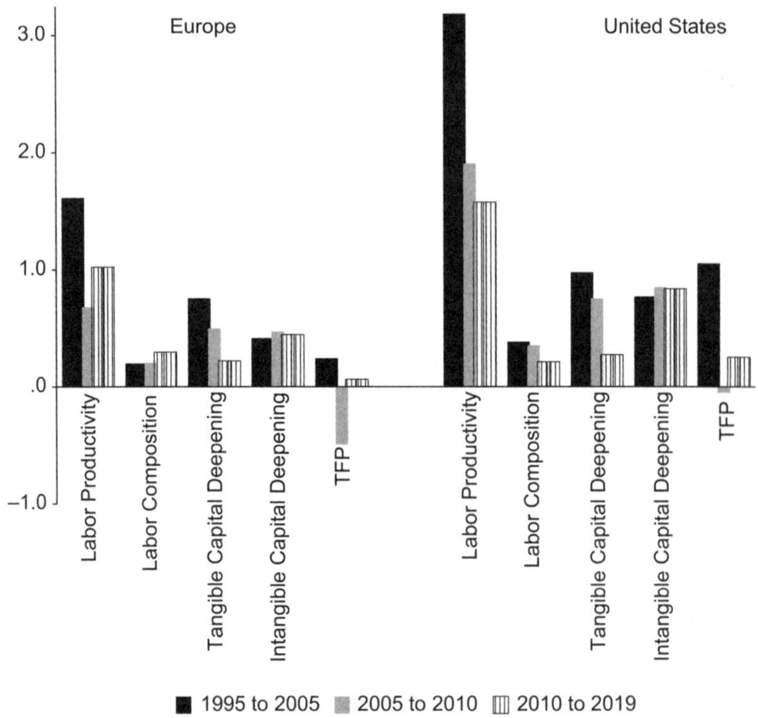

Fig. 7.8 Decompositions of growth in labor productivity, percentage points, annual rate

Note: The bars labeled "Labor productivity" correspond to the value-added weighted industry aggregate shown in the middle set of bars in figure 7.8. European countries include Denmark (DK), Germany (DE), Finland (FI), France (FR), Italy (IT), Netherlands (NL), Spain (ES), Sweden (SE), and the United Kingdom (UK).

Source: EUKELMS & INTANProd. LLEE (2023).

The contribution of the second set of bars (labor composition) reflects the per hour contribution of increases in (employed) human capital, i.e., the contribution of changes in the proportion of high-skilled/high-wage jobs in an economy. Though this effect works in opposite directions in Europe vs the United States, the contribution of changes in labor composition to explaining developments in productivity growth in these regions over the past 20 years is relatively modest.

compared with longer-term averages, i.e., from 1948 to 2005, the drops in the contribution of tangible capital intensity and TFP growth shown in figure 7.8 are in line with historical experience. According to official BLS historical statistics, the contribution of tangible intensity to labor productivity is the same from 1948 to 2005 as it is from 1995 to 2005, and TFP growth is just 0.1 percentage point less. Labor productivity growth was exceptionally high in the United States in the bubble years, however, averaging 0.6 percentage points per year higher compared with growth during the preceding 47 years.

The important takeaway from figure 7.8 is that *direct* contribution of intangible capital deepening does not contribute to the productivity slowdown. The rate at which workers in both Europe and the United States were equipped with intangible capital was well maintained for the period shown in the figure. And the edge down in intangible capital deepening shown in the post-GFR period for the United States reverses direction if we include figures for the pandemic period (2020 and 2021), which are available for the United States but not for Europe; US labor productivity and TFP growth are a tad higher too when the pandemic period is added.[30] That resources continued to be invested in innovation while the growth of TFP slowed suggests that the slowdown story must be about, at least in part, changes in the diffusion of the fruits of those investments across firms and industries in these economies.

Before we turn to discussing innovation diffusion, consider further how we might interpret the fact that the contribution of intangible capital deepening did not slow as productivity growth slowed.

7.7.2 Interpretation of Innovation

When considering innovation, economists typically look to TFP as a measure of underlying technical progress. It seems clear that TFP as a production function "shifter" is capturing innovation, being a residual after subtracting share-weighted paid-for inputs from output, but it is rather hard to talk meaningfully about a residual with practitioners interested in innovation. Innovation strategists typically focus on how individual firms innovate (e.g., develop a new business model, launch a new product) and recognize that business decision-makers need to weigh the costs involved in bringing about change through innovation against retaining profits. Intangible investment captures the cost of implementing and managing innovations.

Whether this connection between innovation and intangible investment helps depends on how innovation at the individual organization level is discerned in economists' productivity measures. In his evidence to the Gutierrez commission (Schramm et al. 2008), Dale Jorgenson explained growth by stressing innovation versus duplication. Consider this by asking, how might the firm Peloton make more sales? One way would be to employ more K and L to produce more bikes and treadmills, i.e., growth via *duplication*. The other path would be to get more sales from existing K and L: mixing new exercise music, developing new software, re-engineering the supply process. Jorgenson called this growth via *innovation*.

The intangible capital framework gives this a natural interpretation (Goodridge, Haskel, and Wallis 2012). Innovation is output less the contribution of K and L, which suggests that innovation reflects the final two terms in (9), or

30. Based on information from the BLS; as of this writing, the EUKLEMS & INTANProd database reports data through 2020 but not 2021.

Table 7.7 Innovation accounting: innovation share of labor productivity growth

		Europe (1)	United States (2)
1.	1995 to 2005	.41	.57
2.	2010 to 2019	.50	.69

Note: Innovation share is the combined contributions of intangible capital deepening and TFP growth to labor productivity growth as a fraction of labor productivity growth.
Source: Equation (10) and figure 7.8.

$$\text{(10)} \qquad \textit{Innovation} = \sigma_Q^R dr + da$$

using the terminology of the upstream/downstream model of section 7.5. This implies that when considering innovation, residually calculated TFP growth (*da*) should not be the sole focal point of analysis but rather a fuller picture includes the appropriated returns intangible investment.

Table 7.7 summarizes the fraction of labor productivity growth accounted for by the combined contributions of intangible capital deepening and TFP growth, which is, in effect, an innovation account (Corrado and Hulten 2014). Seen from this perspective, innovation became a *more relevant* contributor to labor productivity growth in Europe and the United States since 2010 (compare line 2 with line 1). The table also suggests that innovation has been the *dominant* factor contributing to labor productivity growth in the United States since 1995 (column 2).

7.7.3 Diffusion of Commercial Knowledge and Increased Productivity Dispersion

The diffusion of commercially valuable knowledge is the primary determinant of total factor productivity growth (measured *da*) in the intangible capital framework. Cross-country and firm-level econometric work has repeatedly estimated increasing returns (or knowledge spillovers) to intangible capital.[31] In simple terms, these works imply that the proportional relationship, $da \approx .2\ dr$, could be used to represent the costless diffusion of commercially valuable knowledge in market economies. As *dr* (per worker) did not materially slow after 2010, the logical (endogenous) explanation for the slowdown in measured *da* is that factors driving these increased returns ceased to operate as strongly as they previously had.

How should we think about this interpretation? The traditional view of knowledge diffusion is that its potential for boosting market sector productivity growth is determined by an economy's innovation ecosystem. Besides

31. This refers to the aggregate implications of estimates for R&D spillovers reported by Griliches for manufacturing (e.g., Griliches 1992) and for intangible capital spillovers (excluding R&D and software) reported by Corrado, Haskel, and Jona-Lasinio (2017). The latter study used a data set from the late 1990s to the onset of the GFR.

intellectual property rights and their enforcement, innovation ecosystems consist of processes such as the ability of producers to transform new basic knowledge (e.g., research findings and new ideas) into new, useful commercial knowledge in an industry. It also depends on whether there is a healthy degree of Schumpeterian competition in an industry.

This paper has argued that the larger role of (untraded/untradable) big proprietary data used by global productivity "leaders" in the post-GFR period is consistent with a breakdown in knowledge diffusion and weak total factor productivity growth. It is also consistent with increased industry concentration and changes in regulatory frameworks regarding data. If large firms with strong internal cash flows disproportionately invest in, and benefit from, untraded big data, industry concentrations may rise. If regulatory policies prevent third-party trading of data, digital productivity leaders (whether large or small) will be able to distance themselves from competitors via their use of data capital.

These observations on the impact of proprietary big data on TFP deserve further study and econometric analysis. But the empirics developed in this paper are sufficient to frame their likely macroeconomic impact. With post-2010 growth of intangible capital services in nonagricultural market sector industries averaging 3.3 percent per year in Europe and 4.4 percent in the United States, and if data capital accounts for 50 percent of that, a complete cessation of data capital diffusion mechanism could shave 0.33 to 0.44 percentage points per year off measured total factor productivity growth in these regions, respectively. This is a sizable impact and an upper bound, which, note, does not allow for an offsetting potential boost to spillovers to software discussed in the previous section and overexplains the 2010 to 2019 drop in European TFP growth and approaches one-half of the drop in TFP growth in the United States (recall from figure 7.8 these drops were 0.2 and 0.9 percentage points, respectively).

Productivity growth via the costless replication of commercial knowledge is unlikely to have staunched completely, and other structural or policy-induced factors or mismeasurement may have contributed to the productivity slowdown. But our analysis of the increased data intensity of intangible capital, combined with the tendency for data assets to be closely held, suggest that mechanisms that boosted TFP growth in the past may have weakened with the increased use of proprietary big data in production processes.

7.8 Digital Paradoxes Unpacked and Concluding Remarks

The changing nature of the global economy has put a spotlight on intangible capital as a source of economic growth and driver of innovation. But intangible capital itself has been evolving with the digitization of modern economies and increased use of proprietary big data in production processes. At the same time productivity growth—labor productivity and total factor productivity—has slowed, creating what some have called a digital productivity paradox.

We have used an intangible assets approach to address the question of how the increased use of data in economies affects productivity. We argue that data, or more accurately transformed raw digitized records, and the capital services derived from them fit neatly into both the management/technology literature on the data stack and the economics literature on intangible capital. We estimated new measures of industry-level data investments, analyzed new price measures for intangible assets most affected by data, and outlined a simple two-sector growth accounting framework to articulate how much the relative technology gains from the use of data might affect labor productivity growth. Then, using a new multi-country total factor productivity dataset, we documented and analyzed how the slowdown in total factor productivity growth in major developed economies may have been affected by the increased use of proprietary big data.

An econometric analysis found a statically significant overlap between our new "data stack"–inspired estimates of data capital and the estimates of intangible capital in EUKLEMS & INTANProd. The overlap was concentrated in components hypothesized to be strongly driven by modern data use: investments in branding and marketing, marketing research, industrial design, and organization processes and structure. This does not imply that all of the intangible assets in these categories in each industry are, in fact, data assets, but rather that the conceptual notion that data capital strongly overlaps with available estimates of intangible capital is statistically grounded.

Our modeling of the economic impacts of data capital produced two results and associated predictions not featured in prior works. Both results stem from the fact that modern data capital, though inherently nonrival, reflects the rise of proprietary big data and its use in production primarily as an "innovation in the method of innovation." Our analysis implied that the efficiencies associated with modern data capital lower prices for intangible assets and that the proprietary nature of big data strengthens the (partial) appropriability of the intangible asset class. The first-order impacts of these results on productivity are that the use of data capital boosts labor productivity growth (the efficiency effect) but that the increased data intensity of intangibles weakens commercial knowledge diffusion and diminishes TFP growth (the appropriability effect).

In stepping through all of this—from how we should conceptualize and measure big data as an asset to framing its first-order impacts on macro productivity growth—we shed light on several frequently mentioned paradoxes of modern digital economies. The first is that the much-touted efficiency gains promised for businesses as they incorporate AI and big data into decision-making likely *are* present in economies, but they are not so readily "seen." Data investments overlap mainly with components of intangible capital that are not included in national accounts investment, and thus the size and relative efficiency of data investments are not very apparent in our macrodata.

This paper argued that the relative efficiency of data capital is captured by changes in the relative price of data-intensive intangible assets (sign reversed). Price research on data-intensive intangibles is underdeveloped, and an important implication of this paper is that the measurement of these asset prices deserves more attention as data technologies and data use gain more traction in business processes. This paper reported *relative* price declines for branding, marketing, and organizational change that ranged from 2.2 to 3.2 percent per year in the United States. Though these price declines are not nearly as dramatic as drops in relative prices for IT capital during the late 1990s and early 2000s, this paper also found that data investment is rather large—about 8 percent of market sector gross value added on average for the countries studied in this paper (and a figure validated by a very recent survey conducted in the United Kingdom). Combined with the fact that most data assets are produced in-house, i.e., are domestic production, and that most data assets are intangibles not included as investment in national accounts, the potential for data capital to contribute to "unseen" growth in labor productivity is significant.

In our work in this paper, we used a multi-country data set that covers all intangibles and incorporates price measures that capture at least some of the efficiency effects of data capital. The implied boost to labor productivity stemming from these effects was about 0.2 percentage points in countries with significant investments in intangibles. But the calculations also reveal that the boost to labor productivity from the use of data capital appears to be offset by the appropriability effect that diminishes aggregate TFP, perhaps in absolute amounts by as much as 0.3 or 0.4 percentage points per year. This is an upper bound and our discussion of the impacts of data on the production processes for intangibles noted that spillovers to software may have increased in the age of big data.

One might ask whether data capital's (negative) appropriability effect is an economic rationale for what some describe as the downside (or paradox) of the digital transformation of modern economies: the unleashing of winner-take-all forces that stifle the spread of innovations. There are several points to make here, the first of which is that in the context of the intangible capital framework, an increase in the complexity of new marketing, design, and organizational assets that makes them harder to copy is not per se anticompetitive (any more than is the introduction of a newly engineered, complex polymer). It's rather that such science and engineering breakthroughs are more often disclosed (via patents) whereas data knowledge is more likely to be held closely as a trade secret. Second, the winner-take-all view that recent growth has been slowed by diminished competition is often framed as a correlate of rising industry concentration and market power, but measures of industry concentration have been rising for a very long time—100 years according to Kwon, Ma, and Zimmerman (2023)—suggesting the use of big data and digital business model platforms is not a fundamental factor affecting the rise in industry concentration.

Finally, the winner-take-all, excessive market power view is typically supported by empirics that do not account for all intangibles (or neglect them entirely), leading observers to misstate the degree of excess profits in an economy. Here we account for all intangibles, and when this is done, as shown in Corrado et al. (2022a, figure 4), the realized after-tax rate of return in in private industry in the United States showed no material increase after 1995. And while the rise of proprietary big data may be staunching knowledge diffusion and diminishing the rate of TFP growth, these outcomes can be reversed by policies that promote open public data and industry data sharing (Jones and Tonetti 2020).

A full explanation for the recent productivity slowdown perhaps remains elusive, but we are hopeful that the new measurements and findings reported in this paper demonstrate that the increased importance of data assets in intangible capital is a factor in the explanation.

Acknowledgments

Paper originally prepared for the NBER/CRIW Conference on Technology, Productivity, and Economic Growth, March 17–18, 2022. The authors are grateful to the OECD Economics Directorate and the European Commission's DG ECFIN for partial financial support of work reported in this paper. For acknowledgments, sources of research support, and disclosure of the authors' material financial relationships, if any, please see https://www.nber.org/books-and-chapters/technology-productivity-and-economic-growth/data-intangible-capital-and-productivity.

References

Aghion, Philippe, and Peter Howitt. 1992. "A Model of Growth Through Creative Destruction." *Econometrica* 60 (2): 323–51.

Arrieta-Ibarra, Imanol, Leonard Goff, Diego Jiménez-Hernández, Jaron Lanier, and E. Glen Weyl. 2018. "Should We Treat Data as Labor?" AEA Papers and Proceedings 108 (May): 38–42.

Awano, Gaganan, Mark Franklin, Jonathan Haskel, and Zafeira Kastrinaki. 2010. "Investing in Innovation: Findings from the UK Investment in Intangible Assets Survey." NESTA Index Report.

Akcigit, Ufuk, and Sina T. Ates. 2021. "Ten Facts on Declining Business Dynamism and Lessons from Endogenous Growth Theory." *American Economic Journal: Macroeconomics* 13 (1): 257–98.

Andrews, Dan, Chiara Criscuolo, and Peter N. Gal. 2016. "The Best versus the Rest: The Global Productivity Slowdown, Divergence across Firms and the Role of Public Policy." OECD Productivity Working Papers 5. OECD Publishing.

Autor, David H. 2013. "The 'Task Approach' to labor Markets: An Overview." *Journal of Labour Market Research* 46 (3). DOI 10.1007/s12651–013–0128-z.

Babina, Tania, Greg Buchak, and Will Gornall. 2022. "Customer Data Access and Fintech Entry: Early Evidence from Open Banking." Stanford University Graduate School of Business Research Paper, March 31. https://ssrn.com/abstract=4071214 or http://dx.doi.org/10.2139/ssrn.4071214.

Babina, Tania, Anastassia Fedyk, Alex He, and James Hodson. 2022. "Artificial Intelligence, Firm Growth, and Product Innovation." https://ssrn.com/abstract=3651052 or http://dx.doi.org/10.2139/ssrn.3651052.

Baruffaldi, Stefano, Brigitte van Beuzekom, Helene Dernis, Dietmar Harhoff, Nandan Rao, David Rosenfeld, and Mariagrazia Squicciarini. 2020. "Identifying and measuring developments in artificial intelligence: Making the impossible possible," OECD Science, Technology and Industry Working Papers, No. 2020/05, OECD Publishing, Paris, https://doi.org/10.1787/5f65ff7e-en.

Basu, Susanto. 2019. "Are Price-Cost Markups Rising in the United States? A Discussion of the Evidence." *Journal of Economic Perspectives* 33 (3): 3–22.

Bontadini, Fillipo, Carol A. Corrado, Jonathan E. Haskel, Massimiliano Iommi, and Cecilia Jona-Lasinio. 2023. "EUKLEMS & INTANProd: Industry Productivity Accounts with Intangibles." LUISS Lab of European Economics. Deliverable D2.3.1, February 2023. https://euklems-intanprod-llee.luiss.it/wp-content/uploads/2023/02/EUKLEMS_INTANProd_D2.3.1.pdf.

Bontadini, Fillipo, Carol A. Corrado, Jonathan E. Haskel, Massimiliano Iommi, Cecilia Jona-Lasinio, and Tsutomu Miyagawa. 2024. "Intangible Capital, TFP Growth and Green Shoots in New Productivity Data." *International Productivity Monitor* (Spring issue): 3–37.

Brynjolfsson, Erik, and Andrew McAfee. 2014. *The Second Machine Age: Work, Progress, and Prosperity in a Time of Brilliant Technologies*, first edition. New York: W. W. Norton & Company.

Byrne, David and Carol Corrado. 2017a. "ICT services and Their Prices: What Do They Tell Us about Productivity and Technology?" *International Productivity Monitor* 33 (Fall): 150–81.

Byrne, David, and Carol Corrado. 2017b. "ICT Asset Prices: Marshalling Evidence into New Measures." Finance and Economics Discussion Series 2017–016. Washington: Board of Governors of the Federal Reserve System. https://doi.org/10.17016/FEDS.2017.016r1.

Byrne, David, Carol Corrado, and Dan Sichel. 2021. "The Rise of Cloud Computing: Minding Your P's, Q's and K's." In *Measuring and Accounting for Innovation in the Twenty-First Century*, Studies in Income and Wealth, volume 78, edited by C. Corrado, J. Haskel, J. Miranda, and D. Sichel, 519–51. Chicago, IL: Chicago University Press.

Chiarello, Filippo, Paola Belingheri, and Gualtiero Fantoni. 2021. "Data Science for Engineering Design: State of the Art and Future Directions." *Computers in Industry* 129: 103447.

Colecchia, Alessandra, and Paul Schreyer. 2001. "ICT Investment and Economic Growth in the 1990s: Is the United States a Unique Case? A Comparative Study of Nine OECD Countries." OECD STI Working Paper 2001/7. Paris: OECD Publishing.

Corrado, Carol. 2024. "Intangible Capital: What It Is and Why It Matters." In *The Measure of Economies: Measuring Productivity in an Age of Technological Change*, edited by Marshall Reinsdorf and Louise Sheiner, 89–139. Chicago, IL: University of Chicago Press.

Corrado, Carol, Chiara Criscuolo, Jonathan Haskel, Alexander Himbert, and Cecilia Jona-Lasinio. 2021. "New Evidence on Intangibles, Diffusion and Productivity." OECD STI Working Paper 2021/10 (Juy). Paris: OECD Publishing. https://doi.org/10.1787/de0378f3-en.

Corrado, Carol A., Peter Goodridge, and Jonathan E. Haskel. 2011. "Constructing a Price Deflator for R&D: Calculating the Price of Knowledge Investments as a Residual." https://ssrn.com/abstract=2117802.

Corrado, Carol, Jonathan Haskel, Massimiliano Iommi, and Cecilia Jona-Lasinio. 2022a. "The Value of Data in Digital-Based Business Models: Measurement and Economic Policy Implications." OECD Economics Department Working Papers, No. 1723, August. Paris: OECD Publishing. https://doi.org/10.1787/d960a10c-en.

Corrado, Carol, Jonathan Haskel, Massimiliano Iommi, and Cecilia Jona-Lasinio. 2022b. "Measuring Data as an Asset: Framework, Methods and Preliminary Estimates." OECD Economics Department Working Papers, No. 1731, November. Paris: OECD Publishing. https://doi.org/10.1787/b840fb01-en.

Corrado, Carol, Jonathan Haskel, and Cecilia Jona-Lasinio. 2017. "Knowledge Spillovers, ICT, and Productivity Growth." *Oxford Bulletin of Economics and Statistics* 79 (4): 592–618.

Corrado, Carol, Jonathan Haskel, Cecilia Jona-Lasinio, and Massimiliano Iommi. 2022. "Intangible Capital and Modern Economies." *Journal of Economic Perspectives* 36 (3): 3–28.

Corrado, Carol, Charles R. Hulten, and Daniel Sichel. 2005. "Measuring Capital and Technology: An Expanded Framework." In *Measuring Capital in the New Economy*, Studies in Income and Wealth, volume 66, edited by C. Corrado, J. Haltiwanger, and D. Sichel, 11–46. Chicago, IL: University of Chicago Press.

Corrado, Carol, Charles R. Hulten, and Daniel Sichel. 2009. "Intangible Capital and U.S. Economic Growth." *Review of Income and Wealth* 55 (3): 661–85.

Corrado, Carol A., and Charles R. Hulten. 2014. "Innovation Accounting." In *Measuring Economic Sustainability and Progress*, Studies in Income and Wealth, volume 72, edited by Dale W. Jorgenson, J. Steven Landefeld, and Paul Schreyer, 595–628. Chicago, IL: University of Chicago Press.

Coyle, Diane, and David Nguyen. 2018. "Cloud Computing and National Accounting." Economic Statistics Centre of Excellence (ESCoE) Discussion Paper DP-2018–19. London, UK: Economic Statistics Centre of Excellence (ESCoE).

Crouzet, Nicolas, and Janice C. Eberly. 2019. "Understanding Weak Capital Investment: The Role of Market Concentration and Intangibles." NBER Working Paper No. 25869. Cambridge, MA: National Bureau of Economic Research.

De Rassenfosse, Gaétan, and Adam B. Jaffe. 2017. "Econometric Evidence on the R&D Depreciation Rate." NBER Working Paper No. 23072. Cambridge, MA: National Bureau of Economic Research.

De Ridder, Maarten. 2019. "Market Power and Innovation in the Intangible Economy." Discussion Papers, No 1907, Centre for Macroeconomics (CFM). https://EconPapers.repec.org/RePEc:cfm:wpaper:1907.

Economist. 2017. "Leader: The World's Most Valuable Resource Is No Longer Oil, But Data." *Economist*. The Economist Group Limited, May 6.

Goodridge, Peter, Jonathan Haskel, and Harold Edquist. 2021. "We See Data Everywhere Except in the Productivity Statistics." *Review of Income and Wealth* 68 (4): 862–94. https://doi.org/10.1111/roiw.12542.

Goodridge, Peter, Jonathan Haskel, and Gavin Wallis. 2012. "UK Innovation Index: Productivity and Growth in UK Industries." NESTA Working Paper 12/09.

Griliches, Zvi. 1992. "The Search for R&D Spillovers." *Scandinavian Journal of Economics* 94 (Supplement): S29–47.

Haskel, Jonathan, and Stian Westlake. 2018. *Capitalism without Capital: The Rise of the Intangible Economy*. Princeton, NJ: Princeton University Press.

Hughes-Cromwick, Ellen, and Julia Coronado. 2019. "The Value of US Government Data to US Business Decisions." *Journal of Economic Perspectives* 33 (1): 131–46.

International Monetary Fund (IMF). 2019. "The Rise of Corporate Market Power and Its Macroeconomic Effects." In *World Economic Outlook* (April), Chapter 2, 55–76. https://www.imf.org/en/Publications/WEO/Issues/2019/03/28/world-economic-outlook-april-2019.

Jones, Charles I. 2005. "Growth and Ideas." In *Handbook of Economic Growth*, edition 1, volume 1, edited by Philippe Aghion and Steven Durlauf, 1063–1111. Amsterdam: Elsevier.

Jones, Charles I., and Christopher Tonetti. 2020. "Nonrivalry and the Economics of Data." NBER Working Paper No. 26260. Cambridge, MA: National Bureau of Economic Research.

Jorgenson, Dale. 1963. "Capital Theory and Investment Behavior." *American Economic Review* 53 (2): 247–59.

Ker, Daniel, and Emanuele Mazzini. 2020. "Perspectives on the Value of Data and Data Flows." OECD Digital Economy Papers 299. OECD Publishing.

Kwon, Spencer Yongwook, Yueran Ma, and Kaspar Zimmermann. 2023. "100 Years of Rising Corporate Concentration." University of Chicago, Becker Friedman Institute for Economics Working Paper No. 2023–20, February. https://ssrn.com/abstract=4362319 or http://dx.doi.org/10.2139/ssrn.4362319.

Lall, Subir, and Li Zeng. 2020. "Intangible Investment and Low Inflation: A Framework and Some Evidence." IMF Working Paper WP/20/190, September.

Lev, B. 2019. "Ending the Accounting-for-Intangibles Status Quo." *European Accounting Review* 28(4): 713–36. DOI: 10.1080/09638180.2018.1521614.

Li, Wendy C. Y., and P. J. Chi. 2021. "Online Platforms' Creative 'Disruption' in Organizational Capital—The Accumulated Information of the Firm." Moon Economics Institute Discussion Paper, No. 1, August.

Li, Wendy C. Y., Makoto Nirei, and Kazufumi Yamana. 2019. "There's No Such Thing as a Free Lunch in the Digital Economy." BEA Working Paper No WP2019-2. Washington DC: US Department of Commerce, Bureau of Economic Analysis.

LUISS Lab of European Economics (LLEE). 2023. "EU KLEMS & INTANProd database." LUISS University [producer]. Accessed February 25, 2023. https://euklems-intanprod-llee.luiss.it/.

Mandel, Michael. 2019. "Building the New Manufacturing Stack." *Forbes*, August 20. https://www.forbes.com/sites/michaelmandel1/2019/08/20/building-the-new-manufacturing-stack/?sh=623f722b561f.

Maslej, Nestor, Loredana Fattorini, Erik Brynjolfsson, John Etchemendy, Katrina Ligett, Terah Lyons, James Manyika, Helen Ngo, Juan Carlos Niebles, Vanessa Parli, Yoav Shoham, Russell Wald, Jack Clark, and Raymond Perrault. 2023. "The AI Index 2023 Annual Report." April. AI Index Steering Committee, Institute for Human-Centered AI, Stanford University, Stanford, CA.

Mayer-Schönberger, V., and K. Cukier. 2013. *Big Data: A Revolution That Will Transform How We Live, Work, and Think*. Houghton Mifflin Harcourt.

Nguyen, David, and Marta Paczos. 2020. "Measuring the Economic Value of Data and Cross-Border Data Flows: A Business Perspective." OECD Digital Economy Papers No. 297. Paris: OECD Publishing.

Nordhaus, William D. 2021. "Are We Approaching an Economic Singularity? Information Technology and the Future of Economic Growth." *American Economic Journal: Macroeconomics* 13 (1): 299–332.

Open Data Institute. 2016. "Research: The Economic Value of Open versus Paid Data." Accessed March 2021. https://theodi.org/article/research-the-economic value-of-open-versus-paid-data.

Organisation for Economic Co-operation and Development (OECD). 2013. "Exploring the Economics of Personal Data: A Survey of Methodologies for Measuring Monetary Value," OECD Digital Economy Papers No. 220, OECD Publishing, Paris.

Oulton, Nicholas. 2012. "Long Term Implications of the ICT Revolution: Applying the Lessons of Growth Accounting and Growth Theory." *Economic Modelling* 29 (5): 1722–1736.

PriceWaterhouseCoopers LLP. 2019. "Putting a Value on Data." Report. https://www.pwc.co.uk/data-analytics/documents/putting-value-on-data.pdf.

Robbins, Carol, Gizam Korkmaz, Ledia Guci, José B. Santiago Calderón, and Brandon L. Kramer. 2021. "A First Look at Open-Source Software Investment in the United States and in Other Countries, 2009–2019." Paper presented the IARIW-ESCoE Conference, Measuring Intangible Capitals and their Contribution to Growth, November, RSA House, London.

Roca, Ciara. 2021a. "How To Build a Modern Data Stock from the Ground Up." Fivetran blog, July 8. Accessed August 25, 2021. https://fivetran.com/blog/how-to-build-a-modern-data-stack-from-the-ground-up.

Roca, Ciara. 2021b. "What Is the Modern Data Stack?" Data Insights, October 5. Accessed August 25, 2021. https://fivetran.com/blog/what-is-the-modern-data-stack.

Romer, Paul M. 1990. "Endogenous Technological Change." *Journal of Political Economy* 95 (5): S71–S102.

Santiago-Calderón, Jose B., and Dylan Rassier. 2022. "Valuing the US Data Economy Using Machine Learning and Online Job Postings." Paper prepared for the NBER/CRIW Conference on Technology, Productivity, and Economic Growth, March 17–18, 2022, Washington, DC.

Schramm, Carl J., Ashish Arora, Rajesh K. Chandy, Kathleen Cooper, Dale W. Jorgenson, Donald S. Siegel, David L. Bernd, et al. 2008. "Innovation Measurement: Tracking the State of Innovation in the American Economy: A Report to the Secretary of Commerce by the Advisory Committee on Measuring Innovation in the 21st Century Economy." Department of Commerce.

Silk, Alvin J., and Ernst R. Berndt. 2003. "Scale and Scope Economies in the Global Advertising and Marketing Services Business." NBER Working Paper No. 9965. Cambridge, MA: National Bureau of Economic Research.

Squicciarini, Mariagrazia, and Marie Le Mouel. 2012. "Defining and Measuring Investment in Organisational Capital: Using US Microdata to Develop a Task-based Approach." OECD Science, Technology and Industry Working Papers 2012/5. Paris: OECD Publishing.

Statistics Canada. 2019a. "Measuring Investment in Data, Databases and Data Science: Conceptual Framework." June. Ottawa, Canada: Statistics Canada.

Statistics Canada. 2019b. "The Value of Data in Canada: Experimental Estimates." July. Ottawa, Canada: Statistics Canada.

Stiroh, Kevin J. 2002. "Are ICT Spillovers Driving the New Economy?" *Review of Income and Wealth* 48 (1): 33–57.

The Conference Board. 2021. "Skills Growing in Demand for Tech Jobs." March 11. Accessed January 4, 2023. https://www.conference-board.org/topics/help-wanted-online/skills-growing-in-demand-for-tech-jobs.

Timmer, Marcel, Robert Inklaar, Mary O'Mahony, and Bark van Ark. 2011. "Productivity and Economic Growth in Europe: A Comparative Industry Perspective." *International Productivity Monitor* 21 (Spring): 3–23.

United Nations Digitalization Task Team for the SNA 2025 (DZTT). 2023. "DZ.6 Recording of Data in National Accounts." Accessed March 15, 2023. https://

unstats.un.org/unsd/nationalaccount/RAdocs/DZ6_GN_Recording_of_Data_in_NA.pdf.

United Nations Globalization Task Team for the SNA 2025 (GZTT). 2023. "G.9 Payments for Nonproduced Knowledge-Based Capital (Marketing Assets)." Joint Thirty-Eighth Meeting of the IMF Committee on Balance of Payments Statistics and Eighteenth Meeting of the Advisory Expert Group on National Accounts, March 7–10, 2022. Last accessed March 15,2023. https://unstats.un.org/unsd/nationalaccount/aeg/2022/M18/M18_10_G9.pdf.

Varian, Hal. 2019. "Artificial Intelligence, Economics, and Industrial Organization." In *The Economics of Artificial Intelligence: An Agenda*, edited by Ajay Agrawal, Joshua Gans, and Avi Goldfarb. Chicago, IL: University of Chicago Press.

World Economic Forum. 2011. "Personal Data: The Emergence of a New Asset Class." Report by the World Economic Forum retrieved from https://www3.weforum.org/docs/WEF_ITTC_PersonalDataNewAsset_Report_2011.pdf.

Zhang Daniel, Saurabh Mishra, Erik Brynjolfsson, John Etchemendy, Deep Ganguli, Barbara Grosz, Terah Lyons, James Manyika, Juan Carlos Niebles, Michael Sellitto, Yoav Shoham, Jack Clark, and Raymond Perrault. 2021. "The AI Index 2021 Annual Report." AI Index Steering Committee, Human-Centered AI Institute, Stanford University, Stanford, CA.

8

Valuing the US Data Economy Using Machine Learning and Online Job Postings

José Bayoán Santiago Calderón and Dylan G. Rassier

8.1 Introduction

With the recent proliferation of data collection and uses in the digital economy, the understanding and statistical treatment of data stocks and flows is of interest among compilers and users of national economic accounts. During the last revision of the *System of National Accounts* (SNA) (United Nations 2010), which is the international standard for national economic accounts, the treatment of data stocks and flows was a topic of discourse among statistical agencies and international organizations, who ultimately settled on the treatment of *databases* as a subcategory of software in capital formation (Ahmad 2004, 2005). Current global efforts for the next revision of the *SNA*, expected to be published in 2025, have a renewed focus on the valuation and recording of the information content of databases—i.e., the embedded *data*—in response to the presumed rapid increase in data stocks and flows over the last decade and longer.

The value of data is implied in the profits and market values of some firms. In 2020, two of the largest global data firms—Alphabet Inc. (Google) and Meta Platforms Inc. (Facebook)—had a combined net income before tax of $81.3 billion, which amounted to 3.7 percent of US corporate profits before tax. In November 2021, the combined market capitalization of the two firms was $2.9 trillion, which amounted to 7.5 percent of the market

José Bayoán Santiago Calderón is a research economist in the Analysis and Research Group at the Bureau of Economic Analysis.

Dylan G. Rassier was Chief of National Accounts Research and Analysis at the Bureau of Economic Analysis when this chapter was written.

capitalization of all S&P 500 firms.[1] While the value of data may be implied in these measures, data stocks and flows are not visible in national economic accounts under the current *SNA* treatment. Moreover, understanding and measuring the value of data present challenges to economic statisticians.

In this paper, we measure the value of own-account data stocks and flows for the US business sector by summing the production costs of data-related activities implicit in occupations. Production costs include labor costs, capital costs, and intermediate consumption. To estimate production costs, we apply a markup to an estimate of the wage bill for data-related activities, which is consistent with the Bureau of Economic Analysis (BEA) methodology for own-account software. Our method augments the traditional sum-of-costs methodology for measuring other own-account intellectual property products (IPPs) in national economic accounts by proxying occupation-level time-use factors using a machine learning model and the text of online job advertisements (Blackburn 2021).

The occupation-level time-use factors can be decomposed into two components: (1) the fraction of jobs in an occupation engaged in qualifying activities based on data-relevant skills revealed in the job advertisement; and (2) the average share of time allocated to the data-relevant activities. Using online job advertisements from Burning Glass Technologies (BGT), skills in the BGT taxonomy that are relevant to data-related activities are identified, including data entry, storage, analysis, and management. The fraction of jobs in an occupation engaged in qualifying activities is given by the fraction of BGT job advertisements that contain at least one of the data-relevant skills. The average time allocation is based on the distance of an occupation to known data-intensive occupations that serve as "landmark" occupations (e.g., data entry keyers or statisticians). A doc2vec model is then trained on the job advertisement text for each occupation to obtain a numerical representation of what the occupation-level job postings convey. Using the numerical representation, occupation-level pair-wise distances are obtained to measure how "close" or similar an occupation is to the landmark occupations. The product of the similarity to a landmark occupation and the ratio of job openings with identified data-relevant skills serves as the proxy for the occupation-level time-use factor. We then apply the time-use factors to the product of average annual wages and annual number of employees by occupation at the 3-digit North American Industry Classification System (NAICS) level available from the US Bureau of Labor Statistics (BLS) Occupational Employment and Wage Statistics (OEWS) to calculate the

1. Net income before tax comes from each firm's 10-K filings with the US Securities and Exchange Commission for year-end December 31, 2020. Corporate profits come from BEA's National Income and Product Accounts table 6.17D (https://apps.bea.gov/iTable/iTable.cfm?reqid=19). Market capitalizations come from YCHARTS (GOOG, https://ycharts.com/companies/GOOG; FB, https://ycharts.com/companies/FB) as of November 19, 2021.

wage bill (i.e., wages and salaries, excluding employee benefits) for data-related activities.

The main challenges for measurement of own-account data stocks and flows that we address in the paper are similar to challenges imposed by other own-account IPPs that are already included in capital formation in the *SNA* and the US National Income and Product Accounts (NIPAs). First, the scope of capital formation is not yet well defined for own-account data. Second, own-account data and other own-account IPPs are at risk of multiple counting from sources such as overlap among categories of IPPs and non-rival use of data. A third challenge is what proportions of the sum-of-costs should be accounted for by labor costs, capital costs, and intermediate consumption in light of the role that capital services play in the collection, storage, analysis, and management of data. Finally, own-account data are not transacted in active markets, which means there are no observed transactions that are useful for measuring prices and depreciation. We discuss each of these challenges and our approach to addressing them in section 8.4 of the paper.

Our experimental results indicate that annual current-dollar investment in own-account data assets for the US business sector grew from $84 billion in 2002 to $186 billion in 2021, which yields an average annual growth rate of 4.2 percent. Cumulative current-dollar investment for the period 2002–2021 was $2.6 trillion. Annual current-dollar investment in own-account data for the period averaged 1.0 percent as a share of business sector value-added, 5.0 percent as a share of investment in private fixed assets, and 20.2 percent as a share of investment in IPPs. Likewise, the historical-cost net stock of data assets grew from $205 billion in 2002 to $421 billion in 2021, which yields an average annual growth rate of 3.8 percent. Using an experimental price index that we developed for data, the average annual growth rate in real data investment over the period was 7.5 percent, which yields an average annual increase in real business sector value-added growth of 4 basis points and an increase in growth in real investment in IPPs of 31 basis points. In contrast, growth in real data investment is lower than growth in real investment in software, which yields a decline in average annual growth of real investment in software of 26 basis points. For NAICS sectors, the largest dollar investments were made in Professional, Scientific, and Technical (PST) Services (NAICS 54), Manufacturing (NAICS 31–33), and Finance and Insurance (NAICS 52). The largest increases in average real value-added growth by NAICS sector shows up for Management of Companies (NAICS 55) and PST Services (NAICS 54).

The next section summarizes the *SNA* background on the treatment of own-account data stocks and flows and related literature. Section 8.3 provides details on our measurement, including source data and methodologies. Section 8.4 identifies challenges associated with measurement of own-account IPPs and how we address those challenges for own-account data. Section 8.5 reports our core experimental results and some additional experimental results of interest. Section 8.6 concludes.

8.2 National Accounts Background and Related Literature

8.2.1 System of National Accounts

The 1993 version of the *SNA* includes only a brief paragraph on the inclusion of "large databases that the enterprise expects to use in production over a period of time of more than one year" as part of the computer software category of capital formation (United Nations 1993, paragraph 10.93). There is no mention of embedded information content (i.e., data) in *SNA 1993*. Leading up to the 2008 version of the *SNA*, an *SNA* group of statistical agencies and international organizations considered the inclusion of embedded data in capital formation. To guide the discussions, Ahmad (2004) outlined two components of databases—supporting software and data stored in the database—and summarized practical challenges that countries encounter while trying to implement the vague *SNA 1993* recommendation. In light of the challenges, Ahmad (2005) described two definitions for databases considered by the *SNA* group. One definition included the value of the information content to be stored in databases as long as the information had a useful life of more than one year, and one definition did not include the value of the information content. The group recommended that the latter definition is preferable because the former definition would "open the door to the capitalization of knowledge" (Ahmad 2005, 2). Based on the summary outlined in Ahmad (2005), the group primarily considered databases maintained by statistical agencies.

The recommendation that was ultimately written into *SNA 2008* includes databases and computer software as separate categories of intellectual property products in capital formation (United Nations 2010, paragraphs 10.109–10.114). If a database is developed for own use, *SNA 2008* recommends a sum-of-costs approach to value the database. The sum-of-costs includes the cost of preparing data in a format that conforms to the database but excludes the cost of acquiring or producing the data. In addition, the sum-of-costs excludes the value of the database management system (DBMS), which is included instead with computer software. If a database is developed for sale or for license, the value should be determined by the market price, which includes the value of the information content. Thus, *SNA 2008* recommends an inconsistent treatment for data in capital formation depending whether a database is developed for own use or for sale or license. In addition, the value of data acquired or produced for inclusion in databases is not to be treated as intermediate consumption in the sum-of-costs approach for own-account databases, which is inconsistent with the inclusion of intermediate consumption in the usual sum-of-costs measurement. The overall conclusion drawn by the *SNA* group was that if data are an asset, they are a non-produced asset whose value should be limited in national accounts to measures of purchased goodwill. Thus, there should be no value of data reflected in production measures.

8.2.2 US National Accounts

The US national accounts are consistent with the *SNA* recommendations on intellectual property products, including computer software (US Bureau of Economic Analysis 2020). Similar to general practice in other countries, the US accounts do not include a separation between software and databases (i.e., the software that houses data) in published capital stock and flow measures. The value of any data included in purchased software is included in measures of investment and capital stock. The value of any data in own-account software is excluded from measures of investment and capital stock.

BEA estimates three categories of software: (1) prepackaged; (2) custom; and (3) own-account. Benchmark estimates of prepackaged and custom software are determined using a commodity flow method based on receipts reported in the US Economic Census for Software Publishers (NAICS 5112), Data Processing and Hosting (NAICS 518), and Computer Systems Design (NAICS 5415). For non-benchmark years, estimates are based on receipts reported in the Census Bureau's Service Annual Survey. Benchmark estimates of own-account software are determined using a sum-of-costs methodology based on wage data in the BLS OEWS for four occupations—Computer Programmers, Computer Systems Analysts, Software Developers, and Software Quality Assurance Analysts—and based on the Economic Census. For non-benchmark years, estimates are primarily based on the OEWS data. In addition to labor costs and intermediate consumption, own-account software includes a cost for capital services (Chute et al. 2018).

8.2.3 Related Literature

Two strands of literature provide additional context for this paper. The first is literature on the value of data, which not only suggests that data have value but also suggests that the value of data may, at least in part, be a result of a production process rather than non-produced, which is the current perspective in national economic accounts. The second is emerging literature from statistical agencies, international organizations, and other sources that is beginning to recognize the likelihood that some data are produced assets and to generate renewed focus for recording and valuing data stocks and flows.

8.2.3.1 Value of Data

Varian (2018) describes a data pyramid that is a variation of the data-information-knowledge-wisdom (DIKW) hierarchy introduced by Ackoff

(1989) and subsequently used in information science and economics (Rowley 2007; Boisot and Canals 2004). The data pyramid is used to illustrate the relationships among data that are stored as bits, information that is stored in documents, and knowledge that is stored in the human mind (Mokyr 2013). Related to the data pyramid is the data value chain presented in OECD (2013) and subsequently expanded in Moro Visconti et al. (2017). The data value chain illustrates a production process for data from an unstructured form that has very little value to a structured form that can be leveraged in a business model or other usage (Bakhshi et al. 2014). The stages of the chain include collection, storage, processing, distribution, and usage. The Moro Visconti et al. (2017) version of the data value chain focuses on business users at the last stage of the chain with the monetization of data via a business model, which may be data-dependent or data-neutral. Data-dependent business models, such as online platforms, rely heavily on data for sources of revenue and profits (Li et al. 2019; Nguyen and Paczos 2020). Data-neutral firms do not depend on data for revenue but can still realize benefits from data that help improve existing products or offer new products. The OECD (2013) version of the data value chain includes business users and also includes government, non-profit, and household users.

Hughes-Cromwick and Coronado (2019) outline the value of US government data to business decision-making. Likewise, the value of household data is evident in literature on the economics of personal privacy, which has re-emerged as an area of interest as summarized in Acquisti et al. (2016).

Farboodi and Veldkamp (2021) construct a growth model of the data economy in which data is an information asset that contributes to growth by reducing uncertainty and helping firms choose better production techniques via forecasts. The model demonstrates short-run increasing returns due to a feedback loop within the firms. However, long-run diminishing returns result in the absence of traditional technological progress in the Solow (1956) growth model because better forecasts are not a tool that can logically sustain long-run growth. In contrast to Farboodi and Veldkamp (2021), Jones and Tonetti (2020) model data contributing directly to productivity and generating long-run growth.

8.2.3.2 Recording and Valuing Data Stocks and Flows

Under the second strand of literature, statistical agencies and international organizations are renewing efforts to introduce guidelines for recording and valuing data as a produced asset in national economic accounts. Ahmad and van de Ven (2018) and Reinsdorf and Ribarsky (2020) provide background on the historical treatment of data stocks and flows and offer preliminary thoughts on moving forward with changes to the *SNA*. Rassier et al. (2019) also summarize considerations for treatment of data stocks and flows and present cursory estimates of data-related flows based on official statistical sources for the US economy. Statistics Canada (2019b) carefully defines and categorizes data, databases, and data science and presents experimental estimates for each category using a sum-of-costs measurement methodology for the Canadian economy. The Australian Bureau of Statistics and the Netherlands Central Bureau of Statistics have compiled measures of data stocks and flows based on the Canadian methodology. Each of these previous efforts have resulted in preliminary guidance that is currently being considered by the *SNA* community (United Nations Inter-Secretariat Working Group on National Accounts 2022).

Goodridge et al. (2021) are the first to provide a harmonized set of cross-country estimates for data assets in European Union countries and then estimate the contribution of data capital deepening to growth in productivity. They find that about 43 percent of employment engaged in capital formation of software and data is unaccounted for in measured own-account software and databases, and the missing piece of capital formation is growing faster than the measured piece. Goodridge et al. (2021) also provide a summary of previous economic literature on information and knowledge.

8.3 Data and Methods

The *SNA* recommendation for valuing IPPs that lack an observable market transaction is a cost-based approach including labor costs, capital costs, and intermediate consumption. For market producers, capital costs include a net return to fixed assets (or "normal profit") in addition to consumption of fixed capital. Our strategy builds on BEA's sum-of-costs methodology for own-account software. Estimates of aggregate production costs for data-related output have the general form

$$C_{i,t} = \alpha \sum \tau_{\omega} W_{\omega,i,t} H_{\omega,i,t} \tag{1}$$

where for each occupation ω, industry i, and year t, we calculate the wage bill by multiplying the annual number of employees ($H_{\omega,i,t}$) by the average annual wage ($W_{\omega,i,t}$) and an occupation-specific time-use factor (τ_{ω}) that reflects the time-effort that the occupation allocates to data-related activities. The parameter α is a markup that reflects employee benefits (not included in the wage bill), capital costs, and intermediate consumption, which yields the full production costs. The rest of this section discusses our estimation of each of the elements in equation 1.

8.3.1 Employment and Wage Data

The US Bureau of Labor Statistics (BLS) has 12 survey programs that provide information on pay and benefits. We prioritize having wage data at an occupational level specific enough to capture the activities of interest.[2] The BLS Occupational Employment and Wage Statistics (OEWS) program produces employment and wage estimates annually for around 800 occupa-

2. Pay Measure Comparison, https://data.bls.gov/apps/compensation-comparison-matrix/home.htm.

tions and is well suited for our purpose. In addition, the historical data temporal coverage dates back to the early 2000s, allowing us to generate a longer time series. Occupational data collected by the US federal statistical system is generally collected, calculated, and disseminated based on the Standard Occupational Classification (SOC) system. Employees are assigned to an occupation based on the work they perform and not on their education or training. The OEWS data are an SOC-based occupational system that uses SOC codes to assign occupations at levels for which the data are published. Some SOC codes are aggregated into a single OEWS occupational code for reporting purposes. The OEWS system allows the data to be linked to other systems such as the US Department of Labor (DOL) Occupational Information Network (O*NET) (Hopson 2021). The OEWS program reports data using the North American Industry Classification System (NAICS). We use estimates at the NAICS 3-digit subsector levels that are representative of privately owned business establishments, which excludes government and nonprofit institutions serving households (NPISH).[3]

To generate data-related employment and wage estimates for 2002–2021, we use model-based estimates (Dey et al. 2019) for 2015–2020 and official estimates for the period 2002–2014 and 2021 (US Bureau of Labor Statistics 2021). We use estimates of the average annual wage and annual number of employees for privately owned establishments at the NAICS 3-digit level. The wage series use several versions of the underlying occupational and industry systems across time. In order to obtain a consistent time series, we use the OES 2021 hybrid structure crosswalk[4] and rely on the OES 2010–2011 classification crosswalk[5] to account for the temporary codes in those two years. For example, if multiple occupations are aggregated in the latest taxonomy (OEWS 2021), the estimated average annual wage is an average of available wage data weighted by the employment estimates for the corresponding occupations. In cases when an occupation is attributed to multiple 2021 codes, which may occur due to special hybrid-code estimates, those are equally distributed among the corresponding 2021 codes. The resulting series provide us the employment and wage numbers by occupation, year, and industry.

8.3.2 Time-Use Factors

Time-use factors are important to the sum-of-costs methodology as they provide measures of time-effort allocated to the activities of interest such as data-related activities. Time-use factors have been used to examine quality of service, job satisfaction, and other outcomes in various domains such as education, health, and security. For example, the OECD Teaching and

3. The sectors and subsectors identified as NPISH include Educational Services (NAICS 61), Health Care and Social Assistance (NAICS 62), Arts, Entertainment and Recreation (NAICS 71), and Religious, Grantmaking, Civic, Professional, and Similar Organizations (NAICS 813).

4. See https://www.bls.gov/oes/soc_2018.htm.

5. See https://www.bls.gov/oes/2010_and_2011_oes_classification.xls.

Learning International Survey (TALIS) collects data on the time-use allocation of teachers among categories: (1) Administrative and leadership tasks and meetings; (2) Curriculum and teaching-related tasks and meetings; (3) Student interactions; (4) Parent or guardian interactions; and (5) Interactions with local and regional community, business and industry. In the area of health, studies have collected information on the share of time physicians spend on direct care with patients or administrative work (Woolhandler and Himmelstein 2014). While most data on time-use allocations is collected in surveys, other methods include direct observation of the work performed such as rides with police officers (Parks et al. 1999). For data as an asset, we estimate time-use factors using a methodology developed in Blackburn (2021) for data-relevant skills, which are reflected in activities including entry, storage, analysis, and management of data. Examples of specific activities include data cleaning, data wrangling, data manipulation, and data science. Following Blackburn (2021), the time-use factor τ can be decomposed as follows

$$\tau_\omega = \frac{l_\omega}{L_\omega} s^*_\omega = \rho_\omega s^*_\omega \tag{2}$$

where the time-use factor for occupation ω is the product of the fraction of employees that engage in activities of interest (ρ_ω) and an estimate of how much time the occupation allocates to the activities (s^*_ω). Without time-use factors, the sum-of-costs methodology relies on identifying specific occupations assumed to best embody the activities of interest.

8.3.2.1 *Online Job Advertisements*

The method uses online job advertisement data from Burning Glass Technologies (BGT) to estimate time-use factors for a broad range of occupations.[6] The data not only contain the job advertisement text but also enhancements, including deduplication, identified skills, degree requirements, location, and information on the employer (e.g., industry). BGT also uses their own-developed occupational autocoders to identify the occupation of the job advertisement.[7]

Lancaster et al. (2021) look at the data quality, suitability, and representativeness of BGT job advertisement data for research purposes. The study confirms several findings in the literature such as the over-representation of certain occupation groups in the BGT job advertisement data. One aspect of the BGT data that distinguishes them from other alternatives is the focus on skills rather than occupations as the main unit of analysis for understanding

6. Online job advertisements have been used in applications related to labor, education, and credential research. Examples of online job advertisement providers include Burning Glass Technologies, Indeed, and the National Labor Exchange (NLx) Research Hub. These providers collect job postings in "real-time" from various websites.

7. The NLx Research Hub uses the O*NET SOC Code AutoCoder™ (https://www.onetsocautocoder.com).

the job market (Lightcast 2023). The BGT skills taxonomy includes over 17,000 skills as well as various skill properties such as whether a skill refers to data or software (or both).

This strategy uses the BGT job advertisement data to estimate equation 2. The first component refers to the fraction of employees in an occupation who engage in data-related activities. The concept is operationalized with the following definition:

$$\hat{\rho}_{\omega} = \frac{\sum_{j=1}^{L_{\omega}} \mathbb{1}(\hat{y}_j)}{L_{\omega}} \tag{3}$$

where $\mathbb{1}(\hat{y}_j)$ denotes $\exists\, s : s \in S$, meaning s is a subset of skills identified for job advertisement y_j, and S is the set of skills identified as data relevant. In other words, a ratio is computed as the fraction of job advertisements with at least one of the data-relevant skills out of all job advertisements (L_{ω}) for each occupation. Blackburn (2021) manually identified 203 BGT skills that are data relevant, which excludes any skill deemed a software skill as a way to minimize potential overlap with capital formation in software. The top 80 data-relevant skills by frequency are presented in table 8.1.

A two-step approach is used to estimate (s_{ω}^{*}). The first step identifies the occupations with the highest rate of employees engaged in data-related activities (ρ_{ω}) based on the BGT skills. Occupations with a ρ_{ω} of at least 0.50 are denoted "landmark" occupations and assigned full time-effort. Table 8.2 shows the 17 occupations determined to be landmark occupations. Many of the occupations are obvious landmark candidates such as *data entry keyers* and various research and analyst occupations. Some of the occupations are less obvious as landmarks. For example, *wellhead pumpers* may not be an occupation immediately associated with data, but their job activities rely on monitoring and assessing data in order to act on that information promptly. For non-landmark occupations, s_{ω}^{*} is estimated as the cosine similarity to the closest landmark occupation. Mathematically,

$$\hat{s}_{\omega}^{*} = \max_{w \in M} \left\{ \frac{A_{\omega} \cdot A_{w}}{\| A_{\omega} \| \| A_{w} \|} \right\} \tag{4}$$

where M is the set of landmark occupations, A_{ω} (i.e., omega) is a numerical representation of occupation ω, and A_{w} (i.e., double-u) is the mathematical representation of occupation w (i.e., one of the landmark occupations). The effective time-use factor then becomes

$$\hat{\tau}_{\omega} = \hat{\rho}_{\omega} \hat{s}_{\omega}^{*} = \frac{\sum_{j=1}^{L_{\omega}} \mathbb{1}(\hat{y}_j)}{L_{\omega}} \max_{w \in M} \left\{ \frac{\hat{A}_{\omega} \cdot \hat{A}_{w}}{\| \hat{A}_{\omega} \| \| \hat{A}_{w} \|} \right\}. \tag{5}$$

The estimate for the full production costs of data-related activities for a given industry i at time t is then as follows:

$$\hat{C}_{i,t} = \alpha * \sum \frac{\sum_{i=1}^{L_{\omega}} \mathbb{1}(\hat{y}_i)}{L_{\omega}} \sum_{\omega \in \Omega} \left[\frac{\sum_{j=1}^{L_{\omega}} \mathbb{1}(\hat{y}_j)}{L_{\omega}} \left(\max_{w \in M} \left\{ \frac{\hat{A}_{\omega} \cdot \hat{A}_{w}}{\| \hat{A}_{\omega} \| \| \hat{A}_{w} \|} \right\} \right) \hat{W}_{\omega,i,t} \hat{H}_{\omega,i,t} \right]. \tag{6}$$

Table 8.1 BGT skills identified as data relevant

3D Seismic Data	Data Dictionary System
Accenture Data Governance Framework	Data Documentation
Advanced Data Entry	Data Encryption
Assessment Data	Data Engineering
Big Data	Data Entry
Big Data Analytics	Data Entry Prioritization
Billing Data Analysis	Data Evaluation
Biological Database Search	Data Exploitation
Business Intelligence Data Modeling	DFHSM
Cascading Big Data Applications	Data FlowDiagrams (DFDs)
Climate Data Analysis	Data Governance
Clinical Data Abstracting	Data Integration
Clinical Data Analysis	Data Integrity
Clinical Data Exchange	Data Lakes/Reservoirs
CDISC	Data Loss Prevention
Clinical Data Management	Data Management
Clinical Data Review	Data Management Platform (DMP)
Clinical Data Understanding	Data Manipulation
Clinical Database Development	Data Mapping
Clinical Research Data Accuracy and Integrity	Data Migration
Cloud Security Data Protection and Privacy	Data Mining
Columnar Databases	Data Mining Industry Knowledge
Conceptual Data Models	Data Modeling
Customer Data Integration	Data Modeling Star/Snowflake Schema
Customer Service Database	Data Multiplex System (DMS)
Data Acquisition	Data Munging
Data Acquisition Systems	Data Operations
Data Analysis	Data Platform as a Service
Data and Safety Monitoring Board	Data Pre–Processing
Data Architecture	Data Privacy
Data Archiving	Data Protection Industry Knowledge
Data Buffers	Data Protection Planning
Data Capture	Data Protection Strategy
Data Center Hardware	Data Quality
Data Cleaning	Data Quality Assessment
Data Collection	Data Reports
Data Communications	Data Science
Data Compression	Data Security
Data Conversion	Data Security Classification

Note: Top 80 skills by frequency out of 203 data relevant skills identified manually (Blackburn 2021).

8.3.2.2 Sample Design and Description

The BGT data enable observation of over 239 million job advertisements in the United States for 2010–2019. The data include over a thousand O*NET SOC 2010 occupations. The data are used to train an autocoder model for O*NET SOC 2010 using job text to obtain the numerical representation for each occupation such that we can compute pair-wise similarity between occupations. The sample design uses the occupation distribution

Table 8.2 **Landmark occupations**

O*NET SOC 2010	Description	Time-use factor
43–9021.00	Data Entry Keyers	0.94
15–1111.00	Computer and Information Research Scientists	0.77
15–1141.00	Database Administrators	0.75
15–1199.06	Database Architects	0.72
19–1029.01	Bioinformatics Scientists	0.68
19–4061.00	Social Science Research Assistants	0.67
15–2041.00	Statisticians	0.66
15–1199.07	Data Warehousing Specialists	0.63
15–2041.01	Biostatisticians	0.63
15–1199.08	Business Intelligence Analysts	0.61
53–7073.00	Wellhead Pumpers	0.60
19–3022.00	Survey Researchers	0.59
43–9111.01	Bioinformatics Technicians	0.58
43–9111.00	Statistical Assistants	0.54
29–2092.00	Hearing Aid Specialists	0.54
15–2041.02	Clinical Data Managers	0.54
43–3021.01	Statement Clerks	0.50

Note: For landmark occupations, the similarity to the nearest landmark is one, and thus the time-use factor $\hat{\tau}_\omega$ is the same as $\hat{\rho}_\omega$.

across NAICS 3-digit subsectors based on the annual number of employees in privately owned establishments from OEWS for 2015–2020. If observations available at the occupation-industry level are below the target (1,500 × percentage of occupations in a NAICS 3-digit subsector), all observations are included. Otherwise, we sample from the valid observations a targeted sample of 1,500 observations equally distributed based on the sequential order of the job posting dates. We only include occupations for which at least 100 job ads are available, meaning there is complete information for the job text, job posting date (ISO 8601), O*NET SOC 2010, and NAICS subsector. The sample design aims to be representative of the business sector in terms of the occupation-industry interactions and composition as well as temporal changes, while also maintaining desirable properties for modeling, such as avoiding extreme unbalanced classes or making inferences based on limited data. Our goal is different from traditional autocoders, which may emphasize some metric like accuracy and may prefer to focus on having better performance for frequent occupations over having acceptable performance for less frequent occupations.

Considering the observations with complete information (O*NET SOC 2010 and NAICS 3-digit codes are not always available), we sample occupations for which at least 100 observations are available and limit the observations included per occupation to around 1,500. We also exclude military occupations (SOC major group 55) and those that are exclusive to the public sector like legislators and postal service employees. The sample includes 959

O*NET SOC 2010 occupational codes that have between 101 and 1,548 observations.

The final sample comprises 1.12 million observations for which we recover the job advertisement text as well as the skills for each of the job advertisements. We split the data set by applying a clustered sampling design based on occupation-industry subsector with 90 percent of the sample being used as the training set and 10 percent as the test set.

8.3.2.3 Machine Learning Model

The modeling approach uses the doc2vec (Le and Mikolov 2014) implementation in gensim v4.0.1 (Řehůřek and Sojka 2010) for Python (van Rossum and Drake 2009) v3.8.5. The modeling technique uses paragraph vectors to capture the semantics of documents as an alternative to "bag-of-words" or "bag-of-n-grams" representations. In our case, each job advertisement is represented not just by applying a tokenization to the text but by also including indicators for each job advertisement. After training the model, each occupation is represented by a multidimensional numerical abstraction. Once the model has been fitted, we extract the features that are a 1,000-dimensional numerical representation of each O*NET SOC 2010 code. The pair-wise cosine distance is then computed to obtain the occupation similarity matrix. The similarity matrix allows us to find the most similar landmark occupation.[8]

8.3.2.4 Validation

Model Validation. Occupation autocoders are automated models that can predict occupation codes based on inputs such as job advertisements and job titles. One common autocoder regarded as a gold standard is the O*NET-SOC AutoCoder developed by R.M. Wilson Consulting, Inc. for the US Department of Labor. There are various ways to evaluate the performance of a multi-class classifier. For example, the classifier accuracy claims for the O*NET-SOC AutoCoder are stated based on the inputs, whether it operates on a job advertisement and job title or on just a job title. For job titles and job advertisement text, the model accuracy for predicting O*NET SOC 2021 codes is 85 percent based on their internal test results. Since the model is using just the unstructured job advertisement text, we expect the performance to be lower than the gold standard using additional information. Another consideration is that the labeled data are also based on the BGT autocoder for O*NET SOC 2010 codes which in turn contains errors from the BGT autocoder. Given the licensing terms and industry practices, properly assessing the performance of these tools is difficult. For example,

8. The cosine similarity can take values in the [–1,1] interval, but in practice yields cosine distances in the [0,1] interval avoiding the need for other transformations such as angular similarity.

a measure of accuracy can be significantly driven by unbalanced classes. Performing well for common occupations in a sample will result in better accuracy even if the performance for many occupations is not as good if those occupations are less common. For the purpose of obtaining a good numerical representation for each occupation, it is more valuable to have good performance for many occupations rather than great performance for a select few. One metric we compute is the unweighted average F1 score on our test set (out-of-sample) of around 120,000 observations for which the model predictions yield an estimate of 0.5 on a 959-dimensional classification problem.

Validation of Landmark Occupations. An alternative strategy for obtaining representative occupations and similarities between occupations is to use the O*NET program. The O*NET tasks file provides estimates of how frequently certain occupations perform job work activities. For example, for the occupation *data entry keyers* (43–9021.00) in the O*NET v26 data, there is a task relevant to data-related activities: "Compile, sort, and verify the accuracy of data before it is entered." For this occupational task, the O*NET data provide a breakdown of how frequently the task is performed: *Yearly or less* (1.49), *More than yearly* (0), *More than monthly* (2.67), *More than weekly* (41.69), *Daily* (18.6), *Several times daily* (18.6), *Hourly or more* (35.54). Each task can then be assigned an indicator of whether it is considered data-relevant or not and estimate a time-use factor for each occupation. Some of the heuristics we employ include assigning the frequency for each task per occupation to the category with the highest value (daily, several times daily, or hourly). At each of the different frequency categories, we compute the fraction of tasks deemed data-relevant. We then collapse the ratios assigning relative values of 10 percent, 20 percent, and 70 percent to daily, several times daily, and hourly, respectively. This back-of-the-envelope heuristic is used as an additional check on our rankings. Martin and Monahan (2022a) present an alternative methodology to work with O*NET data to obtain time-use factors for green jobs (Martin and Monahan 2022b). To assess whether the landmark occupations are reasonable, we compute Spearman's rank correlation coefficient and obtain a value of around 0.22. The correlation coefficient reveals a negligible correlation, but the machine learning model seems to provide more reasonable rankings than the O*NET-based model.

Time Use Temporal Variation. The estimation of time-use factors used online job advertisements for the period 2010–2019. The estimates are applied to the full series from 2002 to 2021. This approach assumes a representative time-use factor for the full period and restricts potentially significant dynamics such as time-use factor trends both at intensive or extensive margins. For example, more occupations taking on work activities related to the formation of data assets or occupations increasing their time-effort allocation to those tasks. There are generally limitations with job advertisement data available for pre-2010. An additional challenge to estimating time-variant time-use factors is the low number of advertisements for various occupations that are not highly represented in job advertisement data. Relaxing the time-invariant assumption and assessing appropriate temporal periods could be a beneficial extension to this work.

Suitability of Job Advertisements. There are two potential issues related to the suitability of the BGT job advertisement data for our methodology and estimates. The first potential issue refers to the results being highly dependent on the BGT process to compile their job ads data. We examined the variability of replicating the time-use factors using a different job ads data set, namely the National Labor Exchange (NLx) Research Hub. We compared only the pair-wise similarity between occupations as the NLx data did not include the "skills taxonomy." The differences were marked but could potentially be caused by how we generated the samples for training the autocoder. The NLx data did not provide the industry classifications for the job postings, which did not allow us to generate a sample representative of the occupation distribution among sectors.

The second potential issue related to job advertisement suitability is the assumption that job advertisements, which are a prospective employer-provided description of expectations, accurately reflect the current functions of the workforce. To assess this assumption, we are currently exploring the American Community Survey (ACS) public use file of occupation and industry write-ins (2019). The public use file includes the raw write-in responses used to assign occupations to respondents as well as their employer's industry classification. These responses are brief summaries of their main job responsibilities/work activities from current employees. The files also include the assigned occupation and industry coding based on the responses.

8.3.2.5 Mapping Occupational Codes

Using equation 5, we obtain O*NET SOC 2010 level estimates for the time-use factors. However, employment and wage data are collected and prepared with OEWS Employment Projections (EP) 2021 codes. We use the crosswalk files to map the O*NET SOC 2010 codes to the SOC 2010 codes and then to OEWS 2021 codes (see subsection 8.3.1 for additional information on the process and data files). If multiple occupations are mapped to a single OEWS-EP 2021 code, the time-use factor for that occupation is the mean value for all mapped occupations. We then obtain time-use factor estimates for 736 OEWS 2019 occupation codes. These estimates tend to be quite low with a mean lower than 10 percent and a 95 percent quantile of 8 percent. The larger values are almost exclusive to the landmark occupations shown in table 8.2.

8.3.3 Markup and Additional Adjustments

Markup. We estimate the full production costs by multiplying the data-related wage bill by a markup (i.e., the α in equations 1 and 6) that is designed to reflect employee benefits, capital costs, and intermediate consumption, none of which are included in the wage bill. Observing publicly available information, firms engaged in data aggregation, data sales, and other data-related market activities appear generally to be classified to industries in Information (NAICS 51) and Professional, Scientific and Technical (PST) Services (NAICS 54).[9] Based on these observations, we use Data Processing and Hosting (NAICS 518), Other Information Services (NAICS 519), and Computer Systems Design (NAICS 5415) as the representative industries for the markup.

We calculate α as a composite ratio of compensation, intermediate consumption (excluding materials), consumption of fixed capital (CFC), and net operating surplus to wages and salaries using data summed for select industries from BEA's annual industry accounts. In other words, the composite ratio is weighted by the size of the chosen industries. The average annual ratio is 2.52. For our experimental results, we use 2.52 as a time-invariant markup for each year 2002–2021.

Additional Adjustments. We do not have an estimate of own-account data output that is used up in current production versus own-account data output that is used in capital formation. Thus, we reduce the full production cost estimate by 50 percent to capture capital formation.

We also adjust for potential overlap between data assets and R&D assets by reducing the estimated time-use factor for data-relevant activities based on ratios of R&D employees. Likewise, in addition to excluding software skills in the estimation of time-use factors, we assign a zero percent time-use factor for data-relevant activities to the occupations BEA uses to estimate own-account software—Computer Systems Analysts (15–1211), Computer Programmers (15–1251), Software Developers (15–1252), and Software Quality Assurance Analysts (15–1253)—to avoid potential overlap between data assets and software assets.[10] Finally, we adjust for overlap between own-account data and purchased data by further reducing the adjusted production cost estimate for Data Processing and Hosting (NAICS 518) by 50 percent.

We choose 50 percent as a placeholder for capital formation and purchased data adjustments to reflect our acknowledgment of the adjustments until future empirical evidence comes available. Table 8.3 summarizes the effective factors that are applied to the wage bill to calculate investment in data assets for our core experimental results. Section 8.4 has more discussion on the markup and additional adjustments.

9. For example, Axciom, Facebook, Localeze, and Burning Glass Technologies appear to be classified to NAICS 51 industries. In addition, Alphabet, Foursquare, Infogroup, Nielsen, Automatic Data Processing Inc. (ADP), The NPD Group, and International Data Corporation (IDC) all appear to be classified to NAICS 54 industries. Exceptions are the credit bureaus, which are classified to Administrative & Support Services (NAICS 56) industries.

10. Occupational codes correspond to the BLS OEWS/EP 2021 taxonomy.

Table 8.3 **Effective factors applied to the wage bill**

NAICS	Markup	Capital formation	Purchased data	Effective factor
518	2.52	0.50	0.50	0.63
All other	2.52	0.50	N/A	1.26

Note: The table summarizes by NAICS subsector the effective factors that are applied to the wage bill to calculate the full production costs. *All other* excludes NPISH and general government: Educational Services (NAICS 61), Health Care and Social Assistance (NAICS 62), Arts, Entertainment and Recreation (NAICS 71), Religious, Grantmaking, Civic, Professional, and Similar Organizations (NAICS 813), and Public Administration (NAICS 92).

8.4 Addressing Measurement Challenges

The main challenges for measurement of own-account data stocks and flows that we address in the paper are similar to challenges imposed by other own-account IPPs that are already included in capital formation in the *SNA* and the US NIPAs. We identify here four challenges and how we address the challenges for own-account data.

8.4.1 Scope of Costs in Capital Formation

The scope of costs to include in capital formation is important for own-account data and other own-account IPPs.[11] The stages of the data value chain (OECD 2013, Moro Visconti et al. 2017) yield insights into activities that underlie the production process for data—including collection, storage, processing, distribution, and usage—some of which are reflective of costs that embody capital formation. The scope that has been recently introduced by the OECD (2021) is that capital formation should include both recording and processing costs and the costs of procuring access to data. Procurement costs may include either explicit purchases or the value of "free" digital products exchanged for access.[12]

We address this challenge by identifying skills in the BGT taxonomy that are relevant to data-related activities, including data entry, storage, analysis, and management. These skills are embodied by the occupations that underlie our estimates of the data wage bill. In addition, we reduce the full production cost estimate for data by 50 percent to account for data-related output that is used up in the current period and never becomes capital formation.[13]

11. For example, OECD (2010) identifies eight stages of activities in the production of own-account software: feasibility analysis, functional analysis, detailed analysis, programming, tests, documentation, training, and maintenance. Of the eight stages, only costs for functional analysis, detailed analysis, programming, tests, and documentation are within scope for capital formation.

12. The latter procurement costs are identified in Farboodi and Veldkamp (2021) as a measurement challenge, and their model moves beyond price-based valuation by assigning a value to goods and data that have a zero transaction price.

13. Another approach would be to use a depreciation rate for data that reflects a more rapid decline in value of investment flows as a result of obsolescence. However, such an approach

8.4.2 Multiple Counting

Own-account data and other own-account IPPs are at risk of multiple counting from several sources.

8.4.2.1 Overlap Among Categories of IPPs

One source of multiple counting is overlap among categories of IPPs that are separately measured, such as data, software, and research and development (R&D).

Software. We address the overlap between data and software by estimating the time-use factors for data, which are intentionally based on unique data-relevant skills that are distinguishable from software-relevant skills. In addition, we completely exclude from the data wage bill the wages of the occupations that BEA uses to estimate own-account software–Computer Programmers, Computer Systems Analysts, Software Developers, and Software Quality Assurance Analysts.[14] For comparison with data-relevant skills presented in table 8.1, table 8.4 presents the top 80 BGT skills identified as software relevant. Likewise, table 8.5 shows the top time-use factors for occupations engaged in software-related activities to compare with landmark occupations for data reported in table 8.2.

While tables 8.1 and 8.4 demonstrate no overlap for BGT skills by design, there is overlap of seven occupations with high time-use factors in tables 8.2 and 8.5. The occupations that show up in both tables include Business Intelligence Analysts, Computer and Information Research Scientists, Database Administrators, Database Architects, Data Warehousing Specialists, Geographic Information Systems Technicians, and Statisticians. In addition, the data and software time-use factors sum to more than 100 percent for the first five occupations, which implies the occupations and their time-use factors may be used to measure either data- or software-related activity but not both. However, there is no overlap between landmark occupations for data and the occupations BEA currently uses to estimate own-account software.

Overlap is expected when activities are intertwined. One example is software and R&D. Based on the 2018 Business Enterprise Research and Development Survey (BERD) table 19 (https://ncses.nsf.gov/pubs/nsf21312/table/19#data-tables), $165.6 billion (37.5 percent) of domestic R&D was software products and embedded software R&D.[15] In the NIPAs, this overlap

would disregard the accounting difference between intermediate consumption and consumption of fixed capital.

14. The time-use factors for these occupations are relatively modest—each less than 20 percent—and we think the occupations may reasonably embody some data-related activities that accompany own-account software development but are not included in BEA's measures of own-account software. However, we choose to completely exclude the occupations for a more conservative estimate.

15. According to guidance in the BERD survey, R&D activity in software includes (1) software development or improvement activities that expand scientific or technological knowledge;

Table 8.4 BGT skills identified as software relevant

.NET	Microsoft Sql Server Integration Services
Active Server Pages (ASP)	Microsoft Visio
Agile Development	Middleware
AJAX	MySQL
Amazon Web Services (AWS)	Object−Oriented Analysis and Design
AngularJS	Oracle
Apache Hadoop	Oracle PL/SQL
Apache Tomcat	PERL Scripting Language
Apache Webserver	Platform as a Service (PaaS)
Application Design	Python
ASP.NET	Relational DataBase Management System
Atlassian JIRA	Ruby
C++	Salesforce
COBOL	SAP
Computer Engineering	SAS
Crystal Reports	Scrum
Debugging	Shell Scripting
Eclipse	Software Architecture
Enterprise Resource Planning (ERP)	Software as a Service (SaaS)
Extensible Markup Language (XML)	Software Development
Extensible Stylesheet Language XSL	Software Engineering
Firmware	Software Testing
Git	SQL
HTML5	SQL Server
Hypertext Preprocessor (PHP)	SQL Server Reporting Services (SSRS)
IBM WEBSPHERE	Systems Analysis
Informatica	Systems Development Life Cycle (SDLC)
Java	Teradata DBA
Java Server Pages (JSP)	Transact-SQL
JavaScript	Unified Modeling Language (UML)
JavaScript Object Notation (JSON)	UNIX
jQuery	UNIX Shell
JUnit	User Acceptance Testing (UAT)
Linux	User Interface (UI) Design
Microsoft Access	Visual Basic
Microsoft Azure	Visual Studio
Microsoft C#	VMware
Microsoft Operating Systems	Waterfall
Microsoft Project	WebLogic
Microsoft SQL	Windows Server

Note: Top 80 software skills by frequency identified from landmark occupations.

Table 8.5 Top time-use factors for software

O*NET SOC 2010	Description	Time-use factor
15–1133.00	**Software Developers, Systems Software**	**0.95**
15–1132.00	**Software Developers, Applications**	**0.94**
15–1131.00	**Computer Programmers**	**0.85**
15–1121.00	**Computer Systems Analysts**	**0.82**
15–1134.00	Web Developers	0.65
15–1199.02	Computer Systems Engineers/Architects	0.60
15–1199.08	Business Intelligence Analysts	0.55
15–1199.06	Database Architects	0.55
15–1141.00	Database Administrators	0.52
15–1199.01	Software Quality Assurance Engineers and Testers	0.52
15–1199.09	Information Technology Project Managers	0.50
15–1143.00	Computer Network Architects	0.49
13–1111.00	Management Analysts	0.48
15–1199.07	Data Warehousing Specialists	0.46
15–1111.00	Computer and Information Research Scientists	0.45
15–1142.00	Network and Computer Systems Administrators	0.41
15–1199.00	Computer Occupations, All Other	0.40
15–1122.00	Information Security Analysts	0.40
11–3021.00	Computer and Information Systems Managers	0.39
17–2061.00	Computer Hardware Engineers	0.38
15–1199.04	Geospatial Information Scientists and Techs	0.38
15–1199.03	Web Administrators	0.37
15–1152.00	Computer Network Support Specialists	0.37
15–1151.00	Computer User Support Specialists	0.36
15–2041.00	Statisticians	0.34
13–2099.01	Financial Quantitative Analysts	0.32
15–1199.11	Video Game Designers	0.32
15–1143.01	Telecommunications Engineering Specialists	0.32
17–3029.07	Mechanical Engineering Technologists	0.30
17–1011.00	Architects, Except Landscape and Naval	0.30
13–2051.00	Financial Analysts	0.28
15–1199.10	Search Marketing Strategists	0.28
13–1081.02	Logistics Analysts	0.28
17–2199.08	Robotics Engineers	0.27
27–1021.00	Commercial and Industrial Designers	0.27
27–3042.00	Technical Writers	0.27
17–3031.02	Mapping Technicians	0.27
15–1199.05	Geographic Information Systems Technicians	0.27

Note: Bold occupations denote landmark occupations that are by design the same occupations BEA currently uses to estimate own-account software. Software Developers (systems software) and Software Developers (applications) are combined into Software Developers and Software Quality Assurance Analysts in SOC 2018.

is included with R&D investment and excluded from software investment. There may also be job activities at the intersection of data, software, and R&D, such as software programming to prepare a data set for research. Observing independently estimated time-use factors that together exceed 100 percent is not problematic in itself for our estimates because we know that own-account software estimation is limited to four specific occupations with relatively low time-use factors. However, the outcome does suggest an incentive to jointly estimate own-account data and own-account software to ensure consistency and prevent double counting if the scope of own-account software is expanded to include more occupations in the future.

Research & Development. In contrast to software, the BGT skills data set does not include R&D-relevant skills to distinguish them from data-relevant skills, which may yield some overlap between data assets and R&D assets. For example, Goodridge et al. (2021) and Statistics Canada (2019a) both argue that data science activities meet the *SNA* and OECD (2015) definition of R&D. However, Goodridge et al. (2021) suggest that data science is not included in measured R&D in practice by some countries because R&D is generally measured based on surveys designed for known performers of traditional scientific R&D activities. Likewise, Statistics Canada (2019a) suggests that the survey they use to measure R&D needs to be examined for updates because the survey was developed years ago and is biased toward the selection of firms engaged in more traditional forms of R&D activities, such as pharmaceutical firms, and biased away from a growing number of firms in diverse industries engaged in data science activities.

For R&D measures in the US national accounts, the survey used to collect information on performance of business R&D is the BERD survey.[16] The 2019 BERD survey explicitly includes software development or improvement activities that expand scientific or technological knowledge and construction of new theories and algorithms in the field of computer science. In addition, the 2019 BERD survey asks respondents to report the percentage of domestic R&D expenditures paid for and performed by them that was

and (2) construction of new theories and algorithms in the field of computer science. Likewise, the BERD survey requires that R&D activity in software exclude (1) software development that does not depend on scientific or technological advance, such as supporting or adapting existing systems, adding functionality to existing application programs, and routine debugging of existing systems and software; (2) creation of new software based on known methods and applications; (3) conversion or translation of existing software and software languages; and (4) adaptation of a product to a specific client, unless knowledge that significantly improved the base program was added in that process.

16. The 2019 BERD survey defines research and development as follows: "*Research* is defined as experimental or theoretical work undertaken primarily to acquire new knowledge or understanding of phenomena and observable facts. Research may be either 'basic,' where the goal is primarily to acquire new knowledge or understanding of a given topic without a specific commercial application in mind, or 'applied,' where the goal is to solve a specific problem or meet a specific commercial objective. *Development* is defined as the systematic use of research and practical experience to produce new or improved goods, services, or processes. In simple terms, the intended output of research is ideas and the intended output of development is products."

for artificial intelligence (AI), which includes speech recognition, machine vision, machine learning, text analytics, and natural language generation and processing. Thus, data science may not be absent in practice from the BERD survey and may be included in BEA's measures of R&D based on the BERD survey.

To adjust for potential overlap between data assets and measured R&D assets in our estimates, we reduce the time-use factor for data-relevant activities based on an estimate of the ratio of employees whose main work activity is R&D. We use a sample from the National Survey of College Graduates (NSCG), National Survey of Recent College Graduates (NSRCG), and Survey Doctorate Recipients (SDR) from 1993 to 2013 to estimate by occupation group the ratio of employees whose main work activity was R&D (Minnesota Population Center 2016). We then develop a crosswalk between the survey occupation groups and those in the latest taxonomy of the BLS OEWS/EP codes. We matched 249 out of the 834 occupation codes used in the wage bill with 26 of the NSF survey codes. For these 249 occupations, we adjust the time use factor as follows:

$$\hat{\tau}'_\omega = \hat{\tau}_\omega (1 - \hat{\rho}'_\omega) \tag{7}$$

where $\hat{\tau}'_\omega$ is the time-use factor for occupation ω adjusted for R&D, $\hat{\tau}_\omega$ is the original time-use factor, and $\hat{\rho}'_\omega$ is the corresponding share of employees for occupation ω in the NSF surveys that reported R&D as the primary work activity based on the share of time allocated to it.[17]

8.4.2.2 Non-Rival Use of Data

Another source of multiple counting is overlap between own-account data and purchased data, which is also a source of multiple counting for software and R&D. We address this challenge by further reducing the adjusted production cost estimate by 50 percent for Data Processing and Hosting (NAICS 518), which is the NAICS code with data-related activities closest to those we measure under our methodology.[18]

Finally, a source of multiple counting that has been cited as a concern specifically for data as an asset is that the same piece of information can be used in multiple databases. However, a single piece of information is transformed when it is added to a record with other pieces of information. Likewise, we

17. As an alternative, we also consider completely excluding from the data wage bill the wages of four SOC 2010 occupations that appear to be R&D occupations based on "research" in the descriptions: Computer and Information Research Scientists (SOC 15–1111), Operations Research Analysts (SOC 15–2031), Survey Researchers (SOC 19–3022), and Social Science Research Assistance (SOC 19–4061). However, we think the occupations may reasonably embody some data-related activities that accompany R&D, and we are not able to determine if excluding these four occupations based on "research" is as comprehensive as adjusting based on the ratios.

18. The reduction for Data Processing and Hosting (NAICS 518) to adjust for non-rival use of data is in addition to the reductions for software and R&D overlap.

are not valuing pieces of information but rather the activities associated with making the information available in a record, which is unique to every firm for own-account measures.

8.4.3 Measuring Capital Costs

A challenge that may be more relevant (but not unique) to data stocks and flows is how to measure the capital cost component in the sum-of-costs. There is a question of what proportions of the sum-of-costs should be accounted for by labor costs, capital costs, and intermediate consumption, given the role of capital services in the collection, storage, analysis, and management of data.

We apply a markup of 2.52 to the wage bill as explained in section 8.3.3. Since the markup is a weighted composite ratio of compensation, intermediate consumption (excluding materials), CFC, and net operating surplus, we can decompose the markup into the proportionate share of each component in the sum-of-costs. The decomposition is presented in table 8.6.

8.4.4 Prices and Depreciation

Own-account data are not transacted in active markets, which means there are no observed transactions that are useful for measuring prices and depreciation. We utilize international guidelines and US practice for deflating and depreciating own-account software and databases as a starting point for deflating and depreciating own-account data, which reflects the inclusion of own-account data as a subcategory of software and is consistent with preliminary guidance emerging from the *SNA* community's current work on revising the *SNA*.

Prices. In the absence of deflators for own-account software, OECD (2010) recommends that deflators for custom software be used as a proxy until own-account software deflators are developed. In addition, OECD (2010) suggests three options for own-account database deflators. One option is to use a price index of a related activity for which there is a price

Table 8.6 **Weighted composite ratio for full sum-of-costs**

	Ratio	Share (%)
Compensation	1.15	46
Intermediate consumption	0.81	32
Consumption of fixed capital	0.29	11
Net operating surplus	0.27	11
Markup	2.52	

Note: All data are from BEA's annual industry accounts. Intermediate consumption excludes materials. The table reports the simple average for 2002–2021 of each annual measure summed for NAICS 518–519 and NAICS 5415 divided by annual wages and salaries summed for the same industries.

index of reasonable quality. The other two options are an input cost index, one with zero productivity growth and another with an adjustment based on productivity growth of a similar industry. BEA does not compile a price index for own-account databases because own-account databases are not measured separately from own-account software in the US NIPAs. For own-account software, BEA currently compiles a price index from a weighted average of the prepackaged software price and a BEA input cost index (US Bureau of Economic Analysis 2020). The input cost index is compiled from BLS data on wage rates for Computer Programmers and Computer Systems Analysts and the intermediate consumption associated with the production of software. The input cost index reflects an explicit adjustment for changes in productivity that is based primarily on a BLS total factor productivity index.[19]

To address the lack of prices for own-account data, we develop an experimental price index. The price index follows BEA's own-account software price index methodology by estimating a composite wage rate series and an intermediate input cost series. For the wage series we use the effective wage bill from our estimates of investment in data assets. In other words, we use the time-use factors for each occupation in the business sector adjusted for R&D and software overlap. To obtain the composite wage rate series we use the following equation:

$$r_t = \frac{\sum W_{\omega,i,t} H_{\omega,i,t} \hat{\tau}'_\omega}{\sum H_{\omega,i,t} \hat{\tau}'_\omega} \tag{8}$$

where the composite wage rate at year t, r_t, is given as the effective wage bill over the number of employees. $W_{\omega,i,t}$ denotes the average wage for occupation ω at year t for industry i and $H_{\omega,i,t}$ the number of employees for the same occupation, industry, and year. Lastly, $\hat{\tau}'_\omega$ is the effective time-use factors adjusted for overlap with software and R&D.

In addition to the composite wage rate, the input-cost price index includes a cost component for intermediate inputs based on intermediate consumption for Data Processing and Hosting (NAICS 518) and Computer Systems Design (NAICS 5415). We also adjust the input-cost price index for total factor productivity growth published by BLS for Data Processing and Hosting and Computer Systems Design, which are weighted by industry gross output. Finally, we combine our productivity-adjusted input-cost index in a simple average with the average industry price index weighted by industry gross output for Data Processing and Hosting and Computer Systems

19. When BEA first introduced capital measures of own-account software into the NIPAs in 1999, an input cost index was compiled from a weighted average of compensation rates for Computer Programmers and Computer System Analysts and the intermediate consumption associated with their work (Moulton and Sullivan 1999). No productivity adjustment was made.

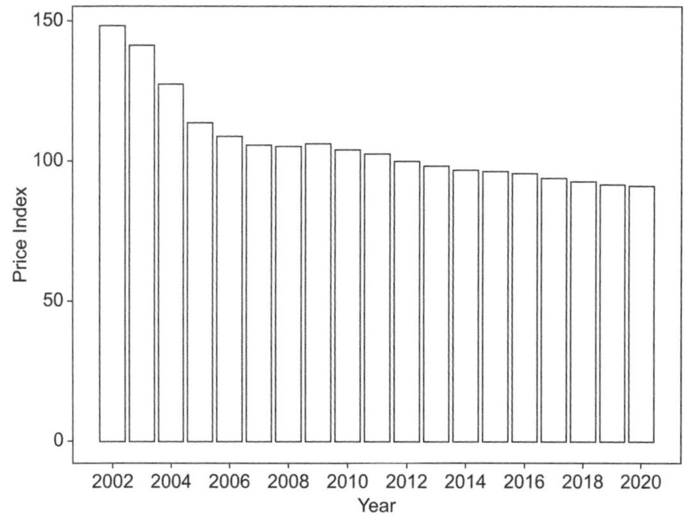

Fig. 8.1 Own-account data price index

Design. The resulting experimental price index for own-account data is presented in figure 8.1, where 2012 is the base year.

Depreciation. OECD (2009) recommends several options for determining depreciation parameters for an asset class, which generally requires information on prices or service lives. One option uses information on the service life and makes an additional assumption about the functional form of the depreciation pattern. A functional form that is commonly used for pragmatic reasons is the geometric model of depreciation, which yields a pattern of constant percentage decline in an asset's value. In the absence of econometric estimates of the geometric depreciation rate, the geometric depreciation rate can be estimated using a simple declining balance method as $\delta = R/S$, where R is an estimated declining balance rate and S is an average service life (Hulten and Wykoff 1996). The declining balance rate may be either estimated econometrically or is sometimes assumed to be 2. For software and databases, OECD (2010) recommends the average service life be obtained by surveying software users, surveying software suppliers, or hiring software consultants. BEA does not compile a measure of depreciation for own-account databases but does compile a measure of depreciation for own-account software for the US Fixed Assets Accounts (FAAs). To estimate depreciation for own-account software, BEA uses a five-year service life and a declining balance rate of 1.65 to determine the geometric depreciation rate. The service life is based on estimates of the relationship between computer expenditures and software expenditures, anecdotal evidence about how long software is used before replacement (including an

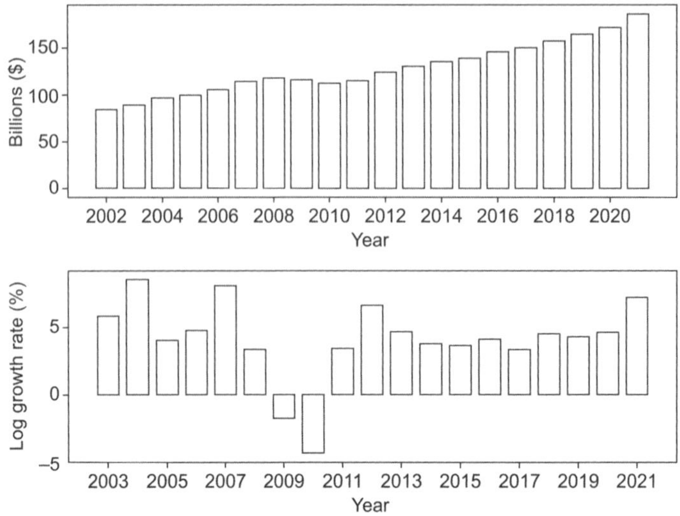

Fig. 8.2 Current-dollar annual investment in data assets

informal survey of business uses of software), and tax-law-based service lives of software.[20] The declining balance rate is borrowed from the Hulten-Wykoff methodology that is used for most equipment in the FAAs (Hulten and Wykoff 1981; Hulten, McCallum et al. 1981; Wykoff and Hulten 1979; Fraumeni 1997). To address the lack of depreciation rate for own-account data, we use BEA's current geometric depreciation rate of 0.33 for own-account software as a proxy.

8.5 Results

8.5.1 National Aggregates

8.5.1.1 Experimental Current-Dollar and Historical-Cost Estimates

Experimental estimates for aggregate business sector current-dollar investment in data assets for 2002–2021 are presented in figure 8.2. The upper panel in the figure reflects current-dollar levels and the lower panel reflects current-dollar log growth rates. Estimated current-dollar investment in 2002 is $84 billion and in 2021 is $186 billion. Growth of current-dollar investment is as high as 8.6 percent for 2004 and as low as –4.4 percent for 2010. The average annual growth rate in current-dollar investment for 2003–2021 is 4.2 percent. Prior to the recession of 2007–2009, the average annual growth rate for 2003–2007 was 6.3 percent, which declined to

20. A summary of BEA's depreciation estimates is available at: https://apps.bea.gov/national/pdf/BEA_depreciation_rates.pdf.

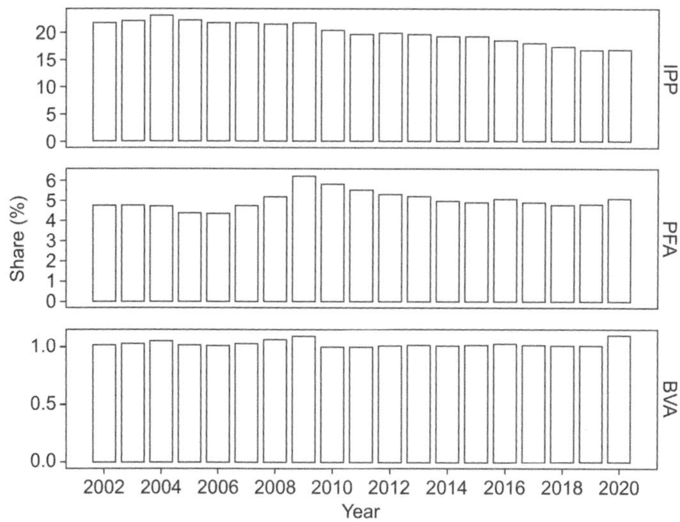

Fig. 8.3 Investment in data assets as a share of NIPA aggregates

Note: The numerator for each share is the current-dollar investment in data assets. The denominator for each share is the current-dollar NIPA aggregate plus the current-dollar investment in data assets. Business sector value-added (BVA) is from line 2 of "National Income and Product Accounts: Table 1.3.5. Gross Value Added by Sector" (https://apps.bea.gov/iTable/?reqid=19&step=3&isuri=1&select_all_years=0&nipa_table_list=24&series=a&first_year=2002&last_year=2021&scale=-9&categories=survey&thetable=). Investment in intellectual property products (IPP) is from line 1 of "Fixed Assets Accounts: Table 3.7I. Investment in Private Intellectual Property Products by Industry" (https://apps.bea.gov/iTable/iTable.cfm?reqid=10&step=3&isuri=1&table_list=139&series=q&first_year=2002&allyears=0&tabledisplay=&scale=-99&last_year=2020), adjusted to exclude NPISH by subtracting lines 66, 67, and 72. Investment in private fixed assets (PFA) is from line 1 of "Fixed Assets Accounts: Table 3.7ESI. Investment in Private Fixed Assets by Industry" (https://apps.bea.gov/iTable/?reqid=10&step=3&isuri=1&table_list=139&series=q&first_year=2002&allyears=0&tabledisplay=&scale=-99&last_year=2020), adjusted to exclude NPISH by subtracting line 66, 67, and 72.

3.4 percent for 2008–2021. Average annual growth for the ten-year period 2012–2021 was 4.7 percent.

Current-dollar investment in data assets as a share of NIPA current-dollar business sector value-added (BVA) is reported in figure 8.3. The share of data investment for the period averages 1.0 percent of business sector value-added. We also report in figure 8.3 current-dollar investment in data assets as a share of NIPA current-dollar investment in IPPs and as a share of NIPA current-dollar investment in private fixed assets. Data investment as a share of investment in IPPs declines over the period from 22.0 percent in 2002 to 16.9 percent in 2020—the share averages 20.2 percent for the period. Data investment as a share of investment in private fixed assets is 4.8 percent in 2002 and 5.1 percent in 2020 with some variation over the period—the share averages 5.0 percent for the period.

Experimental estimates for aggregate business sector historical-cost

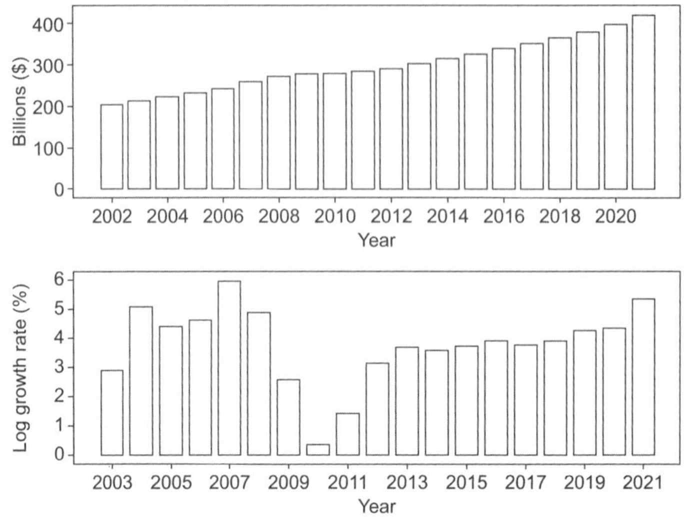

Fig. 8.4 Historical-cost annual net stocks of data assets

net stocks of data assets for 2002–2021 are presented in figure 8.4. The historical-cost net stocks are calculated using a perpetual inventory method (PIM) with geometric depreciation. The PIM is a sum of annual depreciated historical-cost investment in data assets. Annual historical-cost investment in data assets prior to 2002 is backcast using the annual growth in current-dollar investment in own-account software as an indicator. Depreciation of annual historical-cost investment is calculated using BEA's depreciation rate for own-account software of 0.33, assuming new investment in data assets is placed in service at midyear. The calculation for annual depreciated historical-cost investment, i.e., net stock N, in year t for investment I placed in service in year h can be summarized as follows:

$$N_{t,h} = I_h\left(1 - \frac{\delta}{2}\right)(1 - \delta)^{t-h}. \tag{9}$$

The upper panel in figure 8.4 reflects historical-cost levels and the lower panel reflects historical-cost log growth rates. Estimated historical-cost net stock in 2002 is \$205 billion and in 2021 is \$421 billion. Growth of historical-cost net stocks is as high as 6.0 percent for 2007 and as low as 0.4 percent for 2010. The average annual growth rate in historical-cost net stocks for 2003–2021 is 3.8 percent.

We report the historical-cost net stocks of data assets as a share of the FAA historical-cost net stocks of IPPs and as a share of the FAA historical-cost net stocks of private fixed assets in figure 8.5. Data stocks as a share of IPP stocks decline over the period from 15.6 percent in 2002 to 12.0 percent in 2021—the share averages 13.9 percent for the period. Data stocks as a share of private fixed assets stocks is 1.4 percent in 2002 and 1.3 percent in

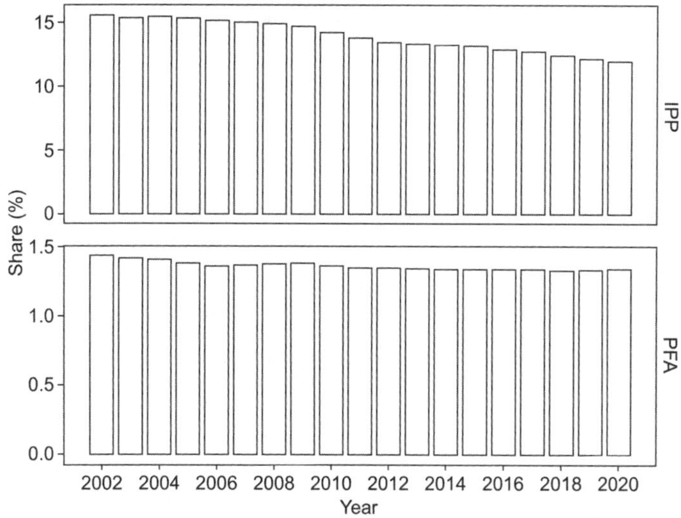

Fig. 8.5 Net stocks of data assets as a share of FAA aggregates

Note: The numerator for each share is the historical-cost net stock of data assets. The denominator for each share is the historical-cost FAA aggregate plus the historical-cost net stock of data assets. Net stocks of intellectual property products (IPP) are from line 1 of "Fixed Assets Accounts: Table 3.3I. Historical-Cost Net Stock of Private Intellectual Property Products by Industry" (https://apps.bea.gov/iTable/?reqid=10&step=3&isuri=1&table_list=139&series=q&first_year=2002&allyears=0&tabledisplay=&scale=-99&last_year=2020#eyJhcHBpZCI6MTAsInN0ZXBzIjpbMSwyLDNdLCJkYXRhIjpbWyJ0YWJsZV9saXN0IiwiMTMxIl0sWyJDYXRlZ29yaWVzIiwiUHVibGljRkFBIl1dfQ==), adjusted to exclude NPISH by subtracting lines 66, 67, and 72. Net stocks of private fixed assets (PFA) are from line 1 of "Fixed Assets Accounts: Table 3.3ESI. Historical-Cost Net Stock of Private Fixed Assets by Industry" (https://apps.bea.gov/iTable/?reqid=10&step=3&isuri=1&table_list=139&series=q&first_year=2002&allyears=0&tabledisplay=&scale=-99&last_year=2020#eyJhcHBpZCI6MTAsInN0ZXBzIjpbMSwyLDNdLCJkYXRhIjpbWyJ0YWJsZV9saXN0IiwiMTMwIl0sWyJDYXRlZ29yaWVzIiwiUHVibGljRkFBIl1dfQ==), adjusted to exclude NPISH by subtracting lines 66, 67, and 72.

2021 with some variation over the period—the share averages 1.4 percent for the period.

8.5.1.2 Real Growth

We compare the log growth in real US aggregate measures with and without our experimental estimates of business sector investment in data assets for 2003–2020. Real aggregate measures include business sector value-added, private sector investment in IPPs, and private sector investment in software. We recalculate measured aggregate prices using Törnqvist expenditure shares. We report average and cumulative annual growth in table 8.7.

The average annual growth in real data investment for 2003–2020 is 7.5 percent and the cumulative annual growth for the period is 134.4 percent. When data investment is added to business sector value-added, the average annual change in real value-added growth over the period is an increase of 4 basis points, and the cumulative annual change is an increase of 74

Table 8.7 **Growth in real measures with and without investment in data assets 2003–2020 (%)**

	Average			Cumulative		
	With data	W/o data	Δ	With data	W/o data	Δ
Data	7.47			134.42		
Value-added	1.99	1.95	0.04	35.89	35.15	0.74
IPPs	5.28	4.97	0.31	95.08	89.48	5.60
Software	7.45	7.71	−0.26	134.07	138.72	−4.65

Note: The table reports average and cumulative log growth rates in real data investment along with changes in growth for business sector real value-added, private sector real investment in IPPs, and private sector real investment in software with and without data investment for 2003–2020. Aggregate price indexes are recalculated using Törnqvist expenditure shares.

basis points. When data investment is added to IPP investment, the average annual growth in real investment in IPPs for 2003–2020 is 31 basis points higher, and the cumulative average annual growth is 560 basis points higher. In contrast, the growth of real investment in data is lower than software investment, so the declines in average annual growth in real investment in software for the period is 26 basis points and in cumulative average annual growth is 465 basis points.[21]

In relation to other types of capital formation, data as an asset seem to grow relatively faster than R&D and entertainment, literary, and artistic originals. However, the software category of IPPs grows faster than data. One plausible explanation for this result is the complementary relationship between data and software. Software is an indispensable asset used for data-related activities such as transformations and analysis of data (e.g., data science). This could explain why software investment growth outpaces data investment growth because data assets increase the demand for software to make use of the data assets.

8.5.1.3 Shares of Investment by Occupation

In order to assess overlap between our estimates of data investment and investment in other IPPs—i.e., R&D and software—we calculate shares of investment in data by occupation. Table 8.8 reports shares of investment in data for occupations with more than 0.5 percent share for 2002–2021. We choose the cutoff to fit the table onto a single page. The 40 occupations in table 8.8 account for 68.4 percent of our investment estimate for the period. There are over 600 additional occupations included in our estimate but excluded from table 8.8. We note two observations in table 8.8. First, even if an occupation makes the list of landmark occupations in table 8.2 does

21. Goodridge et al. (2021) report labor productivity with and without data investment for 13 European Union countries and find a modest average increase in labor productivity of only 5 basis points with data investment for 2011–2016. The largest average annual increase by country is 9 basis points attributable to Germany, and the largest average annual decrease by country is 9 basis points attributable to Estonia.

Table 8.8 **Occupational shares of investment in data 2002–2021**

OEWS 2021	Description	Share (%)
43–9061	Office Clerks, General	5.68
13–1111	Management Analysts	5.27
11–1021	General and Operations Managers	4.48
43–9021	Data Entry Keyers	4.26
11–3021	Computer and Information Systems Managers	4.15
43–3031	Bookkeeping, Accounting, and Auditing Clerks	3.28
43–4051	Customer Service Representatives	3.21
43–6014	Secs and Admin Assistants, Except Legal, Medical, and Executive	2.85
13–1161	Market Research Analysts and Marketing Specialists	2.68
15–1242	Database Administrators	2.58
15–1243	Database Architects	2.38
15–1244	Network and Computer Systems Administrators	2.18
11–3031	Financial Managers	2.17
13–2011	Accountants and Auditors	2.03
43–1011	First-Line Supervisors of Office and Admin Support Workers	1.73
15–1299	Computer Occupations, All Other	1.41
11–2021	Marketing Managers	1.12
15–1241	Computer Network Architects	1.12
11–9041	Architectural and Engineering Managers	1.05
15–1232	Computer User Support Specialists	0.94
11–1011	Chief Executives	0.90
13–1071	Human Resources Specialists	0.89
15–1221	Computer and Information Research Scientists	0.85
17–2112	Industrial Engineers	0.81
13–1082	Project Management Specialists	0.79
13–2051	Financial and Investment Analysts	0.77
41–4012	Sales Reps, Wholesale and Manufacturing, Except T&S Prods	0.71
51–9061	Inspectors, Testers, Sorters, Samplers, and Weighers	0.71
11–2022	Sales Managers	0.71
15–1212	Information Security Analysts	0.69
43–3021	Billing and Posting Clerks	0.68
13–2054	Financial Risk Specialists	0.68
43–5071	Shipping, Receiving, and Inventory Clerks	0.66
41–3091	Sales Reps of Servs, Except Ads, Insurance, Fin Servs, and Tvl	0.64
43–6011	Executive Secretaries and Executive Administrative Assistants	0.60
13–1199	Business Operations Specialists, All Other	0.59
15–2031	Operations Research Analysts	0.59
13–1020	Buyers and Purchasing Agents	0.52
53–7062	Laborers and Freight, Stock, and Material Movers, Hand	0.51
43–5061	Production, Planning, and Expediting Clerks	0.51
	Total	68.38

Note: Shares of investment in data are included for occupations with at least 0.5 percent share.

not imply the occupation will account for a large share of the investment estimate. Two landmark occupations that do not make the cutoff for table 8.8 are *wellhead pumpers* and *hearing aid specialists*, which may be useful references to calculate a numeric similarity for non-landmark occupations but do not appear to play a big role in data investment. In contrast, landmark occupations like *data entry keyers* and *database administrators and architects* account for a large share of the data investment estimate. Second, R&D occupations and software occupations are mostly absent from table 8.8, which reflects the adjustments to exclude R&D employees and software occupations. Occupations with lower shares such as *computer and information research scientists* and *computer network architects* may contribute to capital formation in data as well as capital formation in R&D and software, but occupations with the highest shares are unlikely to contribute to capital formation in R&D and software.

8.5.2 NAICS Sector Aggregates

8.5.2.1 Experimental Current-Dollar Estimates

Experimental estimates for current-dollar investment in data assets by NAICS sector for 2002–2021 are presented in table 8.9. Table 8.10 reports

Table 8.9 Current-dollar investment in data assets by NAICS sector 2002–2021

NAICS	Description	($B)
11	Agriculture, Forestry, Fishing and Hunting	4
21	Mining, Quarrying, and Oil and Gas Extraction	29
22	Utilities	28
23	Construction	95
31–33	Manufacturing	353
42	Wholesale Trade	183
44–45	Retail Trade	141
48–49	Transportation and Warehousing	81
51	Information	159
52	Finance and Insurance	338
53	Real Estate and Rental and Leasing	51
54	Professional, Scientific, and Technical Services	646
55	Management of Companies and Enterprises	179
56	Administrative & Support and Waste Management & Remediation Services	210
72	Accommodation and Food Services	36
81	Other Services (except Public Administration)	30
	Total	2,563

Note: Current-dollar estimates summed for 2002–2021 by NAICS sector. Estimates for NPISH and general government are excluded: Educational Services (NAICS 61), Health Care and Social Assistance (NAICS 62), Arts, Entertainment and Recreation (NAICS 71), Religious, Grantmaking, Civic, Professional, and Similar Organizations (NAICS 813), and Public Administration (NAICS 92).

Table 8.10 **Average annual growth in current-dollar investment in data assets by NAICS sector 2003–2021**

NAICS	Description	(%)
11	Agriculture, Forestry, Fishing and Hunting	3.24
21	Mining, Quarrying, and Oil and Gas Extraction	4.07
22	Utilities	2.95
23	Construction	4.42
31–33	Manufacturing	2.14
42	Wholesale Trade	2.92
44–45	Retail Trade	2.37
48–49	Transportation and Warehousing	4.22
51	Information	4.17
52	Finance and Insurance	3.71
53	Real Estate and Rental and Leasing	3.95
54	Professional, Scientific, and Technical Services	6.24
55	Management of Companies and Enterprises	6.24
56	Administrative & Support and Waste Management & Remediation Services	3.43
72	Accommodation and Food Services	3.71
81	Other Services (except Public Administration)	3.95

Note: Annual log growth rates for current-dollar investment averaged for 2003–2021.

the average annual growth in current-dollar investment in data assets by NAICS sector for 2003–2021. The current-dollar estimates as a share of current-dollar value-added by NAICS sector for 2002–2021 are shown in figure 8.6. Since our methodology starts with an estimate of the occupation-based wage bill, results by NAICS sector reflect industries that employ occupations engaged in data-related activities.

For the period 2002–2021, table 8.9 shows the total current-dollar investment in data was $2.6 trillion. The largest dollar investments were made in Professional, Scientific, and Technical (PST) Services ($646 billion), Manufacturing ($353 billion), and Finance and Insurance ($338 billion). The smallest dollar investments were made in Agriculture, Utilities, and Mining.

Table 8.10 demonstrates that average annual growth in current-dollar investment in data assets was as low as 2.1 percent for Manufacturing and as high as 6.2 percent for Management of Companies and PST Services. Average annual growth rates by NAICS sector exceeded the aggregate average annual growth rate of 4.2 percent for Construction (4.4 percent), Transportation and Warehousing (4.2 percent), PST Services (6.2 percent), and Management of Companies (6.2 percent).

In figure 8.6, the largest shares of NAICS sector value-added show up for Management of Companies (NAICS 55), Administrative Services (NAICS 56), PST Services (NAICS 54), and Finance and Insurance (NAICS 52). The smallest shares of NAICS sector value-added show up for Agriculture

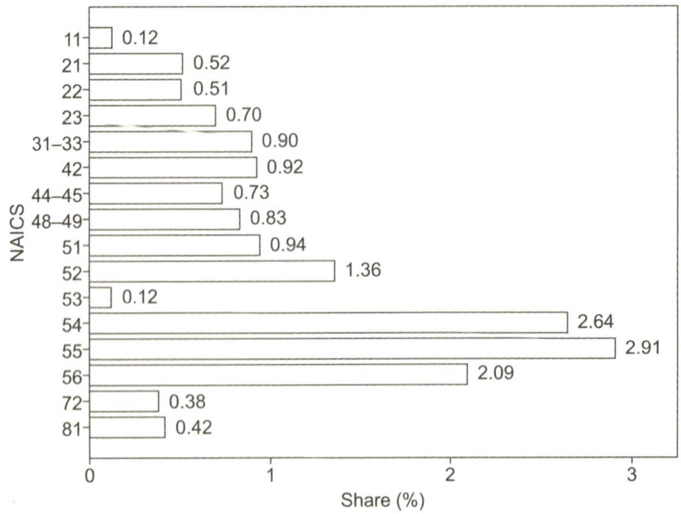

Fig. 8.6 Investment in data assets as a share of value-added by NAICS sector 2002–2021

Note: The numerator for each share is the current-dollar investment in data assets summed for 2002–2021. The denominator for each share is the current-dollar investment in data assets plus NAICS sector value-added summed for 2002–2021 from the U.S. Bureau of Economic Analysis, "Interactive Access to Industry Economic Accounts Data: Table 1 Value Added by Industry" (https://apps.bea.gov/iTable/?reqid=150&step=2&isuri=1&categories=gdpxind#eyJhcHBpZCI6MTUwLCJzdGVwcyI6WzEsMiwzXSwiZGF0YSI6W1siY2F0ZWdvcmllcyIsIkdkcHhJbmQiXSxbIlRhYmxlX0xpc3QiLCIxIl1dfQ==).

(NAICS 11), Real Estate (NAICS 53), Accommodation and Food Services (NAICS 72), and Other Services (NAICS 81).

8.5.2.2 Real Growth

We compare the log growth in real value-added for NAICS sectors with and without our experimental estimates of business sector investment in data assets for 2003–2020. We recalculate measured NAICS sector prices using Törnqvist expenditure shares. We report average and cumulative annual growth in real value-added growth by NAICS sector in table 8.11. Consistent with the result for business sector real value-added in table 8.7, the change in average annual growth is positive for each NAICS sector. When data investment is added, the largest increases in average real value-added growth show up for Management of Companies (NAICS 55, 19 basis points), PST Services (NAICS 54, 17 basis points), Finance and Insurance (NAICS 52, 7 basis points), and Administrative Services (NAICS 56, 8 basis points). Increases in cumulative real value-added growth are also largest for those NAICS sectors. The smallest increases in average and cumulative real value-added growth show up for Agriculture (NAICS 11), Min-

Table 8.11 **Growth in real value-added with and without investment in data assets by NAICS sector 2003–2020 (%)**

	Average			Cumulative		
NAICS	With data	W/o data	Δ	With data	W/o data	Δ
11	2.57	2.57	0.00	46.28	46.24	0.04
21	2.52	2.50	0.02	45.32	44.95	0.37
22	1.66	1.64	0.02	29.93	29.55	0.38
23	–0.68	–0.73	0.05	–12.22	–13.2	0.98
31–33	1.65	1.61	0.04	29.69	29.06	0.63
42	1.54	1.50	0.05	27.81	26.98	0.83
44–45	1.17	1.14	0.03	21.03	20.52	0.51
48–49	1.44	1.39	0.05	25.92	25.01	0.91
51	5.41	5.40	0.02	97.47	97.16	0.31
52	1.61	1.54	0.07	28.92	27.63	1.29
53	1.91	1.91	0.01	34.45	34.32	0.13
54	3.05	2.89	0.17	54.98	51.95	3.03
55	2.57	2.38	0.19	46.35	42.89	3.46
56	2.73	2.65	0.08	49.11	47.65	1.46
72	–0.51	–0.54	0.03	–9.2	–9.68	0.48
81	–1.15	–1.19	0.03	–20.74	–21.33	0.59

Note: The table reports average and cumulative log growth rates in real value-added by NAICS sector with and without data investment for 2003–2020. NAICS price indexes are recalculated using Törnqvist expenditure shares.

Table 8.12 **Current-dollar investment in data assets for NPISH 2002–2021**

NAICS	Description	($B)
61	Educational Services	149
62	Health Care and Social Assistance	329
71	Arts, Entertainment, and Recreation	23
813	Religious, Grantmaking, Civic, Professional, and Similar Organizations	51
	Total	552

Note: Current-dollar estimates summed for 2002–2021.

ing (NAICS 21), Utilities (NAICS 22), Information (NAICS 51), and Real Estate (NAICS 53).

8.5.2.3 Non-Profit Institutions Serving Households

While core experimental results for the paper are limited to the business sector, table 8.12 reports supplemental experimental results for current-dollar investment in data assets for NAICS sectors that represent the NPISH sector. For the period 2002–2021, table 8.12 shows the total current-dollar investment in data by NPISH was $552 billion. The largest dollar investments were made in Health Care and Social Assistance ($329 billion), which is fourth largest when compared with the business sector. The second largest dollar investments by NPISH were made in Educational Services ($149 billion).

8.6 Conclusions

In this paper, we measure the value of own-account data stocks and flows for the US business sector by summing the production costs of data-related activities implicit in occupations. In our experimental estimates, we find that annual current-dollar investment in own-account data assets for the US business sector grew from $84 billion in 2002 to $186 billion in 2021, which yields an average annual growth of 4.2 percent. Cumulative current-dollar investment for the period 2002–2021 was $2.6 trillion. Overall, our results indicate that business sector investment in own-account data grew moderately faster than other business sector economic activity and slower than business sector investment in software.

The method we use in the paper augments the traditional sum-of-costs methodology for measuring other own-account intellectual property products in national economic accounts by proxying occupation-level time-use factors using a machine learning model and the text of online job advertisements (Blackburn 2021). The method appears to be a feasible method for identifying occupations engaged in data-related activities and for estimating the time-effort that occupations allocate to data-related activities. The time-use factors we develop for occupations engaged in own-account data appear to have some overlap with the time-use factors we develop for occupations engaged in own-account software, which suggests an incentive to jointly estimate own-account data and own-account software to ensure consistency and prevent double counting if the scope of own-account software is expanded to include more occupations in the future.

In the future, we plan to expand the scope of estimation to include the NPISH and government sectors. In addition, this paper focuses on estimating current-dollar values and uses the depreciation rate for BEA's measures of own-account software as a proxy to calculate net stocks. Thus, important areas of development in the future will be a price index and depreciation rate specific to own-account data. Likewise, an important area for further development will be estimates of purchased data assets and more precise adjustments for data output used in capital formation.

Acknowledgments

The views expressed in this paper are those of the authors and do not necessarily represent the US Bureau of Economic Analysis (BEA) or the US Department of Commerce. We thank Christopher Blackburn, a former research economist at BEA, for developing the machine learning approach we use in the paper (Blackburn 2021). We also thank Marshall Reinsdorf,

Jon Samuels, Brian Sliker, Brenda Bugge, John Haltiwanger, Eleanor Dillon, Josh Martin, and other participants at the NBER-CRIW conference and pre-conference on Technology, Productivity, and Economic Growth for valuable comments. For acknowledgments, sources of research support, and disclosure of the authors' material financial relationships, if any, please see https://www.nber.org/books-and-chapters/technology-productivity-and-economic-growth/valuing-us-data-economy-using-machine-learning-and-online-job-postings.

References

Ackoff, Russell L. 1989. "From Data to Wisdom." *Journal of Applied Systems Analysis*
16 (1): 3–9.

Acquisti, Alessandro, Curtis Taylor, and Liad Wagman. 2016. "The Economics of Privacy." *Journal of Economic Literature* 54 (2): 442–92. doi: 10.1257/jel.54.2. 442.

Ahmad, Nadim. 2004. "The Measurement of Databases in the National Accounts." Second Meeting of the Advisory Expert Group on National Accounts, December 8. SNA/M2.04/04. New York, USA: United Nations Statistics Division. https://unstats.un.org/ unsd/nationalaccount/aeg/m2–04.asp.

Ahmad, Nadim. 2005. "Follow-Up to the Measurement of Databases in the National Accounts." Third Meeting of the Advisory Expert Group on National Accounts, July 19. Vol. SNA/M1.05/19.1. UNESCAP, Bangkok. https://unstats.un.org/unsd/ nationalaccount/aeg/m1–05.asp.

Ahmad, Nadim, and Peter van de Ven. 2018. "Recording and Measuring Data in the System of National Accounts." Meeting of the Informal Advisory Group on Measuring GDP in a Digitalised Economy, November 9. Vol. SDD/CSSP/WPNA(2018)5. Working Party on National Accounts. OECD Statistics, Data Directorate Committee on Statistics, and Statistical Policy. https://www.oecd.org/officialdocuments/publicdisplaydocumentpdf/?cote=SDD/CSSP/WPNA(2018)5&docLanguage=En.

Bakhshi, Hasan, Albert Bravo-Biosca, and Juan Mateos-Garcia. 2014. *Inside the Datavores: How Data and Online Analytics Affect Business Performance*. March. Nesta. https://www.nesta.org.uk/report/briefing-inside-the-datavores/.

Blackburn, Christopher J. 2021. "Valuing the Data Economy Using Machine Learning and Online Job Postings." The Sixth World KLEMS Conference 2021, March 17. Vol. Digital Economy. Virtual. https://scholar.harvard.edu/files/jorgenson/files/ valuing_data_klems.pdf.

Boisot, Max, and Agustí Canals. 2004. "Data, Information and Knowledge: Have We Got It Right?" *Journal of Evolutionary Economics* 14 (1): 43–67. issn: 0936–937, 1432–1386. doi: 10.1007/s00191-003-0181-9.

Chute, Jason W., Stephanie H. McCulla, and Shelly Smith. 2018. "Preview of the 2018 Comprehensive Update of the National Income and Product Accounts." *Survey of Current Business* 98 (4).

Dey, Matthew, David S. Piccone Jr, and Stephen M. Miller. 2019. "Model-Based Estimates for the Occupational Employment Statistics Program." *Monthly Labor Review*. August 27. issn: 19374658. doi: 10.21916/mlr.2019.19.

Farboodi, Maryam, and Laura Veldkamp. 2021. "A Growth Model of the Data Economy." NBER Working Paper No. 28427. Cambridge, MA: National Bureau of Economic Research. doi: 10.3386/w28427.

Fraumeni, Barbara M. 1997. "The Measurement of Depreciation in the U.S. National Income and Product Accounts." *Survey of Current Business* 77 (7). July. https://apps.bea.gov/scb/pdf/national/niparel/1997/0797fr.pdf.

Goodridge, Peter, Jonathan Haskel, and Harald Edquist. 2021. "We See Data Everywhere Except in the Productivity Statistics." *Review of Income and Wealth*. September 28. issn: 0034–6586, 1475–991. doi: 10.1111/roiw.12542.

Hopson, Amy. 2021. "Mapping Employment Projections and O*NET Data: A Methodological Overview." *Monthly Labor Review*. August 19. issn: 19374658. doi: 10.21916/ mlr.2021.18.

Hughes-Cromwick, Ellen, and Julia Coronado. 2019. "The Value of US Government Data to US Business Decisions." *Journal of Economic Perspectives* 33 (1): 131–46. doi: 10.1257/jep.33.1.131.

Hulten, Charles R., Janice McCallum, and Urban Institute, eds. 1981. *Depreciation, Inflation, and the Taxation of Income from Capital*. Washington, DC: Urban Institute Press.

Hulten, Charles R., and Frank C. Wykoff. 1981. "The Estimation of Economic Depreciation Using Vintage Asset Prices." *Journal of Econometrics* 15 (3): 367–96. doi: 10.1016/0304–4076(81)90101–9.

Hulten, Charles R., and Frank C. Wykoff. 1996. "Issues in the Measurement of Economic Depreciation Introductory Remarks." *Economic Inquiry* 34 (1): 10–23. doi: 10.1111/j.1465-7295.1996. tb01361.x.

Jones, Charles I., and Christopher Tonetti. 2020. "Nonrivalry and the Economics of Data." *American Economic Review* 110 (9): 2819–58. doi: 10.1257/aer.20191330.

Lancaster, Vicki Ann, Devika Mahoney-Nair, and Nathaniel Ratcliff. 2021. "Review of Burning Glass Job-ad Data." TR 2021–013, March 10. Proceedings of the Biocomplexity Institute. doi: 10.18130/V3-KADT-5D77.

Le, Quoc, and Tomas Mikolov. 2014. "Distributed Representations of Sentences and Documents." *Proceedings of the 31st International Conference on Machine Learning*, volume 32, edited by Eric P. Xing and Tony Jebara, 1188–196. Proceedings of Machine Learning Research 2. Bejing, China: PMLR, https://proceedings.mlr.press/v32/ le14.

Li, Wendy C.Y., Nirei Makoto, and Yamana Kazufumi. 2019. "Value of Data: There's No Such Thing as a Free Lunch in the Digital Economy." Working Paper, February 19. Bureau of Economic Analysis.

Lightcast. 2023. The Lightcast Open Skills Taxonomy: Understanding a Fast-Changing Labor Market. https://4906807.fs1.hubspotusercontent-na1.net/hubfs/4906807/The%20Lightcast%20Open%20Skills%20Taxonomy%20Aug%202023.pdf.

Martin, Josh, and Ellys Monahan. 2022a. "Developing a Method for Measuring Time Spent on Green Tasks." Office for National Statistics. Economy—Environmental Accounts. March 7. https://www.ons.gov.uk/economy/environmentalaccounts/articles/developingamethodformeasuringtimespentongreentasks/march2022.

———. 2022b. "Research into 'Green Jobs': Time Spent Doing Green Tasks, UK: 1997 to 2019." Office for National Statistics. Economy—Environmental Accounts. March 7. https://www.ons.gov.uk/economy/environmentalaccounts/articles/researchintogreenjobstimespentdoinggreentasksuk/1997to2019.

Minnesota Population Center. 2016. *IPUMS Higher Ed*, edited by National Science Foundation and Matthew Sobek. Version Number: 1.0 Type: dataset. doi: 10.18128/D100.V1.0. http://highered.ipums.org.

Mokyr, Joel. 2013. "The Knowledge Society: Theoretical and Historical Underpinnings." Ad Hoc Group of Experts Meeting on Knowledge Systems for Development. New York, USA: United Nations Department of Economic and Social Affairs. https://web.archive.org/web/20051216205602/http://www.unpan.org:80/dpepa-kmb-ksranda.asp.

Moro Visconti, Roberto, Alberto Larocca, and Michele Marconi. 2017. "Big Data-Driven Value Chains and Digital Platforms: From Value Co-Creation to Monetization." *SSRN Journal*. issn: 1556–068. doi: 10.2139/ssrn.2903799.

Moulton, Brent R., and David F. Sullivan. 1999. "A Preview of the 1999 Comprehensive Revision of the National Income and Product Accounts: New and Redesigned Tables." *Survey of Current Business* 79 (9). September. https://apps.bea.gov/scb/pdf/NATIONAL/ NIPA/1999/0999niw.pdf.

Nguyen, David, and Marta Paczos. 2020. *Measuring the Economic Value of Data and Cross-Border Data Flows*. Digital Economy Papers Vol. 297. OECD. doi: 10.1787/6345995e-en.

OECD. 2009. *Measuring Capital: OECD Manual 2009*. Second edition. Paris: OECD. https://unstats.un.org/unsd/nationalaccount/docs/OECD-Capital-e.pdf.

———. 2010. *Handbook on Deriving Capital Measures of Intellectual Property Products*. Paris: OECD. https://unstats.un.org/unsd/nationalaccount/docs/OECD-IPP.pdf.

———. 2013. "Exploring the Economics of Personal Data: A Survey of Methodologies for Measuring Monetary Value." OECD Digital Economy Papers 220. April 2. doi: 10.1787/5k486qtxldmq-en.

OECD. 2015. *Frascati Manual 2015: Guidelines for Collecting and Reporting Data on Research and Experimental Development*. The Measurement of Scientific, Technological and Innovation Activities. Paris: OECD. doi: 10.1787/9789264239012-en.

———. 2021. "An Update on Recording and Measuring Data in the System of National Accounts." 15th Meeting of the Advisory Expert Group on National Accounts. April 7. Vol. SNA/M1.21/7.4. Virtual. https://unstats.un.org/unsd/nationalaccount/aeg/2021/M15.asp.

Parks, Roger B., et al. 1999. "How Officers Spend Their Time with the Community." *Justice Quarterly* 16 (3): 483–518. doi: 10.1080/07418829900094241.

Rassier, Dylan G., Robert J. Kornfeld, and Erich H. Strassner. 2019. "Treatment of Data in National Accounts." BEA Advisory Committee. Vol. Measuring Data in the National Accounts. BEA's headquarters in Suitland, Maryland. https://www.bea.gov/system/files/2019–05/Paper-on-Treatment-of-Data-BEA-ACM.pdf.

Řehůřek, Radim, and Petr Sojka. 2010. "Software Framework for Topic Modelling with Large Corpora." English. *Proceedings of the LREC 2010 Workshop on New Challenges for NLP Frameworks*, 45–50. http://is.muni.cz/publication/884893/en. Valletta, Malta: ELRA.

Reinsdorf, Marshall, and Jennifer Ribarsky. 2020. "Measuring the Digital Economy in Macroeconomic Statistics: The Role of Data." ASSA 2020 Annual Meeting, January 3. Vol. Big Data: Value, National Accounts, and Public Policy. San Diego, CA. https://www.aeaweb.org/conference/2020/preliminary/2179.

Rowley, Jennifer. 2007. "The Wisdom Hierarchy: Representations of the DIKW Hierarchy." *Journal of Information Science* 33 (2): 163–80. doi: 10.1177/0165551506070706.

Solow, Robert M. 1956. "A Contribution to the Theory of Economic Growth." *Quarterly Journal of Economics* 70 (1): 65. doi: 10.2307/1884513.

Statistics Canada. 2019a. *Measuring Investment in Data, Databases and Data Science: Conceptual Framework*. June 24. 13–605-X201900100009. https://www150.statcan.gc.ca/n1/pub/13-605-x/2019001/article/00008-eng.htm.

———. 2019b. *The Value of Data in Canada: Experimental Estimates*. July 10. 13–605-X201900100009. https://www150.statcan.gc.ca/n1/pub/13-605-x/2019001/article/00009-eng.htm.
U.S. Bureau of Economic Analysis. 2020. "Chapter 6: Private Fixed Investment." *NIPA Handbook: Concepts and Methods of the U.S. National Income and Product Accounts*. https://www.bea.gov/resources/methodologies/nipa-handbook.
U.S. Bureau of Labor Statistics. 2021. *Occupational Employment Statistics: National Industry-Specific and by Ownership*. https://www.bls.gov/oes/tables.htm.
U.S. Census Bureau. 2024. American Community Survey Public-Use File. 2019. [Public-Use Sample of Occupation and Industry Write-ins from ACS 2019]. Industry and Occupation Indexes (census.gov). https://www.census.gov/topics/employment/industry-occupation/guidance/indexes.html.
United Nations. 1993. *System of National Accounts 1993*, revised edition. Brussels/Luxembourg, Washington, DC, Paris, New York. https://unstats.un.org/unsd/nationalaccount/sna1993.asp.
———. 2010. *System of National Accounts 2008*. July 19. United Nations. doi: 10.18356/4fa11624-en.
United Nations Inter-Secretariat Working Group on National Accounts. 2022. *Recording of Data in the National Accounts*. https://unstats.un.org/unsd/nationalaccount/RAdocs/DZ6_GN_Recording_of_Data_in_NA.pdf.
van Rossum, Guido, and Fred L. Drake. 2009. *Python 3 Reference Manual*. Scotts Valley, CA: CreateSpace.
Varian, Hal. 2018. "Artificial Intelligence, Economics, and Industrial Organization." *The Economics of Artificial Intelligence: An Agenda*, edited by Ajay Agrawal, Joshua Gans, and Avi Goldfarb. 399–419. Chicago, IL: University of Chicago Press. http://www.nber.org/chapters/c14017.
Woolhandler, Steffie, and David U. Himmelstein. 2014. "Administrative Work Consumes One-Sixth of U.S. Physicians' Working Hours and Lowers their Career Satisfaction." *International Journal of Health Services* 44 (4): 635–42. doi: 10.2190/HS.44.4.a.
Wykoff, Frank C., and Charles R. Hulten. 1979. *Tax and Economic Depreciation of Machinery and Equipment: A Theoretical and Empirical Appraisal, Phase II Report*. 28. Washington, DC: The U.S. Treasury Department Office of Tax Analysis. https://home.treasury.gov/system/files/131/WP-28.pdf.

9

An Occupation and Asset-Driven Approach to Capital Utilization Adjustment in Productivity Statistics

Josh Martin and Kyle Jones

9.1 Introduction

Estimates of multi-factor productivity (MFP) have long been known to be procyclical, which is to say they fall during economic downturns and increase during economic booms. One reason for this procyclicality is that the intensity of use (utilization) of labor and capital vary over the business cycle, but this is largely unobserved and therefore typically not accounted for.

The coronavirus pandemic, which began in 2020, was an economic shock that resulted in large and sharp reductions in economic output across most countries of the world. While measured labor input also fell, most standard measures of capital input did not fall. The preferred measure of capital input for productivity analysis is capital services, which re-weights measures of the capital stock by an estimated user cost of capital, giving more weight to assets used more intensively in production. Both capital stocks and capital services, as usually measured by national statistical agencies and researchers, respond slowly to economic events. Since output fell sharply in 2020 but capital input as measured did not, MFP appeared to fall sharply.

In reality, the capital services input to production surely did fall, due to a fall in capital utilization—national lockdowns to prevent the spread of the virus rendered some capital assets unusable, clearly reducing their utilization. Adjusting capital services measures for a sharp fall in capital utilization during 2020 would arguably better reflect reality. This would reduce or eliminate the measured fall in MFP, since now both output and inputs would

Josh Martin is an Economic Advisor at the Bank of England, and a research associate with the Economic Statistics Centre of Excellence (ESCoE).

Kyle Jones is an economist at the Office for National Statistics.

fall. In order for MFP to be useful as an economic measure, it might be preferable to separate changes in capital utilization from all the other things that MFP usually measures, including technological progress.

On the assumption that one wants to adjust for variations in capital utilization, the question becomes how best to do so. There is a reasonable literature on this topic, but no internationally agreed approach. The most widely used method is due to Basu, Fernald, and Kimball (2006) (henceforth BFK), which uses average hours worked to proxy for variations in labor and capital utilization, on the assumption that firms adjust along both observed and unobserved margins simultaneously. This approach is simple to implement but, we feel, has a number of conceptual drawbacks.

In this paper we develop a new conceptual framework to enhance the BFK method for estimating capital utilization. While BFK uses the hours worked of all workers to adjust capital utilization of all capital assets, we assign types of workers (occupations) to types of capital (assets), and adjust only the relevant types of capital for variations in hours worked of only the relevant types of workers. We also restrict the variation in capital utilization, for some assets more than others, on account of an ongoing flow of capital services even in the absence of associated hours of work.

We are particularly motivated by official statistics on MFP produced by the UK Office for National Statistics (ONS). The ONS produces (at time of writing) quarterly MFP estimates for the UK market sector, published with approximately a three-month lag after the end of the reference quarter. As such, quarterly estimates of MFP covering the period affected by the coronavirus pandemic were being published during the period when UK government was reacting to the economic effects of the pandemic. In order for these statistics to be useful in this context, we judged it would be important for these statistics to account for the fall (and subsequent rebound) in capital utilization.

Parts of MFP measurement in most national statistical institutes, including the UK ONS, rely on assumptions and parameters that do not vary over time or are simply unmeasured. The measured user cost of capital, part of the capital service measure, may also not respond to shocks in the short or medium run, or respond in the opposite direction to what would be expected (see section 9.3.1). As such, short-run movements in capital utilization are very unlikely to be captured in current measures. Given this, we view some merit in adjusting measures of MFP for capital utilization, especially in times of shocks and structural breaks—the coronavirus pandemic clearly presents such an occasion.

The paper proceeds as follows. In section 9.2, we provide a brief review of the literature on adjusting for capital utilization in productivity statistics. Section 9.3 presents our conceptual framework for our capital utilization adjustment, and some key parameters. Section 9.4 briefly describes the data and methods to estimate our utilization series. Section 9.5 provides some brief analysis of the results, and comparisons against other measures. Section 9.6 discusses shortcomings of the results and concludes.

9.2 Literature

The reason that no national statistical institutes, to our knowledge, implement a capital utilization adjustment into their regular productivity statistics is that it is difficult to measure to a reliable standard. The OECD Manual on Measuring Productivity (OECD 2001) states that while accounting for utilization can explain some of the procyclical nature of productivity calculations, variations in the utilization of capital inputs are ineffectively measured and so there is no generally accepted approach. There is, however, some literature on potential methods.

On reviewing the literature, we recognize five main strands, which we describe briefly below. See also Berndt and Fuss (1986) for the earliest applications, Basu, Fernald, and Kimball (2006) for a discussion of the literature to that point, and Comin et al. (2022) for an outline of more recent literature.

9.2.1 Labor Hours Worked

Arguably the most promising and widely used method to adjust for variable capital utilization is using some measure of hours worked of labor to proxy for utilization of capital. This method develops from Foss (1981), Bils and Cho (1994), Shapiro (1996), Basu and Kimball (1997), Basu, Fernald, and Shapiro (2001), and Basu, Fernald, and Kimball (2006) (BFK). The central assumption in BFK is that profit-maximizing firms operate along both observed and unobserved margins simultaneously, such that variations in the observed margin (average hours worked) can proxy for variations in the unobserved margins (labor effort and capital utilization). The idea can also be motivated by adjustment costs (such as higher wages for labor working longer hours), and faster depreciation of capital when used more intensively (higher utilization).

This can be interpreted intuitively—workers are required to work capital, and so if labor works less, the capital will work less. In this sense, the capital and labor measures gain a symmetry: true labor input is the stock of labor (employment) adjusted by a utilization rate (average hours worked per worker); likewise, the capital measure is the stock of capital adjusted by a utilization rate (also average hours worked per worker). Gorodnichenko and Shapiro (2011) discuss some measures other than average hours per worker that could be interpreted in a similar way, such as number of shifts, and number of temporary workers employed.

Goodridge, Haskel, and Wallis (2013) implement the BFK method on annual UK data between 2001 and 2010. They find that the utilization effect is small, with a considerably smaller coefficient on the utilization term than in BFK for the United States. While they do find a smaller fall in TFP during the 2008–09 downturn with the utilization adjustment, reducing the degree of procyclicality a little, the effect is small, and TFP is still estimated to fall considerably. Groth, Nuñez and Srinivasan (2006) also apply the BFK method to data for UK industries for 1971 to 2000.

Inklaar (2007) implements the BFK method for France, Germany, and the Netherlands, and compares the results with those for the United States from Basu and Fernald (2001). They find that the BFK utilization adjustment does not reduce the procyclicality of TFP in services industries in the European countries, and speculate that this may be due to differences in the measurement of average hours worked across countries, or differences in labor market practices.

Fernald (2014) implements the BFK method to estimate a quarterly utilization-adjusted TFP measure for the US market sector. This is one of few studies, to our knowledge, that apply a utilization adjustment at quarterly frequency. The UK ONS also applied a simplified BFK-type adjustment to their official quarterly multi-factor productivity estimates for the United Kingdom during the coronavirus pandemic, described in ONS (2021b).

9.2.2 Intermediate Inputs Use

In their seminal work on US productivity, Jorgenson and Griliches (1967) applied a capital utilization adjustment based on the use of electric motors in US manufacturing in TFP estimates for 1945 to 1965. Denison (1969) objected to the method,[1] arguing that it would be inappropriate to adjust the whole capital stock of the United States (across all assets and industries) by the use of electric motors in manufacturing—an assumption Denison described as "truly magnificent in its implausibility" (p.22). Christensen and Jorgenson (1970) then applied the electric motors utilization adjustment just to non-residential structures and equipment assets, resulting in a much smaller role for utilization in US TFP.

Burnside, Eichenbaum, and Rebelo (1995) use energy-usage as a proxy for capital utilization in detailed US manufacturing industries using quarterly data. This follows the assumption that increased usage (increased utilization) of machinery would require more energy. Basu (1996) considers materials input in a similar way.

9.2.3 Model-Based Approaches

Burnside and Eichenbaum (1996) and Larsen, Neiss, and Shortall (2001) (henceforth LNS) exploit an assumed relationship between the capital stock, capital investment, and utilization. Intuitively, when the capital-to-output ratio is low, the capital utilization rate should be high—when there is less capital available, relative to output, it must be used more intensively. Con-

1. Denison also criticized the Jorgenson-Griliches utilization measure on a range of other grounds, including the weighting procedure and implicit assumptions. The detailed criticisms of their measure are not relevant here.

versely, when utilization is high, the firm must invest in more capital to expand production, raising the capital stock and reducing the relative utilization rate. Higher utilization could therefore be seen to lead investment (Shapiro, Gordon, and Summers 1989).

LNS define capital utilization as in the equation below, which is a rearrangement of Burnside and Eichenbaum's (1996) model such that the capital-to-output ratio is more obvious.

$$U^t = \left[\frac{1-\alpha}{\delta\phi}\frac{1}{K_t/Y_t}\right]^{1/\phi}$$

where K_t is the capital stock at time t, Y_t is real output at time t, α is the share of labor in income, δ is the steady-state depreciation rate, and ϕ is the elasticity of depreciation with respect to utilization.

The model-based estimates of capital utilization in Burnside and Eichenbaum (1996), for the United States, and LNS, for the United Kingdom, track survey-based measures for capacity utilization[2] reasonably well. In both cases the survey data cover only manufacturing industries, whereas the LNS implementation of the model covers the whole economy, so the result may not be generalizable. LNS's capital utilization adjustment reduces the procyclicality of their measured UK TFP growth by about 50 percent.

9.2.4 Survey-Based Approaches

In more recent literature, Comin et al. (2022) propose an estimation method that relies on a survey-based utilization proxy: specifically, responses from firms on their current capacity utilization given as a percentage.[3] An equivalent question has been asked of firms in services industries only since 2011, and they backcast this using the manufacturing industry data.

There is an important distinction between *capacity utilization* (covering all factors of production, including labor) and *capital utilization*. Survey measures, which generally ask about *capacity utilization*, will reflect to at least some degree the utilization of labor and other factors of production. Where the utilization of labor and capital differ (for the reasons we set out in section 9.3.3) this makes survey-based *capacity utilization* measures imperfect measures of *capital utilization*. However, if profit-maximizing firms adjust along all margins simultaneously, as argued by BFK, then this could still be an appropriate measure of capital utilization.

Comin et al. (2022) apply capacity utilization adjustments to annual data for the United States, Germany, Spain, France, Italy, and the United Kingdom. They compare the BFK utilization approach with an approach using

2. The Confederation of British Industry (CBI) and British Chamber of Commerce (BCC) surveys in the United Kingdom, and figures from the Federal Reserve in the United States.

3. In the United Kingdom this question, in the CBI business survey, is "What is your current rate of operation as a percentage of full capacity?" See Lee, Mahony, and Mizen (2020) for an account of the CBI business surveys.

survey measures of utilization, and suggest that the survey measures produce more sensible results. Consistent with Inklaar (2007), they find that the BFK method works best in manufacturing, and in the United States, but produces unintuitive results outside of manufacturing, and especially in some European countries. Their results for the United Kingdom using the BFK measure are particularly unintuitive, and while the survey-based measure gives more sensible results, they are arguably the weakest among the six countries they consider.

9.2.5 The "Model Response" Philosophy

One contrary interpretation of productivity is that an underutilization of capital *is* a drop in productivity. A failure to fully utilize the capital of an industry would be interpreted as a fall in productivity of that industry. In many other situations, that would seem appealing—frictions in business structures that prevent effective utilization of assets could indeed be interpreted as a productivity loss, and improvements that allow for increased utilization could indeed be thought of as a productivity gain. This is similar to arguments made by Denison (1969), who describes many reasons why utilization of capital may change, arguing that most would already be accounted for in conventional input measures of labor and capital, and others that could readily be considered as subsets of measured productivity growth. However, Denison states that he would prefer to treat such changes in capital utilization as changes in productivity, since they do not relate to the "saving-investment process" (p.21) which governs the capital input measure, and thus capital income. This interpretation likely works well in "normal times."

However, this seems unintuitive during the coronavirus pandemic, when an inability to use capital is *not* as a result of business inefficiency but rather exogenous factors. The drop in output with respect to available capital input here could be thought of as theoretical spare capacity driven by weak demand, unexpectedly poor market conditions, or some unexpected shock. In this situation, it would seem perverse to label this as a fall in productivity, rather than a fall in measured inputs. It does however reflect a somewhat philosophical debate on the meaning of productivity.

Moreover, in the medium term, the other components of the growth accounting framework should adjust, such that changes to the demand for capital are accounted for. This idea is due to Berndt and Fuss (1986) and Hulten (1986). For instance, if office buildings are less beneficial to businesses after the coronavirus pandemic, then the stock of buildings will shrink through reduced investment and increased scrappage. Put another way, the rate of return on buildings will fall (relative to other options) and as a result the supply of buildings will fall to re-introduce equilibrium to the asset market. This will reduce capital services due to negative growth of the productive stock. It will also lead to a shift in the composition of capital in the capital services index, since the user cost share of buildings will be lower.

There will also, *ceteris paribus*, be a decrease in capital income, and thus a reduction in the weight given to capital in the production function. All of these effects would decrease measured inputs, just as a capital utilization adjustment would.

9.2.6 Our Contribution

To summarize, the above sections give an overview of the main methods in the literature to adjust for capital utilization. Most use measures best suited for manufacturing industries, either explicitly (survey questions that only cover manufacturing) or implicitly (use of intermediate inputs or hours worked, which are assumed proportional to capital utilization, which both conceptually and empirically seems to work best in manufacturing). Much of the literature has been conducted in the United States, and using annual data.

Our contribution to this literature is to implement a new method for calculating capital utilization, building on the hours-based measures, in particular the BFK model. We do so by taking a more granular look into the relationship between different types of labor (occupations) and capital (assets), accounting for heterogeneity across assets, industries, and workers. In doing so we hope to address various concerns in the literature, including the relevance of the utilization measures outside of the manufacturing industry. We also do so at quarterly frequency, unlike many past studies.

We sidestep the philosophical debate, and consider options to adjust for capital utilization, on the assumptions that one does wish to. We critique the "model response" view in the context of current measurement in section 9.3.1.

9.3 Conceptual Framework and Approach

In this section we outline the growth accounting framework and how a capital utilization adjustment enters, the problems we see with the "standard" hours-based approach of BFK, and our modification to the method that we believe overcomes these shortcomings.

9.3.1 The Growth Accounting Framework

In the growth accounting framework, used by many national statistical institutes and other researchers to measure productivity, capital and labor are the measured inputs. Changes in output that deviate from changes in the measured inputs (labor and capital) are taken to be changes in productivity.

The production function can be thought of in the following terms:

$$(1) \qquad Y = f[L(l_1, l_2, \ldots, l_n), K(k_1, k_2, \ldots, k_n), \ldots, A]$$

where L is an aggregator function for types of labor l, and K is an aggregator function for types of capital k, and A is an index of technology. A simple L function treats all hours worked as equivalent, so is simply a summation.

A more complex L function[4] considers types of labor l that differ by age, sex, education, and/or industry, with aggregation by their shares of total labor renumeration.

We use ONS growth accounting estimates throughout, applying our capital utilization adjustment onto existing official measures. ONS follow standard practice and international guidance (e.g., OECD 2001), and use a Cobb-Douglas production function, such that output Y is expressed as a function of capital K and labor L weighted together as shown:

$$Y = AL^{\alpha}K^{1-\alpha} \tag{2}$$

where A is a measure of multifactor productivity (MFP), and α is the output-elasticity of labor. As is standard, ONS use the labor share of income that predominates in the industry for α, which varies over time. Assuming constant returns to scale, the capital share is $1 - \alpha$. Labor income is compensation of employees (wages and salaries plus other non-wage labor remuneration) and the labor share of mixed income,[5] and capital income is gross operating surplus (capturing consumption of fixed capital and net operating surplus) and the capital share of mixed income.

Taking logs and differentiating equation (2) with respect to time, and let n denote "change in the natural log," then the change in output is given by:

$$\Delta Y = \Delta A + \alpha\Delta L + (1 - \alpha)\Delta K \tag{3}$$

The capital aggregator function K is a measure of capital services, which is a weighted index of the growth of the capital stock, where the weights are given not by their shares of the value of the stock but by user cost shares. This has the effect of giving a greater weight to assets which are used more intensively in production, and therefore wear out quicker (depreciate quicker). The asset classes are the types of capital k.

The capital services measure is constructed as a Törnqvist index, using two-period rolling average user cost shares, to weight the growth of the productive stock. The capital services index can thus be given as:

$$\Delta K_{i,t} = \sum_a (\Delta PS_{i,a,t}) \times \overline{UCS}_{i,a,t} \tag{4}$$

where $\overline{UCS}_{i,a,t}$ is the two-period average user cost share measure in industry i, for asset a, at time t; and $UCS_{i,a,t} = (UC_{i,a,t} / \sum_a UC_{i,a,t})$, i.e., the user cost share of asset a in industry i at time t is the user cost of asset a in industry i at time t, divided by total user costs among all assets in industry i at time t.

The quality of the capital services measure is inherently linked to the quality of the capital stocks measure. Capital stocks are calculated using

4. The functional form of the labor aggregator function is not central to the argument, so we omit it for brevity.

5. Mixed income (the income of the self-employed, which is effectively both labor and capital income) can be divided between capital and labor income in a number of ways. One approach, used by the ONS, is to divide it into labor and capital income using the shares calculated from the corporate part of the industry.

the Perpetual Inventory Method (PIM) whereby a time series of investment data is cumulated, retired, and depreciated. The key inputs are long time series of current price capital investment data (with breakdowns by industry and asset), suitable price indices (deflators), and a set of parameters that determine the rate of retirement and depreciation of the capital stock over time. The retirement and depreciation rates are often expressed through asset life lengths, which can (but rarely do in practice) vary over time due to the composition of the broad asset class, and changes in the characteristics of the assets. See ONS (2020) for details on the measures we use here.

The user costs are approximated by the rental prices of the assets. Rental prices are rarely observed, as many assets have thin or nonexistent rental markets. Instead, it is typical to estimate the rental price following Hall and Jorgenson (1967), which can be summarized as:

$$(5) \qquad UC = PS \times [RoR + d - (1 + d)p]$$

where PS is the value of the productive capital stock, RoR is the rate of return on capital, d is the depreciation rate, and p is the price change of a new asset (i.e., the price change for reasons other than depreciation). The productive stock is the value of the stock of the given asset, in the given industry, and the given point in time. The depreciation rate is usually the one used to calculate the productive stock, and is often specific to the asset, industry, and time period. The price changes are often taken as the change in the deflator for investment in the asset.

The rate of return can be found endogenously, if user costs are set to exhaust a known total for capital income. This is common practice in national statistical institutes, including ONS,[6] to ensure consistency within the framework. It can also be given exogenously, often based on market rates. On the assumption of profit maximization behavior, the rate of return does not usually vary by asset, but can vary by industry.

When assets are under-utilized, demand for the assets should fall, and thus we expect the rental price to fall. In the Hall and Jorgenson (1967) framework, the fall in the rental price could come from any of the components of the user cost equation, although measuring any of these in real time is challenging or impossible. We explore the three components in turn.

1. If an asset is under-utilized, this might be because the rate of return on the asset has fallen. For instance, during the coronavirus pandemic, the rate of return on buildings likely fell due to increased homeworking, government-imposed restrictions, and changed consumer preferences. Assuming market equilibrium, demand for other assets would respond and the average rate of return across assets stabilize at some lower level. With exogenous rates of return, this may be measured if the necessary data display the expected trends, although exogenous rates of return are often held constant in prac-

6. ONS use a single rate of return across the market sector, rather than one that varies by industry. See ONS (2020) for details.

tice. With endogenous rates of return, this will depend on the response of all the other components, notably measures of capital income.

2. Under-utilization of an asset might change its rate of depreciation, if use and deterioration are linked. National Accounts measures of depreciation conceptually capture both physical wear and tear and "normal" (foreseen) obsolescence (Eurostat 2010). Decreased asset use might slow physical wear and tear, and thus decrease the depreciation rate. Following the user cost framework, this would reduce the rental price on the asset. However, rates of depreciation (often estimated using assumed "asset lives") are usually held constant over long periods of time in standard measurement. NSIs rarely have high-frequency surveys that collect data on asset lives or depreciation rates, so any impact of changes in utilization on depreciation rates is likely to be missed. We return to this in section 9.3.5.

3. Under-utilized assets might see slower price increases or price decreases, as a result of weaker demand. Price changes of new assets are more readily measured as the change in the asset price deflator, and this usually relies on real time data collected by NSIs. This, as well as a fall in the rate of depreciation, would increase the final term of the user cost equation (since it has a negative sign), and thus move in the opposite direction to the other terms.

The net effect is *a priori* ambiguous, but it seems likely that the user cost *should* fall for under-utilized assets. However, in practice the opposite might be true. The fall in depreciation is likely to be missed given the widespread use of constant depreciation rates. An exogenous rate of return might be held constant, and an endogenous rate of return would simply respond to exhaust capital income, which might not fall, dependent on a range of other data collections for the National Accounts—so the measured rate of return is unclear. The fall in prices is most likely to be recorded in real time, and would likely act to increase the user cost. Thus, the measured user cost may actually move in the opposite direction to what it should, at least in the short run.

Optimal growth accounting measures which have real time data on all of these components might well reflect changes in capital utilization correctly, but in practice this will rarely, if ever, be the case. As such, we proceed to think about implementing a capital utilization adjustment in the context of current measurement.

9.3.2 Introducing a Capital Utilization Adjustment into the Capital Services Measure

We modify the capital services measure K to account for utilization by including a multiplicative factor U for each industry:[7]

7. This can also be applied at the asset level to give a capital services index for an asset across industries, e.g., $\Delta\tilde{K}_{a,t} = (1 + \Delta K_{a,t}) \times (1 + \Delta U_{a,t}) - 1$. For brevity, we assume application at the industry level going forward.

$$\Delta \tilde{K}_{i,t} = (1 + \Delta K_{i,t}) \times (1 + \Delta U_{i,t}) - 1 \tag{6}$$

In words, the growth in the utilization-adjusted capital services index in industry i is (1 plus) the growth in the unadjusted capital services series in industry i, multiplied by (1 plus) the growth in the utilization series in industry i (minus 1). This gives an intuitive interpretation: the utilization-adjusted capital services index is approximately[8] the change in the unadjusted capital services index, plus the change in the capital utilization index, and thus changes in the utilization-adjusted index can be approximately decomposed into changes in "potential capital services" (i.e., unadjusted capital services) and changes in utilization.

If U is the same in every period, then this drops out in the construction of the capital services index, and has no effect on productivity. That is, with constant U for all assets, equation (6) collapses to $\Delta \tilde{K}_{i,t} = \Delta K_{i,t}$.

The industry capital utilization measure is constructed as a Törnqvist index, using two-period rolling average user cost shares, to weight the growth of asset utilization measures within each industry. The growth of this index is then:

$$\Delta U_{i,t} = \sum_{a} (\Delta U_{i,a,t}) \overline{UCS}_{i,a,t} \tag{7}$$

where $\Delta U_{i,a,t}$ is the (change in the) capital utilization measure in industry i, of asset a, at time t. This gives an aggregate capital utilization index for each industry. Note that for some assets we will assume constant utilization, that is $\Delta U_{i,a,t} = 0$.

As previously discussed, the introduction of the capital utilization term U is unnecessary if the user costs are measured using real time data and reflect changes in capital utilization. However, in practice, this is rarely if ever true. As such, we view this approach as a reasonable alternative. We continue to use user cost shares here, consistent with the unadjusted capital services measure in (4), since we still want the index to reflect a relatively higher weight for shorter lived assets. The capital utilization term U thus attempts to embody the changes in the user costs that should take place from a change in utilization, but do not as a result of imperfect measurement.

The addition of a utilization index in this way is similar to the method employed by Fernald (2014), but the aggregation by asset is, we believe, unique to this paper, since other methods typically make use of a single utilization measure covering all assets within an industry or economy.

9.3.3 The Problem with the "Standard" Hours-Based Approach to Capital Utilization Adjustment

While an hours-based approach to capital utilization adjustment (as in BFK) is most promising and most widely recognized, it suffers from several conceptual drawbacks.

8. Ignoring the interaction term, since unadjusted capital services changes are small, and utilization changes are usually also small, so the interaction term is approximately zero.

First, the utilization series is based on hours worked of *all* workers. This assumes that all workers use capital in proportion to their hours worked—that is, people who work more hours use more capital, but everyone who works any hours uses some capital. Clearly this is untrue—some people use capital to a far greater extent than others. Contrast a machine operative in a manufacturing firm with a worker in the finance department of the same firm: the machine operative will clearly use much more capital than the finance worker, but their hours are treated equivalently in the standard (BFK) approach.

Relatedly, the method assumes that reductions in hours worked by some staff can be offset by increases in hours worked of other staff for the same capital asset. In some way, this implies interchangeable skills in the workplace. Consider a two-worker firm, where one uses capital (call her the "woodworker") and one does not (call her the "manager"). Assume both work equal hours in the first period, but the woodworker drops their hours by half in the second period—the capital utilization rate would only fall by a quarter, although the person using the capital drops their hours by half. If the manager increased their hours by an equivalent amount in the second period, then average hours (and therefore the standard hours-based capital utilization adjustment) would be the same as in the first period, but if the manager does not use capital this should be irrelevant to the capital utilization rate.

The standard (BFK) method also assumes that all types of capital are affected equally. That is, for any change in hours worked, utilization of all types of capital change equivalently. Returning to our previous two-worker firm, this time let us distinguish between two types of capital (call them machines and computers), and let us assume the woodworker uses machines, and the manager uses computers. If the woodworker drops their hours, the standard hours-adjustment would reduce utilization of both machines and computers, even though the woodworker does not use computers. Again, this is a shortcoming of the standard method.

Most obviously, the standard (BFK) model assumes that hours worked and capital utilization move in tandem to the same degree. The coronavirus pandemic makes it evident that this is not true—homeworkers can work as many hours as before the pandemic, but without using as much of their business's capital (e.g. they do not need to use the business's building). Similarly, any capital that operates without human intervention fails this assumption, such as automated machines and software, and copyright assets (which produce income based on the behavior of consumers, rather than that of the asset owner).

Finally, the standard application of the hours-based method will typically result in falling utilization of assets over time in a deterministic way, as average hours worked have fallen in most developed countries over recent decades. Through increases in standards of living, improved labor market regulation, and the introduction of newer assets which require less labor to work effectively,[9] average hours worked have been on a steady downward trend over the long run. When changes in average hours worked are used as the measure of capital utilization, this therefore also implies that capital utilization is slowly falling over time, which is a challenging view. We see these trends as structural changes, rather than variations in capital utilization, and therefore want to abstract away from them to leave just cyclical variation. Comin et al. (2022) make a similar point regarding movement in hours worked for reasons other than changes in utilization, especially regulatory changes.

In sum, the standard hours-based method (the BFK method) assumes all workers use all types of capital equally (proportionately to their user cost shares), and any changes in hours of any worker affect all types of capital equally. This method is probably best suited to traditional manufacturing industries, where workers operate machines near one-to-one, and there is a clear relationship between the hours of the worker and those of the asset. For most of the modern economy, however, this is likely to be a poor proxy, an argument also made by Inklaar (2007).

To improve on the standard method, and overcome many of the shortcomings described above, we propose two innovative modifications: using the hours of only certain occupations for certain assets; and adjusting utilization of different assets to different degrees.

9.3.4 Occupation-Asset Matching

First, we consider only the hours worked of occupations that would be expected to use given assets. In the case of general use assets such as buildings, we take the hours worked of the whole industry. For specific assets such as transport equipment or machinery, we select only a subset of occupations. This overcomes the issue described above, whereby all workers are assumed to use all capital equally—now, only the hours of relevant occupations will be considered, and the hours worked of other occupations will have no effect on the utilization of that type of asset. The average hours worked of a factory floor worker will be far more representative of the utilization of a machine than the average hours worked of a desk-based worker in the same industry. This also overcomes an issue associated with homeworkers, especially relevant during the coronavirus pandemic, since workers that can work from home are likely not those that will be needed to use assets *in situ*.

A summary of the occupations matched to the assets in this method are

9. For instance, older aircraft needed three or four pilots, and now they all use two because they are better machines which can do much more of the work themselves. You would not want to take this introduction of more efficient equipment to mean that the asset was underutilized. Thanks to Joe Murphy for this insight.

given in table 9.1.[10] Some assets have broad use, and therefore we use hours worked across the whole industry (all workers are assumed to "use" buildings to the same degree when present). Strictly, this should be office-based hours, which we estimate based on workers' reported homeworking activities, but these follow a similar pattern to all hours worked (aside from the period of the coronavirus pandemic). Utilization of ICT, telecoms equipment, and software and databases, are proxied using desk-based occupations; and utilization of transport equipment proxied by transport related occupations (drivers, etc.). Utilization of most intangible assets and cultivated assets are assumed not to vary (see section 9.3.5) so do not have occupations matched.

The most challenging asset class is "other machinery and equipment" (OME) which covers a very heterogenous set of assets, including manufacturing machinery, medical equipment, industrial cleaning equipment, mining and agricultural machinery and equipment, fixtures and fittings (e.g. lighting equipment), office furniture, and more besides. To tackle this broad range, we split the class in two:

- "heavy OME," encompassing all substantial, valuable, long-lasting and highly productive assets, including manufacturing machinery, medical equipment, industrial cleaning equipment, mining and agricultural machinery and equipment
- "light OME," everything else in the asset group, including fixtures and fittings, office furniture, shelving and storage equipment, etc.

In many services industries in the United Kingdom, "light OME" accounts for 90 percent or more of the OME capital stock (ONS 2019). Given the broad nature and use of many of these assets, it is difficult to think of a single occupation that would not use at least some "light OME." As such, we assign occupations to the "heavy OME" but use the hours worked of all workers for "light OME." We combine these categories according to the share of the "heavy OME" occupations in total hours worked in the industry, giving these occupations twice their normal weight, since the asset life of "heavy OME" assets is usually at least twice that of "light OME" (ONS 2019).

9.3.5 Variations by Asset

To account for the different degrees to which utilization can fall for different assets, we appeal to the concept of depreciation. As argued in section 9.3.1, our capital utilization measure is trying to compensate for the lack of adjustment in the user cost equation when it is estimated using imperfect data. One of the factors of the user cost equation that should respond is the rate of depreciation.

In many cases, the depreciation of the asset is intrinsically linked to its

10. See section 9.4.1 and appendix B, http://www.nber.org/data-appendix/c14745/appendix.pdf, for more.

Table 9.1 Assets and associated occupations

Asset	Occupations	Comments
Other buildings	All (non-homeworking hours)	All workers in business owned buildings, hence non-homeworking hours only
Structures	All	This class includes roads and a range of public infrastructure, used indirectly by most workers
"Heavy" other machinery and equipment (OME)	A range that use agricultural, manufacturing, construction or other substantial machinery or equipment	See text for more details
"Light" other machinery and equipment (OME)	All	"Light" OME encompasses office furniture, shelving, etc. and it is difficult to think of any occupations that use none of these types of capital
IT hardware and telecoms equipment	Primarily office-based occupations, and other occupations that use ICT equipment	
Transport equipment	Drivers, pilots, etc. and all occupations where transport equipment is integral to their role, including flight attendants and car mechanics	Heavily concentrated in certain industries
Cultivated assets	N/A	No variation
Software and databases	As for IT hardware and telecoms equipment	
Entertainment, literary and artistic originals	N/A	No variation
Research and development	N/A	No variation
Mineral exploration and evaluation	All	Only present in the mining and quarrying industry, where utilisation of the asset reflects the degree of activity and hence is well proxied by all hours worked

Note: Since MFP estimates produced by the ONS are for the market sector only, table 9.1 excludes weapons systems, transfer costs, and dwellings assets. A full list of occupation codes matched to the three assets with distinct definitions (ICT equipment and software, "heavy" OME, and transport equipment) is in appendix B.

use. Repeated use of a machine or vehicle contributes to its deterioration through wear and tear. However, depreciation is not due only to physical wear and tear; it is due also to "normal" (foreseen) obsolescence (Eurostat 2010). The degree to which depreciation rates (and asset life lengths) reflect these two factors differs dramatically by asset class. Intangible assets, for instance, do not physically deteriorate at all—the entirety of the depreciation is therefore due to obsolescence. On the other hand, manufacturing machinery and vehicles are known to wear out long before they cease to be useful, as evidenced by thriving secondhand markets.

The balance between use-based depreciation (physical wear and tear) and time-based depreciation (obsolescence) is a good match for the argument in section 9.3.3: that some assets can vary in utilization more than others. Since depreciation does not depend entirely on use, neither should our utilization measures. Put another way, even with perfect data, the rate of depreciation in the user cost equation would not fall to zero even with zero use of the asset, due to continued obsolescence.

In addition, some assets continue to provide capital services even when not actively used. For instance, buildings continue to offer capital services in the form of shelter and storage for other capital assets and inventories, and perhaps even some services in the form of branding for the firm, even when not used by workers; in other words, buildings are always used to some extent. Some machines, and especially intangible assets, are automated, and therefore function without the need for labor hours. Other types of equipment continue to offer services in the form of storage and protection for assets, even when not actively managed. The meaning of *use* is somewhat unclear in the case of cultivated assets (such as dairy cattle and orchards), which will continue growing and developing over time regardless.

In the case of intangible assets, they do not physically deteriorate at all, and all depreciation is due to obsolescence by definition. Some software and databases are "used" by workers, although many are automated and most could be used by homeworkers, so hours worked are probably a poor proxy for utilization in this case. Similarly, mineral exploration and evaluation assets are "used" by mining and quarrying firms to inform operations, and reduced mining operations would preserve the value of the information asset for longer; however, such considerations are generally made over the medium term, and as such changes in hours in the short run are somewhat disconnected from the asset.

More broadly, if there is any obsolescence, which is surely true for all assets to a greater or lesser extent, then there will be some depreciation and therefore some "user cost" at all times—as such, some capital services must be delivered. Utilization adjustments of less than 100 percent therefore seem appropriate in all cases.

The true extent of the role of each factor in depreciation of each asset is unknown, but we postulate a sensible set of factors that account for the heterogeneity of assets. Table 9.2 provides a summary. We believe it should

Table 9.2 **Assumed use-based deterioration factors by asset**

Asset	Typical depreciation rate	Assumed use-based deterioration factor	Rationale
Other buildings	c. 5%	20%	Depreciation mainly due to obsolescence and weathering over time. Continues to provide services in the form of shelter/storage even when not used. Use may even reduce deterioration.
Structures	2–5%	50%	Clearly some depreciation of roads and other public infrastructure through repeated use but given long asset lives, much of the depreciation is also due to obsolescence and weathering over time.
Transport equipment	15–20%	80%	Mostly due to use, since many mechanical parts that wear out through repeated use, e.g., miles on a car. As with all assets, some obsolescence and weathering over time. May be possible to estimate through analysis of secondhand markets for cars.
Other machinery and equipment	10–15%	80%	Mostly due to use, since many mechanical parts that wear out through repeated use. As with all assets, some obsolescence and weathering over time.
Telecoms equipment	c. 20%	20%	Have relatively short asset lives, mostly due to high rates of obsolescence due to technological change. Use largely due to consumers rather than producers, and many assets will be automated.
IT hardware	c. 40%	20%	Have relatively short asset lives, mostly due to high rates of obsolescence due to technological change. Strain on processors from use can lead to failure of components, although more likely due to time. Assets can be fragile.
Cultivated assets	c. 40%	0%	Meaning of *use* in this case is somewhat unclear, but assets will continue growing and developing over time regardless of harvesting. Effective management and use (harvesting) may even reduce deterioration.
Software and databases	c. 40%	20%	As an intangible, no physical wear and tear is possible, but the rate of obsolescence could be linked to use—since reduced use might delay the extraction of value from database assets. Utilization could also vary, as some software and database assets will be actively used by workers.
Mineral exploration and evaluation	c. 20%	20%	As an intangible, no physical wear and tear is possible, but the rate of obsolescence could be linked to use—since reduced use might delay the extraction of value from the information assets.
Entertainment, literary and artistic originals	c. 20%	0%	Depreciation based solely on obsolescence over time, linked to royalties from, and sales of, licenses to use and copies of the asset. Driven by demand and consumers, rather than owners.
Research and development	20–30%	0%	Depreciation based solely on obsolescence over time, linked to product cycles of relevant products. Driven by demand and consumers, rather than owners.

Note: Since MFP estimates produced by the ONS are for the market sector only, table 9.2 excludes weapons systems, transfer costs, and dwellings assets. Depreciation rates given are typical but vary by industry in ONS capital stocks and capital services measures.

be possible to estimate at least some of these factors through analysis of data in secondhand markets (especially for cars, for instance), although this is beyond the scope of the present paper.

9.3.6 Bringing It All Together

From sections 9.3.4 and 9.3.5 we have argued that:

- Only certain occupations use certain assets, and therefore the hours worked of those workers alone are suitable to adjust for the utilization of those assets; and
- Only certain assets are subject to variations in utilization, and to different degrees, and should continue to depreciate due to the passage of time to a greater or lesser extent, regardless of use.

This framework provides a novel way to apply a capital utilization adjustment.

Our asset utilization measures are constructed by:

$$\Delta U_{i,a,t} = \left(\frac{r_{i,a,t}}{r_{i,a,t-1}} - 1\right) \times F_a \tag{8}$$

where $r_{i,a,t}$ is the ratio of actual hours worked to a baseline measure in the relevant occupation group for asset a, in industry i, at time t; and F_a is the use-based deterioration factor (as described in section 9.3.5) for asset a (these do not vary over time or by industry by assumption). Recall that for some assets we assume constant utilization, that is $r_{i,a,t} / r_{i,a,t-1} \equiv 1$.

Then the industry utilization measure is constructed as in equation (7), restated below:

$$\Delta U_{i,t} = \Sigma_a(\Delta U_{i,a,t}) \times \overline{UCS}_{i,a,t}.$$

While this still rests on the estimation of the degree of change in asset use (embodied in r), it does so to a lesser extent, and in a more appropriate way. As such, it overcomes, we believe, many of the shortcomings of the standard hours-based method (the BFK method) described in section 9.3.3, namely that hours worked and capital utilization move in tandem to the same degree. It does this by applying these adjustments only to assets which have such a link between workers and utilization. Using the hours worked of particular occupations, as outlined in section 9.3.4, further improves the method by ensuring the hours worked measures are as appropriate as possible for that asset, overcoming the other shortcomings described in section 9.3.3.

9.4 Data and Methods

In this section we discuss the methods and data used to estimate the series described in section 9.3, namely the assignment of occupations to assets, and the estimation of hours worked of these groups (including office-hours worked).

9.4.1 Assignment of Occupations to Assets

We assigned each of the 369 Unit Group occupations (4-digit level) from the UK Standard Occupation Classification (SOC) 2010 to the asset classes used in ONS capital stocks and capital services measures, using our judgment guided by a number of resources. First, in order to gain a detailed understanding of the nature of the assets, we used the descriptions of assets given in international guidance, including the European System of Accounts (ESA) 2010 (Eurostat 2010), the System of National Accounts (SNA) 2008 (United Nations et al. 2009), OECD Measuring Capital Manual (OECD 2009), and the Classification of Products by Activity (CPA) revision 2.1. Second, we used resources available from the ONS website to explore each of the 369 4-digit SOC 2010 codes, to gain an understanding of the tasks performed by workers in these occupation groups. Finally, we used data from the US O*NET database on the tasks performed by detailed occupations, constructing measures of asset use and converting the data to the UK occupational classification. More details of the sources and process are given in appendix B.[11]

Figure 9.1 shows the proportion of hours worked within our occupation-asset groups, in each section-level industry from the SIC 2007 industry classification. Since occupations can be in more than one asset group, or none at all, the bars will not add to 100 percent within each industry, nor across industries. Rather, the proportion represents the fraction of hours worked in that industry which our method suggests are worked by people who use the relevant asset. The data are for hours worked in 2018.

The proportions in figure 9.1 accord with expectations—transport assets are used most in the transport industry (H), followed by agriculture (A) (which includes fishing), water and waste (E) (which includes waste collection services, e.g., garbage trucks), and retail (G) (which includes the motor trades industry).[12] ICT assets are used widely, but most in business services industries (K, L, M) and the ICT services industry (J), unsurprisingly, and least in agriculture (A), transport (H), and accommodation and food services (I). "Heavy" OME is used most intensively in all the production industries. The healthcare industry (Q) also has a higher "heavy" OME share, reflecting medical machinery and equipment. Note that the industry aggregation used in figure 9.1 hides some variation at lower levels, shown in figure B1 in appendix B.[13]

11. See http://www.nber.org/data-appendix/c14745/appendix.pdf.

12. Public admin (O) also has a relatively large transport share, which is likely due to the police and military in this industry. However, since our measures focus on the market sector, we omit section O entirely.

13. See http://www.nber.org/data-appendix/c14745/appendix.pdf.

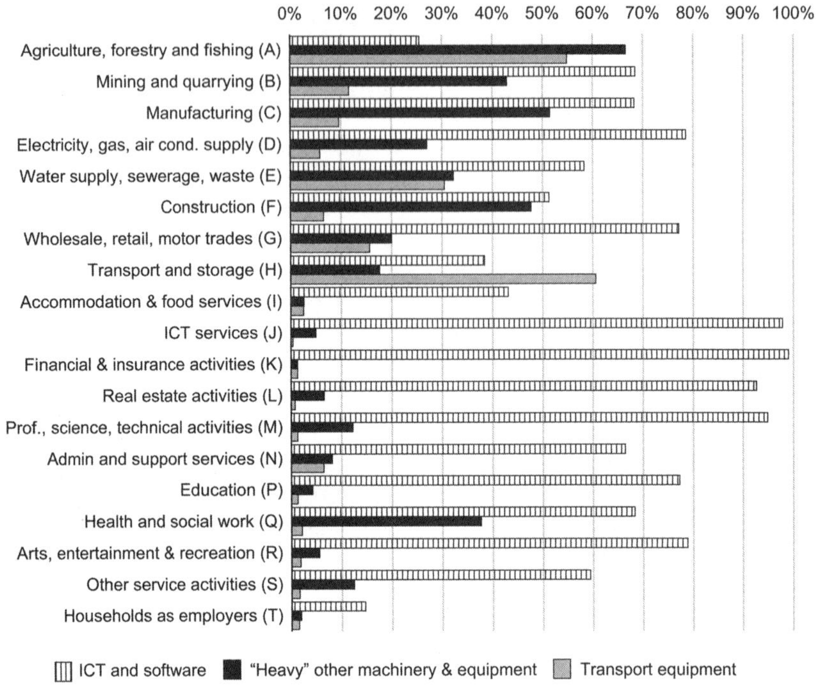

Fig. 9.1 Proportion of hours worked in each occupation-asset group, by industry, 2018

Notes: Letters given in brackets are sections of the UK Standard Industrial Classification (SIC) 2007. See table 9.1 for associated occupation types, and online appendix B for more details on the assignments, and more detailed industry results.

Source: UK Labour Force Survey, authors' calculations.

9.4.2 Estimating Hours Worked

We estimate hours actually worked of these asset-occupation groups at quarterly frequency using data from the UK Labour Force Survey (LFS). To do this, we aggregate all hours worked of occupations within an asset group, by industry, using the total hours actually worked variable (*ttachr*). To generate a long time-series, this requires converting the industry (SIC) and occupation (SOC) classifications at the relevant points, which we do using standard modal mappings at the most detailed level available.

We also compute total usual hours worked of each group in the same way. This allows us to estimate a utilization level in an intuitive way: the ratio of hours actually worked to hours usually worked. Absences from work for any reason (sickness, holiday, strikes, enforced closure or lockdown, etc.) should appear as a deviation of the actual from the usual, and therefore a reduction in the utilization rate. Conversely, an increase in hours relative to

Table 9.3 **Homeworking hours**

Homeworking status	Proportion of hours assumed to be worked at home	Comments
Mainly work at home	90%	Equivalent to one day a week in the office every other week, on average
Recently worked from home	25%	Equivalent to one day a week at home for most, and some for a little longer, on average
Occasionally work at home	5%	Equivalent to one day at home a month, on average
Never work at home	0%	

Source: Authors' judgment, informed by various sources including Felstead and Reuschke (2020).

the usual (due to overtime, or a reduction of the aforementioned absences) would increase the estimated utilization rate.

To estimate homeworking hours (since we measure the utilization of buildings as the inverse of homeworking hours), we use variables on homeworking behaviors collected on the LFS.[14] Following ONS (2021a), we define four homeworking statuses, based on three homeworking questions:

- Mainly work away from the office—respond that the place they "mainly work" is *not* "separate to their home" (such as an office)
- Recently worked from home—respond that the place they mainly work is "separate to their home" but that within the last week they worked at least some time "in their own home"
- Occasionally work at home—respond that they mainly work "separate to their home," and within the last week they did not work "in their own home" but respond that they do "ever" [sometimes] work from home
- Never work at home—the remainder after the above have been assigned

We then assign a fraction of each person's hours worked to be homeworking hours, depending on their homeworking status, as shown in table 9.3. Our buildings utilization measure is based on all hours worked that are not estimated as homeworking hours. Prior to 2008, we do not have access to the data on "recently" or "occasionally" homeworking, so we extend the series using the trend in the mainly homeworking group by industry, which follows a similar trend in the years after 2008 (except in 2020, for obvious reasons).

Although buildings make up a large fraction of the capital stock in the

14. Some of the necessary variables are collected from only from Wave 1 respondents, and are therefore available only in the Annual Population Survey (APS) dataset. We combine the necessary variables from the APS dataset with the quarterly LFS responses, merging on personal identifiers.

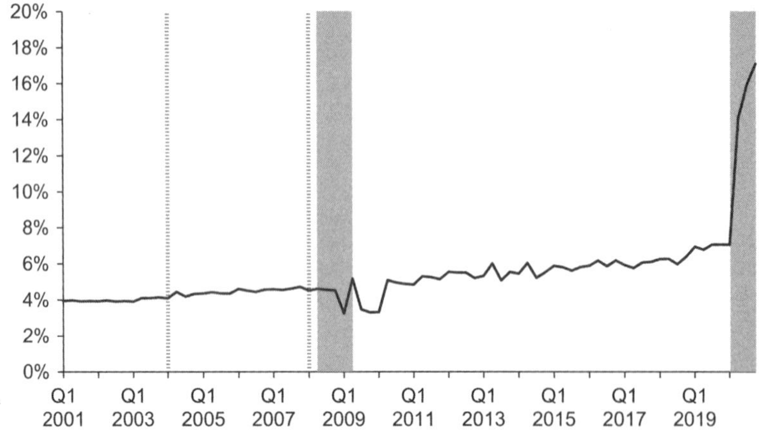

Fig. 9.2 Estimated fraction of hours worked at home in the whole economy, 2001 Q1 to 2020 Q4

Notes: Breaks in methods shown by dotted lines: in Q1 2004, due to switch from LFS (before) to APS (after); in Q1 2008, due to switch from only "mainly" homeworking behavior (before) to include lower-intensity homeworking behaviors (after). Recessions shown by gray shaded areas.

Source: UK Labour Force Survey, authors' calculations.

United Kingdom, they make up a smaller fraction of the capital services index (due to their relatively lower weighting in user costs) and a yet smaller impact on our capital utilization measure. This is because of the use-based deterioration factor for buildings we adopt (see table 9.2), where we assume that buildings are employed largely constantly over time, irrespective of whether workers attend them. In our method, only 20 percent of the overall utilization of buildings is allowed to vary according to the hours worked by workers in business-owned buildings; the other 80 percent is assumed to be constant, as a result of buildings being employed to provide storage and shelter for other capital goods and inventories, and ongoing branding services.

Figure 9.2 shows the fraction of hours worked in the whole economy estimated to be worked at home, which is the inverse of our utilization measure for buildings. This rises slowly over time, from around 4 percent in the early 2000s, to about 6–7 percent in recent years. The economic downturn is visible in this data, albeit with an unusual pattern, and the coronavirus pandemic results in a massive increase in homeworking.

The trends by industry (not shown) are as expected, with industries like professional services and ICT industries, which employ relatively more occupations that are better able to work from home, exhibiting far higher degrees of homeworking than other industries. The creative, arts and entertainment activities industry has the highest share, at around a quarter of all hours worked in that industry done at home. The homeworking share in almost every industry is flat or increasing over time, with the exception of a few small industries. The methods changes and classification conversions occasionally cause increased volatility in the back series.

In comparison to other sources, our estimates may underestimate the "true" fraction of hours worked at home during the pandemic due to the wording of the homeworking questions on the LFS. Respondents that did not work from home before the coronavirus pandemic but did so due to national lockdowns during 2020, may not have responded that they "mainly" worked from home. The relevant question on the LFS refers to the respondent's "usual" place of work, and respondents might have considered their status at that time as "unusual." Instead, they might say that they worked from home in the reference week, but did not mainly work from home—in this case, we would allocate only 25 percent of their hours to homeworking (table 9.3). This might be a reasonable assumption pre-pandemic, but certainly not during 2020, when workers were mostly entirely working from home, or entirely working away from home (or on furlough). We do not vary the factors in table 9.3 over time given lack of data on which to calibrate such an adjustment.

Following the coronavirus pandemic, the ONS has made changes to the LFS, and now asks the number of hours an individual works remote. As such, implementing our method in future could use a more accurate measure of homeworking hours. One benefit of the LFS is the long and relatively consistent time series it allows, necessary to apply our method over time.

Alternative methods of measuring the homeworking rates, such as the ONS-run Opinions and Lifestyles Survey,[15] estimate that around 35 percent of individuals were working fully from home in 2020 Q4 (the last quarter shown in figure 9.2), with a further 10 percent working at least some of their hours from home. This could suggest that the "true" fraction of hours worked from home could be larger than we present.

An underestimate of homeworking hours in our estimates would mean that the utilization of non-residential buildings would not fall enough. However, an underestimate of homeworking (an overestimate of utilization of non-residential buildings) might be preferable, since it would offset the (unmeasured) role of "potential capital," as proposed by Eberly, Haskel, and Mizen (2021). They argue that capital owned by households, such as residential dwellings, home office furniture, etc. are unmeasured capital inputs that are used to a greater extent during the pandemic due to increased homeworking.

15. In the Opinions and Lifestyle Survey respondent were asked, "In the past seven days, have you worked from home because of the coronavirus (COVID-19) pandemic?" and "In the past seven days, have you left home for any of the following reasons?" where "work" was included as an option. Working status can then be derived from these two questions.

9.4.3 Adjusting the Baseline

It is important to de-trend actual hours worked in some way, else changes over time may reflect changes in technology or productivity that lead to fewer hours being worked per person in some industries, instead of variation in capital utilization. Usual hours worked is an attractive baseline, since it relates specifically to workers and their perceptions of "usual"—allowing for changes in contracts, working arrangements, and behaviors over time. It is available at the same frequency and granularity as the actual hours worked variable, and is simple to implement.

However, using usual hours worked from the contemporaneous period, without adjustment, as the baseline proved to be problematic. Not only was it somewhat volatile, but it responded "too quickly" to shocks such as the 2008/09 financial crisis. When workers were laid off, their actual and usual hours fall to zero, and hence the impact on the ratio of the two (and hence the utilization measure) was essentially nil. We wanted such a scenario to generate a temporary fall in utilization, until the business could adapt by selling/scrapping their capital and/or hiring workers to use existing capital again.

We tested a number of adjustments:

1. Use usual hours worked, but smooth it with a filter (such as a Hodrick-Prescott filter) within each industry and asset class. Depending on the specifications and parameters, this would create a smoother and more-slowly-adjusting baseline, and hence a temporary fall in utilization when actual hours fall. However, this adds choices and processing steps to an already complicated process, and could lead history to be revised with every update due to the nature of filters like these. Kurmann and Sims (2021) document large revisions in the utilization-adjusted TFP measures produced by John Fernald for the United States (e.g., Fernald 2014), who uses this "de-trending" approach. We look to avoid this issue.[16]

2. De-trend hours actually worked, and use variations around the trend (with no role for usual hours worked)—this would have a similar effect to (1), with the series now based around 1 rather than 0.8–0.9 (although we view our method as unable to produce an estimate of the "level" of capital utilization). It has the same drawbacks as (1), with additional steps and decisions to be taken and potential for frequent revision to the backseries.

3. Account for the hours worked of people no longer in the industry in the baseline—for instance, those made redundant. Assuming firms take x periods to respond to loss of labor by re-hiring workers or selling capital, in the short run, the hours worked of previously employed workers could be included in the baseline. This would require rolling forward the hours usually worked by people who have left jobs (for a variety of reasons) for x quarters. This would not be susceptible to future revisions, although it does

16. We are grateful to Ana Galvão for this suggestion.

require some careful data processing and some assumptions to be made on the hours worked of those no longer working.

4. Apply a simpler "smoothing" approach to usual hours than (1), such as taking a four-quarter (backward looking) rolling average, or using a one- or two-period lag—these are also not susceptible to future revisions, and are much easier to implement. A choice must be made about how long the lag or average should be, although some choices are intuitive.

We tested five adjustments: de-trending usual hours using a filter; the addition of previously employed worker-hours; a four-quarter (backward looking) rolling average of usual hours; and one-period and two-period lags of usual hours. We did not test option (2) above, since we quickly discounted using a filter based on the criticisms of the approach in Kurmann and Sims (2021).

Figure A1 in appendix A shows the resultant capital utilization series for each of the adjustments, for the market sector aggregate and for manufacturing.[17] We adopted the four-quarter backward looking rolling average of usual hours as our central case. Thus, we see the business as slowly updating their expectations based on the norm over the course of the preceding year, which seems reasonable. Figure A2 in appendix A also shows our central case (using the four-quarter backward looking rolling average of usual hours as the baseline) and the "no adjustment" (using the contemporaneous usual hours worked data) for each SIC 2007 industry section (letter-level industry).

9.5 Results

9.5.1 Trends in Asset Utilization Rates for the Market Sector

We apply the trends in asset utilization rates and homeworking hours with the use-based deterioration factors in table 9.2 and the user cost weights in the ONS MFP system (ONS 2021b) to derive an overall estimated capital utilization adjustment for each industry, and the market sector as a whole (see sections 9.3.1, 9.3.2, and 9.3.6 for algebra). Figure 9.3 shows the market sector capital utilization series, indexed to Quarter 1 2002 = 100, with and without the four-quarter rolling-average adjustment described in section 9.4.3.

Across the market sector as a whole, capital utilization varies between about +2 percent and –2 percent in each quarter between 2001 and 2008, and between about +1 percent to –1 percent between 2008 and 2019. The reduction in volatility could be due to somewhat artificial changes in the data from this point onwards: perhaps due to the SIC conversion used for the historic data causing a break at this point. The smaller changes from 2008 onwards feel more realistic, but we have no clear evidence for preferring one period or the other.

17. See http://www.nber.org/data-appendix/c14745/appendix.pdf.

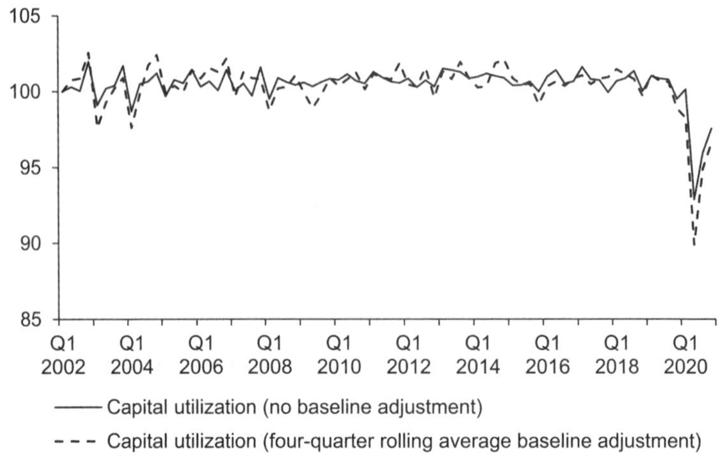

Fig. 9.3 Capital utilization, with and without the four-quarter rolling average adjustment to the baseline, UK market sector, Q1 2002 to Q4 2020, not seasonally adjusted, indexed to Q1 2002 = 100

Notes: Weighted by user cost shares from ONS MFP system—across assets within each industry, and across industries in the market sector. See sections 9.3.1, 9.3.2, and 9.3.6 for algebra.

Source: UK Labour Force Survey, ONS, authors' calculations.

The series is not especially cyclical—the 2008/09 economic downturn is characterized by a reduction in volatility and seasonality, but no substantial or sustained dip in utilization.[18] This is for two reasons: first, in many industries, there was no noticeable fall in hours worked in that period—the characteristic "labor hoarding" phenomenon; and second, if there was a fall in actual hours worked, then usual hours worked tended to fall a similar amount, and hence the ratio between them was relatively unchanged. Our rolling-average adjustment to the baseline mitigates this somewhat, although this does not appear to be enough to generate a significant effect at the market sector level.

The coronavirus pandemic is very visible, with a drop in utilization of some 10 percent overall in Quarter 2 2020, before rebounding. This is by far the largest movement in the series, although less than some might have expected. This reflects the targeted use of occupations and the asset-use factors which subdue the effects of our hours-based utilization measures, to account for some degree of continued asset-use at all times.

The data are not seasonally adjusted, and show some interesting seasonality, summarized in table 9.4. Utilization tends to increase in Quarters 2 and 4, and decrease in Quarters 1 and 3. Lower utilization in Quarter 1 could be

18. Note that the series are not seasonally adjusted, and we might see a larger effect on a seasonally adjusted basis.

Table 9.4 **Seasonal characteristics of the utilization adjustments**

Quarter	Average quarter-on-quarter utilization change, whole economy	Number of industries consistent with whole economy change	Median quarter-on-quarter utilization change, across industries	Industries with largest negative effects	Industries with largest positive effects
1 (Jan to Mar)	−0.34%	48	−0.08%	Water transport, travel agency, air transport	Repair of household goods, insurance
2 (Apr to Jun)	0.30%	48	0.20%	Water transport, insurance, water supply	Fishing, air transport, forestry
3 (Jul to Sep)	−0.13%	47	−0.20%	Education, manuf. of rubber products, repair and instal. of machinery	Air transport, fishing, manuf. of coke/petrol, water transport
4 (Oct to Dec)	0.16%	43	0.19%	Fishing, air transport, travel agency	Education, water transport, rental and leasing

Note: Averages 2002 to 2019.
Source: UK Labour Force Survey, ONS, authors' calculations.

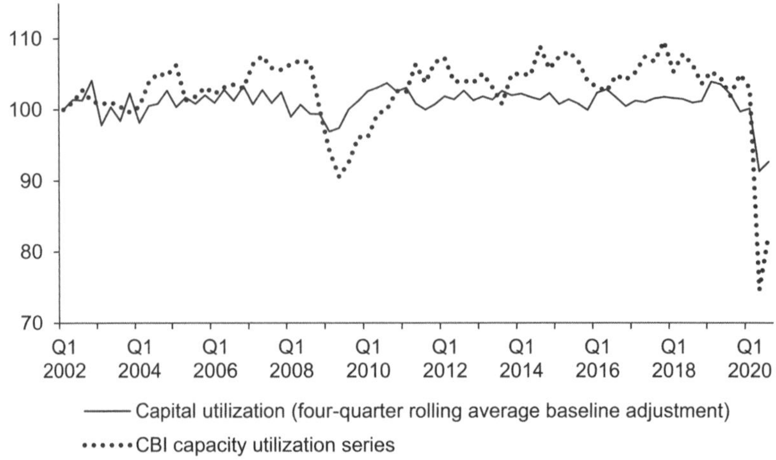

Fig. 9.4 Comparison of hours-based capital utilization (manufacturing industry) and CBI utilization (manufacturing and mining), Q1 2002 to Q3 2020, not seasonally adjusted, indexed to Q1 2002 = 100

Source: Confederation of British Industry (CBI), UK Labour Force Survey, ONS, authors' calculations.

due poor weather disrupting operations, winter illnesses, and low demand after the Christmas period; Quarter 3 overlaps the UK school summer holidays so could exhibit a larger degree of absence for holidays. Meanwhile Quarter 4 is likely to be characterized by increased operations in the run-up to Christmas and other festivals; and Quarter 2 is the quarter with least disruptions for any of the above reasons. Typical seasonal industries (such as water transport and air transport) demonstrate the strongest seasonal effects, but the pattern is widespread.

9.5.2 Trends at Industry Level

As noted in section 9.2, there are other methods and sources used in the literature to measure capital utilization. Figure 9.4 compares the hours-based measures constructed in this paper, for the manufacturing industry, with the data from the CBI survey on capacity utilization (covering the manufacturing and mining industries). Besides the period of the coronavirus pandemic, the series are essentially unalike—the CBI series is far more cyclical than our measure, including during the 2008/09 downturn. However, the CBI is strictly one of *capacity utilization* which includes the utilization of other factors of production like labor—this could influence the measure.

Figure 9.5 shows the median, minimum, and maximum quarterly change across the 62 industries[19] in the ONS MFP system (unweighted by size and

19. These are largely industry divisions of SIC 2007, with some aggregations thereof.

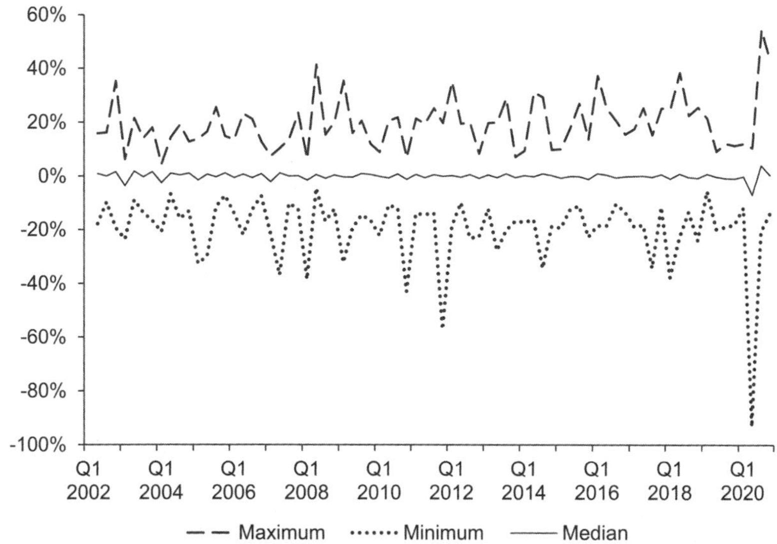

Fig. 9.5 Distribution of quarter-on-quarter changes in capital utilization by detailed industry, 2002 Q2 to 2020 Q4

Notes: Industries are the 62 industries in the ONS MFP system—mostly two-digit industries (divisions) from SIC 07 with some aggregations of 2-digit industries.

Source: UK Labour Force Survey, ONS, authors' calculations.

capital intensity of industry). The median change in Q2 2020 is the largest over the period covered, but smaller than may be expected, at around –7 percent, with a median 4 percent rebound in Q3 2020. The impact of the coronavirus pandemic is very heterogeneous: in some industries, there is a very large decrease in utilization (up to 93 percent in the air transport industry), but in some industries utilization actually increases on the previous quarter. The relatively small median impact is partly because some industries were not especially affected by the national lockdowns and were able to keep operating (including many business services industries) and partly due to the use-based deterioration factors in table 9.2: recall that some assets have no adjustment at all.

9.5.3 Sensitivity to Asset-Use Factors

One of the most uncertain aspects of our approach is the use-based deterioration factors in table 9.2, which subdue the impact of changes in hours worked on capital utilization, and vary by asset. To assess the sensitivity of the results to these factors, figure 9.6 shows the market sector capital utilization series with and without applying these factors.

The capital utilization series without applying the asset-use factors from table 9.2 is similar to our central estimates, with the exception of the impact

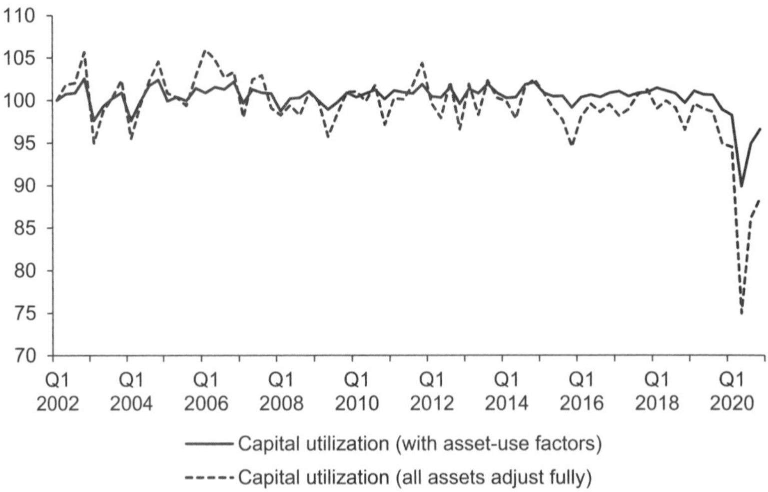

Fig. 9.6 Comparison of capital utilization series with and without asset-use factors, market sector, Q1 2002 to Q4 2020, not seasonally adjusted, indexed to Q1 2002 = 100

Notes: Both series use the four-quarter backward looking adjustment to the baseline.
Source: UK Labour Force Survey, ONS, authors' calculations.

of the coronavirus pandemic, where it is far larger. Utilization falls around 20 percent in Q2 2020 in the series without factors, and only about 10 percent in the version with factors; both series recover about half of their respective declines in Q3 2020. The series without factors is slightly more volatile, and falls slightly over time, especially in recent years, largely due to the larger impact of the gradual shift towards homeworking, which reduces utilization of buildings (which have a relatively large weight).

At the industry level, the impact of the factors is more significant, reflecting the differences in asset mix in each industry. Figure 9.7 shows the quarter-on-quarter change in capital utilization in Q2 2020 by industry with asset-use factors, without factors (but still using the occupation-asset matching approach introduced in this paper), and the simple change in average hours worked (the approach used in the official MFP estimates from the ONS, as in ONS 2021b, a simplified version of the BFK method). The approaches are well correlated across industries.

The average absolute quarter-on-quarter change is smallest in the variant with asset-use factors, and largest in the variant without asset-use factors, with the ONS approach (simplified BFK) somewhere between. This reflects that the occupation-asset matching relies on detailed industry-by-occupation data from the LFS[20] which can be more volatile, and so without

20. A multi-purpose, household survey, not designed for this sort of detailed modeling work.

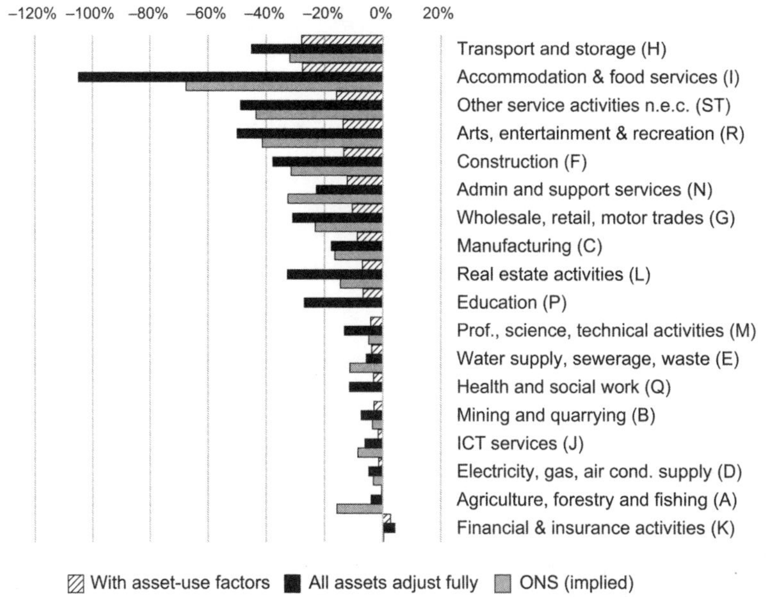

Fig. 9.7 Comparison of capital utilization changes by industry, with and without asset-use factors, and a simplified-BFK approach, quarter-on-quarter growth rate, Q2 2020

Notes: ONS data are implied from the difference between adjusted and unadjusted capital services data. No ONS estimate available for Education (P) or Health and social care (Q) due to suppressions. The ONS estimate for the finance industry (K) is zero. Data are in natural log changes, hence can be less than 100 percent.

Source: UK Labour Force Survey, ONS, authors' calculations.

the subduing effect of the asset-use factors, this can lead the method to produce more noisy results. As such, we recommend that the occupation-matching approach introduced in this paper should only be used in conjunction with the asset-use factors, which also help to subdue some of the volatility introduced by these low-level data.

9.5.4 Impact on MFP Estimates

The impact of the adjustment on MFP estimates is small but broadly in line with expectations. Figure 9.8 shows quarter-on-same-quarter-a-year-ago growth rates of MFP with and without the utilization adjustment, using the official unadjusted MFP estimates from the ONS (ONS 2021b) as the baseline.

The introduction of the capital utilization adjustment makes no material difference to the trend, but does lead to some small differences in MFP in a few points: a trough in growth in 2005 becomes more pronounced, and the weakness in growth in 2015 is staved off a few quarters. There is no obvious impact on the 2008/09 downturn at this level, although there are small

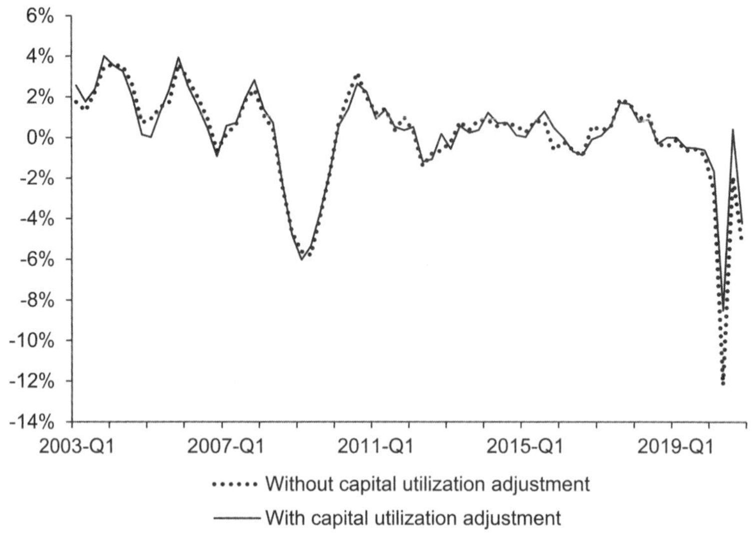

Fig. 9.8 Comparison of MFP growth rates with and without a capital utilization adjustment, quarter-on-same-quarter-a-year-ago growth rates, market sector, Q1 2003 to Q4 2020

Source: UK Labour Force Survey, ONS, authors' calculations.

impacts for some industries (including manufacturing). The fall during the coronavirus pandemic is moderated considerably—from around 12 percent to around 8 percent in Quarter 2 2020.

In line with the literature, the adjustment makes the MFP series less procyclical (given by the correlation between the growth rates of GVA and MFP) although only slightly; this holds with and without including 2020.

The effect varies by industry according to the utilization series and the capital intensity of the industry. Figure 9.9 shows the quarter-on-quarter change in MFP in Q2 2020 by industry, not adjusted for capital utilization, adjusted with our central measure, and adjusted with the ONS approach (simplified BFK). The effect of introducing the adjustment tends to be proportionately larger in more capital-intensive industries. The adjustment introduced in this paper (with asset-occupation matching and asset-use factors) tends to be less severe than the simple hours-methods (as used by the ONS), in line with the findings from figure 9.7.

Correlations between output and MFP growth are weaker (i.e., MFP is less procyclical) when applying the capital utilization adjustments than when not, in line with the literature, in almost[21] all industries. This is true for

21. The only exception (at this level of industry aggregation) is the government services industries (OPQ), which is fractionally better correlated—although this is a small and unusual industry group, since it is only the market sector elements of these industries, which are imperfectly measured.

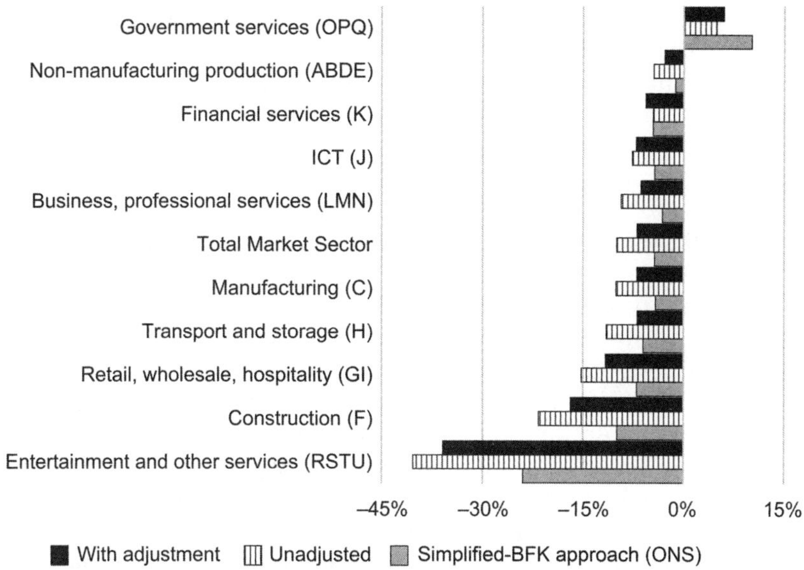

Fig. 9.9 Comparison of MFP quarter-on-quarter growth rates by industry, with and without a capital utilization adjustment, and a simplified-BFK approach, Q2 2020

Source: UK Labour Force Survey, ONS, authors' calculations.

quarter-on-quarter and quarter-on-same-quarter-a-year-ago growth rates, with and without including the period of the coronavirus pandemic.

9.6 Discussion

We believe that our innovations to the more standard hours-based measures to adjust for capital utilization (the BFK method) are conceptually well grounded, and should improve the validity of that method. In particular, we account for heterogeneity across industries and assets for the first time, addressing Denison's (1969) critique. The matching of occupations to assets is a conceptual enhancement on the existing literature, although the allocations would benefit from external review and could be further refined. The method does rely on a number of assumptions, which are currently not supported by sufficient evidence. However, in practice in this application, the results produced by this method do not display key features that we would like them to.

Aside from the conceptual advantages, there are some positives from these measures. We judge that the results covering the period of the coronavirus pandemic in 2020 are of a broadly sensible shape and magnitude. This is the period when an adjustment for variations in capital utilization is arguably most necessary, so the fact that the method produces sensible results, both in the aggregate and by industry, is somewhat reassuring.

This method can also be estimated at quarterly frequency, and on the same timescales as official MFP estimates in the United Kingdom produced by the ONS, making it suitable for use in official statistics applications (see further discussion below). It will not be subject to revision over time that would be the same if using a filter of hours actually worked, and thus avoids the criticism of Kurmann and Sims (2021).

The main shortcoming is that the resultant estimates of capital utilization do not match trends present in other sources, principally business surveys. While one should not cling too closely to one's priors, the estimates produced by this method do not "feel right." A major issue is the lack of a strong effect during the 2008/09 downturn, although this is present to a small degree in some industries. Another is that the series shows very little cyclical variation, such that the impact on MFP measures is minimal. That said, we are measuring an unobservable and difficult-to-measure variable, and we do not have a reliable benchmark to compare against. As such, we cannot be sure whether our results are any more or less accurate than others.

The reason for the lack of 2008/09 dip is that usual hours worked responded similarly to actual hours worked in most industries, meaning the ratio between the two, which drives our utilization measure, is largely unchanged. We have argued that it is important to de-trend actual hours worked in some way, else changes over time may be due to changes in technology or productivity that lead to fewer hours being worked per person in some industries. Usual hours worked is an attractive baseline, since it relates specifically to workers and their perceptions of "usual"—allowing for changes in contracts, working arrangements and behaviors over time. It is available at the same frequency and granularity as the actual hours worked variable, and is simple to implement. However, using usual hours worked unadjusted was problematic, and the adjustments we trialed made relatively little difference (see figures A1 and A2 in appendix A, http://www.nber.org/data-appendix/c14745/appendix.pdf, for more details). We suspect further improvements to the "baseline" would improve the estimates—using a longer window for the baseline (rather than the four quarters we used) might help.

Another potential concern is how the approach would fair in other countries with different labor markets, especially those that had different labor market policies during the coronavirus pandemic. For instance, the United States did not operate a government-supported furlough scheme as in the United Kingdom, so unemployment increased far more during 2020 in the United States than in the United Kingdom. However, hours worked responded similarly in both countries.

For the baseline in our calculation, we use "usual hours worked" of employed workers, averaged over the current and preceding three quarters (i.e., a four-quarter rolling average). Since furloughed workers are still in employment, they are still asked about their "usual hours worked" in UK labor market surveys and thus will still appear in our baseline. By contrast, in the United States, since the equivalent workers will no longer be employed, their "usual hours worked" would not be included in our baseline. As such, the measured fall in capital utilization (the ratio between actual hours and the baseline) will be less in the United States than the United Kingdom. Our four-quarter average adjustment will ensure the baseline adjusts slowly in both countries, which partly mitigates this effect, but not completely.

A further consideration is that lower utilization of business capital might be offset by greater utilization of non-business capital. For instance, the move to homeworking during the coronavirus pandemic clearly reduced the utilization of business-owned buildings, but would have increased the utilization of household-owned capital, especially dwellings (houses) as well as home furniture and ICT technology. Eberly, Haskel and Mizen (2021) term this "potential capital." This potential capital is not included in the capital input measures in standard productivity analysis, so an increase in its utilization would not be accounted for. Accounting for a fall in utilization of business-owned buildings during the coronavirus pandemic, but failing to account for the offsetting increase in utilization of household-owned capital would risk reversing the bias in measured MFP rather than eliminating it. The relatively low use-based deterioration factor we apply to buildings (see table 9.2) might therefore be helpful in avoiding an overly strong effect of homeworking on total capital utilization.

This paper was motivated by the coronavirus pandemic, which led to large and sharp movements in economic variables, including (as measured) MFP. Standard measures of capital services and MFP, such as those produced by national statistical institutes like the ONS in the United Kingdom, are not responsive to shocks in the short-term. Quarterly MFP measures in particular will be susceptible to variations in capital utilization due to idiosyncratic factors. Implementing an adjustment for the change in capital utilization may improve the usefulness of such measures. More thought should be given to whether, and how, national statistical institutes adjust their MFP measures for variations in capital utilization—at all times, or just during economic shocks such as the coronavirus pandemic.

Acknowledgments

We are grateful to Joe Murphy, Emma Hickman, Jakob Schneebacher, Russell Black, Chloe Baker, Rebecca Riley, Susanto Basu, Carol Corrado, Paul Schreyer, and an anonymous referee for helpful comments. We also benefitted from discussion at the NBER CRIW Conference on Technology, Productivity, and Economic Growth in March 2022 in Washington, D.C. (and an earlier conversation with speakers), at the Economic Statistics Centre of Excellence (ESCoE) annual conference in May 2021, at an ESCoE research seminar in January 2022. Most of the work was done while both authors were employed at the Office for National Statistics (ONS). Any views expressed are solely those of the authors and cannot be taken to represent those of their respective employers. This paper should therefore not be reported as representing the views of the Bank of England, or members of the Monetary Policy Committee, Financial Policy Committee or Prudential Regulation Committee. Any errors are our own. For acknowledgments, sources of research support, and disclosure of the authors' material financial relationships, if any, please see https://www.nber.org/books-and-chapters/technology-productivity-and-economic-growth/occupation-and-asset-driven-approach-capital-utilization-adjustment-productivity-statistics.

References

Basu, S. 1996. "Procyclical Productivity: Increasing Returns or Cyclical Utilization?" *Quarterly Journal of Economics* 111 (3): 719–51.

Basu, S., and M. Kimball. 1997. "Cyclical Productivity with Unobserved Input Variation." NBER Working Paper 5915. Cambridge, MA: National Bureau of Economic Research.

Basu, S., and J. Fernald. 2001. "Why Is Productivity Procyclical? Why Do We Care?" In *New Developments in Productivity Analysis*, edited by C. Hulten, E. Dean, and M. Harper. NBER Studies in Income and Wealth, vol. 63, 225–96. Chicago: University of Chicago Press.

Basu, S., J. Fernald, and M. Kimball. 2006. "Are Technology Improvements Contractionary?" *American Economic Review* 96 (5): 1418–1448.

Basu, S., J. Fernald, and M. Shapiro. 2001. "Productivity Growth in the 1990s: Technology, Utilization or Adjustment?" NBER Working Paper 8359. Cambridge, MA: National Bureau of Economic Research.

Berndt, E. R., and M. A. Fuss. 1986. "Productivity measurement with adjustments for variations in capacity utilization and other forms of temporary equilibrium." *Journal of Econometrics* 33 (1-2): 7–29.

Bils, M., and J. Cho. 1994. "Cyclical Factor Utilization." *Journal of Monetary Economics* 33: 319–54.

Burnside, C., and M. Eichenbaum. 1996. "Factor Hoarding and the Propagation of Business Cycle Shocks." *American Economic Review* 86 (5): 1154–174.

Burnside, C., M. Eichenbaum, and S. Rebelo. 1995. "Capital Utilization and Returns to Scale." *NBER Macroeconomics Annual 1995* 10: 67–110.

Christensen, L., and D. Jorgenson. 1970. "US Real Product and Real Factor Input, 1929–1967." *Review of Income and Wealth* 16 (1): 19–50.

Comin, D., J. Quintana, T. Schmitz, and A. Trigari. 2022. "A New Measure of Utilization-Adjusted TFP Growth for Europe and the United States." NBER Working Paper 28008. Cambridge, MA: National Bureau of Economic Research.

Denison, E. 1969. "Some Major Issues in Productivity Analysis: An Examination of Estimates by Jorgenson and Grilches." *Survey of Current Business* 49 (5, Part II): 1–27. Office of Business Economics, Department of Commerce.

Eberly, J., J. Haskel, and P. Mizen. 2021. "'Potential Capital,' Working from Home, and Economic Resilience." NBER Working Paper 29431. Cambridge, MA: National Bureau of Economic Research.

Eurostat. 2010. “European System of Accounts: ESA 2010.” Publications Office of the European Union, Luxembourg. doi:10.2785/16644.

Felstead, A., and D. Reuschke. 2020. “Homeworking in the UK: Before and During the 2020 Lockdown.” WISERD Report. Cardiff: Wales Institute of Social and Economic Research. Accessed 30 August 2021. https://wiserd.ac.uk/publications/homeworking-uk-and-during-2020-lockdown.

Fernald, J. 2014. “A Quarterly, Utilization-Adjusted Series on Total Factor Productivity.” Working Paper Series 2012–19. Federal Reserve Bank of San Francisco.

Foss, M. 1981. “Changes in the Workweek of Fixed Capital. U.S. Manufacturing, 1929 to 1976.” Washington: American Enterprise Institute.

Goodridge, P., J. Haskel, and G. Wallis. 2013. “Can Intangible Investment Explain the UK Productivity Puzzle?” *National Institute Economic Review* 224: R48–R58.

Gorodnichenko, Y., and M. Shapiro. 2011. “Using the Survey of Plant Capacity to Measure Capital Utilization.” US Census Bureau Center for Economic Studies Paper No. CES-WP-11–19.

Groth, C., S. Nuñez, and S. Srinivasan. 2006. “Productivity Growth, Adjustment Costs and Variable Factor Utilisation: The UK Case.” Bank of England Working Paper, no. 295.

Hall, R., and D. Jorgenson. 1967. “Tax Policy and Investment Behavior.” *American Economic Review* 57 (3): 391–414.

Hulten, C. 1986. “Productivity Change, Capacity Utilization, and the Sources of Efficiency Growth.” *Journal of Econometrics* 33 (1–2): 31–50.

Inklaar, R. 2007. “Cyclical Productivity in Europe and the United States: Evaluating the Evidence on Returns to Scale and Input Utilization.” *Economica* 74 (296): 822–41.

Jorgenson, D., and Z. Griliches. 1967. “The Explanation of Productivity Change.” *Review of Economic Studies* 34 (3): 249–83.

Kurmann, A., and E. Sims. 2021. “Revisions in Utilization-Adjusted TFP and Robust Identification of News Shocks.” *Review of Economics and Statistics* 103 (2): 216–35.

Larsen, J., K. Neiss, and F. Shortall. 2001. “Factor Utilization and Productivity Estimates for the United Kingdom.” Bank of England Working Paper No. 162.

Lee, K., M. Mahony, and P. Mizen. 2020. “The CBI Suite of Business Surveys.” ESCoE Technical Report 08. London: National Institute of Economic and Social Research.

National Center for O*NET Development. “O*NET OnLine.” https://www.onetonline.org/. Accessed August 30, 2021.

OECD. 2001. *Measuring Productivity—OECD Manual: Measurement of Aggregate and Industry-level Productivity Growth*. Paris: OECD Publishing.

OECD. 2009. *Measuring Capital OECD Manual, second edition*. Paris: OECD Publications. https://www.oecd.org/sdd/productivity-stats/43734711.pdf. Accessed August 30, 2021.

Office for National Statistics. 2019. “National Accounts Articles: Changes to the Capital Stock Estimation Methods for Blue Book.” ONS website article. https://www.ons.gov.uk/economy/nationalaccounts/uksectoraccounts/articles/nationalaccountsarticles/changestothecapitalstockestimationmethodsforbluebook2019. Accessed August 30, 2021.

Office for National Statistics. 2020. “Volume index of capital services (VICS) QMI.” ONS website article. https://www.ons.gov.uk/economy/economicoutputandproductivity/productivitymeasures/methodologies/volumeindexofcapitalservicesvicsqmi. Accessed April 25, 2022.

Office for National Statistics. 2021a. “Homeworking Hours, Rewards and Opportunities in the UK: 2011 to 2020." ONS website article. https://www.ons.gov.uk/employmentandlabormarket/peopleinwork/laborproductivity/articles/homeworkinghoursrewardsandopportunitiesintheuk2011to2020/2021-04-19. Accessed August 30, 2021.

Office for National Statistics. 2021b. "Multi-Factor Productivity Estimates." ONS website article. https://www.ons.gov.uk/economy/economicoutputandproductivity/productivitymeasures/datasets/multifactorproductivityexperimentalestimatesreferencetables. Accessed August 30, 2021.

Office for National Statistics. 2022. "Developing a Method for Measuring Time Spent on Green Tasks: March 2022." ONS website article. https://www.ons.gov.uk/economy/environmentalaccounts/articles/developingamethodformeasuringtimespentongreentasks/march2022. Accessed April 25, 2022.

Shapiro, M. 1996. "Macroeconomic Implications of Variation in the Workweek of Capital." *Brookings Papers on Economic Activity* 1996 (2): 79–133.

Shapiro, M., R. Gordon, and L. Summers. 1989. "Assessing the Federal Reserve's Measures of Capacity and Utilization." *Brookings Papers on Economic Activity* 1989 (1): 181–241.

United Nations, European Commission, International Monetary Fund, Organisation for Economic Co-operation and Development and World Bank. 2009. "System of National Accounts 2008." New York: United Nations.

10

Opening the Black Box
Task and Skill Mix and Productivity Dispersion

G. Jacob Blackwood, Cindy Cunningham, Matthew Dey, Lucia Foster, Cheryl Grim, John Haltiwanger, Rachel Nesbit, Sabrina Wulff Pabilonia, Jay Stewart, Cody Tuttle, and Zoltan Wolf

10.1 Introduction

It is well known that productivity varies across establishments, even within detailed industries. For example, Cunningham et al. (2023) found that on average an establishment at the 90th percentile of the total factor productivity (TFP) distribution is about 2.9 times as productive as an establishment at the 10th percentile within four-digit NAICS manufacturing industries. In a survey article, Syverson (2011) discusses several possible sources of productivity dispersion, including difficult-to-measure factors such as differences in managerial talent and differences in the quality of labor and other inputs. In this paper, we explore the role of differences in the characteristics of workers and the tasks they perform across establishments within the same industry.

G. Jacob Blackwood is an assistant professor of economics at Amherst College.
Cindy Cunningham is a research economist at the US Bureau of Labor Statistics.
Matthew Dey is a research economist at the US Bureau of Labor Statistics.
Lucia Foster is Chief Economist and Chief of the Center for Economic Studies at the US Census Bureau.
Cheryl Grim is Assistant Center Chief for Business Research at the Center for Economic Studies at the US Census Bureau.
John Haltiwanger is a professor of economics at the University of Maryland, and a research associate of the National Bureau of Economic Research.
Rachel Nesbit is an economist at RAND Corporation.
Sabrina Wulff Pabilonia is a research economist at the US Bureau of Labor Statistics.
Jay Stewart is a senior research economist at the US Bureau of Labor Statistics.
Cody Tuttle is an assistant professor of economics at the University of Texas at Austin.
Zoltan Wolf is a senior data scientist at New Light Technologies.
Blackwood, Haltiwanger, Nesbit, and Tuttle were also Schedule A part-time employees of the US Census Bureau at the time of the writing of this paper.

Our paper builds on a joint Bureau of Labor Statistics (BLS) and Census Bureau project that developed publicly available productivity dispersion statistics (Dispersion Statistics on Productivity, DiSP) posted on the BLS and Census Bureau websites and a restricted-access data set available to researchers.[1] Consistent with the prior literature, the DiSP data show that the degree of within-industry dispersion varies considerably across industries and over time. A limitation of the DiSP data (as well as much of the related literature) is that the labor input is measured as total hours worked by all workers. Ideally, measurement of establishment-level productivity would also account for the types of workers the establishment employs and the tasks they perform. Our ultimate goal is to address this limitation by integrating establishment-level data from the BLS Occupational Employment and Wage Statistics (OEWS) survey with Census Bureau establishment-level business data.

In this paper, we explore the conceptual, measurement, and specification issues to be addressed for this integration to be successful. In addition, we include an empirical analysis relating within-industry dispersion of productivity measures to within-industry dispersion of task and skill measures for four-digit NAICS manufacturing industries over the 2000–2017 period.

Our productivity dispersion statistics come from the DiSP data (described in detail in Cunningham et al. 2023). We create four types of measures of tasks and/or skills using OEWS and Occupational Information Network (O*NET) data. Our first task/skill measure is a composite index accounting for the pricing of occupations in the labor market. It is related to, but distinct from, the skill-adjusted labor input measure BLS publishes as part of its official TFP measures.[2] Conceptually, it is a counterfactual average establishment wage: the average wage of an establishment if the establishment paid the national mean occupational wage for each occupation it employs. Importantly, this measure reflects the share of employment in each occupation at the establishment level each year. We refer to this as a bundled task/skill intensity index (TSB), because the pricing of tasks is bundled through the occupations.

Our second task/skill intensity index is similarly a counterfactual wage but based on predicted wages from a linear regression of OEWS national occupational wages on five task indexes constructed from work activities and work-context-importance scales in the O*NET (as described in Acemoglu and Autor 2011, 1163). The five task indexes are: non-routine cognitive

1. See Cunningham et al. (2023) for a detailed description of the development of the data sets. DiSP is available at: https://www.bls.gov/productivity/articles-and-research/dispersion-statistics-on-productivity/ and https://www.census.gov/disp. The restricted-access dataset is available for use by qualified researchers on approved projects in the Federal Statistical Research Data Centers (https://www.census.gov/fsrdc).

2. See https://www.bls.gov/productivity/technical-notes/changes-in-composition-of-labor-total-factor-productivity-2014.pdf for a description of the official measure. For a more detailed discussion of the theory and measurement issues behind the labor composition index, see Zoghi (2007).

(analytical), non-routine cognitive (interpersonal), routine cognitive, routine manual, and non-routine manual physical. This counterfactual wage is the average wage of an establishment if the establishment paid the predicted wage for each task it employs (again using the employment shares of each task at the establishment level each year). We refer to this index as an unbundled task/skill index (TSU) because it prices the tasks directly regardless of which occupations accomplish these tasks.

The TSB and TSU measures reflect task differences across establishments as well as the prices of those tasks in the labor market, where prices reflect the skills required to accomplish those tasks (among other things that may determine wages). The major difference between these two measures is the bundled measure (TSB) implicitly accounts for how the tasks are organized into occupations, while the unbundled measure (TSU) does not.

We also create measures that do not use wage information but rather use direct information on the tasks being performed at individual establishments based on the occupational mix. For these measures, we use the establishment values of the five O*NET task indexes described above individually. Finally, we create a measure that is equal to the percent of STEM workers in each establishment (%STEM), based on the occupational mix.

We compare the within-industry labor productivity (LP) and TFP dispersion measures from DiSP to the within-industry dispersion in these task/skill measures. To preview our results, we find the TSB and TSU measures are highly correlated with each other at the establishment level within industries. The TSB measure is also positively correlated with the analytical task index, the interpersonal task index, and the %STEM, but negatively correlated with the non-routine manual physical, routine manual, and routine cognitive task indexes. These establishment-level correlations conform with our intuition about the skills required to perform these composite tasks.

Turning to the relationship between within-industry dispersion in task/skill indexes and dispersion in productivity, we find higher within-industry productivity dispersion is associated with higher within-industry dispersion of TSB, TSU, the analytical task index, and the %STEM. These patterns differ quantitatively across different groupings of manufacturing industries but they are especially strong in the high-tech industries. For example, the elasticity of within-industry TFP dispersion with respect to TSB dispersion is about three times larger in the high-tech manufacturing industries than in the non-high-tech ("non-tech" hereafter) manufacturing industries.

The remarkably high within-industry dispersion of both productivity and task/skill intensities across establishments in high-tech industries implies there is considerable heterogeneity in both the outcomes and the ways of doing business, especially among the most innovative sectors of the economy. It is well known high-tech industries exhibit high productivity growth and are more STEM occupation intensive (see, e.g., Decker et al. 2020). Our findings suggest that the strong relationship in first moments carries over to the corresponding second moments.

While our results are only suggestive, they are promising for the longer-run objective of integrating the OEWS data with the Census Bureau business microdata at the establishment level. The establishment-level analysis will enable us to explore related issues such as the relationship between technology adoption and the task/skill mix of businesses. We will examine this in the next phase of our research, but we provide an overview of the potential for such analysis with establishment-level data integration.

While the integration of the OEWS and Collaborative Micro-productivity Project (CMP) microdata awaits future research, in an initial step to this integration we find that more than 80 percent of between-establishment variation in our skill/task indexes among single- and multi-unit EINS is accounted for by between-taxpayer ID (EIN) variation. In other words, establishments within the same firm and industry exhibit considerable similarity in their skill and task mix indexes. Relatedly, the productivity dispersion literature has found that high-productivity establishments are part of high-productivity firms, for example, see Baily, Hulten, and Campbell (1992). These findings are interesting in their own right, but they also facilitate the planned integration of the OEWS and ASM data at the micro level, because a common identifier is the EIN.

The rest of the paper proceeds as follows. Section 10.2 presents a conceptual framework largely through a review of the literature relating productivity to the skills of workers and tasks they perform. Section 10.3 describes the productivity data, the OEWS data, and our task/skill intensity measures. Section 10.4 presents the results relating within-industry productivity and task/skill dispersion. Section 10.5 provides an overview of next steps. Our concluding remarks are in section 10.6.

10.2 Background and Conceptual Framework

In a standard production function, $Q_{et} = A_{et} \cdot F(L_{et}, K_{et})$—where Q_{et} is output, L_{et} is labor input, K_{et} is capital input, A_{et} is a Hicks-neutral productivity term (often interpreted as technical change), and e and t index establishments and time respectively—the different ways businesses use labor may show up as differences in L, $\partial F / \partial L$, or both. Our objective is to take a first step toward exploring heterogeneity in labor input and its potential effect on productivity dispersion. An establishment may have higher measured productivity than its competitors because it uses a given set of labor inputs more efficiently, or because its production process consists of more advanced tasks (generally) accompanied by more skilled labor.

Within the simple production function specification above, differences in skills and tasks across establishments can be captured by introducing a multiplier, Z_{et}, that can be interpreted as an adjustment that converts labor hours into efficiency units based on skills and tasks. The first argument of $F(\cdot)$ then becomes $Z_{et} \cdot L_{et}$, which accounts for differences across establishments due to differences in the efficiency with which L_{et} is used in production.[3] Both A_{et} and Z_{et} are efficiency parameters. The difference is that while A_{et} increases the productivity of both factors of production, Z_{et} affects only the productivity of labor.

Another approach is to explicitly model labor types in order to analyze the returns to different skills. For ease of exposition, we drop *e* and *t* subscripts for the remainder of this section. The canonical model for understanding skill premia assumes two types of workers, low-skilled and high-skilled (see equation [2] in Acemoglu and Autor 2011):

$$(1) \qquad F = [(A_l L)^{\rho} + (A_h H)^{\rho}]^{1/\rho}$$

where L and H denote low-skilled and high-skilled workers and ρ is a constant that characterizes the substitutability between L and H. A_l and A_h are factor-specific augmenting technology terms. The elasticity of substitution, $\sigma = 1/(1 - \rho)$, is defined as the percentage change in relative demand for low-skilled workers for a percentage change in the relative price of high-skilled workers. If the two types are substitutes, an increase in the relative price of one leads to an increase in demand for the other skill. In the limiting case of perfect substitution, or $\sigma \to \infty$ ($\rho \to 1$), relative wages are constant. In the other extreme, $\sigma \to 0$ ($\rho \to -\infty$), the two labor types are perfect complements, i.e., they can be used only in fixed proportions. The third special case, $\sigma \to 1$ ($\rho \to 0$), yields the Cobb-Douglas production function where fixed shares are paid to each factor. In the constant elasticity of substitution (CES) framework above, σ is a crucial parameter because it determines not only how changes in the supply of labor types affect wages and demand, but also how changes in technology affect L and H. In particular, factor-augmenting technology is encapsulated in A_l and A_h in the sense that technical change may affect the productivity of labor types independently of each other. But new technologies do not replace either type of labor.

A more general version of the model above allows for the possibility of technological advances complementing or fully replacing either labor type (Acemoglu 1998):

$$(2) \qquad F = [(1 - \alpha)(A_l L + B_l)^{\rho} + \alpha(A_h H + B_h)^{\rho}]^{1/\rho}$$

where B_l and B_h denote skill-replacing technologies that are perfect substitutes for the two labor types,[4] and α reflects the distribution of tasks between different types of labor (Card and DiNardo 2002). An increase in α increases

3. Gollop et al. (1987) first demonstrate the potential importance of using efficiency units of labor. The methods developed from this early work have been widely adopted by statistical agencies around the world (see Schreyer 2001). BLS uses a related approach in their total factor productivity measures (see https://www.bls.gov/productivity/technical-notes/labor-composition-for-total-factor-productivity-using-new-method-nov-2022.htm).

4. In the case of skill-complementing technologies, the linear terms of the inner parentheses in equation (2) would have the same harmonic sum structure as in equation (1) but with exponents less than zero, in which case,

$$F = \left\{(1-\alpha)\left[\left((A_l L)^{\rho_l} + B_l^{\rho_l}\right)^{1/\rho_l}\right]^{\rho} + \alpha\left[\left((A_h H)^{\rho_h} + B_h^{\rho_h}\right)^{1/\rho_h}\right]^{\rho}\right\}^{1/\rho}, \text{ with } \rho_l, \rho_h < 0.$$

the productivity of H and at the same time lowers the productivity of L, while A_l and A_h only affect the productivity of the corresponding factor.[5]

Although the models described above have been empirically successful in studying the supply and demand for skills, they have been less successful in explaining phenomena such as the different wage dynamics of high- and low-skill workers, job polarization, diffusion of low-skill-replacing technologies, and automation.[6] Acemoglu and Autor (2011) and others have examined alternative models that define the production process as a set of tasks done by workers with the appropriate skills (e.g., Autor, Levy, and Murnane 2003; Acemoglu and Restrepo 2018a, 2019b).

A common property of these more recent approaches is to make a distinction between tasks and skills. Autor, Levy, and Murnane (2003) show, for example, that information and communication technologies can substitute for workers who perform routine tasks and at the same time complement workers who perform more complex or non-routine tasks. They also show such shifts in tasks associated with computerization and their effects on education demand can explain 60 percent of the shift in demand for college-educated labor in 1970s and 1980s.

In the same spirit, Acemoglu and Autor (2011) conceptualize the production process as a set of activities (tasks) that produce output and frame the firm's decision problem as one where workers' capabilities (skills) are allocated to tasks. They argue the conceptual distinction is justified whenever the mapping between skills and tasks is not one-to-one. This would be the case if a certain worker type can be allocated to different tasks, or if the firm can change the task content of production. The latter gives rise to the possibility of an endogenous response of technology to market conditions, automation, or endogenous technology choice (Acemoglu 1998; Acemoglu and Restrepo 2018a, 2018b, 2019a, 2019b, 2020; Dinlersoz and Wolf 2023).

It is instructive to compare the task-content approach of Acemoglu and Restrepo (2019b) in terms of the implied production function with those discussed above. They write:

$$(3)\quad Q = \Pi(I,N)[\Gamma(I,N)^{1/\sigma}(A_L L)^{(\sigma-1)/\sigma} + (1-\Gamma(I,N))^{1/\sigma}(A_K K)^{(\sigma-1)/\sigma}]^{\sigma/(\sigma-1)}$$

where I is innovation, N is the number of tasks, $\Gamma(I, N)$ is the labor task content of production, and $[1 - \Gamma(I, N)]$ is the capital task content of production. In their model, N tasks are ordered by automatability. All tasks can be performed by either labor or capital. New tasks are represented by an increase in N. Innovation, I, is the cutoff—tasks below I are performed by capital and tasks above I are performed by workers. Thus, innovation (an increase in I) represents an increase in the number and types of tasks that

5. The endogenous technology choice model in Dinlersoz and Wolf (2023) uses a similar but simpler structure.

6. See Acemoglu and Autor (2011), and references therein, for a list of previous studies and overview of this class of models with a detailed description of their strengths and caveats.

can be performed by capital. The Hicks-neutral productivity term, $\Pi(I,N)$, is assumed to be a function of innovation and tasks as well. This approach highlights that proxies for the number and nature of tasks and the relationship between innovation and tasks are important for understanding the production process. This specification also helps clarify that the firm's choice of a production function is defined by the set of tasks, the level of innovation, and the types of factor inputs.

We draw on these papers to help map out a potential link between differences in worker types and productivity. Such a link is relevant because existing measures of productivity dispersion are calculated without explicitly controlling for possible heterogeneity in labor, even though it would be ideal to control for these differences when calculating establishment-level differences in productivity. We take the first steps in this direction by comparing information on occupations and wages from OEWS and O*NET and exploring the relationship between within-industry dispersion in task/skill intensity and within-industry dispersion in productivity.

10.3 Data and Measurement

10.3.1 The Establishment-Level Productivity Database

BLS and the Census Bureau have collaborated to create an establishment-level productivity database (the CMP) for the manufacturing sector from 1972 to 2018.[7] These data are based on the Annual Survey of Manufactures (ASM), the Census of Manufactures (CM), and the Longitudinal Business Database (LBD). The ASM collects data annually and is a five-year panel of manufacturing establishments updated by births in each year.[8] The CM collects data from all manufacturing establishments, except those that are very small, every five years, in years ending in 2 and 7. The LBD is a longitudinally linked version of the Census Bureau's Business Register (see Chow et al. 2021). It provides high-quality longitudinal links and information on the universe of manufacturing establishments. The CMP includes measures of inputs, output, and productivity (see Cunningham et al. 2023). The ASM establishments in the productivity database form the basis for creating the DiSP, which we describe below.

10.3.2 Dispersion Statistics on Productivity (DiSP)

The productivity dispersion measures we use here come from the DiSP, a joint BLS-Census *public-use* experimental data product, which currently includes annual measures for all 86 four-digit NAICS manufacturing industries from 1987 to 2021. These measures tell us how much more productive

7. CMP stands for Collaborative Micro-productivity Project.
8. ASM panels start in years ending in 4 and 9.

one establishment is from another between different points in the productivity distribution within four-digit NAICS manufacturing industries. We use the activity-weighted interquartile range (IQR) and 90–10 dispersion measures for both LP and TFP in our analyses. LP is calculated as the log of real revenue per hour, while TFP is calculated as the log of real revenue per combined unit of all factor input costs (capital, labor hours, energy, and materials).[9]

10.3.3 Task and Skill Concepts

Before discussing our data on tasks and skills, we summarize the basic concepts outlined in section 10.2, relying on the nomenclature from the Revised Handbook of Analyzing Jobs (Employment and Training Administration 1991) and Acemoglu and Autor (2011). *Tasks* are activities that when combined with intermediate goods create a good or service and are the true factors of production we would like to measure. However, because we do not observe time spent in different tasks, we use occupations as proxies. An *occupation* is a job in which "a common set of tasks are performed or are related in terms of similar objectives, methodologies, materials, products, worker actions, or workers characteristics" (Employment and Training Administration 1991, 9). Thus, an occupation can be thought of as a bundle of tasks. In contrast, a *skill* "is a worker's endowment of capabilities for performing various tasks" (Acemoglu and Autor 2011, 1045). Skill is commonly conceptualized in the economics literature as a function of education (and sometimes also experience). Operationally, it is often proxied by some measure of wages projected on observable indicators such as education and experience or, alternatively, wages are projected on occupations as in Acemoglu and Autor (2011) (see figure 10 therein). While there is not a one-to-one correspondence between skills and tasks in this framework, complex tasks

9. Revenue is based on the value of shipments with adjustments for resales and changes in inventories from the ASM and deflated using the industry implicit price deflator from BLS. We use deflators at the highest level of industry detail available in BLS, BEA, and NBER-CES data. See Cunningham et al. (2023) for more details on deflators and the construction of the DiSP. An important issue is how much observed revenue productivity dispersion reflects output and input price differences across establishments in the same narrow industry. Foster, Haltiwanger and Syverson (2008) find considerable price dispersion across establishments for the limited number of detailed industries with comparable physical product data in the Census manufacturing data. They find that dispersion in TFPQ (physical productivity adjusting for plant-level differences in prices) is actually larger than dispersion in the type of revenue productivity measures (they refer to these as TFPR) that we use given the negative covariance between prices and TFPQ (i.e., establishments that are more productive have lower marginal costs yielding lower prices). They also find a high positive correlation between TFPQ and TFPR, which is reassuring for the analyses in the current paper. There may be variable markups across establishments in the same industry that influence revenue productivity dispersion measures. Foster, Haltiwanger and Tuttle (2022) show that identifying such markup variation is complex in the presence of differences in production technologies across establishments. This insight leads us back to the current paper and project seeking to understand such differences by integrating the OEWS microdata with the ASM.

generally require greater skills. The relationship between skills and tasks can vary over time and across businesses, presenting a challenge for productivity measurement and highlighting a need for detailed data on tasks and skills.

10.3.4 Occupational Employment and Wage Statistics (OEWS) Data

We use occupation data from the BLS Occupational Employment and Wage Statistics (OEWS) survey, which is a semi-annual survey sampling approximately 200,000 establishments in May and November of each year.[10] This survey covers all workers, both full time and part time, in private non-agricultural industries.

The survey instrument asks establishments to provide what amounts to a complete payroll record for the pay period that includes the 12th of the sample month. Respondents report occupational wage information for each occupation by recording the number of employees in each of 12 wage intervals.[11] The OEWS survey uses the Office of Management and Budget's occupational classification system, the Standard Occupational Classification (SOC), to categorize workers into around 800 detailed occupations.[12] The SOC system provides much more occupational detail than do household surveys, which are the main sources of information about occupations.

The sample is composed of certainty units, which are generally sampled every three years, and non-certainty units. Official estimates are based on data from the current panel and the previous five panels (because the OEWS is typically released in May, the five panels extend back to the November panel three years earlier). Thus, although estimates are published every year, the OEWS data are not a true time series, because about two-thirds of the sample are the same in any two adjacent years.

The OEWS sampling and weighting methods guarantee total weighted employment equals the BLS frame—the Quarterly Census of Employment and Wages (QCEW)—employment, but there is nothing in the methods to guarantee the implied number of establishments equals the number of establishments on the frame. This makes it difficult to develop dispersion

10. From 1999 to 2001, the program surveyed approximately 400,000 establishments in November of each year. Starting in November 2002, the program switched to semi-annual sampling with 200,000 establishments sampled each May and November. To keep sample sizes roughly consistent across the various years, we combine November and May panels to create a pseudo-annual sample and assign it the May year value. For this reason, we do not have data for 2002.

11. Wages for the OEWS survey represent straight-time, gross pay, exclusive of premium pay. Base rate, cost-of-living allowances, guaranteed pay, hazardous-duty pay, incentive pay including commissions and production bonuses, tips, and on-call pay are included, while back pay, jury duty pay, overtime pay, severance pay, shift differentials, non-production bonuses, employer cost for supplementary benefits, and tuition reimbursements are excluded from the reported wage. For a description of the wage intervals, see https://www.bls.gov/oes/mb3-methods.pdf.

12. From 1999 to 2013, the SOC structure has expanded from 770 occupations to its current 821 occupations.

statistics at the establishment level. Therefore, any analysis attempting to measure establishment-specific effects will have to address this feature of the OEWS weighting scheme. As an alternative to reweighting the data, we use a research dataset created using a modified version of the imputation approach developed by Dey, Piccone, and Miller (2019).

This research data set imputes data for the entire QCEW. For each reference year, they use the same dating convention as is used for the official OEWS release (that is, May of the reference year combined with the five previous panels). For each observation in the QCEW not in the OEWS, they identify 5–10 donor observations based on the characteristics of the establishments. The characteristics include employment, industry (six-digit NAICS), ownership, metropolitan statistical area (MSA), and the amount of time between the reference periods of the observations. Donor establishments are evaluated on each attribute and weights are assigned based on closeness to the recipient on that attribute. In the experimental data series, the weights of the donor establishments are rescaled so they sum to one. The recipient's employment in each occupation is a weighted average of the donor establishments. Wages are determined similarly but are also adjusted for differences in wages by area and wage growth by area and industry.[13]

The Dey, Piccone, and Miller (2019) approach is designed as a potential replacement for the current method for generating official estimates. The main advantage of this approach is every establishment in the QCEW is represented and has an establishment weight of one. The disadvantage is that the staffing pattern for an establishment is an *average* of similar establishments. This makes sense for constructing aggregate estimates, but not for analyzing distributions. The research data set incorporates two key modifications to this method for our analysis, which focuses on distributions.

The primary modification to this method is that occupation employment and wage data at the establishment level are imputed from a single donor. The imputation process involves two stages, a matching stage where potential donors are identified and a selection stage where the best donor is selected. The process is hierarchical, where the conditions for finding acceptable matches are sequentially relaxed. At the most detailed level of the hierarchy, a donor and frame unit will match on industry (six-digit NAICS), ownership (private or type of government), state, and county and will have similar employment levels. As the process continues through the hierarchy, geography is relaxed first and then ownership. It is not until very late in the process, after most of the frame units have already found an acceptable donor, that industry and employment proximity are relaxed. The match-

13. These adjustments are not controls for industry and location. Rather, they are designed to convert the wages of the donor observations so they more closely approximate the recipient establishment's actual wages.

ing stage often results in multiple potential donors. To preserve dispersion, the selection of a particular donor from the set of acceptable matches is random. As above, wages are adjusted to account for differences by MSA and industry.

The second modification that we make is to center the sample on the reference year instead of using data from the five panels prior to May of the reference year (as in the published statistics), so we can integrate the OEWS with other data. For example, under this approach, the sample for May 2017 is constructed using data from the following panels: May 2018, November 2017, May 2017, November 2016, May 2016, and November 2015. This results in a nationally representative sample centered on May 2017. To avoid overlap, we construct these "year samples" at three-year intervals. We are effectively assuming the occupational mix within an establishment is fixed over the three-year interval.

The result is a full data set that we can use to estimate dispersion statistics on an establishment-weighted basis (weight = 1) or an employment-weighted basis (weight = employment). Our sample covers the years 2000, 2005, 2008, 2011, 2014, and 2017.[14] Much of our analysis is restricted to establishments in manufacturing industries, so we can make comparisons with the DiSP.

10.3.5 Bundled Task/Skill Intensity Index (TSB): Counterfactual Wages

Our first index of task/skill intensity is a counterfactual wage equal to the average wage paid by the establishment if the establishment paid the national average occupational wage for all workers in each occupation for each year in the sample. Thus, it accounts for differences in the occupational mix across establishments by attaching a different price to each occupation. By using the national average wage for each occupation, the price of each occupation is the same across establishments. We denote this as a "bundled" task/skill intensity index (TSB) because tasks are bundled into occupations.

Let w_{ejb} and L_{ejb} denote the mean log wage and the number of workers in wage interval b of occupation j in establishment e, respectively. All workers in the same wage interval are assigned the same log wage. Suppressing the time subscript for simplicity, the national mean log wage for occupation j is given by:

$$\overline{w}_{nj} = \frac{1}{\sum_{e \in E_n} L_{ej}} \sum_{e \in E_n} \sum_{b \in B} (w_{ejb} \times L_{ejb}) \tag{4}$$

where B is the set of 12 wage intervals, E_n is the set of all establishments (nationwide, manufacturing, and non-manufacturing), and L_{ej} is the number of employees in occupation j for establishment e. The actual mean log wage for an establishment is:

14. The five-year gap between 2000 and 2005 is due to a change in sampling from annual to semi-annual, which made it impossible to construct estimates for May 2002.

(5) $$\overline{w}_e = \frac{1}{L_e}\sum_{j \in J_e}(\overline{w}_{ej} \times L_{ej})$$

where J_e is the set of occupations employed by establishment e, L_e is total employment in establishment e, and $\overline{w}_{ej} = (1/L_{ej})\sum_{b \in B}(w_{ejb} \times L_{ejb})$. Substituting the national mean log occupational wage, $\overline{w}_{nj}$, for the establishment mean log wage for each occupation, the counterfactual mean log wage for establishment e, $\tilde{w}_e$, is equal to:

(6) $$\tilde{w}_e = \frac{1}{L_e}\sum_{j \in J_e}(\overline{w}_{nj} \times L_{ej}).$$

The TSB measure is a simple measure that provides an index of the tasks employed by the establishment using wages, which proxy for skills, to price those tasks. Although it is a useful measure, it has the property that it does not distinguish between different occupations (with different task sets) paying the same wage. Thus, two establishments might have the same task/skill intensity but very different mixes of occupations. To illustrate this, figure 10.1 plots the TSB measure (on the vertical axis) against an index of the dissimilarity of the occupational mix of the establishment relative to its industry (on the horizontal axis) for establishments in four industries: basic chemicals manufacturing, computers and peripherals manufacturing, semiconductor manufacturing, and big box retailers. The dissimilarity index we use is the absolute value of the sum over all occupations (2-digit SOC) of the distances between the establishment's payroll share for that occupation and the industry-wide payroll share for that occupation.[15] It takes on values between zero and one, with higher values indicating an establishment has a much different occupational distribution than the typical establishment in the industry.

Perhaps the most notable feature of the graphs is the fanning out of the TSB as the dissimilarity index increases. Thus, establishments with occupation mixes differing significantly from the industry average mix also have a wide range of task/skill intensities. But more important for our purposes, for a given level of task/skill intensity, there is considerable variation in the occupational mix. For example, in the basic chemicals manufacturing

15. The dissimilarity index we use is:

$$D_{ie} = \frac{1}{2}\sum_{j \in J_i}\left|\frac{\overline{w}_{ej}L_{ej}}{\sum_j \overline{w}_{ej}L_{ej}} - \frac{\overline{w}_{ij}L_{ij}}{\sum_j \overline{w}_{ij}L_{ij}}\right|$$

where the variables are defined as before and the i subscript indicates industry. The index is scaled to represent the fraction of payments to the different occupations that would have to be reallocated to match the industry distribution of payments across occupations. It is worth noting this index is sensitive to the level of occupational detail. The index will be larger the greater the level of occupational detail. We used two-digit occupation codes, which are fairly aggregated, to calculate these indexes. In addition, we restricted the sample to establishments with 20+ workers.

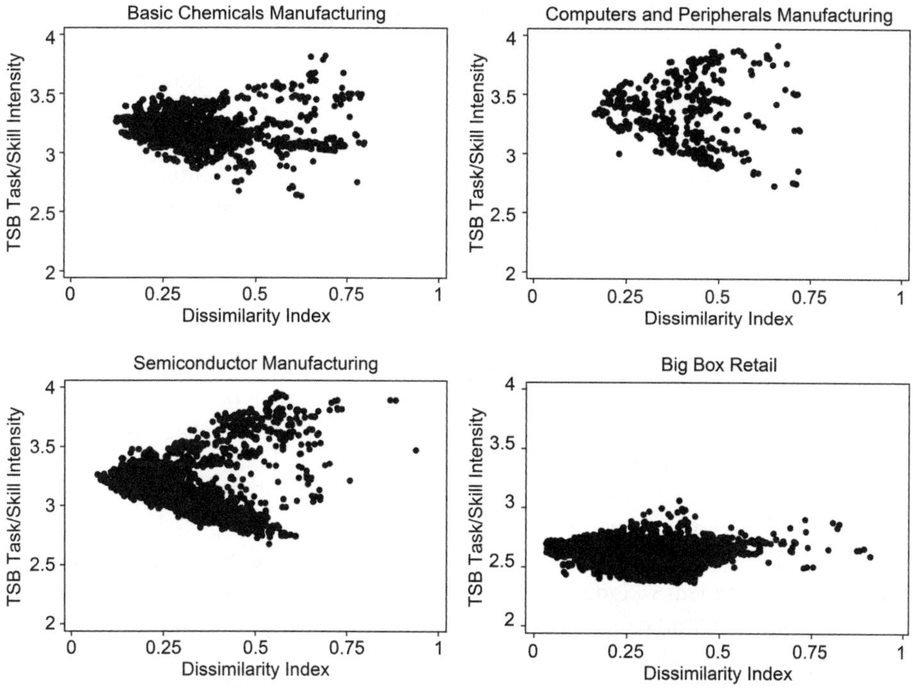

Fig. 10.1 TSB task/skill intensity and dissimilarity indexes in selected industries (2017)

Note: Each dot represents an establishment's indexes in 2017. We exclude establishments with fewer than 20 employees.

Source: Authors' calculations based on the OEWS.

industry, at the mean skill intensity of around 3.2, the dissimilarity index varies from about 0.1 to just over 0.75. There is less variation in the TSB measure and in the dissimilarity index in the big box retail industry than in the other three industries. But there is still considerable variation in the dissimilarity index for a given level of TSB. Thus, although the TSB tells us a lot about differences across establishments in the types of occupations that they employ, it does not account for all the variation in how establishments organize production. There is still much to be learned from looking at differences in the distribution of occupations across establishments.

10.3.6 Unbundled Task/Skill Intensity Index (TSU): Task-Adjusted Counterfactual Wages

Our second task/skill intensity index builds on Acemoglu and Autor (2011), who use O*NET data to operationalize the Autor, Levy, and Murnane (2003) taxonomy of tasks (developed with the O*NET predecessor, the Dictionary of Occupational Titles [DOT]). Autor, Levy, and Murnane developed a two-dimensional categorization of tasks based on whether they are (1) routine or non-routine and (2) cognitive or manual. Routine tasks are those that can be described using a set of rules or specifications; non-routine tasks are those that cannot be described in this manner. They further break down non-routine cognitive tasks into analytic and interpersonal. This yields five categories of tasks: non-routine cognitive (analytical), non-routine (interpersonal), routine cognitive, routine manual, and non-routine manual physical.[16]

The O*NET database is sponsored by the Employment and Training Administration of the Department of Labor and is collected through the National Center for O*NET Development and Research Triangle Institute. The O*NET data are collected from workers in targeted occupations at establishments and contain over 275 variables that describe each occupation.[17] Acemoglu and Autor (2011) use 16 of these variables corresponding to the five task categorizations described above.[18] The O*NET-SOC occupational categories are aggregated to SOC categories, and each variable is scaled and then standardized to mean zero and standard deviation one using employment weights from the OEWS. The five indexes are created by summing the standardized variables for each task category, which are then once again normalized.

We use this methodology to create the same five task indexes for each of the O*NET years where the index variables are available for most occupations (2007, 2008, 2014, and 2017).[19] We merge these five task indexes to

16. Acemoglu and Autor (2011) add a sixth category, offshorability, which we do not include here because it is not a task.

17. O*NET first began surveying jobholders in 2001. Prior to that, past DOT data, collected sometimes decades earlier by job analysts visiting workplaces, were recoded into O*NET variables. Because new surveying was rolled in gradually, the first O*NET completely based on surveys was released in 2008. O*NET re-surveys occupations on a rolling basis over a five-year period. The number of respondents per occupation varies, and respondents are randomly selected to answer a subset of the questionnaire. The value of a particular O*NET variable is the average response over the jobholders who answered that question, so within-occupation variation cannot be observed. See Handel (2016) for more about the history of O*NET and its strengths and weaknesses.

18. Non-routine cognitive (analytical) includes analyzing data/information, thinking creatively, and interpreting information for others. Non-routine cognitive (interpersonal) includes establishing and maintaining personal relationships; guiding, directing, and motivating subordinates; and coaching/developing others. Routine cognitive includes importance of repeating the same tasks, importance of being exact or accurate, and structured vs. unstructured work (reverse). Routine manual includes tasks where the pace of work is determined by speed of equipment, controlling machines and processes, and tasks requiring repetitive motions. Non-routine manual physical includes operating vehicles, mechanized devices, or equipment; tasks where workers use their hands to handle, control, or feel objects, tools, or controls; manual dexterity; and spatial orientation. (See page 1163 of Acemoglu and Autor 2011.)

19. We match two prior years of OEWS data to a given O*NET year to obtain the employment weights. When an occupation is covered in both OEWS years, we average the two years; otherwise, we take the value for the one OEWS year with coverage for that occupation. Thus,

OEWS wage data by occupation and estimate a regression of the national occupational mean log wage for each year on these five task indexes as follows:

$$\bar{w}_{nj} = \alpha + \sum_{k=1}^{5} \beta_k \tau_{jk} + \varepsilon \tag{7}$$

where τ_{jk} is the O*NET measure of task k for occupation j, and $\bar{w}_{nj}$ is defined in equation (4).[20] The coefficients on the task indexes, β_k, are akin to prices in a hedonic regression. We then calculate the counterfactual average establishment wage as:

$$\hat{w}_e = \frac{1}{L_e} \sum_{k=1}^{5} \hat{\beta} \left[\sum_{j \in J_e} (L_{ej} \times \tau_{jk}) \right] \tag{8}$$

where the summation in square brackets is the total amount of task k employed by the establishment and $\hat{\beta}_k$ is the "price" of task k estimated from the regression in equation (7). That is, the TSU measure can be thought of as the average price of tasks performed by employees in the establishment.

We refer to this second measure as an "unbundled" task/skill intensity index (TSU) because tasks (weighted by prices) are aggregated without accounting for how the tasks are bundled into occupations. In contrast, the TSB index uses the occupational mix of an establishment (and the prices of those occupations), so it implicitly takes into account that individual occupations reflect a bundle of tasks. Like the TSB index, there are many combinations of tasks that can result in the same value of the index. We discuss these differences and similarities further below.

10.3.7 Individual Average Task Indexes

In addition to the two task/skill intensity measures based on counterfactual wages, $\tilde{w}_e$ and $\hat{w}_e$, we also develop a set of five task measures based on the average value of the individual O*NET task indexes. Recall, we are using five categories of O*NET tasks: non-routine cognitive (analytical), non-routine (interpersonal), routine cognitive, routine manual, and non-routine manual physical. For each of the five task indexes, we measure an employment-weighted establishment-level average for task index k as follows:

$$\bar{\tau}_{ek} = \frac{1}{L_e} \sum_{j \in J_e} \tau_{jk} \times L_{ej} \tag{9}$$

where k = 1, . . ., 5. Thus, $\bar{\tau}_{ek}$ is the average task k content of all jobs in establishment e. Again, time subscripts are suppressed for expositional convenience. These measures are constructed for each establishment for each year in our sample.

---

the 2007 O*NET is matched to 2005 and 2006 OEWS; 2008 O*NET to 2006 and 2007 OEWS; 2014 O*NET to 2012 and 2013 OES; and 2017 O*NET to 2015 and 2016 OEWS.

20. We first aggregate occupations to a time consistent SOC classification.

10.3.8 STEM Intensity Index (%STEM)

In our final measure, we rely on the definition of occupation as a bundle of tasks and create another alternative task index based on occupation data in the OEWS. We calculate the percentage of STEM workers in each establishment as follows:

$$\%STEM_e = \frac{1}{L_e}\sum_{j \in J_s} L_{ej} \tag{10}$$

where J_s is the set of STEM occupations, with STEM occupations being defined according to the recommendations of the SOC Policy Committee (2010). The %STEM equals the percentage of workers in an establishment who are working in the following sub-domain occupations—life and physical science, engineering, mathematics, and information technology occupations, social science occupations, architecture occupations, health occupations—within the following larger occupation groups: research, development, design, or practitioner occupations, technologist and technician occupations, postsecondary teaching occupations, managerial occupations, and sales occupations. The STEM measure is constructed for each establishment for each year in our sample.

10.3.9 How Do These Task/Skill Measures Differ?

As discussed above, the TSB measure prices the tasks of each occupation as a bundle and therefore indirectly accounts for the fact that the sets of tasks that make up an occupation are complementary and there is a benefit to having them performed by the same person. In contrast, the TSU measure prices the tasks individually and ignores any complementarities between tasks within occupations. We would expect the two measures to be different but highly correlated.

The first row of table 10.1 shows average Pearson correlations between the establishment-level TSB and TSU task/skill indexes for different major sectors. The table entries are the employment-weighted averages of the within-industry correlations pooled over time. As expected, the correlations are high, although there is some variation across sectors. For example, the correlation is higher for manufacturing than for non-manufacturing. There is also a sizable difference between high-tech and non-tech manufacturing industries, with the correlations being considerably higher for high-tech industries ($\rho = 0.911$).[21]

21. Following Wolf and Terrell (2016), we define the high-tech industries as those industries whose share of STEM workers exceeds 2.5 times the national average. This group includes the following 16 four-digit NAICS manufacturing industries: petroleum and coal products; basic chemical; resin, synthetic rubber, and artificial and synthetic fibers and filaments; pharmaceutical and medicine; industrial machinery; commercial and service industry machinery; engine, turbine, and power transmission equipment; other general purpose machinery; computer and peripheral equipment; communications equipment; audio and video equipment; semiconduc-

Table 10.1 **Average industry correlations between establishment-level TSB task/skill intensity and other task/skill measures**

	All Industries	Manufacturing Industries			Non-manufacturing Industries
		All	High-tech	Non-tech	
TSU task/skill intensity	0.719	0.773	0.911	0.741	0.696
Non-routine cognitive: Analytical	0.716	0.752	0.904	0.717	0.700
Non-routine cognitive: Interpersonal	0.509	0.578	0.567	0.580	0.479
Routine cognitive	−0.236	−0.359	−0.571	−0.311	−0.182
Routine manual	−0.426	−0.647	−0.832	−0.605	−0.329
Non-routine manual physical	−0.372	−0.569	−0.828	−0.509	−0.286
%STEM workers	0.433	0.610	0.822	0.561	0.355

Note: Each cell represents the establishment-employment-weighted mean four-digit NAICS industry-wide Pearson correlations of establishment skill/task measures pooling the data across 2000, 2005, 2008, 2011, 2014, and 2017.

Source: Authors' calculations based on the OEWS and the O*NET.

The next five rows of table 10.1 show the correlation of TSB with each of the five task groups. These correlations are insightful because they reveal which type of tasks are more strongly related to the composite index task/skill intensity measures. These individual task indicators also shed light on the high correlation between the TSB and TSU measures. Looking at the second row, we see the correlation between TSB and the O*NET "analytical tasks" measure is nearly the same as the correlation between the TSB and TSU measures. The correlation between the TSB measure and the O*NET "interpersonal tasks" measure is lower, but still high. The other three individual task indicators are negatively correlated with TSB. That is, establishments that have a high composite task/skill intensity generally employ fewer occupations heavy in these tasks.

In the last row of table 10.1, we show the correlation between %STEM and TSB. Again, the correlations are higher for manufacturing than for non-manufacturing and higher for high-tech than non-tech manufacturing industries, with the correlations being considerably higher for high-tech industries.

10.3.10 Dispersion in Tasks/Skills

We calculate two measures of dispersion in establishment-level tasks/skills—the interquartile range (IQR) and interdecile (90–10) range—for each four-digit NAICS industry in each sample year. To account for industry differences in average skills/tasks so we can compare within-industry

tor and other electronic components; navigational, measuring, electromedical, and control instruments; manufacturing and reproducing magnetic and optical media; electrical equipment manufacturing; aerospace products and parts.

dispersion across industries and time, we calculate establishment-level tasks/skills as the deviation from the average tasks/skills in that establishment's four-digit industry. These measures are weighted using establishment employment. We then calculate our dispersion measures, which tell us the degree of within-industry dispersion. For this analysis of summary statistics, we also include the activity-weighted within-industry dispersion in productivity measures from DiSP (see Cunningham et al. 2023, for details). Given the DiSP measures are only available for manufacturing industries, the summary statistics in table 10.2 are only for manufacturing.

Table 10.2 shows summary statistics for our within-industry dispersion measures (productivity and task/skill) for four-digit manufacturing industries. As before, these measures are industry averages pooled over all years. In figures 10.2A and 10.2B, we show the means of the IQR dispersion measures for productivity and select task/skill intensity indexes over time for high-tech

Table 10.2 Summary statistics of industry dispersion measures in the manufacturing sector

	All		High-tech		Non-tech	
	Mean	Std. Dev.	Mean	Std. Dev.	Mean	Std. Dev.
Panel A. IQR Dispersion Measures						
TSB task/skill intensity	0.239	0.088	0.350	0.089	0.205	0.054
TSU task/skill intensity	0.151	0.052	0.194	0.051	0.138	0.045
Non-routine cognitive: Analytical	0.511	0.167	0.654	0.162	0.468	0.143
Non-routine cognitive: Interpersonal	0.551	0.120	0.524	0.082	0.560	0.128
Routine cognitive	0.560	0.165	0.564	0.111	0.558	0.178
Routine manual	0.909	0.220	1.063	0.139	0.862	0.218
Non-routine manual physical	0.630	0.166	0.770	0.105	0.587	0.157
%STEM workers	0.082	0.133	0.282	0.144	0.021	0.031
Labor productivity	0.838	0.328	0.967	0.435	0.798	0.277
Total factor productivity	0.530	0.221	0.672	0.301	0.487	0.169
Panel B. 90–10 Dispersion Measures						
TSB task/skill intensity	0.503	0.167	0.717	0.161	0.437	0.102
TSU task/skill intensity	0.302	0.089	0.390	0.086	0.276	0.071
Non-routine cognitive: Analytical	1.032	0.282	1.310	0.274	0.948	0.225
Non-routine cognitive: Interpersonal	1.115	0.224	1.095	0.166	1.121	0.239
Routine cognitive	1.175	0.289	1.276	0.219	1.145	0.300
Routine manual	1.870	0.383	2.092	0.171	1.803	0.404
Non-routine manual physical	1.313	0.304	1.591	0.188	1.228	0.282
%STEM workers	0.195	0.253	0.582	0.236	0.077	0.082
Labor productivity	1.689	0.504	1.954	0.683	1.608	0.403
Total factor productivity	1.119	0.449	1.414	0.648	1.030	0.319

Note: Industry-employment-weighted means and standard deviations of industry-level dispersion measures for all 86 four-digit NAICS industries in the manufacturing sector pooling the data across 2000, 2005, 2008, 2011, 2014, and 2017.

Source: Authors' calculations based on the OEWS, the O*NET, and DiSP.

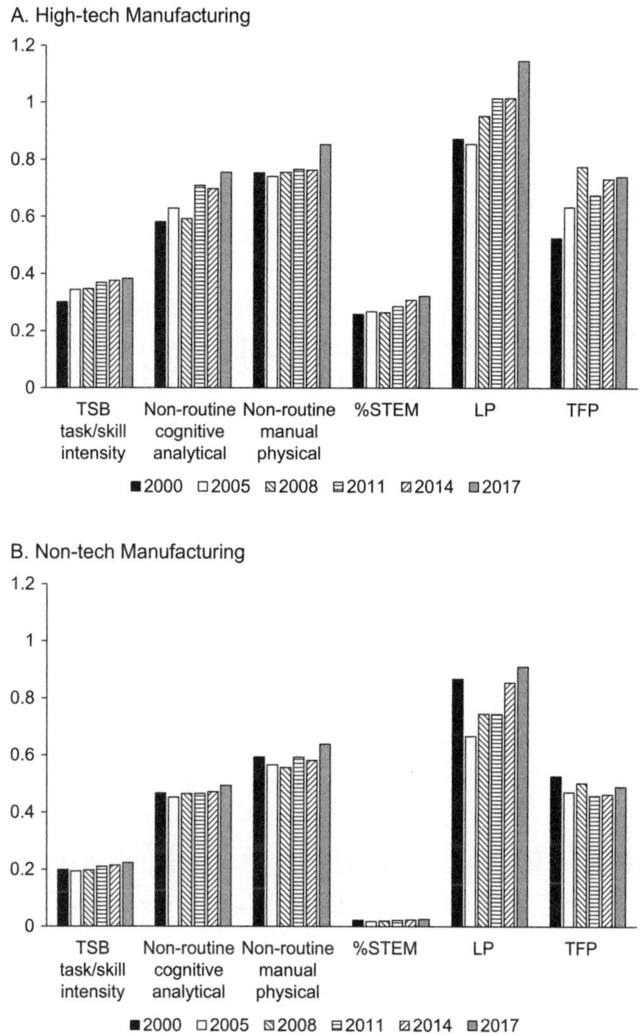

Fig. 10.2 Cross-industry mean IQRs by time and industry type

Notes: Industry-employment-weighted means of industry-level dispersion measures.

Source: Authors' calculations based on the OEWS, the O*NET, and DiSP.

and non-tech industries. For all our measures, we find dispersion is much greater among the high-tech manufacturing industries than the non-tech manufacturing industries. Among the high-tech manufacturing industries, we also observe a gradual increase in each dispersion measure over time, widening the cross-industry dispersion over time. Rising within-industry dispersion in task/skill intensity measures is also present in the non-tech industries, with the notable exception of the %STEM dispersion. Perhaps

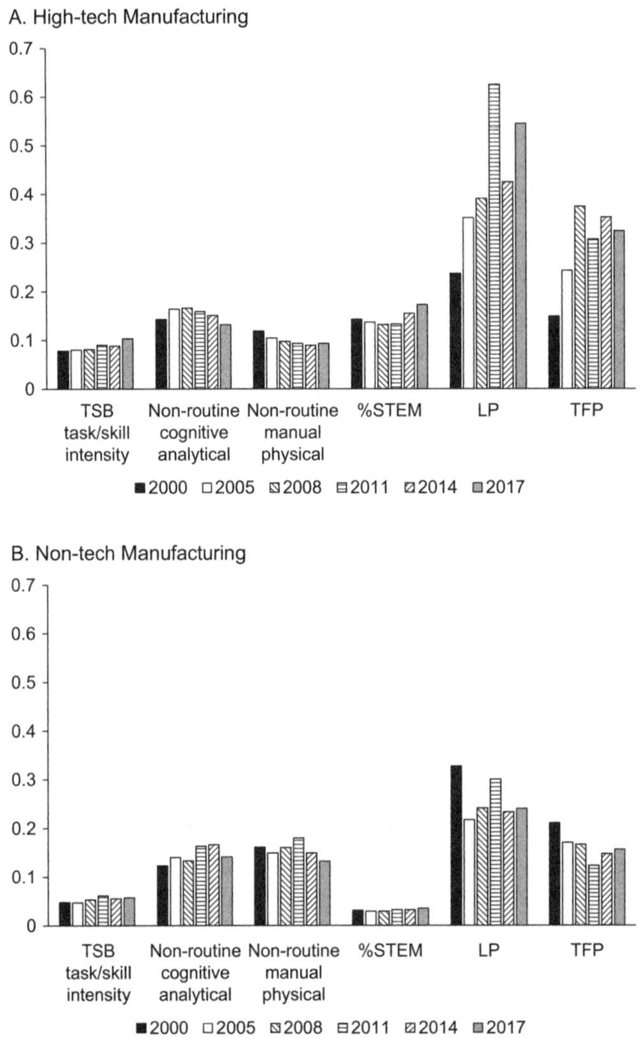

Fig. 10.3 Cross-industry standard deviation in IQRs by time and industry type
Notes: Standard deviations of IQRs of industry-level dispersion measures.
Source: Authors' calculations based on the OEWS, the O*NET, and DiSP.

not surprisingly, there is very little dispersion in %STEM dispersion among the non-tech manufacturing industries.

In figures 10.3A and 10.3B, we show the standard deviations in these dispersion measures, i.e., the dispersion in dispersion. We see higher dispersion in dispersion in the high-tech manufacturing industries than the non-tech manufacturing industries for five of the six measures shown. Figures 10.2 and 10.3 highlight there is dispersion in dispersion both in the cross-section and over time.

Table 10.3 **Correlations between within-industry dispersion in TSB task/skill intensity and dispersion in task measures**

	All Industries	Manufacturing Industries: All	Manufacturing Industries: High-tech	Manufacturing Industries: Non-tech	Non-manufacturing Industries
Panel A. IQR dispersion					
TSU task/skill intensity	0.642	0.748	0.855	0.587	0.636
Non-routine cognitive: Analytical	0.639	0.745	0.865	0.557	0.632
Non-routine cognitive: Interpersonal	0.596	0.057	0.208	0.226	0.608
Routine cognitive	0.294	0.071	−0.011	0.124	0.293
Routine manual	0.253	0.618	0.381	0.630	0.283
Non-routine manual physical	0.331	0.569	0.549	0.371	0.333
%STEM workers	0.280	0.815	0.841	0.245	0.255
Panel B. 90–10 dispersion					
TSU task/skill intensity	0.662	0.798	0.892	0.594	0.655
Non-routine cognitive: Analytical	0.664	0.799	0.874	0.606	0.657
Non-routine cognitive: Interpersonal	0.559	0.146	0.205	0.296	0.571
Routine cognitive	0.341	0.348	0.187	0.371	0.337
Routine manual	0.248	0.574	0.146	0.677	0.294
Non-routine manual physical	0.325	0.596	−0.0001	0.551	0.326
%STEM workers	0.536	0.832	0.856	0.361	0.521

Note: Each cell represents the industry-employment-weighted Pearson correlation between the four-digit NAICS industry-level TSB dispersion measure and the other skill/task dispersion measures correlations pooling the data across 2000, 2005, 2008, 2011, 2014, and 2017.

Source: Authors' calculations based on the OEWS and the O*NET.

In table 10.3, we show the Pearson correlations between the industry-level TSB dispersion measures and the other task/skill dispersion measures, pooled across years. Panel A shows the correlations between the IQR dispersion measures, while Panel B shows the correlations between the 90–10 dispersion measures. In both panels, we see that among all industries, the highest correlations are between dispersion in the TSB and dispersion in the TSU, the analytical tasks measure, and the interpersonal tasks measure. An industry with above-average TSB dispersion is likely to exhibit above-average dispersion in each of these task/skill measures. Among non-manufacturing industries (last column), dispersion measures for these task/skill measures are similarly highly correlated. Among manufacturing industries (second column), the correlations between the TSB and the TSU, analytical tasks, routine manual tasks, non-routine manual physical tasks, and %STEM all exceed 0.5. The interpersonal and routine cognitive tasks dispersions are less likely to be important for TSB dispersion in manufacturing relative to non-manufacturing industries. The main difference between the high-tech and non-tech manufacturing industries is that dispersion in TSU, analytical tasks, non-routine manual physical tasks, and %STEM varies more closely with dispersion in TSB in the high-tech group, while dispersion in routine manual tasks and interpersonal tasks varies more with TSB dispersion in the non-tech group. Those relationships are much stronger for the interdecile range than for the IQR.

With these summary statistics as background, we now turn to the analysis of primary interest—the relationship between within-industry dispersion of productivity and task/skill intensity measures.

10.4 The Relationship between Productivity, Skills, and Tasks

To analyze the link between productivity, skills, and tasks, we consider the relationship between within-industry dispersion measures of productivity, skills, and tasks. Our analysis is descriptive and provides no causal interpretation. As discussed in section 10.2, the relationship between productivity, skills, and tasks likely reflects endogenous relationships between the choice of tasks, factor mixes, and innovation, where innovation can be either product-quality-enhancing or process-enhancing.

We first calculate Pearson correlations between our dispersion measures for manufacturing industries (all, high-tech, and non-tech). In table 10.4, we see the TSB dispersion measure has the highest correlations with our productivity dispersion measures for the entire manufacturing sector, but the %STEM, analytical task, and TSU dispersion measures also have strong positive relationships. Looking at high-tech and non-tech manufacturing industry groups separately, we see the TSB, TSU, and %STEM dispersion measures have higher correlations with the productivity dispersion measures for the high-tech industries than for the non-tech industries. These patterns hold for both the IQR and 90–10 dispersion measures.

It is notable that the correlations for all manufacturing industries are higher than for either high-tech or non-tech industries. This is because the correlations for all manufacturing industries are not an average of the high- and non-tech industry correlations. Rather, they also include differences in dispersion between high-tech and non-tech industries.

Tables 10.5 and 10.6 provide an alternative view of the relationships in table 10.4. These tables present the coefficients, standard errors, and R-squared values from regressions of industry-specific productivity dispersion measures on task/skill-dispersion and task-dispersion measures. All regressions are estimated using ordinary least squares (OLS) by pooling data across years while controlling for year effects. The statistics from these regressions are useful because the coefficients are closely related to the Pearson correlations in table 10.4 and inform us about the explanatory power of the variation in skills and task-content for productivity dispersion. Again, we see positive and statistically significant associations between LP dispersion and the TSB, TSU, and %STEM dispersion measures, with stronger relationships among the high-tech industries relative to non-tech industries.

These patterns are similar for TFP dispersion, but the coefficients are

Table 10.4 **Correlations between productivity measures and within-industry dispersion measures of skill in the manufacturing sector**

	Labor Productivity			Total Factor Productivity		
	All	High-tech	Non-tech	All	High-tech	Non-tech
	Panel A. IQR dispersion					
TSB task/skill intensity	0.520	0.397	0.329	0.454	0.317	0.260
TSU task/skill intensity	0.415	0.314	0.306	0.310	0.229	0.144
Non-routine cognitive: Analytical	0.443	0.320	0.369	0.314	0.184	0.213
Non-routine cognitive: Interpersonal	−0.086	−0.082	−0.027	−0.077	−0.206	0.097
Routine cognitive	0.121	−0.101	0.307	0.091	−0.115	0.355
Routine manual	0.215	−0.026	0.143	0.231	0.249	0.041
Non-routine manual physical	0.275	0.122	0.133	0.243	0.036	0.169
%STEM workers	0.440	0.241	0.012	0.453	0.290	−0.049
	Panel B. 90–10 dispersion					
TSB task/skill intensity	0.551	0.448	0.366	0.564	0.518	0.209
TSU task/skill intensity	0.461	0.351	0.304	0.426	0.349	0.156
Non-outine cognitive: Analytical	0.477	0.367	0.331	0.423	0.317	0.188
Non-routine cognitive: Interpersonal	−0.065	−0.067	0.118	−0.049	−0.142	0.057
Routine cognitive	0.272	0.018	0.367	0.231	0.063	0.326
Routine manual	0.190	−0.028	0.119	0.156	−0.057	0.043
Non-routine manual physical	0.259	−0.018	−0.053	0.195	−0.262	0.033
%STEM workers	0.461	0.233	0.218	0.555	0.422	0.106

Note: Each cell represents the industry-employment-weighted Pearson correlation between within-industry skill dispersion measures and within-industry productivity dispersion pooling the data across 2000, 2005, 2008, 2011, 2014, and 2017. Industries include all 86 four-digit NAICS manufacturing industries.

Source: Authors' calculations based on the OEWS, the O*NET, and DiSP.

smaller in magnitude. A possible explanation for this lies in the fact that LP does not account for the mix of factors used—e.g., capital, which can be substituted for labor. Because factor inputs are embodied in output, all else equal, we would expect LP to be higher in establishments that are more intensive in other inputs. This implies that LP dispersion partly reflects dispersion in, for example, capital intensity. If workers at capital-intensive establishments are more skilled and engage in more complex tasks, then the establishments would have higher TSB. In terms of the second moment, higher dispersion in capital intensity can yield higher dispersion in LP. This discussion highlights reasons why the relationship between TSB dispersion may be weaker with TFP dispersion compared to LP dispersion. We plan to investigate such hypotheses with integration of the OEWS and CMP microdata.

The magnitude of the estimated coefficients in table 10.5 varies considerably across different groupings of industries as well as the alternative task/skill intensity. For example, the elasticity of within-industry TFP dispersion with respect to the TSB dispersion measure (evaluated at means) is more

Table 10.5 **Associations between within-industry dispersion measures of productivity and skill, manufacturing sector (IQR dispersion measures)**

	Labor Productivity			Total Factor Productivity		
	All	High-tech	Non-tech	All	High-tech	Non-tech
TSB task/skill intensity	2.395***	2.816***	1.366***	1.980***	2.300***	0.769***
	(0.421)	(0.826)	(0.288)	(0.454)	(0.718)	(0.209)
	[0.272]	[0.169]	[0.110]	[0.209]	[0.105]	[0.073]
TSU task/skill intensity	3.246***	3.866***	1.534***	2.295***	2.817**	0.493***
	(0.580)	(1.272)	(0.348)	(0.613)	(1.161)	(0.183)
	[0.174]	[0.111]	[0.099]	[0.098]	[0.059]	[0.023]
Non-routine cognitive: Analytical	1.072***	1.242***	0.576***	0.720***	0.688**	0.227***
	(0.176)	(0.386)	(0.108)	(0.182)	(0.342)	(0.065)
	[0.200]	[0.119]	[0.141]	[0.102]	[0.046]	[0.048]
Non-routine cognitive: Interpersonal	−0.444**	−1.375	−0.111	−0.301	−2.325*	0.136**
	(0.213)	(1.058)	(0.123)	(0.219)	(1.358)	(0.067)
	[0.027]	[0.063]	[0.013]	[0.013]	[0.087]	[0.014]
Routine cognitive	0.296**	−0.609	0.388***	0.209*	−0.674	0.306***
	(0.134)	(0.755)	(0.099)	(0.127)	(0.906)	(0.049)
	[0.026]	[0.049]	[0.102]	[0.013]	[0.034]	[0.130]
Routine manual	0.390***	−0.506	0.143**	0.409***	1.184**	0.032
	(0.112)	(0.445)	(0.073)	(0.125)	(0.496)	(0.043)
	[0.055]	[0.049]	[0.028]	[0.059]	[0.074]	[0.004]
Non-routine manual physical	0.667***	0.518	0.177*	0.573***	0.096	0.171**
	(0.143)	(0.545)	(0.103)	(0.138)	(0.516)	(0.072)
	[0.082]	[0.045]	[0.024]	[0.065]	[0.023]	[0.032]
%STEM	1.339***	0.991*	0.030	1.299***	1.321***	−0.235
	(0.305)	(0.512)	(0.349)	(0.304)	(0.333)	(0.326)
	[0.201]	[0.085]	[0.009]	[0.209]	[0.100]	[0.004]

Note: Each cell contains coefficient estimates from a linear regression of within-industry productivity dispersion on within-industry skill dispersion including a constant and year effects. Industry employment weights are used. Standard errors are in parentheses and R-squared values are in brackets. All regressions are estimated using OLS by pooling data on all 86 four-digit NAICS manufacturing industries across years (2000, 2005, 2008, 2011, 2014, and 2017).

Source: Authors' calculations based on the OEWS, the O*NET, and DiSP.

than three times larger in the high-tech grouping of industries than in non-tech industries.[22] This is also true for the TSU and the analytical tasks dispersion measure. In contrast, non-routine manual physical task dispersion is substantially more related to TFP dispersion in the non-tech industries than the high-tech industries.

The regression results for the 90–10 dispersion measures in table 10.6 yield even larger quantitative effects. For example, the elasticities of within-industry TFP dispersion with respect to both the TSB and TSU dispersion

22. The elasticities can be computed combining information from tables 10.2 and 10.5. For example, the estimated coefficients relating the IQR of TFP to the IQR of the TSB measure are 2.30 and 0.77 for high-tech and non-tech, respectively. Using the means from table 10.2, the implied elasticities are 1.20 and 0.32, respectively.

Table 10.6 **Associations between within-industry dispersion measures of productivity and skill, manufacturing sector (90–10 dispersion measures)**

	Labor Productivity			Total Factor Productivity		
	All	High-tech	Non-tech	All	High-tech	Non-tech
TSB task/skill intensity	1.975***	2.609***	1.388***	1.599***	2.558***	0.507***
	(.306)	(0.669)	(0.226)	(0.275)	(0.553)	(0.159)
	[.305]	[0.206]	[0.138]	[0.329]	[0.279]	[0.060]
TSU task/skill intensity	3.166***	3.917***	1.626***	2.326***	3.307***	0.532***
	(0.529)	(1.201)	(0.310)	(0.450)	(0.838)	(0.182)
	[0.214]	[0.127]	[0.093]	[0.191]	[0.133]	[0.035]
Non-routine cognitive: Analytical	1.014***	1.260***	0.565***	0.717***	0.929***	0.200***
	(0.162)	(0.363)	(0.093)	(0.135)	(0.245)	(0.057)
	[0.231]	[0.139]	[0.115]	[0.191]	[0.115]	[0.048]
Non-routine cognitive: Interpersonal	−0.253*	−0.783	−0.130	−0.094	−0.952	0.058
	(0.151)	(0.828)	(0.097)	(0.137)	(0.905)	(0.060)
	[0.014]	[0.025]	[0.014]	[0.007]	[0.048]	[0.011]
Routine cognitive	0.561***	0.090	0.469***	0.375***	0.216	0.246***
	(0.103)	(0.491)	(0.074)	(0.087)	(0.433)	(0.043)
	[0.079]	[0.011]	[0.141]	[0.060]	[0.021]	[0.118]
Routine manual	0.298***	−0.392	0.114*	0.204***	−0.508	0.033
	(0.074)	(0.529)	(0.059)	(0.052)	(0.581)	(0.028)
	[0.041]	[0.015]	[0.022]	[0.033]	[0.028]	[0.011]
Non-routine manual physical	0.521***	−0.150	0.163*	0.323***	−1.103**	0.061
	(0.111)	(0.621)	(0.092)	(0.073)	(0.486)	(0.053)
	[0.074]	[0.012]	[0.021]	[0.049]	[0.091]	[0.013]
%STEM	1.083***	0.853**	0.989***	1.027***	1.378***	0.303*
	(0.218)	(0.422)	(0.352)	(0.171)	(0.248)	(0.185)
	[0.214]	[0.059]	[0.053]	[0.315]	[0.192]	[0.020]

Note: Each cell contains coefficient estimates from a linear regression of within-industry productivity dispersion on within-industry skill dispersion including a constant and year effects. Industry employment weights are used. Standard errors are in parentheses and R-squared values are in brackets. All regressions are estimated using OLS by pooling data on all 86 four-digit NAICS manufacturing industries across years (2000, 2005, 2008, 2011, 2014, and 2017).

Source: Authors' calculations based on the OEWS, the O*NET, and DiSP.

measures (evaluated at means) are more than six times as large in the high-tech industries as in the non-tech industries.

Our results can be thought of as complementary to those of Cunningham et al. (2023), who find that establishment characteristics from the firm dynamics literature (state, age class, and size class) have limited explanatory power for productivity dispersion. In particular, the results in this paper suggest that we will have a better chance of understanding productivity differences if we go beyond the standard establishment characteristics and look at the basic characteristics of workers and tasks.[23]

23. Appropriate caution is needed in making these comparisons, because Cunningham et al. (2023) investigate the relationship between establishment-level productivity and characteristics,

The explanatory power of the regressions estimated over all manufacturing industries indicates that variation in skills and task content is relevant for productivity dispersion. For example, the first row R-squared in table 10.5 shows that the TSB dispersion accounts for about a quarter of the variation in LP dispersion and about one-fifth of the variation in TFP dispersion across manufacturing industries. The second R-squared in column 1 suggests that TSU dispersion accounts for almost one-fifth of the total variation in LP dispersion and about one-tenth of the variation in TFP dispersion. Out of the five task measures, dispersion in analytical task-content is the most relevant for productivity dispersion, indicated by more positive estimated coefficients and mostly higher R-squared values.[24]

The R-squared values for the high-tech and non-tech industries are lower than those for manufacturing overall. As we saw in table 10.4, this implies that it is differences in dispersion between high-tech and non-tech industries driving much of this association rather than within sector differences in dispersion.

Figure 10.4 illustrates the relationships between TFP IQR dispersion and each task/skill IQR dispersion measure by industry (pooled over the years in our sample) for selected measures and also includes the slope of the relationships in 2000 and 2017. Focusing first on the TSB task/skill intensity dispersion measure, we find a positive relationship in the pooled data, but we find the relationship changes over time depending on whether we look at the high-tech or non-tech industries. For high-tech industries, the slope was slightly negative in 2000 but strongly positive in 2017. On the other hand, for the non-tech industries, the relationship was positive in both years but weakened between 2000 and 2017. We find similar patterns using the analytical tasks dispersion. Also, looking at high-tech industries, we find the correlation between TFP dispersion and %STEM dispersion becomes strongly positive in 2017; but for the non-tech industries, there is little dispersion in %STEM and no change over time in the slope.

Patterns are very different using the non-routine manual physical task dispersion measures. Between 2000 and 2017, the negative slope between the TFP dispersion measure and the physical task dispersion measure becomes weaker among the high-tech industries. Among non-tech industries, the rela-

while here we are relating within-industry dispersion in productivity and task/skill characteristics.

24. Our results may be affected by the level of detail in the industry classification because the regression coefficients in tables 10.5 and 10.6 depend on productivity dispersion and the dispersion measures depend on the level of detail at which they are calculated. DiSP is based on four-digit NAICS, at which level the average within-industry standard deviation of TFP over the 1997–2015 period is 0.46 (see table 3 in Cunningham et al. 2023). Using six-digit NAICS, Decker et al. (2020) find this statistic for the relevant TFP measure is 0.35–0.37 (see Panel A of their figure 3). Blackwood et al. (2021) find similar values using four-digit SIC and six-digit NAICS but for a different time-period. Their standard deviation measure is 0.31 (see their table 1). In other words, more detailed industry codes imply lower dispersion, which is intuitive. However, these dispersion measures are similar in magnitude, which suggests using detailed industry codes is likely to have a limited effect on our findings.

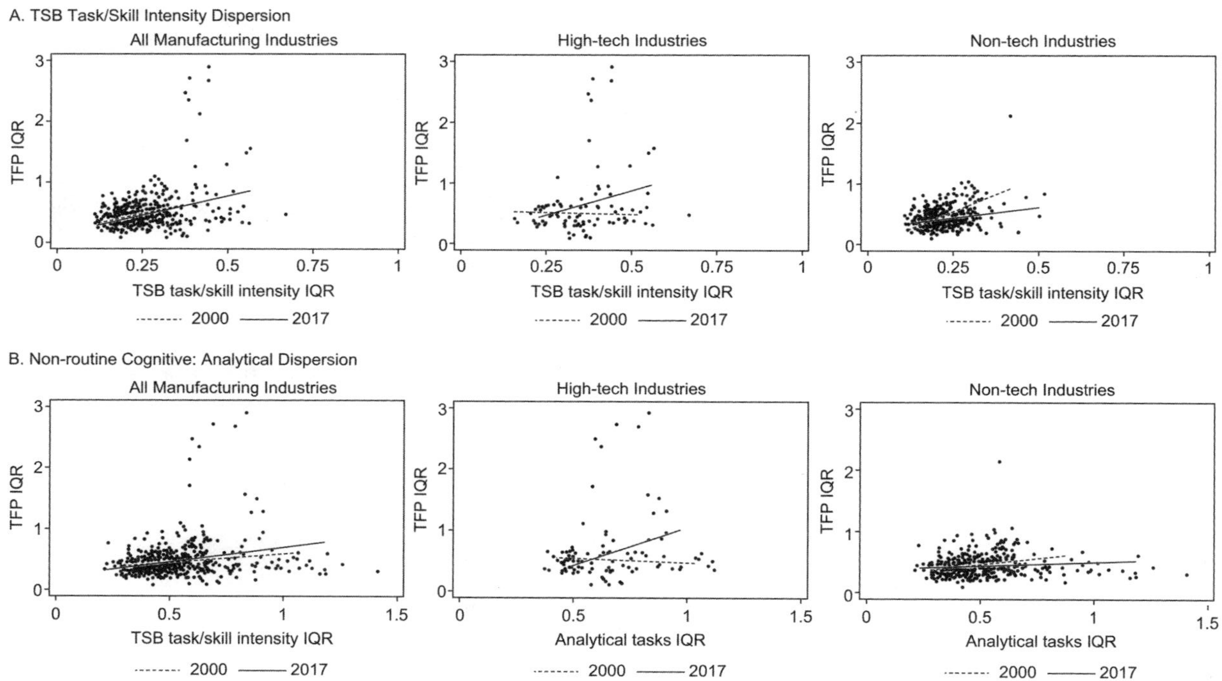

Fig. 10.4 Relationships between TFP dispersion and task/skill dispersion measures

Note: Pooled interquartile range dispersion measures for four-digit NAICS manufacturing industries from 2000, 2005, 2008, 2011, 2014 and 2017 are depicted. Slopes for 2000 and 2017 are also included.

Source: Authors' calculations based on the OEWS, the O*NET, and DiSP.

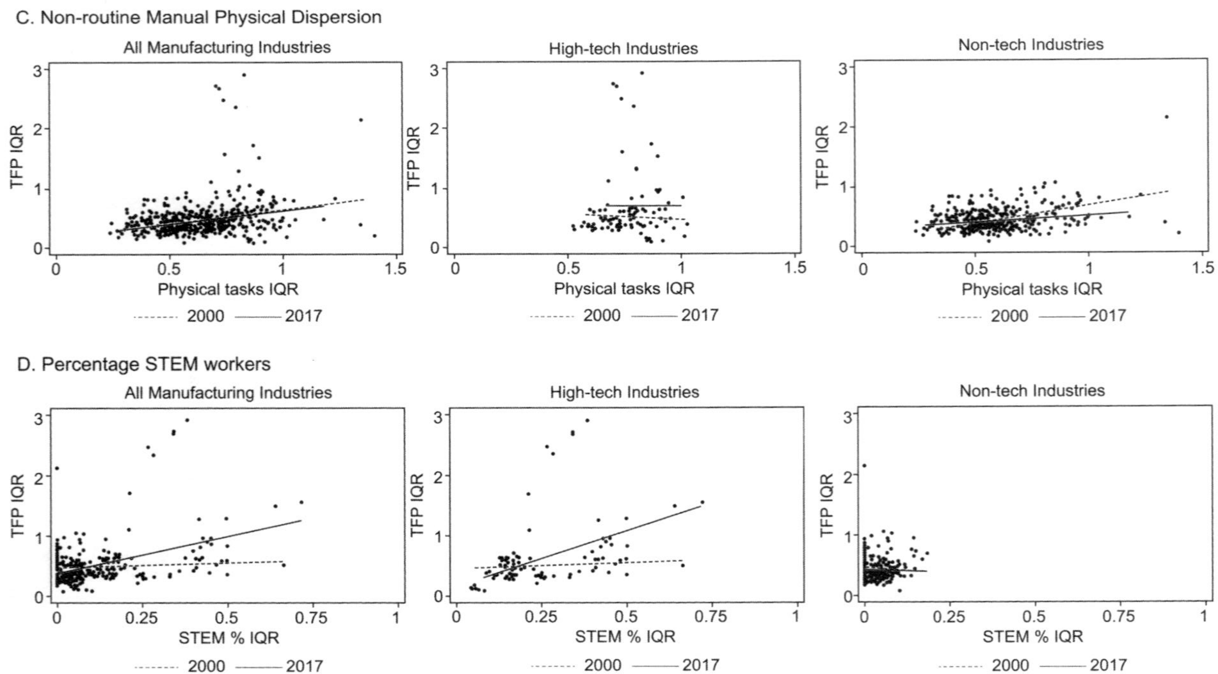
C. Non-routine Manual Physical Dispersion
All Manufacturing Industries
High-tech Industries
Non-tech Industries
TFP IQR
Physical tasks IQR
2000
2017
D. Percentage STEM workers
All Manufacturing Industries
High-tech Industries
Non-tech Industries
TFP IQR
STEM % IQR
2000
2017

Fig. 10.4 (cont.)

tionship is strongly positive, although it is weaker in 2017 than in 2000. When pooling across all industries, we find a strong positive relationship that is similar in both 2000 and 2017. Pooling across industries yields a consistently positive relationship, which highlights again that there are some interesting differences between high-tech and non-tech industry effects at work.

The especially high degree of within-industry dispersion in productivity and task/skill intensity measures and their strong positive relationship in the high-tech industries is striking. It is already well known that high-tech industries have higher than average within-industry productivity growth and higher than average skill/task intensity (as measured for example by the STEM intensity of workers in the industry—see, e.g., Decker et al. 2020). Novel to our analysis is that these first moment relationships have related analogues in within-industry second moments. These innovation-intensive industries exhibit high dispersion in productivity outcomes across businesses accompanied by indicators that these businesses are organized quite differently in terms of their mix of workers. While our results are only suggestive, they offer prima facie evidence that there is likely a high payoff to integrating productivity and occupation data at the establishment level. We turn to the prospects of that integration in the next section.

10.5 Integration of Establishment-Level Productivity and Occupation Data

10.5.1 Challenges in Integrating the OEWS and CMP Microdata

The next step in the larger project is to integrate the establishment-level data in the CMP and the occupation data in the OEWS. In this section, we discuss the challenges that will need to be overcome in this data integration project, along with plans for the types of analyses that can be conducted with this data.

One challenge is the OEWS is drawn from the BLS business register, while the source data underlying the CMP data are drawn from the Census Bureau Business Register. The common identifier on both files is the Employer Identification Number (EIN). Studies have shown that there is a high match rate of EINs across the registers (Fairman et al. 2008; Haltiwanger et al. 2014). Name and address matching can facilitate the next step of establishment-level matching within EINs, but we anticipate that instructive analysis can be conducted using the EIN matches.

When matching OEWS data to the CMP data, we will need to account for the fact that both are samples. We will take two approaches to the analysis. Initially, we will restrict the OEWS sample to non-imputed observations. Because this will result in a large number of non-matches, we will combine the matched CMP-OEWS data with the Census Bureau's Business Register to estimate propensity score weights along the lines of Cunningham et al. (2023). Unlike most reweighting situations, the assumption that data are randomly missing holds—missing data are due to randomness in the OEWS and ASM sampling procedures rather than to the behavior of establishments. It is worth noting the CMP data are essentially a universe for productivity in Economic Census years. Thus, in Census years, we are less constrained by the difference in the sampling of establishments in the OEWS and the ASM.

The second approach is to use the full QCEW-OEWS data set that we use here (that is, including imputed observations). This will result in a match rate of nearly 100 percent and a substantially larger sample. We recognize the imputed QCEW observations may give a distorted picture of the relationship between productivity and the occupational mix. One way to examine this is to see how much the occupational mix varies across establishments within the same EIN in the two OEWS samples. Put differently, it is important to examine whether using imputed observations affects the ratio of within-EIN versus between-EIN variation. Our preliminary analysis discussed in the next subsection reveals some differences but suggests both approaches can shed light on the question.

10.5.2 Within- vs Between-EIN Variation in Skill and Task Indexes Across Establishments

We compute variance decompositions of the between-establishment distributions of the different task and skill measures for each industry in terms of the fraction of the variance accounted for by between-EIN variation. Figure 10.5 shows box-and-whisker graphs of the between-EIN share of total variance for the seven measures in the full (including imputations) QCEW-OEWS data set using all manufacturing industries. Because the shares are very similar across measures, the rest of the analysis will focus on the TSB measure. Figure 10.6 presents four box-and-whisker graphs showing the distribution of the share of between-EIN variation in the four pooled samples defined by (1) whether imputations are included and (2) whether single-unit EINs are excluded. The left two graphs show the between-EIN shares are very high when we include all EINs (single- and multi-unit EINs) and the between-EIN share of total variation is smaller when we include imputed observations. The right two graphs show the between-EIN shares for multi-unit EINs. As expected, the between-EIN shares are lower than when we include single-unit EINs (within-EIN variation is zero for these firms). As with the full sample, the between-EIN share of total variation is lower when we include imputed observations. Put another way, the imputations increase the within-EIN share of total variation in the TSB measure.

Figures 10.7 and 10.8 expand on the distributional statistics shown in figure 10.6 by plotting the between-EIN share of TSB variation when using all imputed data versus the between-EIN share when using only direct or EIN matches. Each dot represents a four-digit industry. Figure 10.7 shows

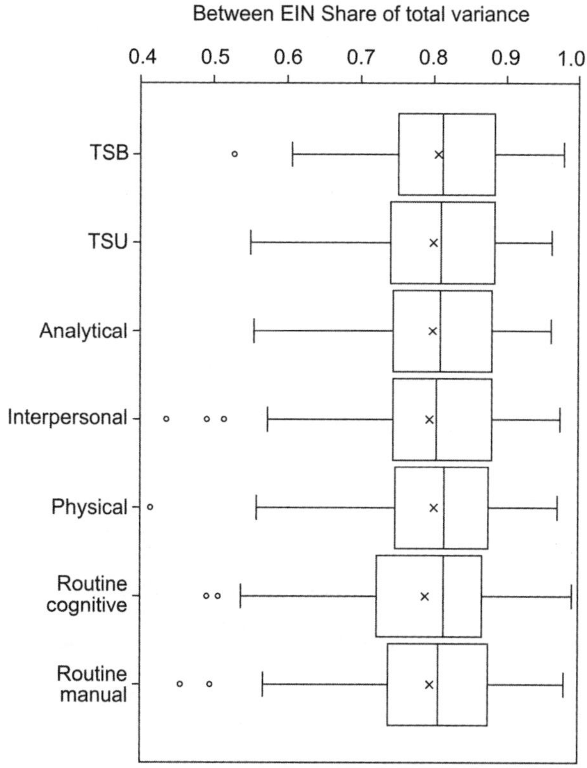

Fig. 10.5 Distributions of between EIN share of total variation, all units imputed or observed, all EINS

Notes: The boxplots represent the distribution of the between EIN share of total variation for all four-digit NAICS manufacturing industries for each skill/task measure. The line in the middle reports the share for the median industry, while the x reports the mean share. The boxes represent the interquartile range, which bound the industries that lie between the 25th and 75th percentiles, respectively. The upper and lower whiskers span the lowest and highest quartiles within 1.5 IQR of the nearest quartile. The dots represent outliers.

Source: Authors' calculations based on the OEWS and the O*NET.

the relationship for all EINs, while figure 10.8 shows the relationship for multi-unit EINs only. For all EINs, whether we include imputed data has very little impact on the between-EIN share of variation. There are more industries where the between-EIN share is lower when including the imputed data, but the observations generally lie fairly close to the 45-degree line. On the other hand, when examining only multi-unit EINs in figure 10.8, including imputed data seems just as likely to increase or decrease the between-EIN share of variation, and the data are not particularly close to the 45 degree line.

These findings are interesting in their own right because they highlight

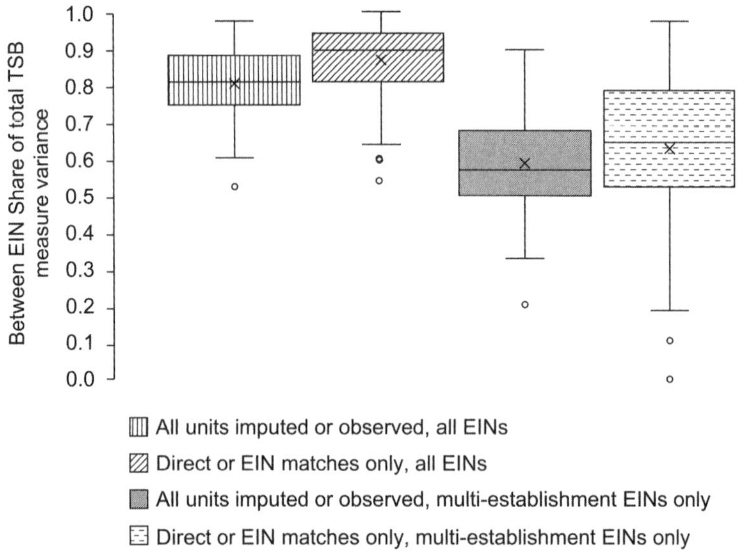

Fig. 10.6 Distributions of between EIN share of total TSB measure variation

Notes: The boxplots represent the distribution of the between EIN share of total variation for all four-digit NAICS manufacturing industries for each skill/task measure. The line in the middle reports the share for the median industry, while the x reports the mean share. The boxes represent the interquartile range, which bound the industries that lie between the 25th and 75th percentiles, respectively. The upper and lower whiskers span the lowest and highest quartiles within 1.5 IQR of the nearest quartile. The dots represent outliers.

Source: Authors' calculations based on the OEWS.

that there is an important common component of task and skill mix across establishments within the same firm. The findings also will greatly facilitate the planned integration of the OEWS and CMP data, because the EIN is a common identifier on the files.

10.5.3 Planned Future Analysis

We will start our planned future analysis of the integrated OEWS and CMP data by examining the joint distribution of establishment-level productivity and our task/skill measures. This exploratory data analysis will examine the joint distribution of productivity and occupational mix through the type of correlation analysis above as well as cluster analysis looking to see whether we can identify distinct patterns relating the productivity and occupational distributions. Exploring the joint distribution will be useful for understanding productivity dispersion given that DiSP does not account for differences in the occupational mix. For example, if the occupation distribution in one group of establishments within an industry is skewed toward high-skilled labor, while it is skewed toward low-skilled labor in another industry, then it is reasonable to calculate dispersion accounting for such dif-

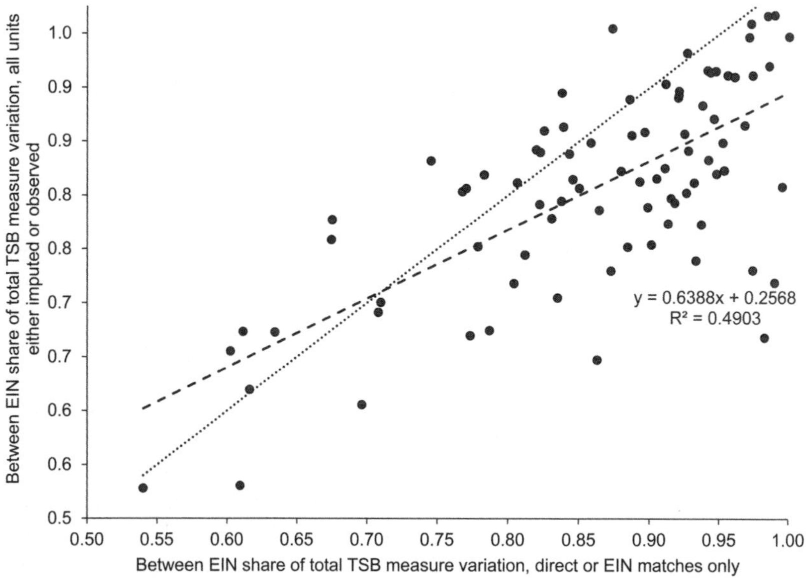

Fig. 10.7 Between EIN share of total TSB measure variation, direct or EIN matches only vs. all units either imputed or observed, all EINs
Source: Authors' calculations based on the OEWS.

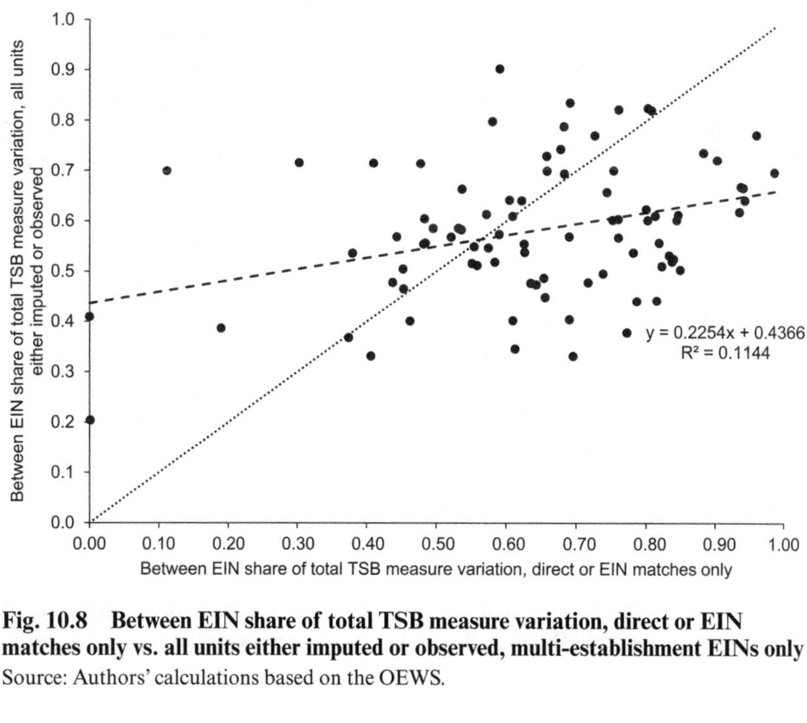

Fig. 10.8 Between EIN share of total TSB measure variation, direct or EIN matches only vs. all units either imputed or observed, multi-establishment EINs only
Source: Authors' calculations based on the OEWS.

ferences either by adjusting the labor input measure or allowing elasticities to vary across clusters, or both. How such clusters should be identified is an open question, but information on occupations from OEWS could provide insights about whether businesses use labor differently within an industry.

For our more structured analysis, we will explore a range of alternative production technologies as considered in section 10.2. A first step is to use the existing DiSP approach but replace total hours with task/skill-adjusted hours. To fix ideas, consider the specification of production in section 10.2: $Q = A \cdot F(Z \cdot L, K)$ where time and establishment subscripts are suppressed for simplicity. One approach would be to use the TSB and TSU measures as proxies for Z. As discussed above, TSB and TSU are task/skill-based indexes that take into account the pricing of those tasks. TSB uses the bundling of tasks through occupations, while TSU uses the pricing of identified tasks associated with the occupation mix. Such an approach is related to but distinct from the discussion in section 10.2 on creating an efficiency units measure of the labor input. An interesting question is: Does measured productivity dispersion decline when we account for differences in the task-content of jobs across establishments? Just as TFP dispersion is less than LP dispersion, we would expect that accounting for task/skill differences would further reduce TFP dispersion. In addition, differences between the TSB and TSU measures can tell us something about the importance of task bundling.

Building on this approach, we plan to estimate a range of functional forms with production technologies specified using tasks. One challenge is how to specify a production technology with multi-dimensional task inputs along with departures from Cobb-Douglas functional forms. A key issue in this regard is that under Cobb-Douglas, the elasticity of substitution between factors is by definition one; deviating from this assumption allows the elasticity to be estimated. Existing studies suggest such generalizations are likely important in this context (see, e.g., Dinlersoz and Wolf 2023; Raval 2019; Oberfield and Raval 2021). The CES models in section 10.2 are a good starting place given the recent insights of Acemoglu and Restrepo (2019b) (e.g., see equation (3), which is from their paper). We anticipate that considering even more flexible functional forms will be of interest. Foster, Haltiwanger, and Tuttle (2022) found that much of the rising mean and variance of measured markups using the De Loecker, Eechkhout, and Unger (2020) production-function-based approach can be accounted for (within manufacturing) by permitting factor elasticities to vary across establishments and time in a flexible manner (e.g., a translog approach with time-varying coefficients). Their findings are relevant for our research because measured markup dispersion is closely related to measured revenue productivity dispersion observed in the DiSP.

A challenge for estimation of the production technology is, as emphasized in section 10.2, that all the factor inputs, tasks, and adoption of specific process- or product-enhancing innovation are endogenous. As such, estimating the production function using OLS is not informative. Much of the recent literature has used control function methods (e.g., De Loecker et al. 2016; De Loecker, Eechkhout, and Unger 2020; Blackwood et al. 2021; Eslava, Haltiwanger, and Urdaneta 2024), which is where we plan to start. A complicating issue is that in the absence of establishment- or firm-level prices, we will need to estimate the revenue function and account for the endogeneity of prices including markups. While a challenge, this issue enhances the interest in helping us understand the causes and consequences of businesses doing business differently.

In a related but distinct set of exercises, we will explore the relationship between observable indicators of technology and changes in the mix of skills and tasks. Berman, Bound, and Griliches (1994) and Dunne, Haltiwanger, and Troske (1997) pursued early versions of such approaches with much cruder data. Dinlersoz and Wolf (2023) is a more recent example where establishment-level indicators of automation are combined with CMP data from a set of manufacturing industries. With integrated CMP-OEWS data, there are rich possibilities. CMP data include time-series-consistent measures of capital, and the ASM contains periodic indicators of the use of advanced technologies (e.g., computer investment). In addition, in more recent years, the Annual Business Survey (ABS) has modules on the adoption of advanced technologies. Analysis of those modules by Zolas et al. (2020) highlights that the adoption of advanced technologies such as robotics, automation, cloud computing, and artificial intelligence is both relatively rare and highly heterogeneous across businesses within the same industries.[25] Using the CES specifications in section 10.2 combined with Shepherd's lemma will permit us to examine the relationship between skill and task mix and the adoption of technologies.

It is likely that factors other than the uneven patterns of adoption of advanced technologies underlie the different choices that businesses make when they organize production. Offshoring and outsourcing are likely at work as well. Of course, the uneven impact of globalization across establishments is likely related to the uneven impact of adoption of advanced technologies.

10.6 Conclusion

Our analysis has barely opened the black box of tasks and skills at the establishment level, but our results suggest that we can gain considerable insights about a potentially important source of differences in measured productivity across establishments within an industry and about the mix

25. Although the data used by Dinlersoz and Wolf (2023) are from the 1990s (Survey of Manufacturing Technologies), they arrive at similar conclusions about robots, automation, and advanced technologies.

of tasks and skills being used in those establishments. Our evidence is only suggestive, as we find industries with high dispersion in within-industry productivity also exhibit high dispersion in a number of the task/skill intensity measures we construct. But we have good reason to believe that we will find a positive relationship between establishment-level productivity and our establishment-level task/skill measures.

More progress on opening the black box awaits integration of the CMP and OEWS data. As we have described, such integration holds great promise for helping us understand how different businesses do business differently. Moreover, opening this black box will also permit a rich exploration of the connection between the adoption of advanced technologies and their impact on the workforce.

Acknowledgments

Any opinions and conclusions expressed herein are those of the authors and do not represent the views of the US Census Bureau or the US Bureau of Labor Statistics. This paper uses public domain DiSP data (the public domain data have been cleared by the Census Bureau Disclosure Review Board, Clearance Number: CBDRB-FY21–305). The authors would like to thank Emin Dinlersoz, Lucy Eldridge, John Eltinge, Susan Houseman, Erich Strassner, and participants at the NBER/CRIW Conference on Technology, Productivity, and Economic Growth for comments. For acknowledgments, sources of research support, and disclosure of the authors' material financial relationships, if any, please see https://www.nber.org/books-and-chapters/technology-productivity-and-economic-growth/opening-black-box-task-and-skill-mix-and-productivity-dispersion.

References

Acemoglu, Daron. 1998. "Why Do New Technologies Complement Skills? Directed Technical Change and Wage Inequality." *Quarterly Journal of Economics* 113 (4): 1055–89.

Acemoglu, Daron, and David Autor. 2011. "Skills, Tasks and Technologies: Implications for Employment and Earnings." In *Handbook of Labor Economics*, vol. 4, Part B, edited by Orley Ashenfelter and David Card, 1043–171. Elsevier: North Holland.

Acemoglu, Daron, and Pascual Restrepo. 2018a. "Modeling Automation." *AEA Papers and Proceedings* 108: 48–53.

Acemoglu, Daron, and Pascual Restrepo. 2018b. "The Race Between Machine and Man: Implications of Technology for Growth, Factor Shares, and Employment." *American Economic Review* 108 (6): 1488–542.

Acemoglu, Daron, and Pascual Restrepo. 2019a. "Artificial Intelligence, Automation and Work." In *The Economics of Artificial Intelligence: An Agenda*, edited by Ajay

Agrawal, Joshua Gans, and Avi Goldfarb, 197–236. Chicago, IL: University of Chicago Press.

Acemoglu, Daron, and Pascual Restrepo. 2019b. "Automation and New Tasks: How Technology Displaces and Reinstates Labor." *Journal of Economic Perspectives* 33 (2): 3–30.

Acemoglu, Daron, and Pascual Restrepo. 2020. "Robots and Jobs: Evidence from US Labor Markets." *Journal of Political Economy* 128 (6): 2188–244.

Autor, David H., Frank Levy, and Richard J. Murnane. 2003. "The Skill Content of Recent Technological Change: An Empirical Exploration." *Quarterly Journal of Economics* 118 (4): 1279–333.

Baily, Martin Neil, Charles Hulten, and David Campbell. 1992. "Productivity Dynamics in Manufacturing Plants." *Brookings Papers on Economic Activity: Microeconomics*: 187–249.

Berman, Eli, John Bound, and Zvi Griliches. 1994. "Changes in the Demand for Skilled Labor within U.S. Manufacturing: Evidence from the Annual Survey of Manufactures." *Quarterly Journal of Economics* 109 (2): 367–97.

Blackwood, G. Jacob, Lucia S. Foster, Cheryl A. Grim, John Haltiwanger, and Zoltan Wolf. 2021. "Macro and Micro Dynamics of Productivity: From Devilish Details to Insights." *American Economic Journal: Macroeconomics* 13 (3):142–72.

Card, David, and John E. DiNardo. 2002. "Skill-Biased Technological Change and Rising Wage Inequality: Some Problems and Puzzles." *Journal of Labor Economics* 20 (4): 733–83.

Chow, Melissa, Teresa C. Fort, Christopher Goetz, Nathan Goldschlag, James Lawrence, Elisabeth Ruth Perlman, Martha Stinson, and T. Kirk White. 2021. "Redesigning the Longitudinal Business Database." Center for Economic Studies Discussion Paper No. 21–08. https://www.census.gov/library/working-papers/2021/adrm/CES-WP-21–08.html.

Cunningham, Cindy, Lucia Foster, Cheryl Grim, John Haltiwanger, Sabrina Wulff Pabilonia, Jay Stewart, and Zoltan Wolf. 2021. "Chaos Before Order: Productivity Patterns in U.S. Manufacturing." *International Productivity Monitor* 41: 138–52.

Cunningham, Cindy, Lucia Foster, Cheryl Grim, John Haltiwanger, Sabrina Wulff Pabilonia, Jay Stewart, and Zoltan Wolf. 2023. "Dispersion in Dispersion: Measuring Establishment Level Differences in Productivity." *Review of Income and Wealth* 69 (4): 999–1032.

Decker, Ryan A., John Haltiwanger, Ron S. Jarmin, and Javier Miranda. 2020. "Changing Business Dynamism and Productivity: Shocks versus Responsiveness." *American Economic Review* 110 (12): 3952–90.

Dey, Matthew, David S. Piccone, Jr., and Stephen M. Miller. 2019. "Model-Based Estimates for the Occupational Employment Statistics Program." *Monthly Labor Review* August.

De Loecker, Jan, Pinelopi K. Goldberg, Amit K. Khandelwal, and Nina Pavcnik. 2016. "Prices, Markups, and Trade Reform." *Econometrica* 84 (2): 445–510.

De Loecker, Jan, Jan Eeckhout, and Gabriel Unger. 2020. "The Rise of Market Power and the Macroeconomic Implications." *Quarterly Journal of Economics* 135 (2): 561–644.

Dinlersoz, Emin, and Zoltan Wolf. 2023. "Automation, Labor Share, and Productivity: Plant-Level Evidence from U.S. Manufacturing." *Economics of Innovation and New Technology*, 33 (4), 604–26.

Dunne, Timothy, John Haltiwanger, and Kenneth R. Troske. 1997. "Technology and Jobs: Secular Changes and Cyclical Dynamics." Carnegie-Rochester Conference Series on Public Policy 46 (1): 107–78.

Employment and Training Administration, U.S. Department of Labor. 1991. *The Revised Handbook of Analyzing Jobs.*

Eslava, Marcela, John Haltiwanger, and Nicolas Urdaneta. 2024. "The Size and Life-cycle Growth of Plants: The Role of Productivity, Demand and Wedges." *Review of Economic Studies* 92 (1): 259–300.

Fairman, Kristin, Lucia Foster, C. J. Krizan, and Ian Rucker. 2008. "An Analysis of Key Differences in Micro Data: Results from the Business List Comparison Project." Center for Economic Studies Discussion Paper No. 08–28.

Foster, Lucia, John Haltiwanger, and Chad Syverson. 2008. "Reallocation, Firm Turnover, and Efficiency: Selection on Productivity or Profitability?" *American Economic Review* 98 (1): 394–425.

Foster, Lucia, John Haltiwanger, and Cody Tuttle. 2022. "Rising Markups or Changing Technology?" NBER Working Paper No. 30491.

Gollop, Frank M., Barbara M. Fraumeni, and Dale W. Jorgenson. 1987. *Productivity and U.S. Economic Growth.* Harvard University Press.

Haltiwanger, John C., Henry R. Hyatt, Erika McEntarfer, Liliana Sousa, and Stephen Tibbets. 2014. "Firm Age and Size in the Longitudinal Employer-Household Dynamics Data." Center for Economic Studies Discussion Paper No. 14–16.

Handel, Michael. 2016. "The O*NET Content Model: Strengths and Limitations." *Journal of Labor Market Research* 49: 157–76.

Oberfield, Ezra, and Devesh Raval. 2021. "Micro Data and Macro Technology." *Econometrica* 89 (2): 703–32.

Raval, Devesh. 2019. "The Micro Elasticity of Substitution and Non-Neutral Technology." *RAND Journal of Economics* 50 (1): 147–67.

Schreyer, Paul. 2001. "OECD Productivity Manual: A Guide to the Measurement of Industry-Level and Aggregate Productivity Growth." Paris: Organisation for Economic Co-Operation and Development.

Standard Occupational Classification Policy Committee. 2010. "Attachment C: Detailed 2010 SOC Occupations Included in STEM." https://www.bls.gov/soc/2010/home.htm.

Syverson, Chad. 2011. "What Determines Productivity?" *Journal of Economic Literature* 49 (2): 326–65.

Wolf, Michael, and Dalton Terrell. 2016. "The High-Tech Industry, What Is It and Why It Matters to Our Economic Future." *Beyond the Numbers: Employment and Unemployment* 5 (8). May. U.S. Bureau of Labor Statistics.

Zoghi, Cindy. 2007. "Measuring Labor Composition: A Comparison of Alternate Methodologies." In *Labor in the New Economy*, edited by Katherine G. Abraham, James R. Spletzer, and Michael Harper. Chicago, IL: University of Chicago Press.

Zolas, Nikolas, Zachary Kroff, Erik Brynjolfsson, Kristina McElheran, David N. Beede, Cathy Buffington, Nathan Goldschlag, Lucia Foster, and Emin Dinlersoz. 2020. "Advanced Technologies Adoption and Use by U.S. Firms: Evidence from the Annual Business Survey." NBER Working Paper No. 28290. Cambridge, MA: National Bureau of Economic Research.

Author Index

Subject Index

The letter *f* following a page number denotes a figure.